2 ᵕ 30

AMERICAN SIGN LANGUAGE

AMERICAN SIGN LANGUAGE
Linguistic and Applied Dimensions
Second Edition

Ronnie B. Wilbur, Ph.D.

Professor of Linguistics
Purdue University
West Lafayette, Indiana

A College-Hill Publication
Little, Brown and Company
Boston/Toronto/San Diego

College-Hill Press
A Division of
Little, Brown and Company (Inc.)
34 Beacon Street
Boston, Massachusetts 02108

Library of Congress Cataloging in Publication Data

Wilbur, Ronnie Bring.
  American sign language.

  Rev. ed. of: American sign languages and sign
systems. ©1979.
    "A College-Hill publicaton."
    Bibliography: p. 331
    Includes indexes.
    1. Sign language. 2. English language — Study and
teaching. I. Wilbur, Ronnie Bring. American sign
languages and sign systems. II. Title. [DNLM:
1. Manual Communication. HV 2474 W666a]
HV2474.W54 1987   419   86-26419
ISBN 0-316-94013-5

Printed in the United States of America.

In baseball, as in any good subject, the question is not one of boundaries. After all, a baseball field is not really a diamond. Fair territory is a 90-degree arc, defined by the foul lines, which extend, theoretically, to infinity. The limits of the baseball world are not intrinsic to the game. All man's occupations extend to the horizon, if we could but see that far.

—Thomas Boswell
How Life Imitates the World Series

To my husband Peter,
Who has helped me to see
Beyond the horizon.

CONTENTS

Preface to the Second Edition

If it can be said that a review of the literature has a theme, the theme of the first edition of this book (*American Sign Language and Sign Systems*, 1979) was the demonstration that sign languages, as represented by American Sign Language, could be analyzed by professional linguists using the frameworks and methods traditionally used only for spoken languages. In the nearly ten years since that first edition was written, the number of linguists involved in sign language analysis and the number of sign languages being analyzed have greatly increased around the world. One obvious reason, then, for writing a revised edition is to include the information that has since become available.

A comparison of this revised edition to the original version will reveal enormous differences. The first section of the original edition contained one chapter each on phonology, morphology, and syntax. By contrast, the present volume contains two chapters on phonology and two on morphology. In essence, entire chapters of the original volume were thrown out and replaced; careful readers may discern some similarity between the present Chapter 2 and the old chapter on phonology, and between the current chapter on syntax and the old one, but the differences outweigh the similarities. The contents of the present chapters on current approaches to phonology, word formation, and sign inflection are virtually all new. The old chapter on psycholinguistics of sign language usage has been replaced by two chapters, one including research with adults and the other with children. Extensive information on deaf culture has also been added to the chapter on sociolinguistics. The result is that the section on linguistic dimensions of sign research now contains eight chapters, as compared to the earlier five. In the applied dimensions section, the major difference is an expansion of the information contained in the chapter on the use of sign language in the education of deaf children.

As with any review of a field of inquiry, it is obviously impossible to provide a summary of every analysis or investigation by every author on every sign language. Certain ones have been summarized, others have been merely alluded to, still others have been referenced without further discussion, and unfortunately some have been omitted (including some that were present in the original edition). In doing so, a theme for the revised edition was created. This theme differs from the theme of the original book, in the sense that there is now *so much* linguistic analysis on sign languages that its existence and feasibility hardly seem worthy of mention. The underlying theme in this revised edition is the great shift in how linguists view the structure of signs. Earlier perspectives on signs treated them as essentially different from spoken words, in the sense that signs were viewed as simultaneous bundles of parameters (handshapes, location, movements, etc.) which behaved as an unanalyzable whole. This oversimplification has given way to the view that there are many signs that are more profitably viewed as analyzable, perhaps parallel to the English word "cat" which may be "decomposed" into three sound segments in sequence. Recognizing the possibility of *analyzability* in sign structure led to further observations, for example that certain signs may be morphologically analyzable, with prefixes and suffixes, parallel to the English word "undeniable," which may be decomposed into several pieces: "un-," "deny," "-able."

The perspective of analyzability has changed how many aspects of sign language linguistics are conducted: the kinds of descriptions of signs themselves, the approach to psycholinguistic studies of memory and perception, the study of sign language acquisition and the notion of what is "complex" for a child. For this reason, after a general overview (Chapter 1), the reader is assaulted with two chapters on sign phonology, the traditional descriptions (Chapter 2) and the current approaches, including such notions as syllables and segments (Chapter 3). Experience has shown me that this is *not* where most readers would prefer to start. Experience has also shown me that without this information, it is impossible to fully appreciate the detail, complexity, and full import of the remaining information. In order, for example, to understand how signs can be productively constructed (Chapter 4), the notion of particular phonological pieces and their relationship to ASL morphemes is crucial. The elegance and importance of a memory study (Chapter 7) that demonstrates that morphological inflections in ASL are separable from the lexical items themselves hinge on the understanding of how phonological pieces can be added simultaneously or sequentially to lexical items without destroying the basic form (Chapters 2, 3, 4, 5). The role of facial expression in sentence structure (Chapter 6), breakdown of the use of space in sign language aphasics (Chapter 7), complexity in child language acquisition (Chapter 8), variation in dialects (Chapter 9) all in some way depend on the reader's familiarity with the analyzability of signs.

Both the original version and this revised version contain a second section on the applied aspects of sign language research. This section contains descriptions of educational signing systems (Chapter 10), implications for deaf students' acquisition of English reading, writing, and speaking skills (Chapter 11), and sign training results with communicatively handicapped people who are not deaf (Chapter 12). Although to a lesser extent, these chapters also depend on the appreciation of analyzability in sign structure. Educational signing systems differ from ASL primarily because educators did not recognize the presence of inflectional morphemes in ASL; artificial ones were invented. Failure to understand the morphological complexity of ASL signs has led many educators to the erroneous conclusion that deaf children's problems with English were due to ASL. Intervention programs with the communicatively handicapped who are not deaf are still struggling to understand what aspects of sign training make it effective with various populations and what characteristics of signs make some easier for these populations to learn than others. Although it has not been made explicit in any of these chapters, the current linguistic perspective on sign structure is as important in the applied domains as it is to the linguists.

In the original edition of this book, I thanked the people "without whom this book would not have been possible." The list of people to whom I am most clearly indebted, but who are "too numerous to mention" here, may be found in the reference section at the back of the book. They are the people who have conducted the basic research and shared their results in print or at conferences, have sent me preprints and unpublished papers, and have helped me run up my long-distance phone bill. Special thanks for this revised edition go to John Bonvillian, Robert Hoffmeister, George Karlan, Vassilis Kourbetis, Scott Liddell, and Wendy Sandler.

However, I am not merely a bibliographer of the field; much of my own research has also contributed to the linguistic and applied debates. Funding from the National Science Foundation (BNS-8317572) and WIRCO have made much of this research possible. My "lab crew" has forged into the great void "where no man has ever gone before" with sometimes only the foggiest idea of what I wanted or why, and has produced quality results with accuracy, reliability, creativity, stamina, and wonderful humor. Special thanks to Lisa Goffman, John Fisher, Sharon Honigman Hellman, Laura Jennings,

Elizabeth Niccum, Theresa Niccum, and Jennifer Windsor, and to my coauthors, Brenda Schick, Susan Nolen, George Allen, and Macalyne Fristoe. Many of the illustrations used in this edition were created by Brenda Schick especially for this volume. Kathy Shuster of K.J. Graphics provided the illustrations of the different signs for "cat" in Chapter 7. The deaf communities in Boston and Indianapolis have also provided invaluable assistance.

For assistance with the revision, Brenda Schick and Peter Bjarkman must be acknowledged for their comments on earlier drafts, with an extra special thanks to Jennifer Windsor, not only for her comments and suggestions, but for her incredible job of cross-checking the references; she was "airsply fair billis!"

My husband, Peter C. Bjarkman, deserves special credit for his good humor and support throughout the duration of this project. Maybe now we can turn our attention to his work.

Ronnie Wilbur

CHAPTER 1

INTRODUCTION

American Sign Language (ASL or Ameslan) is, in the United States, the native language of many deaf people who have deaf parents and is the language used by many deaf adults among themselves. O'Rourke, Medina, Thames, and Sullivan (1975) suggest that nearly 500,000 deaf people and an unknown number of hearing people use ASL, which would make it the third most widely used non-English language in the United States (Spanish, 4.5 million; Italian, 600,000). American Sign Language differs from these other languages, however, because unlike English, Spanish, Italian, and others, ASL is primarily manual/visual rather than oral/auditory.

ASL (like other sign languages) is not derived from any spoken language, although its coexistence with English in a bilingual environment allows it to be influenced in a number of ways (creating new signs borrowed through fingerspelling, initializing a sign by substituting a handshape that corresponds to the first letter of an associated English word, and modifying the word order; see chapters 2–6). Linguists have studied many different sign languages around the

1

world; the consensus is that the influence from the surrounding spoken language is present but limited. ASL's nearest sign language relative is French Sign Language (FSL), a result of the intervention of Thomas Gallaudet and a deaf teacher from France, Laurent Clerc (Chapter 9). These educators brought French signs to the United States in 1817, while others spread French signs all over Europe, influencing such sign languages as Swedish, Latvian, Irish, Spanish, Dutch, Italian, Swiss, Austrian, Russian, and, eventually, Australian (Stokoe, 1972). ASL has been carried to Africa and India in recent years, where it will probably interact with the native sign languages. Woodward (1977) identifies several language families based on hypothesized relationships between known sign languages. In the French sign language family are Old FSL, Modern FSL, Old ASL, Modern ASL, and Danish (recall again that these are *not* related to spoken French). In the British sign language family are British Sign Language (BSL), Australasian Sign Language, Old Catholic Scottish Sign Language, and Modern Scottish Sign Language. Notice that although English is spoken in both America and Britain, the sign languages of the two countries are *not* related, *nor* are they mutually intelligible. Other families identified by Woodward include Asian (Hong Kong, Taiwan, and Japanese) and South American (Costa Rican, Colombian). Egyptian, Indian (studied extensively by Vasishta, Wilson, and Woodward, 1978, and Wilson, 1978), and Malaysian are of unknown affiliation. Others, such as Providence Island Sign (Washabaugh, Woodward, and DeSantis, 1976), appear to be indigenous (that is, to have arisen without any known connection to other sign languages). Mayberry (1978) looked at French-Canadian Sign Language, and the relationship between French Sign Language and ASL has been studied extensively by Woodward and DeSantis (1977a, b). Johnson (1978) investigated the structure of Oregon and British Columbia sawmill signs, which may be related to ASL.

Perhaps the best way to illustrate the expansion of sign language research worldwide is to describe the Third International Symposium on Sign Language Research, which was held in Rome, Italy, in 1983 (Stokoe and Volterra, 1985). Approximately 210 people attended from 22 countries. The conference presentations themselves covered a broad spectrum of sign languages. There were 10 papers directly concerned with the structure of ASL, 2 on Italian Sign Language, 2 on Brazilian Sign Language, 2 on Dutch Sign Language, 2 on Danish Sign Language, and 1 each on Japanese Sign, Russian Sign, Swedish Sign, French Sign, Chinese Sign, Swiss German Sign, British Sign, Providence Island Sign, and Martha's Vineyard Sign.

Several themes pervaded the lectures. These included the complexity of language and thought as evidenced by the structure of sign languages, the similarities and differences among various sign languages and between sign languages and spoken languages, and the role of facial expression and other nonmanual information. There were also specific papers on the acquisition of sign languages, short term memory, perception, kinesiology related to sign language structure, brain function and sign language usage, and the history of ASL and its relationship to French Sign Language. These topics will be dealt with in subsequent chapters.

There have also been a number of recent publications and presentations on sign languages other than ASL. Some are in English, others are in the language spoken in the country where they were written. Several describe the sign language itself, whereas others discuss the sign language in reference to educational issues or provide signs for teachers of the deaf. On British Sign Language, there are three recent publications: Brennan, Colville, and Lawson (1980) — linguistic analysis of BSL; Woll, Kyle, and Deuchar (1981) — BSL linguistics, psycholinguistics, and educational perspectives; and Kyle and Woll (1983) — papers on BSL, Swedish Sign, Norwegian Sign, ASL, and issues related to deafness in general. One volume on Brazilian Sign Language (Hoemann, Oates, and Hoemann, 1981, 1983) is available in both English and Portuguese. Further work on Brazilian Sign Languages (there are at least two distinct languages) is being conducted by Ferreira Brito (1986). Smith and Li-fen (1979), a description of Taiwan Sign Language, is also available in two languages, Chinese and English. More details of the auxiliary system were included in Smith (1986). A description of Danish Sign Language (Engberg-Pedersen, Hansen, and Sorensen, 1981) is available only in Danish. The description of Greek Sign Language by Logiadis and Logiadi (1985) is written entirely in Greek, except for the Table of Contents and one paragraph explaining symbols, which are also written in French and English. Further work on Greek Sign Language and the Greek deaf community is being conducted by Kourbetis (1986; Kourbetis, Hoffmeister, and Greenwald, 1985). The only work on Spanish signing so far is a description for use in the Spanish schools (simultaneous signing and speaking), and is available only in Spanish (Monfort, Rojo, and Juarez, 1982). A dictionary of Israeli Sign Language was published in English by Cohen, Namir, and Schlesinger (1977); it includes extensive explanation and use of a notation system adopted from the Eschol-Wachman dance notation (for a review, see Wilbur, 1978c). In preparation at the time of this writing is a volume on Italian Sign Language (in Italian) by the sign language research group in Rome (Volterra, Radutzky, and their colleagues). A book of translations of information previously published in English and primarily on ASL has also been published in Italian (Montanini-Manfredi, Fruggeri, and Facchini, 1979). Another volume of translations was published in French as a special issue on sign of the journal *Langages* (Grosjean and Lane, 1979). Recent presentations included descriptions of New Zealand Sign Language (Collins-Ahlgren, 1986) and Japanese Sign Language (Kanda, 1986).

The kinds of relationships between sign languages, such as those suggested by Woodward and others, do not imply mutual intelligibility; that is, users of one sign language cannot understand users of another sign language and vice versa. Jordan and Battison (1976) have demonstrated that Modern French Sign Language, ASL, and Danish Sign Language, although related, are not mutually intelligible. The lack of mutual intelligibility is also well demonstrated by the interpreting requirements for the International Symposium on Sign Language Research in Rome. Registrants were not required to indicate their hearing status, thus there is no way to know exactly how many people present were deaf, but the conference organizers estimated the number at 25. The presence of deaf researchers constituted a significant aspect of the conference, not only because of their increased numbers over previous conferences, but also because of the interpreting arrangements that were made to accommodate them. No previous conference has had such extensive interpreting services. The conference itself had two official spoken languages, English and Italian. Spoken French was also used on a limited basis. Standard interpreting facilities (interpreting booths and headsets) were available in the main conference room. For the deaf members of the audience, there were 10 signed languages: Italian, American, British, Danish, Finnish, Swedish, Norwegian, French, Belgian (Flemish), and Thai. A typical presentation presented in Italian would be translated into English by the spoken English interpreter, and then into their respective sign languages by those interpreters following the English on their headsets. The remaining interpreters translated directly from the Italian. Several papers were presented in various sign languages and were translated into either English or Italian by the appropriate sign language interpreter, then into the other spoken language by the respective spoken language interpreter, then into the remaining sign languages by those interpreters.

The fact that deaf people who use different sign languages cannot understand each other sometimes surprises people, who mistakenly think that deaf people are able to communicate with each other in spite of linguistic differences. The truth is that conversations between users of different sign languages are limited in what can be communicated. Although certain things can be communicated by gesturing, pointing, miming, and drawing outlines in the air (things that signers may be more adept at doing, but which hearing people also do, even if they know no sign), more extensive discussions involving topics that are not *here and now* (past or future tense, for example) or that are not concrete (abstract concepts, conditionals, complex negatives) are impossible. Our observation of many deaf people who were present at another conference, the World Federation of the Deaf in Palermo, Sicily (also in 1983), was that almost all had knowledge of English; thus, we saw some people speechreading each other's spoken English and other people who had studied what is called the "International" fingerspelling alphabet attempting to use it to spell English. Frequently, my Italian colleagues (who know English) and I would serve as clumsy interpreters, from ASL, signed English, or fingerspelled English to spoken English to spoken Italian to signed Italian, Italian Sign Language, or fingerspelled Italian and back again. Conversations tended to be limited to functional topics (where people were from, where they were staying, where else they had visited in Europe, where they were eating dinner, what they were having), short in duration, and awkward, although the effort was clearly part of the fun. At the Rome Sign Language Research conference, with its expert interpreters, more sophisticated conversations were possible, including, of course, the contents of the linguistics research papers.

Quite apart from the use of ASL in the United States is the use of a modified form, signed English. The fact that one can sign and speak at the same time has allowed educators to take advantage of the bilingual situation in which American deaf people exist. Taking the signs from ASL and the word order from English, sign language *systems* have been established artificially for teaching English syntax to deaf children. In addition to deliberate modifications by educators, signed English also includes those modifications in signing that result from (1) native speakers of English who are unfamiliar with ASL syntax but have learned ASL signs and fingerspelling, (2) deaf signers' own modifications reflecting the influence of English syntax when in contact with hearing people (for details, see Chapter 9) and (3) possible influences of English on signing structure when hearing children who have deaf parents grow up in a bilingual environment. The larger context in which ASL is used, surrounded by English speaking and English signing hearing people, and the bilingual nature of deaf people themselves must constantly be kept in mind.

BACKGROUND ON EARLY
SIGN LANGUAGE RESEARCH

The early writings on sign language were concerned with its status as a language and its role in the education of deaf children. Later research on ASL and other sign languages was thus aimed at demonstrating (1) that it is indeed a language and (2) that it is beneficial in educating deaf children. More recent linguistic research has shifted away from proving that ASL is a language to concentrating on providing an adequate linguistic description, with the possible subsequent goal of constructing a grammar useful for teaching ASL to nonsigners. However, more recent educational research is still aiming at demonstrating utility of sign language in education. Efficient teaching techniques and maximum utilization of the available modalities remain to be investigated more carefully.

Negative attitudes toward sign languages have arisen from several sources. One is the general lack of understanding of the nature of language itself, as few people have studied linguistics, or know more than one language; the result is a failure to separate "language" from "speech" and to treat one's own native language as the standard for comparison for all others. Another is the absence of a writing system for sign language, because it has led to makeshift ways of recording information about signs. These efforts at writing signs frequently omit crucial information about sign formation. One common technique is to use "glosses"; that is, using a word from the spoken language to "name" the sign, then writing that name each time the sign is used. Glosses do not record how the sign is made; for example, in the sentences "John hit Bill" and "Bill hit John," the verb would be glossed (with capital letters, see p. 15) as HIT for both sentences, even though in each sentence the verb would start and end at different points. Another example of difficulty with glossing was the older practice of writing a dual gloss, such as AIRPLANE/FLY. Researchers did not realize that there was a systematic difference between the formation of associated nouns and verbs (airplane/fly; car/drive; seat[chair]/sit). People assumed that the same sign was made in both situations and that ASL lacked formal noun/verb distinctions. Furthermore, because they depended on their glosses when conducting their analyses, researchers did not think to look harder for such distinctions. The noun/verb distinction in ASL clearly demonstrates that reliance on glosses is inadequate: verbs are usually made with a long, smooth movement, while nouns associated with those verbs are made with short, repeated, tense movements (Supalla and Newport, 1978). Thus, the gloss obscures information about the formation of the sign that is critical to the understanding of the nature of sign language. The use of glosses allowed only crude analyses of the language, and indeed many people did little more than compare a glossed sentence to an English sentence. This resulted in conclusions that ASL consisted of unordered, mimetic gestures and was incomplete, inferior, situation-bound, and concrete. Such terms represent not only a lack of understanding of manual language, but an oral language bias, from which it is exceedingly difficult to escape. These negative attitudes and early linguistic descriptions provided the proponents of oral education for the deaf with the upper hand in the so-called "oral/manual controversy." It was their challenge to those interested in the use of sign language to first prove that sign language was both a language and useful in the education of deaf children (which meant, in addition, to prove that it did not harm deaf children's acquisition of speech; see Chapter 11). The oral language bias inherent in this entire situation is evidenced by the fact that the proponents of manual communication have responded unquestioningly to the challenge while, as Conrad (1975) pointed out, never issuing a similar challenge to the proponents of oral education to demonstrate the effectiveness of their methods for the total development of the deaf child.

The failure to make the initial separation of language from speech goes back far into history, and may be related to the fact that writing was a late innovation, and that even to this day, languages without writing systems still exist. The Bible reports that at the Tower of Babel, the Lord went down and "did there confound their language, that they may not understand one another's speech" (Genesis 11:7). In sharp contrast to this view of oral supremacy, Hewes (1973) has suggested that gestures may have been the origin of language, and speech was a later development.

The education of deaf people has been profoundly affected by the failure to recognize the distinction between language and speech. Siegel (1969) described the character of eighteenth-century educators of the deaf:

The task of educating the deaf was undertaken mainly by charities often manned by fierce evangelical reformers. Filled with enthusiasm and caught up in the evangelical tide which was making deep eddies in English social philosophy, these men of good will and great piety saw their role in terms of Biblical text. The deaf to them were pitiable outcasts whose tongues were tied, and as Christ had opened the ears of the deaf man and had loosened his tongue, so must they try to do.

At the same time, "in France, the situation was quite different, and there was by the end of the XVIIIth century great concern for the total education of the deaf" (Siegel, 1969). By 1790, the Abbé de l'Epée had founded his school for the deaf in Paris, and had developed a modified sign system, a form of signed French, which he called "methodical signs" (Markowicz, 1976).

Both France and England were influenced by John Locke's empirical philosophy, which maintained that the mind worked only on what the senses conveyed to it. Introspection on the part of some Englishmen revealed to them that they thought in words — they spoke to themselves — and they concluded that *speech* conveys information to the mind. Therefore, a person deprived of speech would necessarily be deprived of the means by which to think. However, the French interpreted Locke's writings differently; they concluded that the mind would work on any information conveyed to it by any sense and that deaf people should be able to profit from the visual mode. "That two such opposite philosophies could grow simultaneously in two countries [England — oral, France — manual] which shared so many other ideas certainly warrants an investigation of the historical and intellectual climates which produced these ideas" (Siegel, 1969).

Two recent books by Lane (Lane, 1984; Lane and Philip, 1984) provide the most extensive discussions of deaf history available. Lane (1984) is written as though told by Laurent Clerc, the deaf teacher who came to the United States with Thomas Gallaudet and opened the first school for the deaf at Hartford, Connecticut, in 1817. The book uses as its theme a quote from Victor Hugo: "The one true deafness, the incurable deafness, is that of the mind." The other book, by Lane and Philip (1984), contains a set of essays translated from the original French, written between 1764 and 1840. These essays document the pendulum swings between what Lane (1980) called "replacement" (the replacement of sign language by oral-only methods) and "dialectization" (the deliberate modification of the natural sign language to make it parallel to the word and sentence structure of the spoken language). In this regard, the essays in Lane and Philip (1984) illustrate a quote from Hegel (cited in Lane, 1980): "what experience and history teach is this — that people and governments never have learned anything from history, or acted on principles deduced from it." It is surprising how much of what modern educators and linguists think they invented was created, debated, modified, and discarded before 1900 (for a review, see Wilbur, 1985a; further discussion, Chapter 9).

The conflict between these two diverse methods of educating the deaf continues to this day. In the United States, there has been a rapid increase in total communication (TC) usage (loosely, the simultaneous use of signs and speechreading) in programs for deaf children. Jordan, Gustason, and Rosen (1976) found that 510 programs reported using total communication, some 333 of which (about 65 percent) had changed between 1968 and 1975. (This represents a significant increase in the number of deaf children who are learning a form of signed English, thus providing the potential for greater influences of English syntax on the structure of ASL.) This rise in total communication has been greeted with mixed reviews. On one hand, the establishment of effective communication with young deaf children is viewed to be essential to their socioemotional development as well as to their academic achievement (Chapter 11). On the other hand, there are unanswered questions concerning the potential for processing two modalities at the same time, concern over the greater amount of processing time that signed English takes compared to ASL or to spoken English, concern over the declining emphasis placed on specific speech skills training, and the proliferation of language programs of any kind without considering the individual needs of each particular child. These topics will be discussed in subsequent chapters.

LINGUISTIC INTEREST IN SIGN LANGUAGE

The existence of any unstudied language represents a great attraction to most linguists. For that language to be visual/spatial rather than commonplace auditory heightens their interest. Of primary concern among linguists are the features that all human languages have in common and what might account for these universal characteristics. In this respect, sign languages represent a challenge to theories of linguistic universals, as well as to metalinguistic concepts of "possible grammar." If it were found that proposed constraints on, for example, what syntactic rules may or may not do are valid also for a visual/manual language, confidence in a description of language that incorporates such constraints would be greatly strengthened.

The search for linguistic universals has traditionally included only oral languages (Chinchor et al., 1976; Greenberg, 1966; but see Comrie, 1981). Many attempts to investigate linguistic universals with respect to manual languages thus displayed an oral language bias. In order to fully understand how this bias can affect manual language research, and to emphasize the need for caution when interpreting any research on sign languages, it is instructive to consider an early attempt by Schlesinger (1970) to study Israeli Sign

Language (ISL) to see if manual languages expressed grammatical relations such as subject, object, and indirect object, which are claimed to be linguistically universal.

Schlesinger's experiment was designed to elicit sentences in ISL (which is not related to ASL) that contain three noun phrases ("arguments") in the function of subject, object, and indirect object, as illustrated by the English sentence "John gave the book to Mary," where "John" is the subject, "the book" is the direct object, and "Mary" is the indirect object. The same relations hold if the sentence is reworded as "John gave Mary the book." The *sender* had in front of him a picture that contained a man, a bear, and a girl, in which the man might be handing the bear to the girl, or handing the girl to the bear, etc. The *receiver* had six pictures in which each of the possible combinations was portrayed. The sender had to communicate in sign language to the receiver which picture to choose. Thirty subjects were used. They varied greatly in background; some had a good knowledge of Hebrew (and probably limited knowledge of ISL) whereas others had limited knowledge of Hebrew (and probably were users of ISL). It is also likely that those with good knowledge of Hebrew used signed Hebrew, which is to ISL as signed English is to ASL. The results of Schlesinger's experiment showed a high degree of misunderstanding between sender and receiver. Schlesinger concluded that ISL did not have a means for expressing grammatical relations, because the receivers would pick the wrong pictures and thus indicate that they were not receiving the grammatical information of who was doing what to whom. Therefore, he concluded that grammatical relations must not be linguistically universal.

The same experiment was conducted by Bode (1974) with American Sign Language and the results were very different. Bode used a group of native users of ASL and a hearing control group who used spoken English. She found 86 percent comprehension for the signers and 95 percent for the speakers, the difference being not significant. Schlesinger had an average of 52 percent comprehension for his signers. Why such a large difference? Bode screened her subjects to make sure that all of them were native users of the language, whereas Schlesinger did not. In Israel, this can be a great mistake, since the population is heterogeneous, including immigrants from all parts of the world, some of whom may have only recently arrived in Israel. Stokoe (personal communication) feels that Israeli Sign Language is in fact a convenient fiction for a lingua franca (a working language for people with different linguistic backgrounds) composed of sign languages that came together only shortly before the establishment of Israel. In such a situation, variables like age, education, and residency can be of critical importance. Schlesinger's subjects could not understand the messages sent, not because of a lack of grammatical relations in Israeli Sign Language, but because they were not all using the same language. "The comparable situation in the United States indicates that users of ASL often readily comprehend sentences from signed English, but that users of only signed English have great difficulty understanding ASL. This is primarily due to the fact that the education system insists on teaching English syntax to deaf children in school and that they are consequently familiar with the syntax of signed English. Educational institutions in the United States do not teach American Sign Language or its structure. The result is that deaf individuals may have a range of competency in ASL' (Chinchor et al., 1976). The same situation is probably true in Israel. In any event, the failure to investigate these factors may lead to a lack of validity for experimental conclusions.

Another problem inherent in Schlesinger's study, which will shed light on later reports as well, is his data analysis. He assumed that grammatical relations would be displayed in a linear sequence, thus he choose to analyze only "full sentences," those that contained separate signs for the subject, direct object, and indirect object in linear sequence with the verb. This excluded from analysis any utterances that used a sign language device of establishing positions in space for nouns and moving or orienting the verb sign between them (Chapter 6). The effects that these assumptions had on Schlesinger's overall analysis are discussed more fully in Chinchor et al. (1976). For present purposes, it is only the historical perspective this study provides that is of specific interest. Nor is Schlesinger alone. In Wilbur and Jones (1974), failure to understand the function of pointing in ASL led them to ignore certain signs used by hearing children of deaf parents; thus they missed important stages of development (Chapter 8). Others have framed their descriptions of ASL in terms of comparisons with English. Fant (1972), for example, wrote that ASL has no passive voice, no sign for the verb "to be," and no determiners. By itself, this description is insufficient, because it fails to indicate how such information *is* communicated in ASL.

PROCEEDING WITH SIGN LANGUAGE RESEARCH

This review of the research on sign language and its educational applications is divided into two major parts. Part I concentrates on

structural descriptions of ASL and psycholinguistic and sociolinguistic aspects of its usage. Of necessity, descriptions of sign language must begin with descriptions of the sign itself. Stokoe (1960)
provided a description of sign formation, a "cherology" (coming from
a Homeric Greek morpheme *cher* meaning "handy") parallel to spoken language phonology, which has been built upon, refined, and
modified in subsequent years by himself and others (Chapters 2 and
3). The term "phonology" has been retained in this book because it
has become apparent that traditional notions of segment structures,
their effects on surrounding segments, and their combination into
larger units (spoken words or signs) are appropriate for sign structure as described so far (Chapters 2 and 3). Discussion of historical
changes in sign formation, constraints on sign formation, violation
of constraints for humorous or artistic purposes, and the role of
facial expression are also included in Chapter 2. This chapter is also
the first of several chapters containing separate sections marked
"Primarily for Linguists"; these sections are more technical and assume greater linguistic sophistication than the other sections. These
technical sections are written with the assumption that many readers will skip directly to the chapter summary.

As more research focused on the structure of signs themselves, it
became clear that there are certain similarities between the structure of signing and speech, particularly in terms of timing, rhythm,
and clustering of segments for perception and production. Evidence
accumulated that it is appropriate to talk about syllables and syllable structure in signed languages. Timing and frequency data are
presented in Chapter 3, along with discussion of how particular
pieces of signs are modifiable in certain circumstances (productive
signs versus frozen signs). The technical section in Chapter 3
presents information on syllable structure, tiers and spreading, issues of underlying representations and phonological rules, and suggestions for the organization of the phonological component of ASL
and how that organization might constrain the types of phonological
rules that may occur.

One of the aspects of ASL sign formation that parallels spoken
language word formation (but not English) is the presence of classifiers, a particular kind of pronoun that includes in its meaning more
information than English pronouns do. For example, in English, the
pronoun "it," indicates only that the referent is inanimate and singular. Classifiers include information about the same size, shape,
material, rigidity, configuration, arrangement, or even function of
the referent. In languages that have classifiers, instead of having
one pronoun "it," there are many forms, each one being chosen

according to the characteristics of the object itself. Thus, a pencil might be referred to with a form that would translate into English as "it-the long thin thing" and a basket might be referred to with a form meaning "it-the woven thing" or "it-the thing with the hollow interior" or "it-the thing with the curved exterior." The choice depends on the object and on the forms available in the language itself. Chapter 4 discusses some of the classifiers that are available in ASL and how they parallel those that have been identified for spoken languages. Furthermore, these classifiers are almost always just handshapes, and are therefore able to combine with certain verbs that are just movements (with further details for direction of movement, location of formation, manner of formation, and so on). The combination of classifier handshapes with predicate verb movements creates new signs, referred to as productive signs. Categories of predicates are also discussed in Chapter 4. There are also "families" of signs that are related because they have similar handshapes, movements, locations, or directions of movement; these are presented in Chapter 4 as well.

Once the signs are put together by the processes discussed in Chapter 4, they can be further modified to carry additional information. This additional information can tell more about the subject and object involved or it can tell more about the action itself. Chapter 5 presents both types of modifications and a discussion of how both types can be put onto the same sign without destroying the whole message. The technical section "Primarily for Linguists" deals extensively with how different types of modifications are made in certain ways so that they will not interfere with other types of modifications, thus allowing many pieces of information to be packed into one sign.

Sign language researchers agree that even though many of the most interesting things that can happen in ASL happen to single signs through the types of modifications mentioned above, there are still important observations to be made about sentence structure in ASL. To fully appreciate these observations, it is necessary to understand that languages like English, where sentence structure is heavily dictated by the ordering of words, are not as common as languages in which the ordering is less rigid because the individual words carry many pieces of information about who is doing what to whom. This is true in ASL as well. At one point in time, some researchers suggested that maybe ASL did not have any sentence structure at all because each complex predicate sign contained so much information that sentence structure was irrelevant. Most researchers today recognize that there are constraints on what kinds of ordering can occur in a sentence and that it depends heavily on what other information is present in each sign. There are also complex sentences that have more than one clause in them. These topics are dealt with in Chapter 6. The technical section in this chapter provides linguistic details concerning noun phrases, the verb complex, and other syntactic structures.

Many studies of ASL have concentrated on how deaf native signers use the language rather than on the structure of the language itself. In Chapter 7, many aspects of sign production, perception, and memory are reviewed. Issues related to the often mentioned iconicity of signs are also discussed, including recent perspectives on the metaphorical use of iconicity in sign languages. Also included is the recent focus on the relationship between signing and brain lateralization, with evidence from experimental work and clinical observation of aphasia in deaf signers. Chapter 8 presents the fascinating observations of those who have studied sign language acquisition. In many ways, these studies provide confirmation of the descriptions presented in the earlier chapters and the findings of the experimental studies in Chapter 7.

Chapter 9 includes sociolinguistic aspects of ASL usage and the deaf community, including theories of the history of ASL, variation and dialects in ASL, and modifications of ASL in contact with English. The role of ASL in defining an identifiable community is also discussed. The role of hearing people with respect to the deaf community is approached from two perspectives, that related to hearing children who have deaf parents, and that related to hearing people who have no other connection to the deaf community but with whom deaf people must interact (including teachers of the deaf, interpreters, and sign language researchers).

Part II, Applied Dimensions, contains three chapters. Chapter 10 is concerned with artificial signed English systems, including the most commonly used of these, Signing Exact English (SEE 2) and Signed English (distinguished from signed English in the latter part of Chapter 10). Also included are fingerspelling, which is used very little in ASL but which may be used simultaneously with speech (and no signs) in an educational method called the Rochester Method, and Cued Speech, which is not a sign system at all but an auxiliary system of manual cues for assisting in speechreading. Chapter 11 deals with the education of deaf children and the resulting influence of sign usage on the language development (English and sign language), reading and writing, speech skills, memory, perception, and socioemotional development of deaf students. Chapter 12 focuses on reports of successful language intervention using signs with communicatively handicapped people who are not deaf. This includes autistic children, mentally retarded individuals, multiply handicapped student's and individuals with cerebral palsy. The surprising result of many of these intervention attempts has been that some of these individuals with normal vocalization mechanisms have eventually increased their vocalizations and improved their verbalizations to intelligible levels.

The diversity of topics included in this book reflects the diversity of people who are concerned with deafness and sign language. The information presented here is not all there is to know about ASL or sign language research in general, nor is every paper from every researcher included (a result of time and space requirements). Rather than participating in the continual oral/manual controversy, this author has instead chosen to present available factual information. Where appropriate, the information presented has been questioned. The reader is advised to do the same. Do not assume that the summaries herein contain all of the original authors' data, arguments, or intentions. Particular attention should be paid to the use of words like "seems," "could be," and "may," in which I have avoided stating as fact those things that are still controversial, remain to be investigated, or are insufficiently documented. In many cases, the use of such terms are the original author's, and in no case should their usage be considered negative.

EXPLAINING THE NOTATION

The hardest thing to do with a dynamic, three-dimensional language is to reduce it to two-dimensional linear description. Transcriptions, illustrations, and photographs fall far short of the ideal representation. Several detailed transcriptions have been proposed for describing the formation of signs. The notation in Stokoe, Casterline, and Croneberg's (1965) *Dictionary of American Sign Language* has been retained here. Others (Newkirk, 1975; Sutton, 1976) suggest that a wider variety will be available in the future.

In addition to Stokoe notation, which is discussed early in Chapter 2, a few other conventions are necessary. The glosses (names) of all signs are written in capital letters, e.g., HIT. The English translation (or best approximation thereof) is presented in double quotation marks, e.g., "hit." Complex glosses are connected by hyphens, e.g., SIT-ON-IT "sit on it." Fingerspelled letters are indicated in single quotation marks, e.g., 's'. Fingerspelled sequences are written in lower case with hyphens between each letter, e.g., s-e-a-r-c-h-i-n-g "searching." Fingerspelling sequences that have become actual signs, called fingerspelled loan signs, will be written in capitals (as for signs) with the symbol "#" before them. Thus, b-u-t indicates that three handshapes were made in sequence, whereas # BUT indicates that a sign was made with two handshapes (B and T) and a closing hand motion (see Battison, 1978, for details of how short fingerspelled sequences become modified into signs).

When necessary, descriptions of the formation of the sign are given in parentheses in awkward English. The reader may want to have the Stokoe, Casterline, and Croneberg (1976) *Dictionary of American Sign Language* or the O'Rourke (1973) *A Basic Course in Manual Communication,* or some other sign reference manual, available to see what signs not illustrated here look like. Finally, an asterisk* before a sentence indicates ungrammaticality.

Part I

Linguistic Dimensions

CHAPTER 2

Sign Phonology: Traditional Approaches

This chapter contains several traditional descriptions of sign structure. There is also a technical section entitled "Primarily for Linguists." It is assumed that when this book is used as a text for a basic course in sign language structure for nonlinguists, the technical section will probably be omitted, but that when the book is used to introduce linguists to the linguistic literature on sign language structure or as a reference for more sophisticated readers, the technical section will be of special value. Readers omitting the technical section should skip to the summary at the end.

In order to fully understand the complex structure of ASL, it is necessary to understand the building blocks that are available to form signs and the ways in which those blocks may be fit together. There are several ways in which sign formation can be described, some using older theories of linguistics or different assumptions about the nature of signs. This chapter contains a summary of the traditional descriptions of sign formation, whereas the next chapter contains more modern approaches. One feature that sets the traditional descriptions apart from the more recent models is that traditional perspectives have worked with the assumption, whether explicitly or not, that signs were composed of *simultaneous* bundles of building blocks, whatever those building blocks might be. The more recent approaches have emphasized the *sequential* nature of the arrangement of building blocks, slicing signs in a way that parallels speech. Aside from this fundamental difference in approach, there remains considerable debate about the nature of the building blocks themselves and how to best represent them.

TRADITIONAL BUILDING BLOCKS

In the earliest linguistic description of ASL, Stokoe (1960) used a structural linguistic framework to analyze sign formation. He called it "cherology," based on the Greek root for 'hand', and treated it as analogous to the phonological system of spoken languages. He defined three "aspects" that were combined simultaneously in the formation of a particular sign — what acts, where it acts, and the act. These three aspects translate into the "parameters" or "primes" that other linguists have described — the handshape, the location, and the movement. Stokoe referred to the handshape as the "designator" (DEZ), the location as the "tabulation" (TAB), and the movement as the "signation" (SIG). The notational system that Stokoe developed for writing signs contains symbols for each individual handshape, location, and movement.

Stokoe notation is still used today as a convenient shorthand for writing signs, although linguists cannot use it for many purposes because it does not provide symbols for many phonetic details, such as uneven rate of signing, tenseness or laxness, sharp or soft manner of movement, or facial expressions and other nonmanual components that are crucial to the actual formation of a sign. Instead, Stokoe notation may be thought of as similar to the alphabet for English; using the alphabet, we know how a word is spelled and can look it up in a dictionary, but the alphabet does not contain details of pronunciation such as dialect variation in the vowels, syllable initial aspiration of voiceless stops, or the stress that distinguishes 'permit' the verb (stress on the second syllable) from 'permit' the noun (stress on the first syllable). Speakers of English recognize the word and know how to pronounce it when they see it written in context, but this is because they provide additional information that is not present in the writing itself. Linguists can use Stokoe notation for research to be sure that they are referring to the same sign when they see the notated form, but a person who does not know sign would not actually be able to produce the sign without additional formational information provided by someone who already knows how to sign. Thus, Stokoe notation is *not* like the International Phonetic Alphabet, which can be used with reasonable success to represent the pronunciation of a spoken language. The development of a truly phonetic notation for sign language production is badly needed, both for teaching signs and for research purposes. Several efforts are underway, most notably Liddell and Johnson (1985).

After Stokoe, other analyses of sign language formation suggested additions to the three basic building blocks — handshape, location, and movement. One major parameter, orientation of the palm, was suggested by Battison (1973; Battison, Markowicz, and Woodward, 1975). The difference between the signs CHILDREN and THING is that in the first, the palm of the hand faces down, whereas in the second, the palm faces up. Other formational pieces that are needed to provide a full description of a sign include the contact of the signing hand with another part of the body (including the other hand), the direction of the movement, the speed of signing, the tension in the signing hand, the size of the path of the sign, facial expression, eye gaze, and head tilt, nod, or shake.

HANDSHAPE. ASL handshapes are given in Figure 2–1, and the American manual alphabet used for fingerspelling is given in Figure 2–2. Notice first that there are 36 handshapes in Figure 2–1 but only 26 handshapes for letters of the alphabet (Figure 2–2). Some of the handshapes overlap, others do not. In Table 2–1, the Stokoe notation symbols for the ASL handshapes (Figure 2–1) are presented (Stokoe et al., 1976). It is important to emphasize that although some of the handshapes are named with letter names (A, B, G, etc.), these handshapes are not necessarily identical in formation to the letters of the manual alphabet of the same name (compare, for example, G in Figures 2–1 and 2–2). Furthermore, the use of the letter names for the handshapes used in signing does not mean that there is a connection between the formation of the sign and the letters of the English word that is used to translate that sign. There are some signs whose formation has been modified so that the handshape *does* correspond to the first letter of the English word (initialized signs), but this has been done deliberately and artificially (usually for educational purposes) and will be discussed separately.

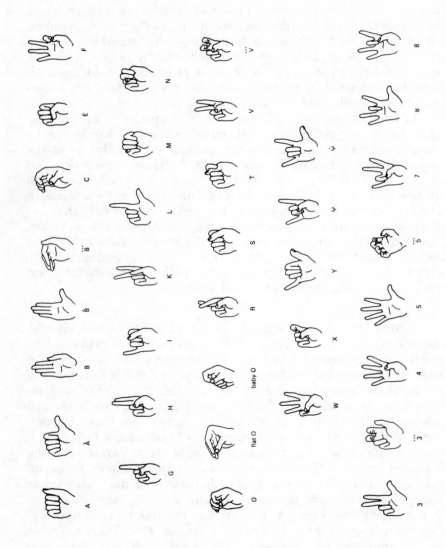

Figure 2-1. ASL handshapes (presented in an order allowing comparison with the Manual Alphabet in Figure 2–2).

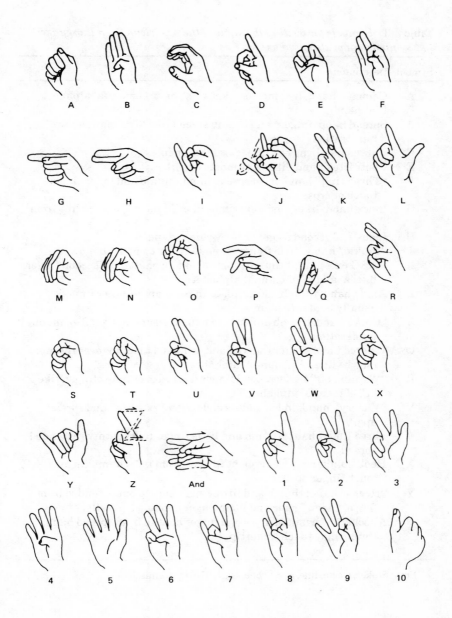

Figure 2-2. The American manual alphabet.

Table 2-1. *Symbols for writing the signs of the American Sign Language:* DEZ *symbols, some also used as* TAB

Symbol	Description
A	Compact hand, fist; may be like 'a', 's', or 't' of manual alphabet
B	Flat hand
5	Spread hand; fingers and thumb spread like '5' of manual numeration
C	Curved hand; may be like 'c' or more open
E	Contracted hand; like 'e' or more claw-like
F	"Three-ring" hand; from spread hand, thumb and index finger touch or cross
G	Index hand; like 'g' or sometimes like 'd'; index finger points from fist
H	Index and second finger, side-by-side, extended
I	"Pinkie" hand; little finger extended from compact hand
K	Like G except that thumb touches middle phalanx of second finger; like 'k' and 'p' of manual alphabet
L	Angle hand; thumb, index finger in right angle, other fingers usually bent into palm
3	"Cock" hand; thumb and first two fingers spread, like '3' of manual numeration
O	Tapered hand; fingers curved and squeezed together over thumb; may be like 'o' of manual alphabet
R	"Warding off" hand; second finger crossed over index finger, like "r" of manual alphabet
V	"Victory" hand; index and second fingers extended and spread apart
W	Three-finger hand; thumb and little finger touch, others extended spread
X	Hook hand; index finger bent in hook from fist, thumb tip may touch fingertip
Y	"Horns" hand; thumb and little finger spread out extended from fist; or index finger and little finger extended, parallel
8	Allocheric variant of Y; second finger bent in from spread hand, thumb may touch fingertip

From Stokoe, Casterline, and Croneberg (1976) by permission.

Notice in Table 2–1 that according to Stokoe, the manual letters 'a', 's', and 't' are not distinctive, but are considered variants of A. In ASL before the introduction of initialized signs, a sign made with the handshape 'a' of the manual alphabet was not distinct in meaning from a similar sign made with the handshape 's' or 't'. Initialization has created several signs from one, by attaching distinctive meanings to the different handshapes borrowed from the manual alphabet. Thus, the sign made with the A handshape, which may be translated as "try, attempt, strive," has been split so that with the 'a' handshape from the manual alphabet it means "attempt," with the 's' manual letter it means "strive," and with the 't' manual letter it means "try." These borrowings are discussed in more detail later in this chapter, and in Chapter 4.

LOCATION. Table 2–2 lists the Stokoe symbols for the location of a sign. A basic distinction is made between those signs made on the body (including so-called "body anchor verbs") and those made in neutral space. All signs must be made within the "signing space" (Battison, 1973; Bellugi and Fischer, 1972; Frishberg, 1975), described by Lacy (1974) as extending from the top of the head to just below the waist (or hip area) on the vertical axis while horizontally and laterally forming a "bubble" in front of the speaker, extending from the signer's extreme right to the signer's extreme left (an arc of

Table 2–2. *Symbols for writing the signs of the American Sign Language:* TAB *symbols*

Symbol	Description
ø	Zero, the neutral place where the hands move, in contrast with all places below
Ö	Face or whole head
∩	Forehead or brow, upper face
Ц	Mid-face, the eye and nose region
∪	Chin, lower face
}	Cheek, temple, ear, side-face
∏	Neck
[ ]	Trunk, body from shoulders to hips
⟍	Upper arm
⟋	Elbow, forearm
ɑ	Wrist, arm in supinated position (on its back)
ᗡ	Wrist, arm in pronated position (face down)

From Stokoe, Casterline, and Croneberg (1976) by permission.

180°). The signing space may be proportionately enlarged for signing to larger audiences ("louder") or confined for purposes of more rapid signing or to be secretive ("quieter") so as not to be "overseen." Few signs are made over the head, behind the ear, or below the waist (Lacy, 1974). Bellugi (1972) reported that when signed English was compared to ASL, the signing that was intended to parallel English was produced in a more compact space in front of the signer's body, whereas when ASL was signed, a larger signing space was used. In addition to the locations listed in Table 2–2 several of the handshapes listed in Table 2–1 may serve as place of formation for signs that involve two hands touching. Thus, the sign NAME involves the touching of one H hand to the other H hand, whereas the sign THAT involves a Y hand touching a 5 hand.

Table 2–3. *Symbols for writing the signs of the American Sign Language:* SIG *symbols*

Symbol	Description	Action
∧	Upward movement	
∨	Downward movement	Vertical action
∿	Up-and-down movement	
>	Rightward movement	
<	Leftward movement	Sideways action
⋛	Side-to-side movement	
т	Movement toward signer	
⊥	Movement away from signer	Horizontal action
Ⅰ	To-and-fro movement	
α	Supinating rotation (palm up)	
ɒ	Pronating position (palm down)	Rotary action
ω	Twisting movement	
η	Nodding or bending action	
□	Opening action (final DEZ configuration shown in brackets)	
#	Closing action (final DEZ configuration shown in brackets)	
ℓ	Wriggling action of fingers	
℮	Circular action	
)(	Convergent action, approach	
x	Contactual action, touch	
ꓵ	Linking action, grasp	
+	Crossing action	Interaction
○	Entering action	
÷	Divergent action, separate	
' '	Interchanging action	

From Stokoe, Casterline, and Croneberg (1976) by permission.

MOVEMENT. Table 2–3 lists the Stokoe parameters for describing the motion of a sign. This is the most difficult area to transcribe. The first three symbols refer to vertical action, the next three to side-by-side motion, the next three to horizontal motion toward or away from the signer, the next three to rotary action, and the rest to complex motions involving either the fingers, the hands, or the lower arms and hands. Notice that two of the symbols refer to closing and opening action and require specification of a final handshape in addition to the initial handshape.

Although the Stokoe notation may look arbitrary and difficult at first, it is actually fairly easy to learn and reasonably logical if the symbols and their meanings are closely compared. For example, the symbol for circular action seems to describe the path that a finger might take while producing a circle in space, and the symbols for up-and-down, side-to-side, and to-and-fro are composed of the symbols for the individual movements upward movement and downward movement, leftward movement and rightward movement, movement toward the signer and movement away from the signer.

CONSTRAINTS ON SIGN FORMATION

In spoken languages, physical constraints make certain combinations of building blocks impossible. For example, a vowel cannot be both [+high] and [+low]. Other combinations are not allowed for purely linguistic reasons, in which case a combination that is not allowed in one language may actually occur in another language. For sign language, there are similar redundancy conditions that specify possible combinations of sign parameters. Violations of these conditions are considered impossible or improbable (nonsense) signs. Just as English has actual words like "brick," possible but nonoccurring words like "blick," and nonoccurring and not possible words like "bnick," ASL also has "blick"-type signs, which may be used creatively in dramatic forms, and "bnick"-type signs which are not used at all (see "Violations of Constraints and Art-sign," this chapter). Some of the conditions on allowable signs may be attributable to constraints placed on the visual mode by the perceptual system and others to the physiology of the hand, whereas some appear to be totally arbitrary.

PERCEPTION AND PRODUCTION CONSTRAINTS. Siple (1978) described the visual field in terms of the optimal visual acuity for signs. The viewer seems to have a "high acuity area" centered on two fixation points, one between the eyes and the other at about the neck or chin. Within this high acuity area, it is easier to detect small differences in handshape (such as between x and baby o), in location (e.g., the small difference between APPLE on the lower cheek and ONION on the upper cheek bone), and in movement (e.g., the sweep downward of the sign GIRL as compared to the sweep upward and outward of the sign TOMORROW, both made with the same handshape and the same location on the cheek).

Outside of the "high acuity area," visual discrimination is not as accurate, depending more on the peripheral vision than the central vision. Because discrimination is more difficult, it is not surprising to find that signs made in this area (trunk, arms, neutral space) do not use fine details of handshape or small differences in location or motion, but instead increase discriminability in a number of ways. These include bigger distinctions in handshapes (for example, using the closed hand s and the open hand b or 5, but not having two signs that differ only in that one has G and the other has H — handshapes that differ only in the number of fingers, which would be difficult to see with peripheral vision), larger movements, increased temporal duration (which can be done by signing a bigger path, repeating the movement more than once, or signing more slowly), and using two hands (signs made in neutral space tend to use two hands whereas signs made on the face, head, or neck tend to use only one).

The anatomy of the hand and arm also contribute to sign structure constraints. Certain combinations of movements are easier or more natural than others. Much could be learned about sign formation from further investigation in this area, but few linguists are conversant with anatomy, physiology, and kinesiology applied to sign language. Mandel (1979) demonstrated that combinations of movements within a sign could be partially explained by the muscles and tendons involved in sign movement. He pointed out that when the fingers are flexed (bent), the wrist tends to extend (straighten) and vice versa. To demonstrate this, let the hand hang loose from the wrist; the fingers will be extended and the wrist will be bent. Make a fist and the wrist will pull up straight. This is not to say that it is not possible to have the fingers and the wrist both bent at the same time, only that to do so requires normal muscle preferences to be overcome. Mandel's analysis of ASL signs and fingerspelled loan signs indicates that the relationship between the wrist and fingers plays a role in what are allowable signs and also in what movement fingerspelled loan signs will acquire.

LINGUISTIC CONSTRAINTS. The constraints on sign formation from the visual perception system and the manual production capabilities restrict the complexity of signs so that they are easily produced and easily perceived against the backdrop of other ongoing activities. The linguistic constraints on allowable signs serve to reduce the overall complexity of signs in a particular language and thus increase the redundancy of sign formation. The result of this is that not all possible combinations actually occur, and certain pieces of information become critical in that other formational characteristics can be predicted from them. A system with controlled complexity and redundancy presumably provides certain advantages to the learner, especially young children.

Battison and colleagues (1975) give several examples of linguistic constraints on ASL sign formation. Some signs involve two sequential contacts with the body. If the body is divided into four major sections — (1) head and neck, (2) trunk, (3) arm, and (4) hand — then only the combinations shown in Table 2–4 are allowed. In addition, although the first contact may occur in a variety of places within each of the general areas, the second contact is more restricted and can only occur in the central part of the general area. Thus, a sign may go from the head to the center of the chest, but not from the head to a shoulder or to a side of the trunk or an edge of the hand. A constraint such as this, which is not required by physical limitations, may aid perception and production of signs, and certainly is one of the important features that distinguishes sign from mime.

Table 2–4. *Permissible contacts with the body for double-contact signs in ASL*

First contact	Second contact			
	Head	Trunk	Arm	Hand
Head	+[a]	+	+	+
Trunk	–	+	–	+
Arm	–	–	+	–
Hand	+	–	–	+

Based on Battison, Markowicz and Woodward, 1975.

[a] + indicates an acceptable sequence, – indicates an unacceptable sequence.

Battison (1974) described two further constraints related specifically to signs formed with both hands. Basically, there are three types of two-handed signs: (1) both hands move independently; (2) only one hand moves but both handshapes are identical; and (3) only one hand moves (the dominant one) and the handshape of the nondominant, nonmoving hand is restricted to one of a limited set of the possible handshapes. For the signs in which both hands move, a symmetry condition exists, specifying that the handshapes and movement for both hands must be identical or opposites (mirror images). For two-handed signs in which the handshapes are not identical (3 above), a dominance condition exists, specifying that the nondominant hand must remain static while the moving dominant hand produces the sign. (The dominant hand is most often considered to be the hand that is used by the signer to make one-handed signs and the moving hand in two-handed signs where only one hand moves. Kegl and Wilbur (1976) diverge from this practice by considering any moving hand to be dominant; thus if both hands are moving, they are both dominant, and if a signer first makes a one-handed sign with his right hand and then a different one-handed sign with his left hand, he has switched dominance.) Furthermore, the nondominant hand can assume only one of the six most unmarked handshapes, which include (see Figure 2–1):

1. s hand: a closed fist
2. b hand: the flat palm
3. 5 hand: the b hand with fingers spread apart
4. g hand: fist with index finger extended
5. c hand: hand formed in a semicircle
6. o hand: fingertips meet with thumb, forming a circle

Battison pointed out that these six handshapes are considered the least marked because they are found in all other sign languages studied to date, they are maximally distinct formationally and perceptually, and they are among the first acquired by children learning sign language (Boyes, 1973). Lane, Boyes-Braem, and Bellugi (1976) noted that these six handshapes constitute "69% of all the entries in the Stokoe et al. dictionary (1965) and 81% of all the entries in a 1-hr. corpus of the signing of a deaf two-and-a-half year old."

In summary, "signs with two active hands must be symmetrical and signs which have different handshapes can only have one active hand. In these cases, a relative complexity in one part of the sign (two hands vs. one hand moving; different handshapes vs. identical ones) is counteracted by a reduction in complexity somewhere else (symmetry; one hand remains still)" (Battison, 1974).

It is important to emphasize that these conditions hold for the citation forms of signs. The citation form is the isolated answer that is given to the question, "What is the sign for X?" In actual signing, grammatical modifications or creative use of signs may result in forms that appear to violate these conditions (Chapter 4).

VIOLATIONS OF CONSTRAINTS
AND ART-SIGN

Some of the existing constraints on the formation of possible signs are linguistic and not physiological. Clearly it is possible for two hands to move along different paths simultaneously (although it is often difficult, e.g., rubbing your stomach while patting your head). The nonuse of all the possible formational combinations provides a reservoir from which puns, rhymes, and art-sign (poetry and song) may be made (Klima and Bellugi, 1975). Challenging Tervoort's (1961) claim that "the spontaneous use of signs in an ironical or metaphorical way is rare to non-existent," Klima and Bellugi investigated manipulation of signs for creative purposes (see also discussion, Chapter 7). In addition to identifying sign puns, several types of sign-play were found (these are creative uses that do not depend on the structure of English). Three basic processes were reported: (1) the overlapping of two signs, (2) the blending of two signs, and (3) the substitution of one value of a regular formational parameter for another.

OVERLAPPING. Overlapping of two signs is possible because there are two hands that can move independently, and although in "straight signing" the symmetry condition prohibits different simultaneous motions, this condition is lifted for creative purposes. For example, to indicate mixed feelings about taking a new job, Klima and Bellugi cite the signs EXCITED and DEPRESSED, produced simultaneously. Both signs are normally two-handed and are related formationally in that they differ only in the direction of motion, DEPRESSED moving down the chest, EXCITED moving up. Thus, to produce both at once, one hand moves down while the other simultaneously moves up. Another way to overlap signs is to form one with one hand and hold the hand in that position while the other hand forms another sign. A third possible way is to start with a two-handed sign, hold one hand in that position, and make another sign with the other hand. These combinations are most effective when the differences between the two signs are minimal, when they use the same handshape, or when the place of formation of the first is the starting point of the second.

BLENDING. Blending of signs can be accomplished by combining the hand configuration of one sign with the movement and location of another sign. This process occurs regularly as a grammatical device in "straight signing" (not sign-play) where the handshape of a noun, pronoun, or numeral is combined with the movement and location of a verb (see Chapter 4). The creation of "name signs" (Meadow, 1977) is similar. Within the deaf community, each individual is given a name sign which is used in place of spelling out the whole name. A single individual may have several name signs, each one given by different groups within the community. The name sign is chosen to include some salient characteristic of the individual; thus if a particular person is the chief programmer at work, the worst player at bridge, and a loving husband at home, he may have three name signs, each of which reflects these different characteristics, although it is just as likely that because all these groups are in the same city, he may have the same sign in all three. Name signs ordinarily consist of the handshape corresponding to the fingerspelled first letter of the name and the movement and location of an appropriate verb, noun, or adjective. For example, Shelley Lawrence's eye winks frequently, and she has been given a name sign consisting of an S handshape and the movement and location of the sign WINK (two hands in front of eyes, one moves down quickly then up). My own name sign is less exciting — an R handshape made at the side of the chin where the signs GIRL, MOTHER, SISTER (a compound of GIRL and SAME) are made, indicating female. Name signs are a good example of signs which, although mentioned in the Appendix, are not listed in the *Dictionary of American Sign Language.* Since they are productively generated by rules, the list of name signs is seemingly infinite.

SYSTEMATIC SUBSTITUTION OF PARAMETERS. The systematic substitution of one of the parameters of a sign is a planned effort to change the meaning of the sign in a recognizable way. The results are signs that do not violate any of the constraints on signs, and thus are possible but not actual signs of the language. Klima and Bellugi (1979) illustrate several types, including (1) change in the hand configuration (using the little finger to make the sign UNDERSTAND instead of the normally used index finger; the little finger changes the

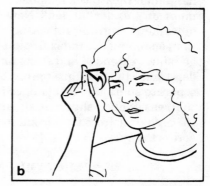

Figure 2-3. The meaning of the sign UNDERSTAND (a) is changed to "understand a little" (b) by using the little finger in place of index finger. From Klima and Bellugi, 1979. Copyright © U. Bellugi, The Salk Institute.

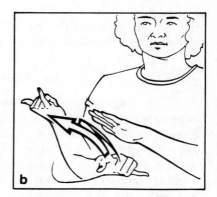

Figure 2-4. The meaning of the sign NEW YORK "New York City" (a) is modified when the dominant hand moves underneath the nondominant hand, indicating "underhanded New York" (b). From Klima and Bellugi, 1979. Copyright © U. Bellugi, The Salk Institute.

meaning from "understand" to "understand a little") (Figure 2–3), (2) changes in orientation (signing NEW YORK (city) with the dominant hand underneath the nondominant hand to indicate a negative comment on "underhanded" New York) (Figure 2–4), (3) changes in movement (signing UNDERSTAND with the reverse motion — rather than snapping the index finger open from a closed fist, the index finger starts extended and shuts into a closed fist; to indicate "don't understand" in straight signing one would sign NOT UNDERSTAND, two separate signs, and (4) changes in location (to indicate a bruised eye that was swollen shut, one signer signed "My eye is deaf" by moving the sign DEAF from its normal location across the cheek to a location across the eye).

HISTORICAL CHANGES

The general linguistic constraints previously discussed are also reflected in historical changes that some signs have undergone. Descriptions of signs are available from as early as 1797 for Old French Sign Language and 1850 for American Sign Language. Significant changes can be seen in signs in the relatively short time since Long (1918). Frishberg (1975, 1976) reports that changes in signs over time have tended to increase the symmetry of a sign, increase the fluidity between parts of a sign, move signs to a more centralized location, and modify the formation of some signs so that the hands are the main conveyor of the information rather than the facial expression or body or head movements.

Increase in Symmetry

Several modifications have occurred which result in increased symmetry. Signs that are made below the neck have tended to change from one-handed to two-handed (cf. modern version of DIE/DEAD, HURRY, ANGRY). Signs that are two-handed have tended toward identical handshapes, although, as mentioned before, two-handed signs in which only one hand moves may still have a different handshape on the nondominant hand. Frishberg (1976) illustrated this tendency with several signs which indicate that it is usually the nondominant hand that changes to the handshape of the dominant hand. The old sign for DEPEND was made with a dominant G hand and a nondominant B hand. The new sign is made with two G hands. Similarly, the old sign for SHORT/BRIEF was made with a dominant H hand and a nondominant B hand and is now made with two H hands. The sign LAST/FINAL provides an interesting counter-example to this trend, in that here it is the dominant hand that has changed.

The old sign was made with a dominant G hand and a nondominant I hand. The current sign is made with two I hands. Two factors are possibly involved. One is the preservation of morphological information, the I hand being made with the fifth finger and the fifth finger being the *last* finger in most counting or listing. Thus to have given up the I hand to become two G hands would have been to lose this morphological information. The other possible factor is avoidance of homonymity. Two signs that are already made with two G hands in motions similar to that of LAST/FINAL are CAN'T and a recent version of TOMATO. This may have provided some resistance to the change to two G hands.

Fluidity

The term "fluidity" refers to the smoothness of the transition from one part of a sign to the next. In compound signs that are recently formed, an indication of compoundness may be the shortness of the interval between the formation of the two signs. As the compound becomes lexicalized, parts of the first and/or second sign may be lost and a tighter bond between the remaining parts may result. Movements, locations, and handshapes may be modified to create a smoother transition. The old sign FOR (as in "this is for you") was made as two separate movements, a G hand first pointing to the forehead then pointing to object (if present) or its established location in space (use of space for this purpose is discussed in greater detail in Chapter 4). The current sign is made as a single smooth movement with the G hand from the forehead out. The sign INFORM is now made with two hands throughout, one slightly higher than the other, retaining the handshape change from BRING. One particularly illustrative example that Frishberg gives is the Toronto sign HOSPITAL. This sign originally was made as a compound, SICK + HOME. SICK was made with two open 8 hands, one at the forehead, the other at the stomach. HOME was itself a compound, originally EAT + SLEEP. (EAT is made with a flat O handshape at the mouth; SLEEP is made with a B hand at the cheek. HOME developed into a two-touch sign using the flat O handshape, touching first near the mouth and then at the cheek (modern versions include two touches both in the same place on the cheek, midway between the two older contacts.)) Thus, HOSPITAL was made as SICK with two open 8 hands at the forehead and stomach followed by HOME made with the O handshape contacting first near the mouth and then on the cheek. The first contact of HOME dropped out, as did the lower hand of SICK, leaving HOSPITAL as an open 8 hand at the forehead, moving to the cheek and changing to an O hand. Eventually the change to an O hand also dropped out, leaving HOSPITAL as a two-touch sign with open ୪ hand, first at forehead, then at cheek. Fluidity of formation increased as the movement changed from two contacts to a continuous contact, starting at the forehead and moving down the side of the head. The place of formation, motion, and handshape have been modified to produce a sign that is more fluid than the compound from which it is derived.

Centralization

In looking at centralization of signs over time, Frishberg (1975) found that signs have moved down from the face, in from the side, and up from the waist. She suggests that this results in the hollow of the throat being a center point of the signing space. She gives several examples: DON'T-CARE, moving down from the forehead to the nose; YOUNG and WILL/FUTURE, moving up from the waist to the shoulder; and FEEL, LOVE, and PLEASE, moving in from the heart to the center of the chest. The only exception to this trend has been that signs made on the face have tended to move outward toward the sides so that the mouth and eyes are more easily seen (presumably an aid to speechreading).

Changing Role of the Head and Face

Over time, signs that previously included head movement as part of their formation have transferred this movement onto the hands or simply have lost the head movement component. The sign PATIENT used to include a lowering of the head as the A hand moved down in front of the lips. Now the head remains still while the hand performs the movement. Frishberg (1975) described the change that occurred in the sign COMPARE. The old sign was made "holding two flat hands facing the signer, separated. The eyes moved from one to the other and then the hands moved together, eyes focused on both at once." The current sign uses the hands only, either rocking alternately, probably a vestige of the former eye movements, or rocking together, a change in movement that can be viewed as an increase in symmetry.

Head tilts and facial expressions play an active role in ASL, more often than not in a larger context than the single sign. Certain signs still retain distinctive facial expression as part of their formation, but these are relatively rare. Head tilt has been observed to indicate relative clauses (Liddell, 1978), whereas facial expression has often been cited as an indicator of negation, question, affirmation, and other functions usually attributed to intonation in spoken languages. These are discussed in detail below and in Chapter 6.

Borrowing from English through Fingerspelling

INITIALIZED SIGNS. The inclusion of a handshape from the manual alphabet in a sign to make that sign somehow "correspond" to an English word is called initialization. Typically, a sign is initialized in several ways, thus creating several distinctive signs from a single ASL sign. Although some deliberate initializations clearly violate rules of allowable sign formation (Chapter 10), others are linguistically permissible and may even be accepted into the daily language. The acceptance of such signs, and other invented signs, varies from person to person. Some deaf people, who have been told most of their lives that signing is "inferior" or "not grammatical," may feel that these signs are "improving" the sign language, that they make the sign language "more precise." Others recognize the artificiality of these signs and stigmatize people who use them as "obviously hearing signers" (even though some deaf people may use them). Upon meeting a new deaf person, I first have to determine if this person will be offended if I sign with him, and then what kind of signing to use. Some people may view my use of obviously initialized signs as a mark of my being non-native; others may view my lack of them as being professionally inappropriate. Flexibility of signing styles is discussed further in Chapter 9.

CREATION OF NEW SIGNS. Battison (1978) reported that short fingerspelled English words may change into signs through a variety of modifications. Medial letters may be lost, leaving only the first and last letters. The remaining handshapes may assimilate according to the number of fingers involved. At the same time, the handshapes may dissimilate along the open/close dimension (i.e., if the first handshape is open, e.g., 5, then the second will be closed, e.g., S, or vice versa). Movements may be added (remember that fingerspelled letters, except 'j' and 'z', do not move except as a transition into the next letter handshape). These may include 1) linear movement (for example, the *new* sign ALL derived from fingerspelled a+l may move down a list to indicate all the items in a list, or sweep across the horizontal plane (from side to side) to indicate all the people or things) or 2) reduplication (repetition, usually of open/close change in handshape). The location may also change (fingerspelled words are made in a constrained box about shoulder height on the same side of the body as the hand that is doing the spelling) to other areas within the signing space. Finally, the sign may add a second hand. These combined changes remove the word from the realm of fingerspelling into the lexicon of signs. Battison suggests that the target of these processes is to produce a double handshape sign (not necessarily made with both hands) which changes its handshape during formation. Spoken languages in need of a vocabulary item may invent new words, compound already existing words, or borrow words from other languages. These processes, which allow borrowing from English (or theoretically any spoken language), provide ASL with the same lexical innovation options as other languages.

FACIAL EXPRESSION AND USE
OF THE HEAD

Turning back to the description of modern ASL, one area that has received a considerable amount of attention is the description of the nonmanual signals that are used in ASL. Stokoe (1960) noted that a side-to-side headshake served the grammatical function of making a negative without having a negative sign (e.g., NO, NONE, DON'T, CAN'T, WON'T/REFUSE) in the sentence. When a negative sign does occur, the negative headshake supports it; when there are no negative signs, the headshake alone is sufficient to change the meaning from positive to negative.

Numerous other functions can be served by parts of the body above the neck. Morphological, syntactic, and semantic functions have been identified for the eyebrows, eye gaze, eye blinks, nose wrinkles, various mouth and cheek positions, and head tilts. Nonmanual signals are used with questions (yes/no, WH-Q, rhetorical), conditionals, relative clauses, topics, and a variety of adverbial functions.

In their study of ASL conditionals, Baker and Padden (1978) report that in conditional statements at least four changes could be observed between the first clause and the second clause: eye blinks, release of nasolabial contraction, brow lowering, and initiation of head nodding. In conditional questions, at least two changes occurred. They report that in both conditional statements ("If it rains tomorrow, I will go to the library") and conditional questions ("If it rains tomorrow, will you go to the library?"), the "if" clause was marked with raising of the eyebrows. In the statements, but not the questions, the "if" clause was followed by an eyeblink. In the conditional statements, the second part would have the brows returned to their normal position, unless the statement was also negative, and changes in gaze direction and head orientation would occur as appropriate. In the conditional questions, the question part continued to have raised eyebrows (part of the "q" marker), gaze at the addressee, and the head foward or cocked to one side. Finally, whereas ASL may have a lexical marker IF or #IF (Baker and Padden noted the fingerspelled i+f) in the first part, it does not have the equivalent of "then" as a sign in the second part.

Baker (1977) also noted that the control of conversational flow involved nonmanual signals. Eye gaze serves a major function in this regard, directing the flow back and forth between signers. The back channel functions that she identified were confirmed in a later study by Wilbur and Petitto (1981, 1983).

Liddell (1977, 1980) identified uses of facial expression and head position in five different contexts: (1) as abstract grammatical markers (topicalization, question, negative, and so on), (2) as adverbs, (3) as parts of lexical items, (4) as part of pantomime, and (5) as indication of emotional states or evaluative judgments of the signer. The abstract grammatical markers are notable because of their precise onset and offset times with respect to the manual signs. These contrast with evaluative and emotional facial expressions which seem to develop as the sign is being produced.

The abstract grammatical marker that Liddell called "t" (a topic marker) is a combination of the head tilted backward slightly and the eyebrows raised. It co-occurs with the topicalized sign, then disappears for the remainder of the sentence. Another distinctive nonmanual clue is "q," the question marker for yes/no questions. It includes a leaning forward of the body, head forward, and eyebrows raised, and is usually held throughout the duration of the question. Others have observed that for WH-questions (who, what, where, etc.), the eyes are narrowed and the eyebrows are squished.

Another nonmanual signal, "n," is a negating signal composed of a side-to-side headshake, and a special facial expression in which a primary feature is the turning down of the corners of the mouth. Liddell identifies "hn," head nod, as a slow, forward head nod which signals assertion and/or existence. Gapping sentences (as in a list, "I brought cake for dessert, Susie the drinks, Bob the silverware, and John the salad," which has the structure NVN, NN, NN, etc.) require "hn" on the second noun in each gapped construction. Liddell suggests that "hn" behaves as a parallel to English "be" and "do," especially in its function when the main verb is missing and for emphasis ("John *did* go to the movies").

Liddell identified three nonmanual signals that function as adverbs in ASL. They are "mm," made with the lips together and slightly pushed out, with a slight head tilt, "cs," made with the shoulder raised and head turned to the side of the raised shoulder and a characteristic facial expression, and "th," made with the lips apart and pushed out with tongue protruding (as when making the English sound "th," hence the name).

The adverb "mm" indicates that everything is normal and proper (e.g., engine running ok, people feeling relaxed and comfortable) and co-occurs with the verb. In the following example, [I:continuous] is Liddell's notation for continuous aspect on the verb:

$$\overline{\text{MAN FISH}}^{\text{[I:continuous]}}\,^{\text{mm}}$$

meaning "the man is fishing with relaxation and enjoyment." If the question "Is the man fishing with relaxed enjoyment?" is asked, the "mm" signal falls within the scope of the "q" signal (which covers the whole sentence):

$$\overline{\overline{\text{MAN FISH}}^{\text{mm}}}^{\text{q}}\,^{\text{[I:continuous]}}$$

Similar descriptions are given for "cs," which seems to have a meaning related to proximity of time or physical distance (e.g., "just yesterday," "brand new," "right behind," etc.) and "th," whose semantic interpretation involved "lack of control, inattention, unintention, and unawareness" (Liddell, 1977) (e.g., "clod," "clumsy," "careless," "make lots of mistakes," etc.).

Coulter (1979) and, more recently, Baker-Shenk (1983) extended the descriptions of nonmanual signals. Baker-Shenk's study is particularly detailed, providing a microanalysis of the facial expressions used in questions. She includes discussion of the muscle groups involved and measurements of the onset and durations of the facial expressions with respect to the hand movements. Head and facial actions tend to occur together and to start before the onset of the manual sign. Baker-Shenk suggests that a simplified statement of her findings would be that the face is observed to move first, then the head, then the hand(s).

One aspect of the use of facial expression and head position in ASL that is not usually made explicit in the various discussions is the extent to which several signals are possible at once. The head position can be made independently of actions of the eyes and eyebrows or of the mouth and cheeks. The mouth and cheeks appear to be used for adverbial ("mm," "cs," "th,") or adjectival (e.g., puffed cheeks for "big/fat") functions at the phrase level, while the nose can express evaluation, and the eyes, eyebrows, and head can serve syntactic functions at the clause or sentence level. The phonetic separation of these different functions at different locations on the face or head allows the simultaneous transmission of more than one signal. Obviously, not all combinations are possible, but the layering of these signals parallels a layering of movement types for the manual signs themselves (Chapter 5).

PRIMARILY FOR LINGUISTS

Distinctive Features

For spoken language, we can describe vowels by their height, their position in the mouth, their roundness (or lack thereof), their nasality (if present), and so on. The descriptors for consonants refer to place of formation, presence or absence of voicing or nasal resonance, and manner of articulation (e.g., stop versus fricative). Each of these features refers to a class of segments which have a particular characteristic in common (the class of voiced consonants, the class of velars, the high vowels). The search for distinctive features for signs aims at providing the same level of descriptive adequacy now available for spoken languages. Several distinctive feature systems have been proposed, with those for handshape receiving the most attention.

Friedman (1976b) rejected the possibility of a distinctive feature analysis for American Sign Language. Other linguists have found distinctive features to be desirable for linguistic description of ASL (Mandel, 1981; Wilbur, 1978; Woodward, 1973a) and psycholinguists have found distinctive features to be useful in studying visual perception of ASL. In their effort to determine the distinctive features that might be involved in the visual perception of signs, Lane and colleagues (1976) presented handshapes masked by visual "snow," and analyzed the perceptual confusions that subjects made using clustering and scaling techniques. They proposed a set of 11 features for the ASL handshapes (see Table 2–5).

Lane and colleagues based their features on the notions of the fingers and/or thumb being either "closed" (as in a fist) or "extended" (as in the number 5). [Compact] hands, then, are closed, with no fingers extended. [Broad] refers to those hands with three or more fingers extended. In their feature system, a handshape cannot be both [compact] and [broad]. The feature [ulnar] refers to handshapes that have at least the fifth finger extended; [full] hands have (at least) four fingers extended. The feature [concave] is used for handshapes with two or more bent fingers (as in c or o). [Dual] hands have only two fingers extended, [index] hands have only the index fingers extended, and [radial] hands have the thumb (and possibly some fingers) extended. [Touch] is used for handshapes in which at least one fingertip is in contact with the thumb (as in F or o). [Spread] hands have two or more fingers that are spread apart, and finally, if two fingers (but not thumb) are overlapping, the feature [cross] is used. Correspondences and differences between this and other feature systems are discussed later. It is important to point out here, however,

Table 2-5. *Features for handshapes*

	Compact	Broad	Ulnar	Full	Concave	Dual	Index	Radial	Touch	Spread	Cross
	+				+				⊕		
	+				+				⊖		
	+				−		+		⊕		
	+				−		+		⊖		
	+				−		−		⊕		
	+				−		−		⊖		
	−	+		+				⊕			
	−	+		+				⊖			
	−	+		−				⊕			
	−	+		−				−		⊕	
	−	+		−				−		⊖	
	−	−	+					⊕			
	−	−	+					⊖			
	−	−	−			+				⊕	
	−	−	−			+				−	⊕
	−	−	−			+				−	⊖
	−	−	−			−		−	+	⊕	
	−	−	−			−		−	+	⊖	
	−	−	−			−		−	−	⊕	
	−	−	−			−		−	−	⊖	

From Lane, Boyes-Braem and Bellugi (1976) with permission.

that these features are perceptually descriptive and their utility in the formation of phonological rules has not yet been tested.

Woodward's (1973a) features are presented in Table 2–6. They are based on articulatory characteristics, and cover a larger number of handshapes than do Lane and colleagues. Woodward defined 10 features that can describe 40 handshapes. The feature [closed], when positively specified, indicates fingers curled into the palm (although some fingers may be extended as the result of other feature specifications), and where possible the thumb is across the fingers, as in the handshape s. In fact, s, is defined as [+closed] and negative for all other features. The feature [thumb] when positively specified moves the thumb from across the fingers to straight up next to the index edge of the hand (A in Figure 2–1). The feature [spread] can refer to either the fingers, if extended, or the thumb. The handshape 5 differs from the handshape B in that the former is specified as [+thumb, +spread] but the latter is specified as negative for both features. The feature [bent] is used for bent fingers that are not in contact with other fingers or the thumb. Each finger extended (and possibly bent) has its own feature. Thus, there is a feature [fore], which when positively specified indicates that the forefinger is extended, and three other features, [mid], [ring], and [pinkie], which are similarly defined. Contact between the thumb and any finger is indicated by the feature [contact], and the crossing of any digit (fingers or thumb) is indicated by the feature [crossed]. Because of the great detail and the large number of handshapes specified by this feature system, it was determined to be the most useful (to date) in allowing a generative analysis of handshapes (Mandel, 1981; Wilbur, 1978a), although the new features proposed by Liddell and Johnson (1985) hold the potential for further generalizations.

Kegl and Wilbur (1976) attempted to determine a set of distinctive features on the basis of articulation, perception, and theoretical descriptive utility. Drawing upon the basic distinction indicated by Lane and colleagues, two features, [extended] and [closed], were defined to refer to maximally opposed handshapes. [Extended] refers to the straight extension of the fingers; [closed] is its opposite, the fingers being curled into a fist (s). Unlike the definition presented by Lane and colleagues, however, a handshape can be both [extended] and [closed], as illustrated by the following set of minimal feature specifications:

[+ extended, + closed] G
[− extended, − closed] O
[+ extended, − closed] B
[− extended, + closed] S

Table 2-6. *ASL DEZ (handshape) symbols with tentative feature representation*

Distinctive feature	S	E	O	C	B	4	T	A	Ȧ	B̈	B₂	5̈	5	ʊ	G	X	D	G₂	G̈	L
Closed	+	+	−	−	−	−	+	+	+	−	−	−	−	−	+	+	−	+	+	+
Thumb	−	−	−	−	−	−	−	+	+	+	+	+	+	+	−	−	−	+	+	+
Spread	−	−	−	−	−	+	−	−	+	−	−	−	+	+	−	+	−	−	−	+
Bent	−	−	−	+	−	−	+	−	−	+	−	+	−	+	−	+	−	−	+	−
Fore	−	−	−	+	+	+	+	−	−	+	+	+	+	+	+	+	+	+	+	+
Mid	−	−	−	+	+	+	−	−	−	+	+	+	+	−	−	−	−	−	−	−
Ring	−	−	−	+	+	+	−	−	−	+	+	+	+	+	−	−	−	−	−	−
Pinky	−	−	−	+	+	+	−	−	−	+	+	+	+	+	−	−	−	−	−	−
Contact	−	+	+	−	−	−	−	−	−	−	−	−	−	−	−	−	−	+	−	−
Crossed	−	−	−	−	−	−	+	−	−	−	−	−	−	−	−	−	−	−	−	−

From Woodward (1973a) with permission

Thus, if no other features are positively specified [+extended, +closed] implies that only the index finger is extended (G), whereas [+extended, −closed] implies that all the fingers are extended and unspread (B). [−Extended, −closed] is the handshape O, where the fingers are not extended straight out, nor are they curled into the palm, but rather are curled slightly away from the palm and meet the thumb. Finally, when no finger is extended and all are curled into the fist with the thumb across the second joint, we have [−extended, +closed], the handshape S. [Thumb] is used for extended thumbs (as in Ȧ) and [pinkie] is used for extended pinkie (as in I or Y). [Bent] is used when any finger is bent (as in X). The features [2adjacent] and [3adjacent] refer to the number of adjacent fingers (not thumb) that are extended (not the total number of extended fingers, however, unless all are adjacent, i.e., none are bent down) and that obey the convention:

Adjacency Convention: If the handshape is [+extended, +closed], start counting adjacent fingers at the index finger. If the handshape is [+extended, −closed], start counting at the pinkie edge. When the proper number of adjacent fingers has been reached, put the next finger down in contact with the thumb (if the handshape is also marked [+thumb] this contact will not be maintained). These features are not relevant to [−extended] handshapes.

This adjacency convention eventually led Mandel (1981) to formulate the finger position constraint. He noted that fingers in a

Distinctive feature	I	Y	⊔	⊔	7	8	H	N	V	R	3	K	M	W	6	F_s	9	F	M_t	N_t
Closed	+	+	+	+	−	−	+	+	+	+	+	+	+	+	−	+	−	+	+	+
Thumb	−	+	−	+	−	−	−	−	−	−	+	−	−	−	−	−	−	−	−	−
Spread	−	+	−	+	+	+	−	−	+	−	+	+	−	+	−	+	−	+	+	−
Bent	−	−	−	−	−	−	−	+	−	−	−	−	−	+	−	−	−	−	+	+
Fore	−	−	+	+	+	+	+	+	+	+	+	+	+	+	+	+	−	−	+	+
Mid	−	−	−	−	−	+	+	+	+	+	+	+	+	+	+	+	+	+	+	+
Ring	−	−	−	−	+	−	−	−	−	−	−	−	+	+	+	+	+	+	+	−
Pinky	+	+	+	+	+	+	−	−	−	−	−	−	−	−	−	+	+	+	−	+
Contact	−	−	−	−	+	+	−	−	−	−	−	−	−	+	+	+	+	+	−	−
Crossed	−	−	−	−	−	−	−	−	−	+	−	+	−	−	−	−	−	−	+	+

handshape fell into two groups, the *selected* fingers and the *unselected* fingers. The selected fingers can be in any of the different positions of a handshape except closed, but they must all be in the *same* position. The unselected fingers may only be all extended or all closed. He suggests that the function served by this division into two groups is to provide a "foreground" of fingers (the selected ones) against a "background" of fingers, but no third or "middle" ground. Perception and production are both served by this, the number of possible feature combinations within a handshape is reduced, and the redundancy can be exploited in the writing of phonological rules. The simplified adjacency principle that he proposed states that "all selected fingers are adjacent unless the specifications force non-adjacency."

Mandel's analysis of handshape includes finger selection features, finger position features that describe the whole handshape, and "detail" features for particular fingers. One interesting aspect of his analysis is his recognition of the fact that the thumb may act either as one of the fingers or separately as a thumb. Other researchers have merely marked the thumb for extended or not. Mandel postulated several thumb position features: [thumbbent], [thumbside], [thumbfront], and [thumbout]. Taken together these features can uniquely specify the position of the thumb separately from the rest of the fingers.

In her analysis of the features of ASL handshape, Boyes-Braem (1981) proposed several features that characterize the handshape in terms of function or shape. Thus, she had features for grasping hands, such as [tip grasp] (e.g., F) and [palm grasp] (e.g., a variant of A) and features for [round], [linear], and [surface] shapes, which refer to the general impression of the overall handshape. Boyes-Braem extended her analysis beyond the phonological level and attempted to determine which of the handshape features also have morphological functions attached to them. She was also concerned with the metaphorical basis for the handshapes and how that affects the surface variations that may occur. Both of these topics will be returned to in later chapters.

Stokoe's values for the description of *location* were given earlier in this chapter. Within his system, signs that did not contact any part of the body were described as being made in neutral space, a location that contrasted with the remaining 11 locations on the body. However, many lexical and grammatical distinctions require that neutral space be further specified. Kegl and Wilbur (1976) chose to distinguish signs in neutral space from signs on the body by use of the feature [contact]. This allowed specification of different locations *within* neutral space by having all signs described with reference to the body areas. (The importance of contact in ASL phonology is an issue that has been pursued in Mandel, 1981; Wilbur, 1978a, 1985b; see next chapter).

The area on (or off) the body can be divided into three major divisions by combinations of three features, [head], [trunk], and [hand] (Table 2–7). Thus, the neck is treated as a special (but not major) area, and the arm is treated as a leftover area in which none of the features is specified positively.

Each of the major areas my be further divided into the center ([central]) and the perimeter ([extreme]) (Table 2–8). The use of the features [top] and [bottom] divides each area into three subareas ([+top], [−top, −bottom], [+bottom]). The feature [dorsal] is only relevant to signs made on or near the arm or hand, since one cannot make signs on the back of the head or trunk. (In the National Theater of the Deaf performance of "Parade," a deaf Nathan Hale, hands

Table 2–7. *Features for major places of formation*

	Head	Neck	Trunk	Hand	Arm
Head	+	+	−	−	−
Trunk		+	+	−	−
Hand				+	−

Table 2–8. *Feature assignments for locations*

Locations					Features				
	Head	Trunk	Hand	Extreme	Central	Top	Bottom	Lateral	Dorsal
Forehead	+	–	–	+	–	+	–	+	
Eyes	+	–	–	–	+	+	–	+	
Center nose	+	–	–	+	+	–	–	–	
Side nose	+	–	–	–	+	–	–	+	
Mouth	+	–	–	–	–	+	+	–	
Upper cheeks	+	–	–	+	–	–	+	+	
Cheeks	+	–	–	–	–	+	–	+	
Chin	+	–	–	+	–	–	+	–	
Ears	+	–	–	+	–	+	–	+	
Shoulder	–	+	–	–	–	–	–	+	
Chest	–	+	–	–	–	–	–	–	
Waist	–	+	–	–	–	+	+	+	
Hips	–	+	–	+	–	+	+	+	
Fingertips	–	–	+	+	–	–	–	–	+
Finger base	–	–	+	+	–	+	–	+	+
Center palm	–	–	+	+	+	+	+	+	+
Fleshy part	–	–	+	+	–	+	–	+	+
Wrist	–	–	+	+	–	+	–	–	+
Edge of hand	–	–	–	+	–	–	–	–	–
Upper arm	–	–	–	–	–	+	+	–	+
Lower arm	–	–	–	+	–	–	–	–	+
Elbow	–	–	–	+	+	–	+	–	+

From Kegl and Wilbur (1976).

tied behind his back, turned his back to the audience and signed, "I regret that I have but one life to give for my country." The audience's response acknowledged their appreciation of this creative violation of normal signing constraints.)

Another relevant feature that has not been included in this matrix would be one that indicated ipsilateral (or contralateral, or perhaps both will be needed) to indicate that the sign is made on the same or opposite side of the body from the hand that articulates it.

Other features are needed for orientation of the palm, orientation of the fingers, contact point of the contacting hand, contacted point on the other hand or body, speed of signing, tenseness of the musculature, size and shape of the path movement, direction of movement, spatial relationship between the two hands, and numerous other details that have only recently begun to receive the attention they deserve.

SUMMARY

Signs may be viewed as a conglomerate of several features or parameters. Signs are subject to physical, perceptual, and linguistic constraints, and may also be highly redundant (e.g., two-handed signs that move identically). Historical changes in sign formation have supported the descriptions given for modern signs, in that signs that did not fit these constraints tended to evolve into signs that did. Violations of these constraints may be used for creative humor. In Chapter 10, unintentional violations of these constraints by artificially created signs used in educational settings are discussed.

ASL, which exists in a bilingual environment, has a productive mechanism for borrowing from English by creating new signs from fingerspelled words. This contributes to an expanding and changing vocabulary. Yet these new signs obey the existing sign constraints and are made up of the same features as existing signs.

Extensive use is made of nonmanual signals involving the face and head. The description and timing of these signals supports the argument that they are grammatical in nature, and not merely embellishments chosen by individual signers whenever they feel like it. Later discussion will expand the description of their syntactic functions.

CHAPTER 3

Sign Phonology: Current Approaches

SEQUENTIAL MODELS

Since Stokoe and colleagues' pioneering work, linguists have pondered the parallelism of the descriptions of sign language and spoken language. Although at first glance this might seem to represent spoken language bias as discussed in Chapter 1, the issue is really more subtle. Until now, linguistic models of language have been shaped entirely by spoken languages, although they were supposed to be models of "language" and not just models of speech. It therefore becomes a relevant question to ask whether current linguistic frameworks can be applied to sign languages. The idea is not to mold the description of sign language into a spoken language framework, but to see if the *structure* of the spoken language framework comfortably fits sign languages. If, for example, the phonological level of a language, as treated in generative phonology, describes the processes involved when elements of the language occur in sequence, then one might expect to find similar processes (assimilation, metathesis) in both spoken and sign languages. Or, if the smallest segmental unit of a language is viewed as a matrix of distinctive features chosen from a universal set of features constrained by marking conventions, then it should not matter whether that segment is spoken or signed. The features themselves will reflect modality differences, but there should be one set from which all spoken languages can choose and another set from which all signed languages can choose. Only certain combinations should be allowable for the languages in each modality, and the phonological rules of deletion, assimilation, or modification should refer only to the features, not directly to the modality that the features represent. Thus, the rules should look similar for signed and spoken languages except for the feature names. Whether this is true or not will require further linguistic investigation. It is clear, however, that the newer descriptions of sign structure reflect more recent models of spoken language phonology (Wilbur, 1986b).

As previously mentioned, a major difference between the traditional approaches to sign description and more recent approaches is the treatment of sign structure as either simultaneous (traditional) or sequential (recent). Previously, each sign was treated as a unit: signs with two locations were referred to as "double location" signs; signs with two contacts were treated as "double contact" signs; signs with two handshapes were treated as though the change in handshape were part of the movement; many signs with two movements were identified as compounds, while the rest were often ignored. The prevailing view was that a sign was composed of a simultaneous bundle of primes/parameters, including the "big four": handshape, location, movement, and orientation (Friedman, 1977; Klima and Bellugi, 1979; Siple, 1978; Stokoe, 1960; Wilbur, 1979).

To talk about the internal structure of a sign required a break with the view of simultaneity. Several early papers suggested that there were syllables in ASL and that these syllables had internal sequential organization (Chinchor, 1978b; Kegl and Wilbur, 1976; Liddell, 1982; Newkirk, 1979, 1980, 1981). Liddell (1982) argued for a sequential notion of signs consisting of two types of segments, movements (M) and holds (H). The remaining information — handshape, contact, orientation, location, and facial expression — would be represented as features that occur simultaneously with each segment, so that there would be a sequence of feature matrices within each sign. Signed syllables could then be of several types, namely M, MH, HM, and HMH.

Wilbur (1982a) argued that movement had to be divided into two types, path movement and local movement. Local movement includes elbow rotation, wrist nod, a variety of handshape changes, and finger flutter. The reason for this division is that a sign can have as its movement either a path alone, or one of the local movements alone, or a combination of path and one of the local movements. Thus, even though there is a need to talk about the sequentiality of movement within a sign, there is still a need to talk about movements that can occur simultaneously. The implication of this is that the cover term "M" for movement may include considerably more complexity than was originally suggested.

This recent work has led in two directions. Liddell and Johnson (in press a,b), for example, discuss the formation of ASL compounds in terms of the rules that affect the two signs that compose the compound. Certain rules delete segments, for example, all holds that are not next to a phrase boundary, but not their associated "articulatory bundles," the features from which the segments are composed. This contrasts with the treatment of compounds in Klima and Bellugi (1979), where compound formation was viewed as a temporal compression process rather than a deletion process (compounding is discussed further in the next chapter).

The second direction is the study of syllables themselves. Although an adequate definition for "syllable" does not exist for either spoken or signed languages, research on syllables is still possible, using a working hypothesis that syllables are clusters of segments that participate as a unit for linguistic purposes such as rhythm or stress assignment, and the fact that people seem to be able to *count* syllables even though they cannot specify exactly where the syllables start and end (Wilbur, 1986a). Coulter (1982) argued that the majority of basic lexical items in ASL were monosyllabic. He suggested that the multisyllabic forms that existed were compounds, reduplicated forms, or fingerspelled loan signs, and that of these, only the reduplicated forms were stable as multisyllabic forms; the others tended to reduce to single syllable forms over time by various of the historical changes discussed in Chapter 2. This analysis seems correct, with the possible addition of certain bidirectional signs that are probably disyllabic (i.e., have two syllables, such as DYE or WASHING-MACHINE) in their basic forms (cf. Supalla and Newport, 1978, for a discussion of unidirectional and bidirectional signs and the notion of basic forms).

It is important to recognize the implications of saying that ASL

has primarily monosyllabic signs. First, the prevalence of monosyllabic signs is one reason why the traditional view of ASL structure
was useful for such a long time. If one avoided the other kinds of
signs, one could make generalizations without confronting the problem of internal structure. Second, because most signs are single syllables, there is not likely to be phonemic lexical stress parallel to
that which distinguishes "permit" the verb (second syllable) from
"permit" the noun (first syllable) in English. Third, affixation, when
it does exist in ASL, does not usually add extra syllables. Instead,
the result is comparable to the addition of the past tense to the English verb "walk" which produces "walked," pronounced as one
syllable.

Before continuing with a review of recent research on syllables,
let us consider the notion of "syllable" in more depth. First, what is
the difference between a syllable and a sign? In many cases, the sign
is a single syllable and the boundaries of the two coincide; in these
cases, there is no significant difference between a syllable and a sign
except for the theoretical notions themselves. In several cases, such
as DYE, WASHING-MACHINE, or BABY, it takes two syllables to
complete the sign. In these cases, the sign is a bigger unit than the
syllable. In certain other cases, such as MOTHER, FATHER, or the
numbers from ONE to NINE, the formation can be specified with a
handshape, a location, an orientation for the hand, and, for some, a
contact. These lexical items do not have their own movement. It is
true that the hand must move to the location for the sign and away
from the location after the sign, but the movement will differ depending on where the hand is coming from and where it is moving
to; the sign itself does not have a particular specification for movement. But every syllable in ASL must have movement. For these
signs, the transition movement to the location of the sign joins with
the sign to produce a full syllable; thus, in these cases, the sign is actually smaller than the syllable.

Now consider a related question: what is the difference between
a syllable and a morpheme? A morpheme is the smallest possible
unit of meaning. In the examples given above, all of the signs that
we mentioned are also single morphemes. Thus, in some cases, the
morphemes and the syllables are the same size, whereas in other
cases the morphemes are either larger or smaller than the syllables.
However, it will be important for our discussion later on to recognize
that signs and morphemes are not the same things. There are many
signs in ASL that are composed of several morphemes; we refer to
these signs as "productive" signs to contrast them with "frozen"
signs. We will discuss these two categories in more detail later; for

the present purposes, it is sufficient to note that a morpheme in ASL may be as small as the feature specification for handshape or location within a single syllable or as large as a two-syllable sign.

DURATION AND FREQUENCY
OF SYLLABLES

SYLLABLE DURATION AND THE NUMBER OF SYLLABLES IN A SIGN. Several investigators have reported duration measurements for signs, and in some cases, for signs that are clearly single syllables, thus providing some syllable duration measurements (Bellugi and Fischer, 1972; Friedman, 1976b; Liddell, 1978, 1982). For those reports where the signs are clearly monosyllabic, the means range from 233 to 835 msec, depending on the context. Liddell (1978) provided additional information on the effects of sentence position and syntactic function on the duration of the monosyllabic signs DOG and CAT. The signs were shortest when they appeared in the medial position in a relative clause, longer when they appeared in initial position, and longest in final position. Syntactic function also affected duration: when the sign was the object of the verb, it was shorter than when it was the subject, or when it was the head of the relative clause. Another factor that affects duration is semantic function. Wilbur and Nolen (1986) reported that pointing signs (personal and deictic pronouns) were longer than nonpointing signs of comparable construction. The composition of a syllable is also important. Wilbur and Nolen (1986) reported that syllables that had a final hold were significantly longer than syllables without a final hold. Pragmatic function is yet another factor that affects syllable duration. When syllables are at the end of a conversational turn, they tend to be much longer than when they are not.

Wilbur and Nolen (1986) also provided extensive information on syllable duration. The mean syllable duration of 889 syllables taken from three signers engaged in conversation was 248 msec; this figure is comparable to the estimated 250 msec for spoken English (Adams, 1979; Hoequist, 1983). The possibility exists that this similarity is a reflection of an underlying timing mechanism for motor movement that may surface not only in speech and in signing, but also in nonlinguistic motor behaviors. This hypothesis needs to be tested more directly, using a variety of linguistic and nonlinguistic tasks.

Wilbur and Nolen (1986) also provided means for syllables in several other linguistic situations. One subject signed a list of signs, once before starting work on an unrelated signing project and again after working for two hours. The mean syllable duration for the first list production was 299 msec, whereas the mean for the second list production was 417 msec. Thus, the same signer can have a different mean duration at different times; this, of course, is parallel to what would be found for speech.

In another situation, 14 signers were asked to sign paragraphs that contained either a stressed or an unstressed target sign. The difference here was not only in the means, which, although significantly different, were similar in magnitude (317 msec stressed and 299 msec unstressed). There was also a significantly greater number of syllables per sign in the stressed condition. What seems to happen is *resyllabification*, the changing of the number of syllables in certain environments. In English, a stressed form of the word "please" can be pronounced as two syllables "puh-leeze." Part of the front of the syllable has been broken off and made into another syllable. This is a common occurrence in ASL.

When compounds are made from simple lexical items, the resulting compound may have two syllables or may be reduced to just one (Coulter, 1982; Liddell, 1985). Wilbur (1986a) reported the results of an analysis of 18 sets of compounds and their associated two sign phrases which had been recorded in Ursula Bellugi's research lab. In each set, two signs appeared in a phrase in isolation (e.g., FACE CLEAN) and in context (HE HAS FACE CLEAN 'He has a clean face'). The same morphemes ('face', 'clean') also appeared in a compound (FACE-CLEAN 'handsome') in isolation and in context (HE FACE-CLEAN 'He is handsome'). The compounds had significantly more syllables per sign than simple lexical items. Also, the signs in isolation (whether simple lexical items or compounds) had significantly more syllables than in context.

Wilbur and Schick (1985) discussed many of the movement modifications that can affect a sign when stressed; some of these modifications can result in a sign being split into two or more syllables. The number of syllables in a sign is also affected by the repetition of the movement for morphological purposes (see Chapter 5). As long as the movement is completely repeated, extra syllables result for each repetition. When the repeated movement is reduced so that the repetitions are not countable, the result is usually one long syllable with several short movements in it. For example, the sign WHO when it occurs at the beginning of a question is made with a complete bending of the index finger. This bending may be repeated, but the repetitions are also full and countable. At the end of a question, WHO is made with the reduced movement, with the finger bending looking more like a finger flutter or tremor and the individual bends uncountable. If there were three full repetitions at the beginning of the question, there would be three syllables. If there were theoretically three reduced repetitions at the end of the question, there still might be only one syllable. Thus, the number of syllables a sign actually has when it is produced will vary depending on the context, the presence or absence of stress or emphasis, and the type of movement it has.

SYLLABLE COMPOSITION AND FREQUENCY OF SYLLABLE TYPES. In addition to reporting the overall duration of syllables, Wilbur and Nolen (1986) investigated the duration of the movement and hold pieces that make up syllables. Recall that syllables can begin and/or end with holds (H) and have movement in between (M), but that the holds are optional. Wilbur and Nolen separated syllables according to whether the movement observed was transitional ("T," between signs) or lexical ("M," identifiable lexical item). Because of widespread compression (Klima and Bellugi, 1979), assimilation (Wilbur, 1979), or spreading (Wilbur, 1986a; Wilbur, Klima, and Bellugi, 1983), a single path movement can *start as transitional and finish as lexical* (TM, with the help of changes in handshape, location, or orientation). Such "combination" syllables are quite frequent in conversational signing. Table 3–1 shows the frequency and duration of six syllable types present in the signing of all three conversational signers. Four additional syllable types were observed infrequently in one signer's data and not at all in that of the other two: HMH, HM, HT, and HTM (there were only 16 syllables in all four of these categories combined). These hold-initial syllable types were also infrequent in the other signing samples.

Table 3–1. *Frequency and duration of syllable components, ranked by overall duration (in msec)*

Syllable Type	N of Sylls	T	M	H	Total	SD
TMH	41	127	137	224	488	246
TH	48	187		154	340	227
MH	73		172	123	295	200
TM	213	131	157		288	154
T	114	203			203	118
M	384		195		195	128

In Table 3-1, the different syllable types are listed in descending order by total duration. The three longest syllables types are those with final holds (TMH, TH, MH), and the difference between their mean duration and that of the three syllable types without final holds (TM), T, M) is statistically significant. The internal proportions of syllables containing final holds appear to follow a pattern. On the average 45 percent of the total duration of the syllables containing final holds was accounted for by the hold portion, with the remaining 55 percent in the movement portion. This was true even for TMH syllables in which the *combination* of T and M accounted for 54 percent of the total duration. Similar patterns were found for the stressed and unstressed target signs. The finding of a pattern to the proportions raises the question of whether there is a hold-to-movement ratio of some kind that is necessary to make the hold perceptually and linguistically salient.

There is also a significant relationship between the duration of a syllable and its frequency in conversation. The shorter the duration, the more frequent the syllable type and vice versa. This relationship probably contributes to overall rhythmic patterns in ASL conversations, although at this time further investigation needs to be done to determine exactly how syllable duration and frequency are related to rhythm.

FROZEN VERSUS PRODUCTIVE FORMS

Clearly, holds and movements contribute to syllable structure. The presence of these segments within a syllable allows certain changes to happen during a single syllable. Some of these changes are purely phonological, for example the closing or opening of a handshape, the distance travelled between two contacts with the body or other hand, the change in rhythm for indicating stress or emphasis. Sometimes, however, there is meaning or grammatical function attached to these changes. Recall that in English, the sound "s" can simply be the last sound in a word, such as the word "glass." There is no meaning attached to the final "s." But when "s" makes the difference between singular and plural, as in "cat" and "cats," then it is performing a morphological function. Similarly, in ASL, various parts of certain signs can have meaning or functions attached to them.

LOCATION. Consider how this works for the locations in a sign. Some signs are made in a particular location throughout their entire production. Signs such as APPLE and ONION are distinguished solely by their locations (ONION right below the eye, APPLE lower on the cheek), and the movement (elbow rotation) does not change location, only orientation of the arm. These two signs need to have only one location specification for their production. Other signs may change locations during their production, but only the starting location and the direction of movement are relevant, the final location being unspecified and unimportant. For example, the sign CAT is made with a closing of the thumb and index finger until they touch, starting at or near the side of the mouth and moving away to the right (for right-handed signers). After the fingers touch, it makes no difference if the hand keeps moving (within reason) or stops, because the end location is not specified as a basic part of the sign's production. Pointing signs have the opposite specification; it is the *end* location that is of interest, not where the hand starts. Finally, other signs may have both their beginning and ending locations specified. One type of sign with both locations specified is the "double contact" sign, as in KING, which starts at one shoulder and moves across the trunk to the opposite hip.

More interesting, however, is another type of sign, primarily consisting of verbs, in which the starting and ending locations must be specified, but the actual locations are not filled in until the sign is put into a sentence context. In these situations, the starting location usually is a place that has been established in space for the subject of the sentence and the ending location is a different place for the object of the action of the verb itself. A verb sign like GIVE will have its beginning and ending points specified, but until it is placed into a particular sentence, the actual locations that it starts and ends at cannot be determined. For "I give you," the sign will start at or near the signer and move toward the receiver; for "John gives Bill," the locations of John and Bill must be determined. If John and Bill are both standing there during the conversation, their actual locations can be used to start and end GIVE. However, if they are not there, the signer must indicate a space for John and a saliently different space for Bill. The sign GIVE would then start at John's space and end at Bill's. For the opposite sentence "Bill gives John," the start and ending locations would be exactly the opposite (see Chapter 5 for further discussion of verb agreement).

What we have, then, is a situation in which the starting and ending locations of a sign may be separate morphemes; that is, they may carry grammatical information that reflects syntactic influences. Furthermore, these separate morphemes are affixes added to the stem; one is a prefix, the other a suffix, but they do not add extra syllables. If signs are viewed as being composed of pieces that can occur either simultaneously or sequentially, then the specification of two different locations for one sign is a simple matter of marking the beginning segment with the first location and the ending segment with the second location. Signs with only one location specification for the entire sign production would have the same specification for location simultaneously marked on all its segments. Signs like CAT, with a starting location and a change in location, would have the starting location marked on the first segment, the direction of movement marked on the movement segment, and then the final segment would be unmarked for location, because the ending location is unknown and unimportant.

HANDSHAPE. A similar situation holds for handshapes. A sign can have a single handshape throughout; the sign GIRL is a typical example. A sign can have two handshapes but not need two specifications, especially if the hand is closing or opening (including bends and flicks). In these cases, the second handshape is almost always predictable given the first one. The handshape S almost always opens to 5; the handshape A almost always opens to B. Conversely, the handshape 5 almost always closes to S and the handshape B almost always closes to A. In the case of bending, whether a single finger is involved or the whole hand, the second handshape will almost always be the bent version of the first handshape (B goes to bent B, G goes to X, which is a bent G, etc.). In these cases, the first handshape must be specified and the type of movement (opening, COUNSEL; closing, TAKE; bending, PIG; flicking, HATE, UNDERSTAND, SPEED) must be indicated, but the final handshape specification can be omitted from the basic form of the sign (but not from a transcription that seeks to record all of the phonetic detail).

This contrasts with a similar but distinct situation, in which the handshape changes from one handshape to another, but the ending handshape is *not* predictable from the beginning handshape, and therefore both must be indicated. This is what would need to be done for a syllabic representation of fingerspelling, where each syllable would have a specific starting handshape and a specific ending handshape. The movement of the syllable would not need to be specified because it is merely the transition from one handshape to the next. Because we are interested here primarily in ASL, we will not pursue this model in general for fingerspelling, but rather confine ourselves to fingerspelled loan signs (Battison, 1978), which are real signs but which do not have the same kind of predictable handshape changes as were previously discussed. The fingerspelled loan sign

#OK would need to have O specified as the first handshape and K speci-
fied as the second. #OK would differ from COUNSEL, then, in that COUN-
SEL would have the starting handshape specified as S and the movement specified as opening, while #OK would have two handshape
specifications (with a "flick" handshape change for the movement).

This type of analysis allows signs to be subdivided into phonological classes so that their behavior in context can be better studied.
Some signs will allow their handshapes to be modified by the following signs, and others will not. Some signs allow the rhythm of their
movement to be changed, and others do not. If, for example, there is
no movement specification, then presumably the movement rhythm
cannot be modified.

We are assuming here that the basic form of the sign has all the
information that distinguishes one sign from another, but does not
contain any of the redundant or predictable information; a description of a sign with all the predictable and redundant information is a
phonetic transcription, but what we are interested in here is a phonemic representation. In this sense, it is possible to talk about signs
that have no handshape specification at all, even though it is obvious that a sign made with the hands must have a handshape. Parallel to the signs that had beginning and ending locations marked but
not actually determined until they occurred in a particular sentence,
there are signs that may have different handshapes depending on
the context in which they occur. In some situations, these signs have
a "fall-back" handshape which is very general and does not provide
extra information to the sentence. An example would be the sign for
CHASE, a two-handed sign that is made in citation form with its fall-
back handshape Å. When signed this way, the signer is not providing
information about who or what is chasing who or what. This contrasts to the forms that occur when such information is included.
The signer may use the 3 handshape on both hands to indicate that
one vehicle chased another. The signer may use the G handshape on
both hands to indicate that one person chased another. The signer
may use the bent V handshape on both hands to indicate that one animal chased another. In addition, because there are two hands and
each one can have its own handshape specification, the signer can
use different combinations of handshapes; for example, 3 on the right
hand and G on the left for a vehicle chasing a person, or bent V on the
right hand and 3 on the left hand for an animal chasing a vehicle,
and so on. When the handshapes carry such meaning and are
changeable within a sign, they are generally referred to as *classifiers*
(Chapter 4). The "fall-back" handshape is merely a very general
classifier.

Classifier handshapes are separate morphemes that combine with verbs to complete the predicate construction. If a verb also has its starting and ending locations specified to agree with its subject and object, there may be at least four morphemes in one syllable: the two locations for the subject and object, the handshape for an additional noun (for example, what is being given), and the movement for the verb itself. Speakers of English are used to thinking of morphemes as being represented primarily by grammatical suffixes such as the plural, possessive, and progressive -*ing,* or by grammatical words such as the auxiliary verbs, infinitive marker *to,* and forms of the verb *be.* But the plural morpheme "s" is only a single segment. In ASL, morphemes may be as small as the feature marking the location of a sign or as large as an entire sign (which may have more than one syllable).

DIRECTION OF MOVEMENT. In the previous discussion, we referred to signs like APPLE that have their own particular location and signs like GIRL that have their own particular handshape. Most signs have their own particular direction of movement. Signs with no movement specification will obviously not have a specification for direction of movement. Frequently, the direction of the movement carries or contributes to the meaning of the sign. The sign EAT moves toward the mouth; obviously that is where food goes when someone eats. The sign APPEAR involves an upward movement of the hand as the extended index finger of the G handshape moves in between the index finger and middle finger of the other hand. Viewed from above, the index finger "appears." The sign DISAPPEAR moves downward; viewed from above, the index finger disappears. Similarly, the sign IMPROVE moves upward between the first and second contact it makes on the arm; GET-WORSE moves downward between the two contacts. These signs contrast with GIRL, for example, which involves movement in which the direction is specified but meaningless.

We have illustrated several different types of signs. Some of the signs have *all* of their production characteristics completely specified in their basic forms; no additions or substitutions will affect these signs and they are referred to as "frozen" forms. Other signs have pieces that are not specified in the basic form and which can be filled in by combining the signs with morphemes that can complete the specifications. These are referred to as "productive" signs. A verb without a specified handshape can combine with a classifier morpheme that specifies only handshape. Complex morphological forms may be built up by combining morphemes that fit together — the morphemes involved must have the appropriate phonological specifications or the combination will be impossible to produce. It should also be mentioned that the constraints on sign formation discussed earlier (symmetry and dominance conditions) are true primarily for frozen forms. Many productive verb predicates may have two moving hands with different handshapes (a violation of the symmetry condition) or a secondary handshape on the nonmoving hand that is not one of the six allowable unmarked handshapes (a violation of the dominance condition). These conditions appear to hold for lexical items that are monomorphemic, but not for productive forms that are multimorphemic.

EFFECTS OF LINGUISTIC STRESS

It is theoretically possible for any sign to be in a context where it carries linguistic stress. Although our knowledge of rhythm and stress is far from complete, two elements of importance can be identified: stress (in terms of beats) and duration (the time elapsed between beats). The most frequently studied stresses are lexical stress, sentential stress, emphatic stress, and contrastive stress. Friedman (1976b) investigated emphatic and contrastive stress in ASL. She observed that numerous changes occurred. First, there tended to be a change in the type of contact that might occur: signs *without* final contact tended to add it, whereas signs *with* final contact tended to lose it. Second, there were changes in the manner of production, both in the rhythmic characteristics (that is, the addition of tension, restraint, faster movement) and in the movement itself. Third, there were duration changes, with the movement faster and shorter, and the holds longer.

Overall, a stressed sign tends to be produced larger, tenser, and more rapidly than its corresponding citation form. In measurements made comparing stressed and unstressed signs, Friedman reported that the mean duration of a stressed sign was 833 msec, compared to 366 msec for unstressed signs. However, the actual movement part of this duration was only 150 msec for the stressed signs compared to 267 msec for the unstressed signs. Holds before the movement averaged 367 msec for the stressed signs compared to 150 msec for the unstressed signs, whereas holds after the movement averaged 617 msec for the stressed signs compared to 100 msec for the unstressed signs.

Changes in motion vary according to the type of movement in the citation form. Motion along a straight line, twisting motion, and motion that involves bending of the wrist are modified to become larger, more rapid, and tenser, whereas other nonstraight movements, such as circular, bending of fingers, bending of knuckles, opening, and closing, become tenser and more rapid, but by their nature of formation cannot become larger. Signs that involved repetition in their citation forms tend to lose that repetition. For example, movements such as bending of the fingers, knuckles, or wrist, wiggling of the fingers, twisting, and circular motions are usually made more than once in citation form, but only once in stressed form. Wiggling movement, in losing its repetition, becomes a straight motion sign, and thus it also becomes larger and more rapid. In addition, it becomes ballistic (forceful thrusting motion), as do many other straight action signs, particularly if their direction of motion is away from the body, up, or down. Upward or outward ballistic straight motion signs may also result in full arm extension (making the sign larger).

Friedman's findings regarding duration were not supported by the results of a recent study on stress. Wilbur and Nolen (1986) did not find the same large differences in mean duration between stressed and unstressed signs, or in their respective movement pieces, but did find that the number of syllables per sign was significantly greater for the stressed than the unstressed versions. Thus, the overall durations of the stressed signs were longer because there were more syllables per sign, not specifically because each syllable was longer.

Looking at the effects of stress on the movements themselves, Wilbur and Schick (1985) did find modifications similar to those reported by Friedman. There are many movements that are possible with the arm, hand, and fingers. In ASL, certain movements are reserved for lexical items. Other movements are used only for morphological purposes (Wilbur et al., 1983; see Chapter 5). Recall that movements can be phonologically divided into path movement and local movement (elbow rotation, wrist movement, a variety of handshape changes, and finger flutter). Table 3–2 shows the 10 possible movement categories for lexical items with some examples.

In the last category, hold only, there are very few signs: NOON, COW, MOTHER, FATHER, FINE, the numbers from 1 to 9, and pointing. In each of these cases, the only movement is that which is necessary to get the hand to the required location for the sign and away again. This type of movement is entirely transitional and has been considered by several researchers to be epenthetic, or inserted by rule. These signs are specified for handshape, location, orientation, contact, and so on, but not for movement.

Wilbur and Schick observed that the type of modifications that a

Table 3-2. *Movement categories for ASL lexical items*

Basic Movement	Example
1. Elbow Rotate	HAPPEN
2. Wrist Movement	LATER
3. Flutter	DIRTY
4. Handshape Change	DOUBT
5. Path and Elbow Rotate	LANGUAGE
6. Path and Wrist Movement	STILL
7. Path and Flutter	FINGERSPELL
8. Path and Handshape Change	DESTROY
9. Path	GIVE
10. Hold (No Movement)	NOON

sign underwent depended on the type of movement it originally had. Table 3–3 shows the most preferred modifications for each movement category (up to three per category).

For categories 1, 2, 3, and 4, which have no path movement, the most common modification was the *addition* of a path movement, except that category 4, handshape change, preferred to repeat the handshape change instead. In the wrist move and elbow rotate categories, the temporal and spatial durations are increased by the addition of path movement and highlighted by the modification of the rhythm to a fast tense stop, what is called "short stop." Also, the handshape change and flutter categories tended to have additional emphasis added by the facial expression. This is consistent with Siple's (1978) observation that the area of greatest visual acuity is on the face, whereas the area of least visual acuity is that part of the signing space monitored by the peripheral vision, which includes the space in front of the chest where these signs are made. To heighten the visual perception of the intended linguistic stress, path is added to make the sign larger, repetition is added to increase its temporal duration, and tension is added to increase its force. In the cases of handshape change and flutter, because they are made with the fingers and it is difficult to enlarge the finger area, or to increase the perceived tension of the fingers, the addition of a marked facial expression serves to highlight the added linguistic stress. Other categories have alternate ways of accomplishing this highlighting; thus, handshape change and flutter are the only two categories in which the use of facial expression forms a significant strategy for marking stress (which is not to say that it does not occur elsewhere, only that it is not relied on as a major marker). Note also that while

Table 3-3. *Movement categories and their most preferred changes*

1. Elbow Rotate	Add Path	Short stop	
2. Wrist Movement	Add Path	Elongate	Short stop
3. Flutter	Add Path	Delete Flutter	Facial expression
4. Handshape Change	Repeat	Facial expression	
5. Path and Elbow Rotate	Elongation		
6. Path and Wrist Movement	Other	Elongation	
7. Path and Flutter	Repeat	Delete Flutter	
8. Path and Handshape Change	Elongation		
9. Path	Repeat	Repeat Contact	Elongate
10. Hold (No Movement)	Other		

the handshape change category repeats the handshape change as a way of increasing temporal duration, the flutter category deletes the flutter in the handshape and adds path movement as a way of increasing temporal and spatial duration.

In those categories with path movement, two strategies emerge, either repetition of the path movement in the path only and path with flutter categories (and a secondary tendency to delete the flutter), or elongation of the path itself to make it temporally and spatially longer in all the categories with path except where path occurs with flutter. Additional modifications of rhythm, such as initial restraint with a fast finish, and of movement, such as the addition of movement flourishes to either the beginning or end of the movement, are also observed, but these occur in less than 25 percent of the productions in any category and are therefore omitted from Table 3-3.

Of particular interest is the hold only category. When these signs are produced in isolation, the only movement is the transition movement, which allows the hand to get to and from the location for the sign. The question is, "How can a sign *without movement* be stressed?"

The sign NOON provided several answers to this question. The sign is normally made with the right arm upright, open palm, fingertips straight up, with the back of the left hand contacting underneath the right elbow, and no movement. *Three* different stressed versions which modified the contact between the two hands occurred in our data. In one version, the left hand repeatedly bounced up to the right elbow and made contact with it; in a second version, the right arm repeatedly moved downward to make contact with a motionless left hand; in the third version, the left hand fingertips moved repeatedly into the side of the right elbow and made contact with it. In each case, a reduced repeated contact was used. (We use the term "tremored" to refer to a reduced repetition, rather than a completely and distinctly rearticulated movement; Liddell, 1986, called this 'local movement,' but we have used the term 'local movement' differently here.) A fourth version of stressed NOON kept the contact constant and instead introduced a small, repeated waving to the right arm. In yet another form, the hold of NOON was maintained while the head moved repeatedly left/right. In each of these cases, the signer has to solve the problem of how to provide the minimum movement necessary for a stressed form to signs that have no lexical movement of their own.

A stressed form of the sign FLIRT showed that certain contacts cannot be reanalyzed as "movement to contact." The unstressed sign FLIRT is made with contact at the thumbtips and finger fluttering (it is in the flutter category, not the hold only category). In one stressed version, the flutter was deleted (as happened in the flutter category); this left *no* lexical movement, creating a derived hold only form. However, tremored contact between the thumb tips did *not* occur and is judged unacceptable as a variant for this sign. Contact between the thumbs continued to be treated as a location and was maintained throughout; instead, the stressed form used a small repeated bouncing up and down of both hands or a repeated wrist nod. Nonetheless, the same tremored contact that is unacceptable for FLIRT is the lexical movement for MEASURE. There are some interesting similarities and differences between FLIRT and MEASURE. Both signs have as variant forms a continuous contact at the thumbtips with a dominant hand wrist nod, usually repeated. As indicated, MEASURE allows tremored thumbtip contact, FLIRT does not. The stressed form of FLIRT that bounces both hands (with continuous thumbtip contact) is not permissible for MEASURE. This can be summarized as Table 3–4:

Table 3-4. *A comparison of allowable forms for FLIRT and MEASURE*

Sign	Wrist Nod	Bouncing	Tremored Contact
FLIRT	+	+	*
MEASURE	+	*	+

The different treatment of contact in these cases reflects two *types* of contact: (1) contact as a *place of formation* (FLIRT), and (2) contact as *part of the movement* specification (MEASURE). The overlap between FLIRT and MEASURE (both allowing the wrist nod form) results from phonological processes that produce similar surface representations. The ambiguity of this situation, which has created significant problems for ASL analysis, is demonstrated nicely by the sign MEASURE, which in certain cases treats contact as location (wrist nod) and in others as a movement specification (tremored contact). In FLIRT, the underlying movement is the flutter, while the contact itself is a location specification. In MEASURE, the underlying movement is "movement to contact." But for the wrist nod variant, MEASURE must allow continuous contact. This is not a peculiarity of MEASURE; "movement to contact" alternates with continuous contact when various signs are reduplicated for morphological purposes. A phonological rule for the reduction of "movement to contact" to continuous contact is necessary to fully describe the phonological modifications to ASL signs. The sign NOON in the various stressed versions with tremored contact represents a situation in which an underlying location specification for continuous contact has been treated by some signers as though it were a movement specification. This is their solution to the problem of how to stress a sign with no lexical movement. Note that not all of the signers chose the tremored contact solution. Others introduced waving of the arm while maintaining continuous contact as the location specification, and still others moved their heads rather than their arms to mark the number of beats they considered necessary to indicate linguistic stress.

In earlier descriptions of ASL sign formation, contact did not receive much emphasis, in part because signs were seen only as either having contact or not having contact, and in part because even those signs that did have contact easily lost it in rapid signing, casual signing, and encumbered signing. Thus, the presence of contact was not considered to provide much information to the phonological characterization of sign formation. In a recent paper on the role of contact in ASL, Wilbur (1985b) noted that contact plays a significant role in compound formation (cf. Klima and Bellugi, 1979; Liddell, 1984a) and handshape prediction (Mandel, 1981; Wilbur, 1978, 1979), in addition to being strongly correlated with certain locations (Friedman, 1976b). The reanalysis of "contact as a location feature" to "contact as a movement type" in the stress data discussed provides the key to understanding the internal organization of ASL phonology, especially the phonological rules involved in augmenting and reducing movement. Details of this organization and the role contact plays in it are presented in a later section.

PRIMARILY FOR LINGUISTS

This section contains several topics that have been briefly discussed or alluded to in the preceding sections. It presumes knowledge of modern phonological theories and familiarity with the preceding descriptions of ASL structure (including Chapter 2).

ON SYLLABLES. Returning first to the issue of syllables, recall that in the earlier discussion of their duration, frequency, and composition, it was assumed that four main syllable types existed: MH, HM, HMH, and M (ignoring the semantic function that would separate movement into transitional or lexical movement). This general model was originally suggested by Liddell (1982, 1984a). Wilbur (1982a) argued for a more complex model, modifying a syllable structure suggested by Cairns and Feinstein (1982) for spoken English. The more complex model included Liddell's three pieces (2 holds and 1 movement), three pieces from Newkirk (1979, 1980, 1981), and one additional piece for local movement. Newkirk's analysis allowed for the first and last piece to be either hold or movement, thus allowing the possibility of three movement pieces in a row. The need for several sequential movement pieces becomes apparent when derivational and inflectional processes are taken into account. There is clear evidence that when path movements are observed in inflected forms, initial portions may have a feature marking the production as [+restrained], or final portions may be marked for increased speed, increased deceleration, or even for a different movement type. In the latter case, the regular movement of the sign seems to be shortened so that the suffixed movement can be squeezed into the same syllable. There are many signs that require some type of internal sequence or differential marking of the pieces. Only a few examples will be discussed here.

The regular movement for the sign CHURCH is simply a contact at the back of the nondominant hand, and it can be argued that there is really no movement specification at all (that this is a member of the hold only category discussed in the section on linguistic stress). A derived form of this sign, meaning "pious," adds a full path movement before the contact (Klima and Bellugi, 1979). An idiomatic derivation from this form yields "narrow-minded"; the full path movement is shortened, made faster and tenser, and bounced back from its brief contact with the back of the other hand.

The sign for ONION is made with an elbow rotation with a knuckle of the index finger making contact with the cheek bone during the entire rotation. Friedman (1976b) cites an emphatic form of ONION, ONIONY, that contains an additional small movement away from the cheek after the twisting movement.

One inflected form of the sign SICK is made with a restrained initial movement followed by a fast finish. Klima and Bellugi (1979) identify this form as the "resultative."

The first two of these cases, "narrow-minded" and ONIONY, require additional specification to the last part of the movement, whereas the third form, the "resultative" of SICK, requires a manner of movement feature on its initial part. Newkirk's analysis postulated a three-part syllable composed of an onset, a core, and an offset. These pieces could be marked for the features [syllabic], [dynamic] (= movement), [path], [restrained], and [tense]. Redundantly, the onset and offset were [−syllabic], whereas the core was [+syllabic]. Any piece marked [−dynamic] indicated the absence of movement, and thus a hold. A piece could be marked as [+dynamic, −path] for local movement (elbow rotation, wrist movement, a variety of handshapes, and finger flutter). Newkirk's treatment of "narrowminded" and ONIONY would be to have the offset marked as [+dynamic] instead of [−dynamic], and to mark the offset with the special features of the added or modified movement. In both cases, the extra bounce or movement away from contact is too small to be [+path], which is reserved for signs with salient paths. For the "resultative" of SICK, the onset would be marked [+dynamic], and also [+restrained]. In addition, all three pieces are marked [+path].

Newkirk's analysis demonstrates the need to be able to mark pieces within the movement itself. Both he and Liddell recognize that syllables can be bounded on both sides by holds. But neither analysis can handle internally marked movements that are preceded and/or followed by holds. To mark a movement onset or offset, Newkirk must change the hold specification ([−dynamic]) to a movement specification ([+dynamic]). Liddell has only a unitary segment M and treats sequences of two movements, even a restrained beginning followed by a fast finish, as a sequence of two M.

The model proposed in Wilbur (1982a) allows for initial and final holds as well as three pieces of sequential movement (Figure 3–1). Parallel to Newkirk's onset and offset when they are marked [+dynamic], Wilbur proposed a pre-peak and a post-peak to precede and follow the peak of the movement, respectively. Parallel to Liddell's HMH structure, Wilbur proposed an onset hold and a coda hold, both of which are optional.

Neither Newkirk nor Liddell can handle situations in which a sign has both a path and a local movement. The local movement is represented by the satellite position, and is placed so as to reflect both its simultaneity with path movement when both occur and its function as the syllable peak when no path movement is present.

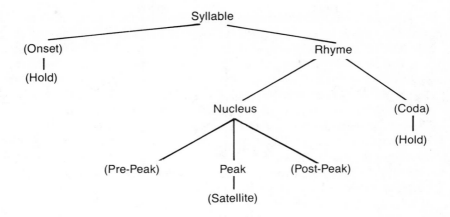

Figure 3-1. Syllable model from Wilbur (1982a).

The syllable model presented in Figure 3–1 was designed after the hierarchical model proposed by Cairns and Feinstein (1982). Hyman's (1984) discussion of an alternative model of syllables in which syllable weight plays a primary role leads to the question of whether the hierarchical structure in Figure 3–1 is linguistically necessary, as suggested by another model in Figure 3–2 (Wilbur, 1986a). (It should be pointed out that the models in Figure 3–1 and 3–2 both use Liddell's holds (H) and movements (M) as the basic segments, where the nucleus = M. Sandler (1986), to be discussed later, has suggested different segments, movements (M), locations (L), and handshapes (C). Wilbur (1986a) also presented syllable models using Sandler's segments. It is too soon to tell which will be the most useful model.)

Hyman argues that the only relevant aspect of syllable structure is the weight units that each syllable has. A light syllable has one weight unit, a heavy syllable has two. In spoken languages, a CV structure has one weight unit, for which Hyman postulates a universal rule of onset formation that ensures the initial C will not have weight. Syllables with long vowels have two weight units, supporting a VV notation. However, spoken languages differ in how they treat CVC structures. Some languages treat CVC as a light syllable, whereas others treat it as a heavy syllable.

As far as ASL is concerned, syllables containing final holds (MH, TH, TMH) are clearly heavy, with the assignment of one weight unit

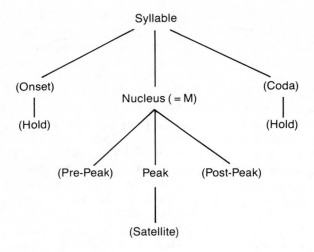

Figure 3-2. Without hierarchical structure (Wilbur, 1986a).

to the movement and one to the final hold. Movement only syllables (M, T, TM) can be either light or heavy. The transition movement syllables (T) are always light, having only one weight unit; these syllables participate in the rhythmic pattern of ASL sentences, carrying demibeats as described in Selkirk (1984), but never carrying a full beat of their own. Their behavior is perhaps best described as parallel to syllables consisting only of epenthetic schwa (i.e., counts as one syllable, does not carry a full beat, cannot carry stress).

The previous generalizations are supported primarily by observations concerning the overall durations as a function of syllable composition (Table 3–1). Although there are other factors that affect syllable salience, such as tension and aspects of acceleration, total duration is certainly a major one. Syllables with short overall durations "don't count" when signers are asked to tap the overall rhythm of signed sentences, but "do count" when signers are asked to count syllables or to tap once for each syllable (Allen, Wilbur, and Schick, 1986).

One unsolved problem is the question of the status of the TM syllables. On the basis of duration alone, these syllables should be treated as heavy. They are significantly longer than the other syllables that do not contain final holds (T, M). They also do not differ significantly in length from the MH and TH syllables, both of which contain final holds. However, as might be predicted from the discussion above, they are significantly shorter than TMH syllables, given that the final hold carries weight of its own. There are two aspects of this problem that will have to be addressed. One is the implication that if TM is a heavy syllable, which means it carries two weight units, then TMH must carry *three* weight units. Some languages, such as Estonian, make three distinctions in syllable quantity, and this may be what is happening here. Or it may be that there is a parallel between ASL and English, which has two levels of syllable weight (light and heavy) and a separate distinction of syllable stress (heavy syllables may be either stressed or unstressed). These two separate distinctions result in three syllable types, light, heavy unstressed, and heavy stressed. At this point, it is not possible to tell whether either of these two analyses fits ASL. The situation is complicated further by the fact, mentioned earlier, that there appears to be a constant relationship between the movement and holds in syllables containing final holds, such that the movement accounts for 55 percent of the total duration and the hold accounts for 45 percent. This relationship was true even for TMH, raising the question of whether these syllables, although longer than TM, are still saliently only two pieces, movement and hold. The second aspect of this problem is simply that there are currently no linguistic arguments for treating TM either as light or as heavy. Thus, although there is psycholinguistic evidence for TM as a heavy syllable because of its duration, there are so far no linguistic ramifications of this analysis.

One final problem needs to be mentioned. There have been so few syllables with initial holds in the data that it is difficult to make any generalizations about their durations, their weights, or their role in ASL phonology. Citation signs were frequently cited as having initial holds, but in many cases, the "hold" was actually a starting contact. Researchers have agreed that for measurement purposes, a hold has to be at least two fields long (33 msec). This eliminates the possibility of mistaking a slowing down prior to direction change as a hold. One implication of the scarcity of hold initial syllables is the lack of a parallel in frequency between spoken CV syllables and signed HM syllables. It is probably true that the initial hold does not carry weight in ASL, but at this point the demonstration is weak at best.

Using a phonological weight framework to discuss the structure of ASL syllables leads to the generalization that there are light syllables, heavy syllables (hold final), and syllables for which the category has yet to be determined (TM). The possibility exists that there may need to be three levels, with units having one, two, or three phonological weights. At the same time, the arguments discussed earlier for the internal structure given in Figures 3–1 or 3–2 are still valid. In addition to whatever weights are assigned at the core level, there still needs to be an indication of the sequential segment possibilities, including three possible sequential segments and one simultaneous movement. In this regard, the syllable structure postulated for ASL differs significantly from that proposed for English by Cairns and Feinstein (1982). In English syllables, the major complexity is found in the onset and coda, which are composed of consonants. The nucleus portion of the syllable consists at most of a vowel and a glide. In ASL, the major complexity is in the nucleus itself, with all the movement pieces, whereas the onset and coda consist of at most a hold.

ON TIERS AND SPREADING. In the literature on ASL phonology, spreading and tiers have both made appearances in a variety of situations. In some cases, their use is purely for notational convenience; in others, they capture significant linguistic generalizations.

Liddell's (1982) proposal concerning ASL segment structure included a sequence of HMH and the simultaneous marking of the remaining information — handshape, contact, orientation, location, and facial expression. Wilbur (1982a) argued not only for the internal structure previously discussed and presented in Figure 3–1, but also that the initial and final holds, which are optional, obtained their feature markings from the adjacent movement pieces by spreading. That is, an initial hold always has the same handshape, orientation, location, and other nonmovement features as its adjacent (following) movement piece (pre-peak), and the final hold is always marked identically to its adjacent (preceding) movement piece (post-peak). Wilbur also argued that in the case of simple path movement, only the peak was fully marked, and the redundant pre-peak and post-peak obtained their features by spreading. The only cases where separate feature matrices need to be marked internal to a syllable are when there is a change in specification: change in movement type, change in location, change in handshape, change in contact, change in orientation, change in facial expression. In an earlier section, syllables containing more than one feature specification were discussed. Verb agreement on the sign GIVE, for example, requires a starting location that agrees with the subject and an ending location that agrees with the (surface direct) object. The difference between a handshape change (e.g., opening, COUNSEL) and a change in handshape (e.g., fingerspelling) was described. In the former case, the satellite is filled with the movement specification for opening; in the absence of a co-occurring path movement, the opening movement fills the peak slot, the features are then spread to the pre- and post-peak slots, and if there are initial and final holds, they obtain their features from the adjacent movement pieces. In the latter cases, the pre-peak is specified for the first handshape, the post-peak is specified for the second handshape, the peak may be unspecified and filled phonetically with epenthetic transition movement; as before, initial and final holds obtain their features from the adjacent movement pieces. By contrast, fingerspelled loan signs, such as #OK, have two handshape specifications *and* a handshape change specification.

A short note on theoretical differences is in order: the above analysis differs from that proposed in Liddell (1984a, b) in that in cases like #OK, Liddell puts his initial nonmovement (e.g., handshape, location) features on an initial *hold* and his final nonmovement features on a final *hold,* spreads those features onto the movement, then deletes the holds (which do not occur on the surface) when they are not adjacent to a phrase boundary. In his analysis, then, initial holds are far more frequent than occur in actual conversation, and have equal status with final holds.

This and several related observations led Sandler (1986) to propose a different perspective on sign structure. She offers an alternative model in which the opposition is between movement (M) and location (L), with handshape (C) on a separate autosegmental tier. The presence or absence of holds would be characterized by a binary feature in the location feature matrix; rather than have holds underlying, there will be some phonetic holds (list rhythm), some phonological holds (at utterance boundary), some morphological holds (ASL aspectual inflections may include final hold as part of their pattern), and pragmatic holds (end of conversational turn, waiting for backchannel nod). Sandler demonstrates that handshape spreading may occur both to the right (typical situations within a syllable, across affixed suffixes) and to the left (compound formation). Sandler's model is consistent with the view of ASL phonology discussed in a later section "On the Organization of the Phonological Component," and is thus preferable to a strictly HMH approach, but it is not clear how her model will mesh with the description of sign syllables given earlier, particularly with the issue of the salience of final holds, illustrated by the constant proportion of movement to hold, and the contribution of final holds to the weight of a syllable. Because Sandler has postulated hold as a feature on the location segment, it is not clear how the weight and proportion data can be represented, although this issue can probably be resolved. Sandler suggests that word internal location gemination would give a sequence of LL that would then share a single feature matrix and would in many respects be parallel to spoken consonant gemination. Wilbur (1986a) presented several possible syllable structures which incorporate Sandler's suggestions.

Wilbur (1985c) uses tiers and spreading to describe the formation of numbers in Italian Sign Language (Sicilian dialect). The number morphemes themselves are obligatorily specified for handshape (like ASL numbers and classifiers) and, in some cases, for orientation. From 11 to 19, a local movement is also necessary. The numbers are essentially hold only signs, thus, except for the numbers from 11 to 19, they are not specified for movement. The segmental tier consists of a series of movement segments, the number being determined by how many digits are to be produced. Each M is associated with a number morpheme on the morpheme tier; each associated M will acquire the signer's choice of list movement — presented with a push forward, rocking side to side, or other small movements. Epenthetic transition movement between different handshapes is inserted by rule. Alternating beat assignment places beats on lexical M and not on transitional T. This is illustrated in Figure 3–3, with several possible syllable types given at the bottom.

Wilbur, Klima, and Bellugi (1983) made several observations concerning tiers and spreading. They noted that several pieces of signs were eligible for phonological or morphological treatment on separate tiers. Local movement, for example, carries the root meaning of many signs and may be spread across path movement when it is added for inflectional purposes. This observation must be modified to restrict the spreading to path movement within the same syllable, and not across syllable boundary onto suffixed path movements such as in the continuative inflection. Handshape, which warrants its own tier as a classifier may be spread across path movement within and across syllable boundaries. The issue remains of whether handshape should be on its own tier when it is not a separate morpheme. Other features that can be spread include contact, location, orientation, and nonmanual signals. It is also not clear that any of these merit their own tiers.

In general, then, linguists have found tiers and spreading applicable to certain processes in ASL. Similar utility has been found for distinctive features, generative phonological rules such as the epenthesis rule cited earlier, and a variety of other spoken language devices. The fact that ASL is a language implies that it will share certain principles of organization with other languages. It is highly likely that parallels between ASL structure and spoken language structure will continue to be found. It is also highly *unlikely* that the study of ASL phonology will help resolve theoretical issues, as more questions seem to be raised than answered.

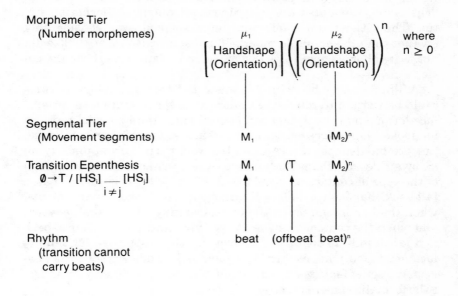

Figure 3-3. Derivation of numbers in Italian Sign Language (from Wilbur, 1985c)

*Source of Holds not discussed; syllables are separated by ".".

75

ON UNDERLYING REPRESENTATIONS AND PHONOLOGICAL RULES. The assumption that ASL had both an underlying (phonemic) level and a surface (phonetic) level has been part of ASL research almost from the beginning (although not used by every researcher). Stokoe's (1960) inventory of notational symbols consisted of only those for which he could demonstrate phonemic status (what he called "cheremic"); variants were delegated to allophonic ("allocheric") status. Thus, the number of handshape symbols was considerably smaller than the actual number of handshapes. However, Stokoe did not write phonological rules to derive the variant forms from the basic forms.

Wilbur (1978a b, 1979) demonstrated that phonological rules could be written to relate the underlying representation to the surface forms and that these phonological rules were parallel to those for spoken languages except for the features to which they referred. Surface handshapes [S], [A], and [Å] were derived from underlying /S/ by a rule that changed thumb feature specifications as a function of the type of contact involved (Figure 3–4). The "elsewhere" (basic, fall-back) handshape is [S], occurring in no-contact environments, when the hands contact on the index or pinky edge or on the wrist, and when the contact is made at the third finger joint. Signs specified for thumb-tip contact will have [Å]; those specified for thumb-face or second joint contact will have [A]. Liddell (1986) has suggested a set of features which would permit these different contacts to be formalized more precisely.

Also important is the existence of a separate phonemic handshape /Å/ which functions as a classifier form and exists in no-contact situations. Thus, surface phonetic [Å] may be either a derived form of underlying /S/ or a surface reflection of underlying /Å/. This situation is a violation of the biuniqueness principle, which classical phonemic analyses sought to maintain, but which generative phonology discarded (Chomsky, 1964). Wilbur (1978a) argued that ASL phonology required an analysis with at least the power of generative phonology, in contrast to Friedman (1976b), who felt that a classical phonemic analysis would be sufficient.

Let us turn now to some of the phonological rules that have been proposed for ASL. Four rules have already been mentioned. One was the rule that derived surface handshapes as a function of contact environments, just discussed. Another was the epenthesis of transition movements between adjacent segments containing different handshape specifications. A third was Liddell's hold deletion rule, which deleted holds that were not adjacent to phrase boundaries. A fourth was the rule that reduced "movement to contact" to "continuous contact," discussed in the section on linguistic stress. Several uses of standard autosegmental spreading have also been mentioned, although not elaborated.

There has also been mention of tremored or rapid, uncountable repetition of certain reduced movements. There appear to be two sources for reduced movements: phonological reduction and morphological reduction. In Chapter 5, several morphological inflections will be discussed; some of these result in movement reductions (e.g., the habitual, approximative). Phonological reductions occur on signs not carrying stress, re-occurring within the same sentence (e.g., WHO in question initial versus question final position), or when reduced for compound formation. Some signs (SICK, SHOES) appear in their citation forms with tremored contact (small, repeated movements to the point of contact). Wilbur (1985c) argued that tremored movement ("gemination") is not specified in the underlying representation of these forms, but rather than tremoring/gemination is an "elsewhere" rule, applying to an underlying representation when no other rules do. The underlying representation of the forms to which tremoring applies specifies a contact in the post-peak and no path or local movement. Such an underlying presentation is incapable of standing by itself as a surface syllable because it does not meet the minimum movement necessary to carry phonological weight (has no movement specification). At least three types of rules could apply to these forms and *block* tremoring: *stress, compounding,* and *reduplication* (for derivational and inflectional purposes). For example, a stressed form of SICK would have only one large movement to contact; a path movement will be inserted to carry the stress and tremoring will be blocked. There is thus an alternation between

$$/S/ \rightarrow [A] \quad / \quad \begin{bmatrix} \text{second joint contact} \\ \text{thumb face contact} \end{bmatrix}$$

$$/S/ \rightarrow [\dot{A}] \quad / \quad \begin{bmatrix} \text{thumb tip contact} \end{bmatrix}$$

Using Woodward's features and a shorthand notation for S, we can write these rules as:

$$\begin{bmatrix} + & \text{closed} \\ - & \text{thumb} \\ - & \text{spread} \end{bmatrix} \rightarrow [\,+\,\text{thumb}] \quad / \quad \begin{bmatrix} \text{second joint contact} \\ \text{thumb face contact} \\ \text{thumb tip contact} \end{bmatrix}$$

Figure 3-4. Phonological Rule from Wilbur (1978a).

forms having one path movement to contact and forms having multiple too-short-to-be-path movements to contact. In compounding, if the form is to be the first part of the compound, only the single short movement appears; in the second part the movement may be repeated or not. Consider as an example the compound meaning "homework." Both HOME and WORK are signs that show up in unstressed forms with tremored movements to contact (the form of HOME referred to here is not the two-touch two-location form, but the form in which multiple touches are made in the *same* location; the multiple touch form is specified only for contact in the post-peak, whereas the two-location form must have two separate location specifications and is thus not eligible for tremoring). In the compound, one touch for "home" and one touch for "work" are separated by a tense, large movement from the location of HOME to the location of WORK. Inflected forms of WORK (e.g., "to work for a long time") undergo various reduplication processes, many of which add path movement (in different shapes — circles, ellipses; see chapter 5). Because only signs lacking path or local movement are eligible for tremoring, these derived forms do not become tremored.

Note that reduplication is different from tremoring in that reduplication processes in ASL display different possible paths and rhythms, each of which carries different morphological information, whereas tremoring appears to be a primarily phonological process, with the resultant forms incapable of carrying stress or having a salient modification to the internal rhythm. For example, aspectual modifications that use reduplication modify the types of contacts. The predicate SIT is made with one single even movement to contact. In certain reduplicated forms for nominalizations the contact becomes continuous and the two hands move together. In the associated noun CHAIR, there is repeated contact, not continuous contact, and the repetitions are countable (usually two). In tremored forms, the number of repetitions is usually not countable and certainly does not appear fixed or deliberate. The difference is that reduplication in ASL is actually a set of morphologically motivated rules (deverbal noun formation for CHAIR, various aspectual modifications for continuative, durative, habitual, etc.) with associated phonological modifications. Tremoring, as an elsewhere phonological rule, will not modify *any* of the significant characteristics of a sign. Note also that even though the distinction between tremoring and reduplication may be neutralized in surface forms like the habitual, which uses rapid, small, repeated movements, the derivations will be different.

A variety of phonological rules was discussed in Wilbur (1979). Many of them were of questionable synchronic productivity, and perhaps are best treated as dialect or stylistic differences, or as fast signing phenomena. Included were several types of assimilations (movement, facial expression, orientation) and finger bending. Of those originally discussed, several still warrant description: assimilation of location (including metathesis), assimilation of handshape, and deletion(s).

Assimilation of location has been observed between two consecutive signs. In each case so far, it has been regressive assimilation, with the second sign conditioning adjustment in the formation of the first sign. For example, in a signed version of "The Three Little Pigs" (Kegl and Chinchor, 1975), while the wolf tries to gain admittance to the house of the three little pigs, he signs LET ME IN repeatedly. In some cases, the formation of LET is modified in that the right hand moves from waist level (where LET is normally signed) to chest height, in anticipation of the formation of the sign ME. In a few cases, both hands of LET were raised to chest height in anticipation of the following sign.

In another example, WE REFUSE, regressive assimilation of location caused the sign WE to *metathesize* its two places of articulation (contact first at right chest, then at left chest, *became* contact first at left chest, then at right chest) in anticipation of the formation of REFUSE at the right shoulder. (This analysis is of course only valid for those dialects that use this form of WE in the first place.) Metathesis provides further support for the sequential model of ASL sign structure. The feature representation for the first location and the feature representation for the second location are switched internal to the sign WE. Furthermore, all of the signs that are eligible for this have the same structure — two locations specified fairly close to each other and no movement specification other than the movement between the two locations/contacts. They are monomorphemic single syllable signs. Other signs that can undergo this rule are FLOWER, DEAF, and PARENTS. Further discussion of metathesis is contained in Johnson (1986).

The example WE REFUSE also illustrates assimilation of handshape, again regressive assimilation. The sign WE is usually made with an H hand (or for some people, with a G hand), or in initialized versions with a W, but in one recorded case it is made with an A hand as an assimilation to REFUSE, which is made with an A. According to Coulter (personal communication), a single handshape sign is susceptible to assimilation with the following handshape, whereas a sign with two handshapes or a handshape change (opening or closing) is not. As yet, the details of this assimilation have not been further formalized.

Battison (1974) described types of deletion that may occur in

ASL and related them to the structural complexity of the signs. He noted four types of deletion: (1) deletion of a contact (also viewed as deletion of a location), (2) deletion of one part of a compound, (3) deletion of movement (e.g., loss of repetition in stressed signs), and (4) deletion of one of the hands in two-handed signs.

It is the latter type that Battison concentrated on. Recall that two-handed signs are restricted in their handshapes and movements by the symmetry condition, allowing three classes of signs: (1) one hand moves, the other stays still, and they both have different handshapes, (2) one hand moves, the other stays still, and they both have the same handshape, and (3) both hands move (and they therefore have the same handshape and same or mirror image movement). Battison reports that these structural groups are correlated with the acceptability of deleting one of the hands. In the first group, deletion of the moving hand is prohibited, probably because the nondominant hand does not provide sufficient information to identify the sign, thereby making the signal unintelligible. Deletion of the nondominant hand in this group of signs is permitted for only a few signs (THAT, WEEK, LATER). In the second group of signs, deletion of the nondominant hand is more readily acceptable, but Battison reports that the signer frequently attempts some type of substitute for the missing hand, perhaps contacting another part of the body or an object, or "ghosting" the movement as though the other hand were there. In the third group of signs, where both hands move, deletion of one hand is more frequent. Frishberg (1975, 1976) reported that deletion of one hand in two-handed signs made near the face was an obligatory diachronic process. Synchronically, it is optional for two-handed signs made in neutral space, with the exception of signs with alternating movement or with crossing of the arms (HUG, BEAR, SKELETON). Deletion is also not allowed if the contact that the two hands make with the body is not symmetrical, as in the sign RESPONSIBILITY, where the contact (for right-handed signers) is at the right shoulder, and is asymmetrical in the sense that the right hand touches the ipsilateral shoulder (the right one) but the left hand touches the contralateral shoulder (the right one) instead of the symmetrical situation where the left hand contacts the ipsilateral shoulder also. As the degree of redundancy increases in two-handed signs (group 1 is the least redundant, group 3 the most), the freedom for deletion increases.

Padden and Perlmutter (1984) describe a similar deletion process, which they refer to as weak drop. Signs that are made with two hands that do not have alternating movement (e.g., one moves up while the other moves down) and that do not contact each other may lose the nondominant hand and be made one-handed. HAPPEN and CELEBRATE can undergo this process, whereas EXPLAIN, JUDGE, or MEAN-ING cannot. The process applies in fast or casual signing.

Bellugi (1975; Klima and Bellugi, 1979) discusses deletion in the context of the process of compounding, which will be dealt with more extensively in Chapter 4. Frishberg (1978) investigated synchronic remnants of compounds that experienced deletion. When deletion of one part of the sign (whether first or second) left behind a sign with a complex movement (like wiggling, twisting) or a sign that is two-handed, symmetrical, with no contact between hands or body, then no further modification of the sign occurred and no trace of the deleted part has been left. However, in many signs, deletion of one part of the sign resulted in a subsequent modification in the formation of the sign, which Frishberg argued is appropriately described as "compensatory lengthening." In spoken languages, it is not uncommon for the deletion of a consonant to be accompanied by the lengthening of a neighboring vowel. In ASL, the deletion of one part of a sign has resulted in a lengthening of a movement, either by repetition or by a complication of the movement (addition of wiggling or circular motion). Thus, when "compensatory lengthening" is not accomplished by the addition of a circular path or local movement, the form undergoes the gemination rule discussed in an earlier section. The loss of one part of the compound, and the subsequent repetition of motion, also led to modifications in the location of certain signs. Usually, this reduced two locations (one for first part of sign, one for second) to a repetition at one location. Frishberg observes that if the former compound involved a crossing of the "major area" boundaries (see Table 2–4 in Chapter 2), the location of the resultant sign was double contact at the former second location (based on discussion in Frishberg, 1975, the physically lower location is expected also). However, if the former compound involved two contacts within the same major area, the resulting location was midway between the two former locations.

ON THE ORGANIZATION OF THE PHONOLOGICAL COMPONENT. The description of ASL phonology presented so far contains distinctive features, segments, syllables, tiers, and phonological rules, including spreading. Recent papers have suggested two organizational aspects that may be specific to ASL. One of these is the relationship between the nonmoving (static) features of the language and their associated moving forms (Wilbur, 1985b). The other is the layering of certain phonological options in accordance with certain lexical or morphological functions (Wilbur et al., 1983). Because of the intimate relationship between the notion of phonological layering and the morphological component, that discussion will be delayed until Chapter 5.

Recall the discussion of the reanalysis of contact as a "movement to contact" specification. The relationship between "contact as location" and "movement to contact" is partially obscured by the terminology used to describe them, location for the former and (path) movement for the latter. In fact, path movement (as opposed to handshape change, flutter, wrist movement, and elbow rotate) is *a change in location*. That is, location and path movement are in direct opposition to each other because one is the dynamic (moving) counterpart of the other. A similar opposition is also apparent between handshape and handshape change. One other opposition is not only obscured by the terminology but also by our way of thinking about it: orientation is often viewed as a somewhat less important characteristic than handshape, location, and movement, whereas wrist movement and elbow rotate are viewed as two less important kinds of movement. Yet wrist movement is a change of orientation of the hand, and elbow rotate is a change of orientation of the arm. This gives three corresponding pairs of static and dynamic characteristics (Table 3–5).

What the above organization does, besides providing some coherence to the sign formation components, is to highlight the oppositional relationships that exist and the role that contact plays as a bridge between location and location change. It is tremored contact that serves as this bridge — a repeated reduced movement that is clearly not static, yet is so slight in its movement that it must be repeated in order to qualify as the minimum movement necessary for a surface phonetic form (Frishberg, 1978). Similarly, repeated reduced forms such as tremored finger bend (also called flutter), as in the question-final variant of WHO, may also serve as a bridge between handshape and its corresponding dynamic form handshape change, whereas the tremor movement found in phonological variants of signs like YES, THAT, FINISH, and YELLOW seems to serve the same func-

Table 3–5. *Static and dynamic correspondences*

Static	Dynamic
Handshape	Handshape Change
Location	Location Change (= Path)
Orientation	Orientation Change (= Elbow Rotate/Wrist Movement)

Table 3–6. *Phonologically-related static, full dynamic, and reduced dynamic forms (Wilbur, 1985b)*

Static	Full Dynamic	Reduced Dynamic
Handshape	Handshape Change	Flutter/Repeat Bend
Location	Location Change	Tremored Contact
Orientation	Orientation Change	Tremor (Wrist/Elbow)

tion between orientation and its corresponding dynamic forms elbow rotate and wrist movement. These are not variants across dialects; rather, they are variants in different phonological environments. This suggests a three column analysis as shown in Table 3–6, as opposed to the two column analysis in Table 3–5.

This organization represents a very different perspective on the relationships among the various sign formation characteristics than does the traditional list of "the big four" and the remaining minor characteristics, inherited from the modifications made to sign description since Stokoe (1960). This organization would predict the fact that there are phonological alterations between the static, full dynamic, and reduced dynamic forms. That is, there will be phonological rules that reduce full dynamic movement to reduced movement, or full movement to static, and reduced movement to static, *or* phonological rules that enhance in the other direction. The point is that if the goal is to specify something about possible phonological alternations in ASL, the organization presented predicts that alternations will occur across the rows in Table 3–6, not down the columns. The full dynamic handshape change form of, for example, WANT alternates with the reduced dynamic finger bend form of WANT in different phonological environments. These predictions are in accordance with the model proposed by Sandler (1986), which postulates movement (M) and location (L) as segments, with a separate hand tier (she refers to her model as the "hand tier" (HT) model, as opposed to Liddell's "movement-hold" (MH) model). The opposition of movement and location is exactly what was predicted earlier, where movement is referred to as location change. Many more details concerning the model and the types of rules consistent with the organization in Table 3–6 remain to be addressed.

Previous analyses involving contact have identified syllable structure constraints, in which certain handshapes co-occur only with certain contacts, certain locations co-occur only with certain contacts, and the type of contact restricts the movement modifications that may occur, for example, under stress (Wilbur, 1985b). If contact is inherently connected to movement, as suggested here, then its central role in the determination of certain handshapes, locations, and movement modifications can be better understood.

SUMMARY

This chapter has presented a variety of approaches to describing the internal structure of signs. Syllable duration and frequency were reported, including the observation that syllables in ASL were approximately the same length as syllables in speech (about 250 msec). Also, syllables with final holds are significantly longer, suggesting that they have status as heavy syllables, whereas syllables consisting of a single movement and no hold could be light or heavy syllables (depending on other factors, such as tension, force, or movement length). Syllables containing combined movements (TM) are of unclear status, and their counterpart with final holds (TMH) may require a third level of phonological weight to distinguish them from other heavy syllables. Linguistic evidence of critical functions played by heavy and light syllables, such as in stress assignment, is still needed.

The effects of linguistic stress on sign movement were described, and a variety of ASL phonological rules, including insertion of transition movements, tremoring of reduced movements, and deletion of the nondominant hand in two-handed signs, was presented.

Signs with internal changes were discussed in relation to the models of sequential segmental structure. The need for sequential internal structure was demonstrated both for simple lexical items and for derived and inflected forms. Several models, including Liddell's MH model, Sandler's HT model, and Wilbur's hierarchical syllable model were outlined.

A number of modern phonological theories have been applied to ASL structure. The examination of their utility in this chapter illustrates the similarity between ASL and spoken languages once the difference in modality is accounted for. Padden and Perlmutter (1984) referred to this as the *minimal difference hypothesis*: "Oral and sign languages have different phonological features. Otherwise, there are no significant differences between their grammars." What we have seen in this chapter is the extent to which this is true. There is, however, one remaining aspect of ASL structure, the layering of phonological characteristics for morphological purposes, which may represent a difference in the structure of signed grammars. This will be discussed in Chapter 5.

Sign Morphology: Word Formation

In the preceding chapter, signs were discussed in terms of their phonological building blocks, and were separated into those with completely specified underlying representations ("frozen") and those with empty specifications that could be filled by combination with other morphemes containing the appropriate phonological specifications ("productive"). It is the productive lexicon of ASL that is the focus of this chapter on word formation. Classifiers, which are represented phonologically as handshape specifications, combine with predicate roots, which are represented phonologically as movement specifications. Location, orientation, the relationship between the two hands, contact, and other important aspects of the total sign production will vary in how they are specified. Some specifications may depend on the syntax, for example, the starting and ending locations will agree with the subject and object; others may depend on the meaning, for example, the orientation and spatial arrangement of the two hands will differ if what is being discussed is a pencil standing in a cup, lying on a table, hidden under a blanket, or being used as a makeshift ruler. Systematic relationships that exist between phonological specifications and morphological and lexical meanings will be highlighted in the discussion that follows.

Several linguistic terms need further clarification before continuing. The term "predicate" refers to a verb form that may include information about its subject, direct object and/or indirect object, as well as information usually represented in English by prepositional phrases and adverbs. This latter information may not appear in ASL as prepositional phrases or separate adverbs, but rather may be included as part of the predicate sign in the form of morphemes with partial phonological specifications (e.g., place of formation, direction of movement, or facial expression). The term "argument" is used by linguists to refer to the nouns in a sentence that perform a grammatical function with respect to the verb (subject, direct object, and indirect object). The terms "agree" or "agreement" refer to a marking on the verb with respect to some aspect of its argument(s). In English, there is number agreement, whereby the verb must be marked with the suffix "–s" if the subject is third person singular, "he walks." Other forms of the verb are unmarked for number (singular or plural) or person (first, second, or third person). More extensive verb markings are found in languages like French, which mark the verb *differently* for first person singular, first person plural, second person familiar singular, second person familiar plural, and so on. In these cases, the agreement is with the subject noun phrase. It is not uncommon for languages to mark their verbs to agree with both the subject and the object noun phrases; many ASL verbs agree with their subjects and objects, as was suggested in the earlier discussion of location specifications in the phonological representation of predicates. Finally, the term "classifier" is used to refer to a particular kind of pronoun (= takes the place of a noun), which provides additional information about its referent other than what English pronouns usually include such as person, number, gender ("he" versus "she"), and case ("he" versus "him" versus "his" versus "himself").

CLASSIFIERS

The Concept of Classifiers

The presence of classifiers in ASL was initially reported by Frishberg (1975). She described them as "certain handshapes in particular orientations to stand for certain semantic features of noun arguments." Since her initial identification, classifiers have received considerable attention in the literature on ASL structure. Kegl and Wilbur (1976) elaborated the notion of classifiers as handshapes that functioned as pronouns in combination with predicates. Others have highlighted classifier participation in the construction of locative predicates (Liddell, 1980; McIntire, 1980), their function as literal or metaphorical themes in ASL verbs (Gee and Kegl, 1982), and their potential use to mark up to two of the various arguments of ASL predicates (Gee and Kegl, 1982; Supalla, 1982, 1985). Kantor's (1980) study of classifier acquisition by deaf children confirms their complexity. An empirical study by Wilbur, Bernstein, and Kantor (1985) reports the prototypical meanings for many of these classifiers and the variation that may occur among signers with respect to nonprototypical uses.

A description of spoken language classifiers provided by Allan (1977) should help to put these forms in perspective. Allan surveyed 50 different classifier languages (English is not a classifier language) and reported that in these languages, classifiers served to focus on certain qualities or features of their noun referent in very precise ways. For example, a classifier might identify a class of objects that is one dimensional, two dimensional, or three dimensional, flexible or rigid, "of prominent curved exterior," long, or round. Other characteristics include animacy, humanness, mobility, and functions.

Allan also noted that there are four kinds of classifier languages, according to where and how the classifiers are used in sentences. ASL is generally believed to be one of the predicate classifier type, that is, unlike Thai, the classifiers in ASL contribute to the construction of the predicate rather than the noun phrase (cf. Kantor, 1980; McDonald, 1982; Wilbur, Bernstein, and Kantor, 1985). In Thai, a noun may be used alone as the subject of a sentence without the equivalent of English "the" or "a." However, if a demonstrative ("this," "that," "these," "those") or quantifier (a number, or "each," "any," "some," "all") modifies the noun, then an appropriate classifier must also be used. If the noun is "boy," the classifier must be "khon," meaning human. If the noun is "pig," the classifier must be "tua," meaning animal. The English phrase "this boy" would be rendered in Thai with the equivalent of "boy khon this," whereas "this pig" would be "pig tua this." In ASL, the classifiers do *not* occur in the noun phrase, but rather as part of the predicate construction, combined with the verb. In ASL, "give a bottle" would require the verb "give" to be combined with the classifier meaning "curved exterior," whereas "give a book" would use a classifier for "flat, movable object." The forms of the verb "give" are thus different because the classifier specifies the handshape, and "give" specifies the movement.

Allan notes that there are seven categories that may be found in spoken language classifiers: (1) material, (2) shape, (3) consistency, (4) size, (5) location, (6) arrangement, and (7) quanta. The last two categories may also occur in nonclassifier languages, but the first five are restricted to classifier languages in the sense that there are specific forms devoted to representing these characteristics in place of the noun itself. It is important to recognize that nonclassifier languages can talk about these features, but do not have special forms to do so. Thus, in English, we have phrases such as "a piece of paper," "a piece of rice," "a piece of glass," "a piece of pie," but "piece" does not carry information about the nouns it quantifies. In classifier languages, the form for "piece" might be different for paper (which is flat), rice (small grains), glass (some languages mark whether the piece is a whole or part of a broken object), and pie (meant to be separated into pieces, unlike broken glass). The seven categories offer classifier languages choices about which aspects of objects to focus on; different languages use different categories, and in some cases, may collapse two categories onto a single classifier form (instead of having a form that means "big" and another form that means "flat surface," the language may have one form that means "big flat surface"). Allan notes that the categories range over all the predictable bases of noun classification except color, taste, smell, and sound.

Further elaboration of Allan's categories will help highlight the extent to which ASL's classifier system coincides with those of spoken languages. In the first of Allan's categories, *material*, there are three subcategories: (1) animacy, which is frequently subdivided into human (which may be further divided into male/female or child/ adult) and nonhuman; (2) abstract and verbal nouns, for example, the English word "jabs" (which is not a classifier) conveys the meaning of 'the actions of jabbing with a pointed needle' ("The nurse gave me two jabs in the arm and it was all over;") and (3) inanimacy, which has many subdivisions. In Thai, an inanimate classifier is used for trees and wooden objects, which is connected with the class of long or saliently one dimensional objects. Other inanimate classifiers include those for bladed or pointed objects, body parts, food, implements, liquids, and boats. Allan (1977) suggests that "boats are perhaps the original vehicles, and the 'boat' classifier is more widely used than any for vehicles in general." It has been suggested that the ASL "vehicle" classifier (a 3 handshape) may have originated as a shape classifier referring to the mast (thumb) and main body/hull (index and middle finger together) of a boat; indeed, the results reported in Wilbur, Bernstein, and Kantor (1985) support this notion, as subjects routinely chose various representations of boats and submarines as preferred meanings for the vehicle classifier.

Allan's second major category is *shape*, usually "saliently one dimensional, two dimensional, and three dimensional." The shape category frequently combines with the consistency category, giving for example, "rope-like," which is composed of 'saliently one dimensional' and 'flexible', whereas "plank-like" would be composed of 'saliently two dimensional' and 'rigid'. Also included under shape are "prominent curved exterior" and "hollow" as minor subdivisions.

The third major category is *consistency*, with three subdivisions: (1) flexible, (2) hard/rigid, and (3) nondiscrete (mush, mud, liquid). The fourth major category is *size*, with large and small as its major subdivisions. In ASL, the combination of the size and shape categories plays a prominent role, so much so that the name "size and shape specifiers" (SASSES — Klima and Bellugi, 1979) has been given to the forms. The fifth category is *location*, used by some languages for such things as fields, villages, or canoe compartments. There do not appear to be subdivisions, nor have any of the ASL classifiers been assigned to this category.

The sixth category, *arrangement*, has three subcategories. The first refers to 'specific and noninherent configuration' of objects, such as pleats, folds, coils, and curls. The second identifies objects in specific positions, such as 'extended perpendicular object' or 'objects in a row'. The third subdivision includes noninherent distribution, such as clumps or heaps. The seventh category, *quanta*, includes grammatical number (singular, dual, plural), collection (mass, uncountable), volume, instance (kind of), partitive (piece of), and measure (dimension, weight, time). Recall that these last two categories are not specific to classifier languages alone.

Classifier Types in ASL

Of the seven categories that Allan identified for classifiers in spoken languages, at least three are clearly represented by the classifiers in ASL. These are (1) material (animate/inanimate), (2) shape (salient one dimensional, two dimensional, three dimensional, vertical/horizontal extent, salient top/underside surfaces, round, flat), (3) size (small/large) and (4) arrangement (heaps, pleats) (Wilbur, Bernstein, and Kantor, 1985). This does not mean that other categories are not expressed in ASL, as there are classifiers that have not been thoroughly investigated and there are also means of expressing some of these concepts without using classifiers. Kegl and Wilbur (1976) provided a list of classifiers for ASL (Figure 4–1). A number of

1. General person (animate): G-hand, usual orientation is fingertip up

2. Person by legs: V-hand, usual orientation is fingertips down for 'stand', 'walk', 'kneel', but may have other orientations

3. Vehicle: 3-hand, orientation is fingertips sideways (as opposed to the numeral '3', which has its citation orientation fingertips up), may be used for cars, motorcycles, boats, trains, etc.

4. Plane: ⨆ handshape, may be used for airplanes

5. Stationary object taller than it is wide (also may be used as dummy general object): Å-hand, used in place of objects such as bottle, house, lamp.

6. Stationary object taller than it is wide that cannot be moved by an independent source or that is intended to be stationary: arm extended upward from elbow to fingertips, B-hand, used for buildings, trees, walls, etc.

7. Flat objects that can be moved: B-hand, palm up, can be used for book, paper, mirror, etc.

8. Flat object that is not supposed to be moved: B-hand, palm down, can be used for bridge, floor, rooftop, ground, etc.

9. Hollow, curved object with rim: C-hand, palm facing sideways, can be used for glasses, cups, jars, etc.

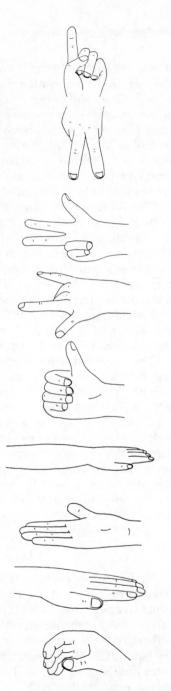

Figure 4-1. Frequently used ASL classifiers. (Drawings ©Brenda Schick, Purdue University.)

additional forms have been suggested by several researchers (Liddell, 1977, 1980; McDonald, 1982; Supalla, 1982, 1985).

Initial descriptions of ASL classifiers grouped all of them into one group — classifiers. Later descriptions identified a second group, the "size and shape specifiers (SASS)" (Klima and Bellugi, 1979; McDonald, 1982; Supalla, 1982, 1985; Wilbur, Bernstein, and Kantor, 1985). The SASS handshapes represented an outline of the noun referent, rather than representing the object itself (Figure 4–2). The term "semantic classifiers" (also called "abstract classifiers") came to be used for those forms that do not outline the size and shape of the object. There are many SASS handshapes, and they are used frequently in ASL conversation. An extended index finger indicates that the referent is straight and thin (Figure 4–2a); extended index and middle finger together indicate a straight and narrow object (Figure 4–2b); the extension of all four fingers indicates a straight and wide object (Figure 4–2c). Small round objects can be depicted as in Figure 4–2d; smaller objects would be indicated by decreasing the circle, curling the bent index finger tighter against the thumb. Larger round objects are depicted by a bent (rounded) index finger and bent thumb (Figure 4–2e). To indicate size, the distance between the fingertip and thumbtip can be varied; if that is insufficient, two hands can be used, with the distance between them becoming the relevant size indicator. A thicker round object would be indicated by using the index finger and middle finger (not shown), and the thickest-/deepest round objects would be represented by the whole hand, as shown in Figure 4–2f. Note that there are no forms with *three* fingers (index, middle, and ring), as these are impossible in ASL (Supalla, 1982).

A third group, the "handle" forms, were identified as those handshapes that provided information about the size and shape of an object by representing the hand configuration required to *handle* the object, rather than outlining the object itself (Figure 4–3) (Boyes-Braem, 1981; McDonald, 1982; Schick, 1985a; Supalla, 1985). Supalla (1985) suggested several other categories of classifiers (body classifiers, body part classifiers), which contain appropriate meanings from Allan's (1977) list, but which, on closer inspection, are not themselves actual classifiers because they do not meet the other criteria (for example, do not participate in the construction of predicates or do not represent a class of objects).

INCREASING DIMENSION →

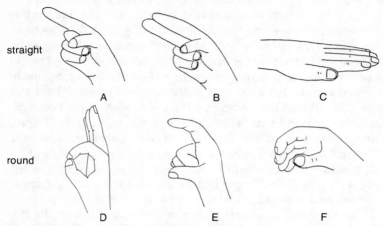

Figure 4-2. Common ASL SASSes for straight and round referents, showing increasing dimension. ©Brenda Schick, Purdue University.

INCREASING DIMENSION →

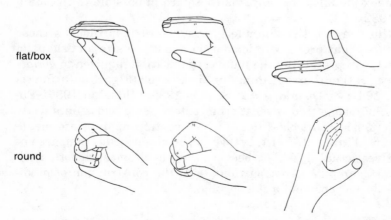

Figure 4-3. Frequently used HANDLE classifiers, showing increasing dimension. ©Brenda Schick, Purdue University.

PREDICATE ROOTS

Recent Analyses

As part of an extensive description of ASL sign formation, Supalla (1982) characterized ASL predicate roots as falling into several categories (1) existence, (2) location, and (3) motion. Existence roots are phonologically realized as holds; location roots are phonologically realized by "stamping" the hand at a particular location; motion roots are characterized by path movement (linear, arc, or circle). These roots, then, are specified phonologically for movement type (or absence of movement), and the handshape specifications come from combining with the classifiers. Supalla argued that complex movement roots can be constructed by combinations of these roots, plus "secondary" movement affixes that indicate direction of movement, frequency (of repetition), and degree of change, either maximum or minimum (for example, degree of change of direction, viz. a hard right turn versus a slight right turn).

Schick (1985a) proposed a different categorization of the productive roots. She argued that Supalla's existence and location roots differ only in the presence of "stamping" for the location root, and that this appeared to be primarily a matter of emphasis, providing focus to the location itself. Thus, she posited a category DOT (= "dot"), which included both location and existence roots. She also posited a MOV (= movement) category, parallel to Supalla's motion category. The movement of the MOV root can indicate path of the referent or extent of the referent (cf. McDonald, 1982). Her third category, IMIT (= imitation), gave formal recognition to the apparent imitation of real world activities by certain signs. The movement of the IMIT root is seen as an idealization of the real world activity, making the movement less of an imitation and more of a "distillation."

Schick noted that each of the nine possible combinations of classifier type (HANDLE, semantic CLASS, SASS) and predicate root (MOV, IMIT, DOT) results in a construction with a different meaning and different syntactic properties.

HANDLE + MOV. HANDLE combined with MOV, for example, produces forms such as GIVE-CUP or RECEIVE-MONEY, which includes the verb (GIVE, RECEIVE) and the direct object of the verb (CUP, MONEY). Because these forms have path movement, they are eligible for verb agreement because they can have specific starting and ending locations. In these cases, the agreement would be with the subject and the indirect object. For GIVE, the starting point agrees with the subject and the ending point with the indirect object, whereas for RE-CEIVE, the starting point agrees with the indirect object and the ending point with the subject; these two types of verbs have been discussed extensively in Padden (1983) and Meier (1982).

HANDLE + IMIT. When the HANDLE handshapes combine with IMIT roots, the combined form contains the verb and, instead of the direct object, the instrument. There is no path movement, so starting and ending locations for verb agreement are not phonologically available. Morphologically, the location specification indicates the place where the activity occurs. Combined HANDLE + IMIT forms include signs such as CLIMB-ROPE, STEER-CAR, PLAY-GUITAR, and COMB-HAIR. The handshape reflects the hand position involved in holding a rope, a car steering wheel, a guitar, and a comb. The movement demonstrates each activity, but the movements are restricted according to the constraints on other, nonimitative movement. Thus, they differ significantly from mime (unlike mime, in signing, only the hands are used, the sign must stay in the signing space, only one local movement per syllable, and so on.)

HANDLE + DOT. When the HANDLE handshapes combine with the DOT predicate root, the resulting form includes the verb, the direct object, and the ending location of the activity. Thus, the verbs are usually "transfer" verbs (such as PUT), and the ending location indicates where the direct object has been put. This differs from MOV verbs where the ending location indicates an agreement marker with one of the verb's arguments (usually indirect object). If a table is indicated at a particular point in space during the conversation, the HANDLE + DOT form PUT-SMALL-OBJECT, made with the "stamping" or "dotting" movement ending at the location of the table, would mean that the small object was put at the location of the table, most probably "on the table."

CLASS + MOV. Semantic classifiers include the handshapes for VE-HICLE (3 hand), PEOPLE-BY-LEGS (v hand held fingertips down), and ANIMAL-BY-LEGS (bent v hand held fingertips down). The combination of semantic CLASS and MOV root results in a form that contains the subject and the intransitive verb. The location specifications are for true locations (marked in English by locative prepositions such as "in," "on," "at"), not for verb agreement. An example would be the form meaning "the vehicle went from a location on the right to a location on the left" (these locations have probably been previously introduced into the conversation). Many of these forms also contain a second hand, which includes a classifier handshape for a reference object (secondary object in Supalla, 1982; "ground" in Schick, 1985a). If the second hand is made with the VEHICLE classifier and placed at a particular location, the first hand can indicate "a car passed another car" by its path movement (= CLASS + MOV). Another form containing a secondary object would be PEOPLE-JUMP-ON-SURFACE, where the moving (= IMIT) hand is made with the v handshape and the nonmoving hand is made with the flat B surface handshape. As with most classifier usage, the only way to know the referent of SUR-FACE is to follow the conversation; either the surface will be identified (bed, trampoline, floor) or it will be possible to tell from the other information in the conversation. (For an empirical investigation of signers' abilities to interpret classifiers, see Wilbur, Bernstein, and Kantor, 1985).

CLASS + DOT. When semantic CLASS handshapes are combined with the DOT predicate root, the resulting form is a stative predicate indicating the existence or location of the subject (represented by the classifier). Typical examples (with a second hand for a secondary object) include: PEOPLE-SIT-FACING-EACH-OTHER, ANIMAL-SIT-ON-SURFACE-WITH-VERTICAL-ORIENTATION (fence), and PERSON-STAND-NEAR-SOLID-UPRIGHT-OBJECT (tree). When a semantic classifier such as VEHICLE is combined with DOT, the resulting form introduces a vehicle into the conversation and provides an approximate location for it for further discussion. The secondary object in "a car passed another car" might be introduced into the conversation by a CLASS + DOT form, which establishes the car that is passed. Then the other hand might produce the CLASS + MOV previously discussed to indicate the car that does the passing. Two people who are standing facing each other would be described with PERSON-BY-LEGS classifiers and DOT predicates at the appropriate places and with the appropriate orientations.

CLASS + IMIT. When the semantic CLASS handshapes are combined with IMIT roots, the resulting form indicates more about the manner of movement than the location of movement. Schick (1985a) cites PEOPLE-FLIP, PEOPLE-ROLL-OVER-SIDE-TO-SIDE, and STUNT-PLANES-FLIP-TOGETHER as examples of CLASS + IMIT..

SASS + MOV. McDonald (1982) identified a group of classifier + predicate forms whose meaning was interpreted as indicating the *extent* of an object, rather than the movement of that object. Schick (1985a) argues that these forms are the result of the combination of SASS handshapes with MOV roots. The MOV root is interpreted to mean the extent of the object that is represented by the SASS handshape rather than movement of the object. These forms are essentially predicate adjectives (R. Johnson, personal communication; Schick, 1985a; Wilbur, Bernstein, and Kantor, 1985). The equivalent English forms might be "there was a continuous line of upright thin things (e.g., people)," "this object is saliently one-dimensional in the vertical direction (e.g., pole)," or "this surface is flat and continuous (e.g., floor, ground, roof)."

SASS + IMIT. When SASS handshapes are combined with IMIT roots, the resulting forms are interpreted as using the object represented by the SASS handshape as the instrument to perform the verb's activity, usually at a location appropriate for the activity itself. Thus, BRUSH-TEETH uses the extended index finger handshape to represent the toothbrush, the activity is performed at the mouth with the teeth showing, and the activity is a back-and-forth movement of the hand. Note that the handshape is NOT the HANDLE form that would be used to represent holding a toothbrush, but rather a SASS form representing "a straight thin thing," that is, the toothbrush. Schick (1985a) noted that there are two subdivisions to this group, those that use a part of the body as their location (BRUSH-TEETH, PUT-ON-HEARING-AID) and those that use the nondominant hand as the ground (PLUG-IN-WALL, CAR-TOW-CAR, PUT-TAPE-ON-X).

SASS + DOT. The last combination with SASS handshapes is with the DOT root. The forms mean something like "an object of this description at this location." Using the F handshape for small, round, flat objects (e.g., coins), the DOT root can be repeated to mean "many small, round, flat objects are located here and here and here" (perhaps a description of the result of spilling a pocketful of change). Two bent L handshapes (bent and rounded index finger and thumb) "dotted" against a vertical surface might mean "a hole in the wall located here."

Using the three categories of classifier handshapes, HANDLE, (semantic) CLASS, and SASS, and the three categories of predicate roots, MOV, IMIT, and DOT, Schick (1985a) observed that the nine possible combinations of classifier and predicate roots yield distinct morphosyntactic forms (Table 4–1).

Thus, a single productive sign in ASL may contain the equivalent of an entire sentence in English. Additional noun, verb, and sentential modifiers can also be provided by facial expressions and head positions. The productive morphology of ASL, combining many morphemes into a single word, places it among the agglutinating or polysynthetic languages of the world.

Table 4-1. *Morphosyntactic interpretations of classifier and predicate roots*

Classifier Type	Predicate Root		
	MOV	IMIT	DOT
HANDLE	(S–) V–O (–IO)	(S–) V–O	(S–) V–O + LOC
CLASS	S–V + LOC	S–V	S–V:be + LOC
SASS	(S–) V:Adj	V–INST	V:Adj – LOC

Reprinted from Schick (1985a).

The Issue of Scale

Early descriptions of ASL classifiers noted that the classifier forms (e.g., PEOPLE-BY-LEGS) tended to be used where the hands might move outside the signing space if a bigger movement needed to be made (Kegl and Wilbur, 1976). The shift from the full flat hand form of WALK to the classifier form PEOPLE-BY-LEGS, together with parallel examples, were referred to by Supalla (1982) as issues of reference frame — either real or abstract. In the real reference frame, every point is analogous to the real world, whereas every point in the abstract reference frame is arbitrary. This shows up clearly when discussing the distance between two objects. If the real reference frame is being used, then the distance indicated by the hands is (more or less) the real distance. When the abstract frame is being used, two cities can be discussed with a distance of one foot between them, but the distance itself is not a direct representation of the distance between the two cities. Thus, in separate conversations, a signer can discuss New York and San Francisco in the same locations that might be used to discuss New York and Philadelphia. However, in the same conversation, Philadelphia would have to be placed closer to New York than to San Francisco.

Schick (1985a) observed that the interpretation of real or abstract scale is predictable in large part by the type of classifier used in the predicate. As a rule, HANDLE classifiers are always interpreted with reference to a real world reference frame; semantic CLASS are always interpreted in the abstract reference frame (Schick uses the term "model space"). She notes that HANDLE classifiers vary discretely in size as a function of the variation in the real world object being referred to, but that semantic CLASS never modify their size, regardless of the relative size of the referent. Thus, the classifier for VE-HICLE may refer to a submarine, a motorcycle, a Cadillac, a Volkswagen, or a toy car, without changing its formation. However, HANDLE-A-BOX varies its formation, both in terms of handshape and hand arrangement (one hand versus two, distance between them). A small box may be handled with an L̈, C, or B handshape, whereas a medium sized box will almost always have two hands, with either the B or 4 handshape, and a large box will always have two hands with either 4 or B handshapes and will be made in such a way as to imply weight or extra size (for example, by pushing movement rather than lifting movement).

SASS forms have a preferred real world interpretation, but can be interpreted in abstract or model space when they are used in conjunction with CLASS, as metaphorical extensions, or when other lexical items in the discourse set the scale (Schick, 1985a). Used alone, the C handshape SASS might be used to mean a cup, or in a different orientation, a cup on its side. The same handshape as a secondary object can mean something large, like a tunnel, in a form with the vehicle classifier, VEHICLE-THROUGH-TUNNEL. In the cup case, the interpretation is real world (the size of the cup is reflected by the size of the handshape), whereas in the tunnel case, the interpretation is abstract or model scale (the tunnel is not really the size of the handshape). There appear to be restrictions on which SASSes can in fact occur with CLASS constructions; when they serve as secondary or ground objects, the most frequent ones are C for containerlike objects (in the case of tunnel, container implies having a hollow interior), B or 5 for surface-like objects, and S or O for solid objects. This observation harkens back to the discussion in Chapter 2 of unmarked handshapes (GOBSC5) and the allowable handshapes on the nondominant hand in frozen lexical items. It has been suggested that many of the frozen lexical items were at one time productive forms following these constraints, which then became fixed in their preferred form and meaning.

Signers switch back and forth between real and abstract scale. Schick (1985a) notes that in the case of PUT-ON-A-HIGH-SHELF, the signer is in real world space because of the HANDLE classifier and cannot sign the sentence "I put the object on the high shelf out of reach." because it is not possible to sign "out of reach" using real world scale, which is restricted to what is within reach. Thus, the signer must switch to model scale to continue the discourse. The signer can use a model scale construction, such as CHAIR PEOPLE-ON-CHAIR 'a person stands on a chair', followed by PUT-OBJECT-ON-HIGH-SHELF-OUT-OF-REACH. In this case, the explicit form PEOPLE-ON-CHAIR is interpreted as moving the agent into model space (in order to change the agent's range of "reachability"). Once the agent is standing on a chair, all subsequent real world signs are interpreted from that position. The signer has shifted the agent's frame of reference. The sign PUT-OBJECT-ON-

HIGH-SHELF-OUT-OF-REACH is made with a HANDLE classifier which normally has real world reference, but the model space interpretation is
based on a shifted frame of reference, namely the extended reach
made possible by the chair. Signers can also shift frames of reference
by using lexical items (frozen forms) such as JUMP ME, PUT-OBJECT-ON-
HIGH-SHELF-OUT-OF-REACH 'when I jumped, I could put the object on the
high shelf out of reach' where JUMP is a lexical item that provides an
extension of the reference frame, again by extending the reaching
height.

OTHER BOUND MORPHEMES

The morphemes that participate in the combinations previously
described are bound morphemes. The defining feature of bound morphemes is that they cannot stand alone but must combine with other
morphemes. In English, the plural suffix, the past tense suffix, the
progressive suffix, the negative prefixes ("un-," "in-," "dis-"), and
the adverbial "-ly" (among others) are all bound morphemes. Classifiers and predicates of motion and location are bound morphemes in
ASL. Classifiers, which are represented phonologically as handshapes, cannot stand alone as a sign. They must be combined with
other morphemes that provide the additional phonological specifications of movement, direction of movement, orientation, location, and
so on. Predicate roots can provide some of these characteristics, and
verb agreement may provide others.

Two predicates, THINGS-GO-PAST and DRIPPY-LIQUID, are not parallel
to any particular English verbs and thus may seem somewhat different from the predicates discussed before. Both forms are good examples of morphemes that were ignored by researchers for a long time
because they were thought to be "visual pictures," a term that does
indeed characterize what they are but which fails to provide a
linguistic description for their formation and use.

Kegl (1978c) identified the defining characteristic of the morpheme THINGS-GO-PAST as its movement in relation to the signer. The
morpheme varies its handshape, location, and orientation according
to its intended referent (Lucas and Valli, 1986, referred to the various surface forms as "predicates of perceived motion"). For example,
when driving a car and watching the telephone poles go by, one sees
a series of straight upright poles approach the car, pass by the car,
and disappear behind the car. Such a description is based not on the
perspective of the car driving past the poles (which obviously do not
move) but on the perceived movement of the poles as seen by a sta-

tionary person sitting in the moving car. The world appears to pass by the person in the car rather than the reality of the car and person passing by a stationary world. The signer, in describing this scene, uses two upright G hands and moves them back and forth (alternately or together), reflecting the approaching and passing of poles. Suppose that instead of sitting in a car, the person is now seated in an airplane. The world goes by underneath, and of course does not appear vertical as the telephone poles did, but appears as horizontal, flat land below. In this case, the morpheme THINGS-GO-PAST is realized with two flat B hands, palms down, moving alternately in toward the signer, back out, and in again, at chest height, and the signer may look down at the hands while they are moving. A bowling ball might go down the alley with the same flat B hands, palms down, but perhaps slightly higher, below the chin (treating the head as the ball). These two representations of THINGS-GO-PAST appear to be completely different signs, but can be seen to be related by the similarity of movement that defined THINGS-GO-PAST.

The other bound morpheme illustrated here is defined by both its movement (wiggling downward movement) and its characteristic handshape ̈5 ̇(or variant ̈4 ̇),thus making it more obvious than THINGS-GO-PAST. It occurs in the signs GRAVY (dripping from the bottomside of the nondominant B hand), DROOL (formed at the side of the mouth), and in occurrences of BLOOD/BLEED. For BLOOD/BLEED, the back of the hand of the nondominant hand is used as a general location, but usually the sign incorporates the location of the body part that is bleeding (e.g., "bleed from the head" would be made at an appropriate spot on the head, "bleed from the upper arm" would be made at the upper arm). One can "bleed from the nose" or even "have a runny nose" with variations of this same sign.

MAKING NEW WORDS FROM OLD

In the preceding discussion, the combination of productive predicate and classifier forms has illustrated how novel signs are constructed to fit specific situations during a discourse. As indicated, some of these productive forms may eventually become fixed in formation and meaning, creating a new frozen lexical item. In the discussion that follows, new lexical items are created by compounding, by idiomatic or regular derivation, and by fitting new forms into an existing pattern for noun/verb pairs.

Compounding

Klima and Bellugi (1979) identified compounds as having two separate parts which are (or were) clearly identifiable lexical items, the composite of which functions as one sign and the meaning of which may differ from what would be predicted from the sum of its two parts. They note that compounds in ASL undergo temporal compression of the two parts, particularly of the first part, such that the entire compound may take only as much time to make as either of its parts signed in isolation. The reduction and weakening occur primarily in the movement of the sign. Signs that are normally made with repeated contact lose their repetition. Full circular motion is reduced to a partial, brief arc. Signs that are made with brushing movement may reduce to a brief contact and may lose contact altogether (if the brushing is normally repeated, a single brush may remain, or may reduce as single brushing movement does, to brief contact or no contact). Other movements (nodding, twisting, opening, closing, alternating) are weakened and reduced. The common pattern of double contact, which Klima and Bellugi refer to as "touch-move away-touch," is reduced to a single contact (especially if both contacts are in the same place) or contiguous contact (by "slurring" the movement and not actually moving away from the point of contact).

Other changes that affect the production of signs in compounds are determined by the number of hands used in the first and second parts of the compound. If the sign is made with one hand for the first part and two for the second, the nondominant hand of the second part may already be in place while the first part is being executed. If the first part has two hands, and the second only one, the nondominant hand may drop or may be held during the second part. If both parts are made with two hands, the compound may actually be made with one (subject to the constraints of deletion discussed by Battison, 1974). If both parts are made with one hand, there is a high likelihood of finding handshape assimilation occurring. The ultimate in compression, of course, is when the two signs merge into one syllable and the fact that it is a compound is no longer obvious, although the history of the sign may still be apparent. Many signs that are treated as compounds probably do not deserve to be grouped with the others. A good example is the sign HOME, which is thought to be derived from EAT and SLEEP, but which is made with a location and movement that do not clearly reflect either former piece. Forms like HOME, then, can be recognized as derived by compound formation historically, but probably should not be considered to be derived by compound formation any longer. Recall also that Coulter (1982) included compounding as one of the "unstable" multisyllabic forms, that is, forms that are likely to reduce to single syllable forms over time; the only stable multisyllabic forms that he identified were reduplicated forms. Nonetheless, for those compounds that are still obviously formed by compound formation, Wilbur and Nolen (1986) documented that compounds had significantly more syllables than simple lexical items (cf. discussion in Chapter 3).

The issue of compounding has been addressed again more recently by Liddell (1985) and Liddell and Johnson (in press a, b). Using the model of sequential segments proposed in Liddell (1984a), compounding is described as a process that chooses specific segments from the first and second signs and puts those segments together to form a new sign. Only one segment is chosen from the first sign, the first piece containing a contact with the body. Liddell (1985) posits the segment selection rule: retain the first contacting hold in the initial sign forming a compound; delete all others.

In their discussion of compound formation, Wilbur, Klima, and Bellugi (1983) noted that when signs were reduced by the compound formation process, local movements (nonpath movements) were left intact, although they might be quickened, shortened, or weakened. Full explanation of the compound process in terms of determining which sign occurs first and which sign functions as the head of the compound remains to be investigated.

Idiomatic and Regular Derivation

The term "idiomatic derivation" refers to derivational processes that produce new forms whose meanings are not predictable given the meaning of the old words from which they are derived. Klima and Bellugi (1979) described several examples of forms that undergo idiomatic derivations. In one case, the sign for QUIET, normally made with a path movement, adds a pivot at the wrist (local movement) and acquires the meaning "acquiesce." The sign WRONG, which is a movement-to-contact sign, adds a twist of the wrist (technically speaking, an elbow rotation) to produce a form meaning "suddenly, unexpectedly." The sign PARK-CAR also adds an upwards twist of the wrist to mean "drive-in-movie." Additional examples can be found in Bellugi and Newkirk (1981) and in Klima and Bellugi (1979).

The examples just given all were modified by the addition of a local movement and the resulting meaning was idiomatic (Wilbur, Klima, and Bellugi, 1983). In more regular cases, the modifications result from the addition or modification of *path* movement. Klima and Bellugi (1979) describe a derivational process that makes predicates from nouns. They indicate that the path movement of the derived sign is made once, fast, and tense, and has a meaning roughly translated as "to act like ___" or "to appear like ___." The sign meaning "China" when modified this way means "to seem Chinese," whereas CHURCH when so modified means "churchy" or "pious." In these cases, the local movement remains unaffected, and the path movement is added or modified. An idiomatic form with a tense movement that bounces back after contact (sometimes called "checked") formed from the modified CHURCH means "narrow-minded."

Noun and Verb Pairs

The earliest linguistic descriptions of ASL failed to recognize the distinction between certain associated noun and verb pairs. Instead, they assumed that no difference existed, frequently using the same gloss for both forms. Supalla and Newport (1978) described the relationship that exists between related noun and verb pairs. The verbs have a large path movement with continuous, hold-final, or restrained offset, and the nouns are all restrained with short repetitions. This relationship holds not only between concrete pairs like DRIVE and CAR or EAT and FOOD, but also with abstract pairs such as COMPARE and a form meaning "comparison" or DERIVE and a form meaning "derivation." Supalla and Newport argue that it is inappropriate to consider the nouns as derived from the verbs or the verbs as derived from the nouns. Rather, they suggest that both the noun and the verb forms are derived from an underlying form that is stripped of the various distinguishing features of either noun or verb. In this respect, these noun/verb pairs should not be thought of as new words derived from old ones, because neither one is the basis for the derivation of the other.

Supalla and Newport (1978) discussed the use of repetition in the formation of deverbal nominals and associated forms. Their discussion includes an aspect of sign formation that has not been characterized extensively, namely, manner of formation. They began by defining two basic types of sign movement — unidirectional and bidirectional. Within the category of unidirectional, they identified three types, *continuous, holding,* and *restrained,* and within the category of bidirectional, only two of these, *continuous* and *restrained.* They illustrated *continuous* with the example of someone swatting frantically after a fly and missing, *holding* as the abrupt end of the motion as the fly is squashed with the fly swatter, and *restrained* as the tense, controlled motion one would use to avoid splattering the fly all over the table (the hand usually bounces back from the contact, reacting to the abrupt stop and tenseness of the muscles). Whether the verb is continuous or holding (verbs tend not to be restrained), the corresponding noun is restrained. Thus, FLY is unidirectional continuous and AIRPLANE is unidirectional restrained. SIT is unidirectional holding and CHAIR is unidirectional restrained. DRIVE is bidirectional continuous and CAR is bidirectional restrained.

RELATED WORD FAMILIES

This section describes a group of related families discussed in Frishberg and Gough (1973a).

Families Related by Motion Differences

Certain signs are related to each other in that their production is identical except for the direction of motion. The opposite pairs APPEAR (index finger moves up through base hand palm-down fingers) and DISAPPEAR (the index finger moves down the base hand palm-down fingers), IMPROVE (dominant hand jumps up nondominant arm) and GET-WORSE (dominant hand jumps down nondominant arm), and CHASE (one A hand approaches other in circling motion) and EVADE (one A hand circles away from other) are clearly differentiated by their opposite direction of movement. In many cases, downward direction tends to be associated with negative meanings (DEPRESSED).

Another group is differentiated by the sharpness or softness of formation (Frishberg, 1972). Soft signs are gentle and repeated; sharp signs are made with extra intensity. MULTIPLY has a soft variant, FIGURE-OUT. YELLOW has both a soft variant, YELLOWISH, and a sharp variant, DEEP-YELLOW (other colors may undergo this process also).

The signs STUDY and CRAM, DIRTY and FILTHY, and AFRAID and TERRIFIED are related by a change from wiggling of the fingers (in the first of each pair) to "spritz" (sharp bursting open of the fingers from a closed fist). Frishberg and Gough (1973a) provide at least 13 such pairs.

Families Related by Handshape Changes

Frishberg and Gough (1973a) discuss a group with initial open hand and final closed flat O, all seeming to have a meaning related to taking of information: COPY, XEROX, TAKE-A-PICTURE, EAVESDROP, LEARN and others. The opposite movement, ending with an open hand, relates the signs INFORMATION, ADVISE, INFLUENCE, CONTAGIOUS, CONSULTANT, and others.

Similar closing motion can be found in another group, in this case with the closed hand either s or F: FIND, PICK-UP, CHOOSE, TAKE, TAKE-UP, ACCEPT, CATCH, MEMORIZE.

A separate group, implying negative emotions and other negative connotations, often employs a flicking of the fingers to an open 5. This group includes BAWL-OUT, HATE, AWFUL, and NOTHING.

Families Related by Handshape

Many signs that express emotions are produced with the open 8 handshape — EXCITE, DEPRESS, FEEL, LIKE, INTEREST(ED/ING), TOUCH — and appear to be related to those negative emotion signs previously mentioned.

WH-words tend to be made either with a G hand or B hand: WHO, WHAT, WHERE, WHEN, and WHAT-FOR are made with G; WHAT, WHERE, and HOW may also be made with B. Frishberg and Gough (1973a) indicate that they found no semantic or syntactic criteria for differentiating the different forms of WHAT and WHERE, although WHERE with the B hand is probably related to the sign HERE, also made with the B hand. The G hand forms may be related to the G hand used for pointing (Hoffmeister, 1977).

The handshape À occurs in two semantically unrelated families. One is a group of negatives: NOT, DENY, REFUSE, BLAME, ALCOHOLIC, SUFFER, STUPID, and others. The other group involves the use of À as a classifier in verbs such as FOLLOW, CHASE, EVADE, FALL-BEHIND, FAR, AHEAD, PASS, BEHIND, and is also seen in the preposition UNDER.

The G handshape serves numerous functions in ASL: as the handshape used to index points in space; as a classifier for people; as the general handshape in many signs, such as WEEK and MONTH, meaning "1 week" and "1 month," and which can be replaced by other numbers; and simply as a handshape in certain signs. Frishberg and Gough (1973a) indicate a group of signs that share meanings or opposites depending on whether the two G hands are parallel to each other (AGREE, ALIKE/SAME, etc.) or pointing at each other (DISAGREE, OPPOSE, HURT, ARGUE).

Another handshape that serves a similar variety of functions to those of G is V. In some signs, it is related in meaning to vision: SEE, LOOK-AT, WATCH, READ, SCRUTINIZE, and WINDOWSHOP. Bent V is found in BLIND, DOUBTFUL, and ORAL/LIPREAD. The bending of the V in the previous forms is a combination of the V for vision and the bending of V to indicate difficulty: PROBLEM, HARD, NERVY, BLIND (hard to see), STEAL,

ANALYZE, DEVIL, DOUBT. Before leaving V in its function as an indicator of vision, it should be mentioned that popular myth suggests that the two fingers of the V hand in such signs as SEE reflect the two eyes. However, it has also been suggested that the V in these signs has come to ASL through the influence of the French signs, which were brought to the United States by Laurent Clerc and Gallaudet. The French sign made with V is said to be an initialized sign (V for VOIR "to see") of an older French sign made with a G hand.

The other use of V is the "legs" classifier (although Frishberg and Gough do not call it this) in such signs as DANCE, STAND, KNEEL, CLIMB, LAY-DOWN, GET-UP, FALL, TOSS-AND-TURN, ROLL-IN-THE-AISLE-WITH-LAUGHTER, RESTLESS, JUMP and so on. Bent V occurs in variations of the verb SIT, as in SIT-IN-A-CIRCLE, SIT-ON-A-BENCH.

Many families have been created through the initialization process. The days of the week, Monday through Saturday, are each represented by a circular motion made in neutral space and a different initialized handshape for the corresponding English name. Thus MONDAY is made with an M, TUESDAY with a T, WEDNESDAY with a W, THURSDAY with an H, and so on. SUNDAY is apparently unrelated to the other days formationally (and seems to be related to the sign PREACH). Signs for royalty include KING with a K, QUEEN with a Q, PRINCE with a P, LORD with an L, and EMPEROR with an E, the only difference between them being the handshape. Similarly, a single sign for group or class or category, originally made with a C hand, has lead to a family with GROUP (G hand), ASSOCIATION (A hand), CLASS (C hand), FAMILY (F hand), ORGANIZATION (O hand), TEAM (T hand), and WORKSHOP (start with W, end with S). It seems that ASL initially had few color terms, probably BLACK, WHITE, RED, and maybe some other color term made in neutral space with a shaking hand. Frishberg and Gough speculate that this proto-color term might have been BLUE, because the motion is possibly related to "waves" or "water." At present, this shaking hand serves for the colors BLUE (B hand), YELLOW (Y hand), PURPLE (P hand), GREEN (G hand), but the sign for RED (made at the mouth) has been initialized for PINK (P hand), and apparently unrelated signs exist for ORANGE and GRAY.

Families Related by Location

One of the most frequently indicated families based on location is the group of signs that separates male and female according to its place of formation on either the forehead or cheek/chin, respectively. Thus, on the forehead there is BOY, MAN, FATHER, GRANDFATHER, BROTHER; on the lower cheek area there is GIRL, WOMAN, MOTHER, GRANDMOTHER, SISTER.

Many negative signs are made under the chin. These include NOT, DENY, NOTHING, NONE, WRONG, UNFAIR.

On the back of the hand, one finds NATION (with N handshape), IN-STITUTION (with I), and CHURCH (with C), probably based on ROCK and MOUNTAIN. Several signs in the same area include a circular motion before contact with the back of the hand, including NATURAL (with N handshape) and ISLAND (with I).

On the back of the wrist there are the signs USE, WORK, BUSINESS, DUTY, APPOINTMENT, HABIT, ESTABLISH.

One obvious group made at the mouth is that related to speech: SHOUT, SCREAM, CURSE, QUIET, SHUT-UP, SECRET, MUTE, WHISPER, THANKS, PRAISE, SAY, TELL, INSULT, ANSWER, TALK, ANNOUNCE, DIALOGUE, PROMISE, TRUE, LIE, and COMMUNICATE.

The nose is often used for derogatory or negative signs: UGLY, STINK, IGNORE, RELUCTANT, BORED, BULLSHIT, DON'T-CARE, FOOL, STRICT, LOUSY, KIDS, FUNNY, and many others.

Families Related by Number Morphemes

The number signs in ASL and their many variants represent a family in the same sense as those discussed by Frishberg and Gough (1973a). A general description of numbers is included in Stokoe and colleagues (1976), Appendix B. They list the cardinal numbers from 0 to 22 and provide information on producing 23-29, 30-99, 100, 1000, and 1,000,000. They note two alternatives for 13 through 15, and 16 through 19 are a combination of 10 plus the proper unit. They also discuss the ordinal numbers and indicate that there are separate forms for "first" through "tenth," but that for higher ordinal numbers, the cardinal number is used followed by the fingerspelled -t+h (a borrowing from English), and that -st, -nd, and -rd are not used. They describe various modifications that may affect numbers, such as changes in orientation to indicate such things as standings in a league or place in a list, and modifications of movement to use in approximations (e.g., shaking the 6 hand to indicate "approximately six").

Chinchor (1978a) and Kannapell (n.d.) have investigated the numeral system in considerable detail. The formation of the numbers from 0 to 1,000,000 is not simply a matter of learning the numbers from 0 to 9 and rules for their combinations. There is considerable variation in their formation, and numerous modifications that may affect them in context.

Chinchor (1978a) notes that, when used to count, the numbers 1 to 5 may be made with the palm facing either toward or away from the signer (depending on the person) whereas the numbers 6 to 9 al-

ways face away from the signer. When signing long strings of numbers (phone numbers, social security numbers, etc.), the palm always
faces away from the signer.

The number 10 is the first number to be made in citation form
with a characteristic movement. The A or Ȧ hand is used and is wig-
gled slightly from side to side. The numbers 11 and 12 are made similarly, in that both are made with the same starting point, a fist facing toward the signer's body, and are produced by the rapid
extension of either the index (11) or the index and middle (12) fingers. The numbers 13, 14, and 15 can be made similarly to 11 and
12, with the proper number of fingers extending rapidly from the
fist, or they can be made with the proper number of fingers extended
(from the fist, palm still facing signer) and waving back and forth.
Another formational process exists for all of the numbers from 11 to
19; they can be made as a compound of the sign 10 (without its wig-
gle) followed by the appropriate digit 1 to 9 (all face palm out). This
latter process does not seem to be widely used. For the number 16 to
19, their formation as a compound of 10 plus a digit can be made
with 10 (A or Ȧ) in its normal upright (thumb up) position or with the
fist turned to the side (thumb faces nondominant side, like manual
alphabet letter A) so that the hand does not change orientation during the actual formation of the numbers. The numbers 16 through
19 may also be made by forming the appropriate single digit, palm
out, and twisting it, similar to the way the number 10 is shook. A
third possible formation for the numbers 16 to 19 is to form the appropriate digit, palm facing out, and to rub the thumb against the
finger that it contacts (i.e., thumb rubs against pinkie for 16, against
ring finger for 17, against middle finger for 18, and against index
finger for 19).

The number 20 illustrates a general process, namely, that the
tens (20, 30, etc.) are made with a digit closing to 0, but at the same
time, 20 is an exception to the general rule in that the digit used is
not the simple digit 2 (v hand) but an archaic form (believed to be
from French Sign Language) of the number 2 (L hand). Thus 20 is
made by the sequence L hand changes to baby O.

The number 100 is made with the number 1 (G hand) followed by
the C hand (with no assimilation). The numbers 200, 300, 400, and
500 may be made similarly as the digit followed by the C hand, but
more frequently involve assimilation so that 200 is made with a v
hand which bends to V̈ (simulating the shape of C while not actually
including all the fingers that C uses), 300 is made with a 3 hand that
bends to 3̈, 400 with 4 bending to 4̈, and 500 with 5 bending to 5̈. From
600 to 900, there is no assimilation between the digit and the following C handshape.

Chinchor (1978a) divides modifications that can affect signs in context into changes in motion, changes in location, and changes in orientation. Each of the changes is either associated with a change in the use of the number itself (e.g., cardinal to ordinal, exact to approximate) or reflects an increased relationship with the noun it modifies.

CHANGES IN MOVEMENT. As indicated earlier by Stokoe and colleagues (1976), the change in production from a sharp, clear formation to a slightly shaking formation reflects a change from precision (exactly 7) to approximation (about 7). For emphasis, the formation of the number is tensed and may move inward toward the signer during its formation. A certain coolness about the number (for whatever contextual reasons) can be indicated by a relaxing of the hand and fingers and a slight flexing of the wrist. A major semantic and functional difference is indicated in the change from cardinal (counting) to ordinal (reflecting order) numerals. The primary change in formation is a pronounced twisting of the numbers 1 to 9, usually from a facing outward position to palm facing the signer. Similarly, numbers can be twisted in this same manner to indicate dollars, although if ambiguity needs to be avoided the sign DOLLAR can always be added. When DOLLAR is used, the twisted numeral is not used; instead the numbers 1–5 are oriented inward and 6–9 are oriented outward. Another modification of movement, shaking, can be used to indicate speed (reputed to represent the movement of the speedometer needle). This shaking is potentially ambiguous with the shaking used to represent approximation.

Changes in the direction of movement can also reflect differences in function. To indicate a stack of $100 bills, the sign 100 can be repeated in a downward moving direction. In counting down a list of things, the numbers also move downward, usually with a change in orientation from fingertips upright to fingertips sideways.

CHANGES IN LOCATION. Chinchor (1978a) indicates that changes in location for number signs may result from one of two processes; the number sign can change its location through assimilation to a preceding or following sign, usually an associated noun (the result of assimilation is still two separate signs), or the number sign can change its location by actually being blended into another sign (creating one sign with the number for its handshape, but with the movement and location of the other sign). Assimilation of location tends to occur when digits follow the sign CENT, which is made on the forehead. The numbers are not actually made on the forehead, but lower in front or to the side of the face; this is quite different from their usual place in neutral space at about shoulder height. Another example of assimilation is the relocation of the number sign to the location of the sign AGE/YEARS-OLD. Number signs can also relocate to indicate the scores of different teams in a game, with their score out in neutral space and our score near the signer's chest.

The process of blending creates a single sign with a number for its handshape. Blending occurs when the number handshape is made at the location of the sign TIME to indicate, for example, 6 o'clock. Numbers can also be blended into time indicators such as HOUR, DAY, WEEK, MINUTE, MONTH, and YEAR. However, such blending is not unrestricted for all numbers. There seems to be a greater degree of freedom for the numbers 1, 2, and 3 to incorporate into other signs, whereas 4 and 5 are generally more restricted (5 even more than 4), being only marginally acceptable to some people and unacceptable to others. The numbers 6 to 9 can blend in only a few instances, and 10 and higher cannot incorporate at all. Zero appears to have blended (and lexicalized) into the sign KNOW to yield a sign made with the zero handshape at the location for KNOW, which means KNOW-NOTHING.

CHANGE IN ORIENTATION. Chinchor (1978a) reported the change in orientation that occurs when the numbers 1 to 5 are used in enumerating objects (palm facing out) and when numbers are used to count down in a list (palm in, fingertips facing sideways instead of up). The use of palm out and the fingerspelling box for producing long strings of numbers can also be considered an orientation change (as well as a change in location from neutral space).

One factor that may affect whether a change in orientation for numbers when enumerating objects will actually occur is the location of the object sign itself. If the sign is made in the peripheral areas of the signing space, the number may assimilate its location to that object and may then adopt an orientation identical to or close to that of the noun sign, thus appearing to contradict the generalization that numbers face inward when enumerating objects. Chinchor (1978a) indicates the phrase 3 CHILDREN as such an example, with the 3 moving to the location of CHILDREN and adopting a downward orientation, rather than an inward one.

General Comments on Word Families

There are several observations that can be made concerning the existence of word families in ASL. The presence of initialized signs and number signs, along with the productive classifier + predicate signs discussed earlier, strongly supports the notion of a separate status for handshape (referred to as a separate "tier" in current phonological theory). Handshape is clearly a separable unit, capable of being replaced by other morphologically meaningful handshapes. In the case of numbers and classifiers, it is clear that the handshape should be treated as having the status of a separate morpheme. In the case of initialized signs, the handshape that the sign was originally made with is replaced by the handshape representing the first letter of the English word equivalent; the original handshape was not a separate morpheme (did not have its own meaning) and it is not clear that the initialized handshape should be treated as a separate morpheme either. It is at the point that this new form is first constructed that the handshape becomes a separable unit (gets its own tier); until that point, the lexical item would have been considered to be frozen. Once the first initialized version of the sign comes into use, the pattern has been set up for other initialized signs to be constructed, leading to the families that have just been discussed. Thus, these previously frozen forms can then participate in a productive, although limited, process.

There is a fine line between saying that a phonological piece (e.g., handshape) contributes to the meaning of a sign and saying that the particular piece is itself a morpheme. In order to be considered a morpheme, there must be some evidence of separability and productive function. When a form has lost its separability or its meaning is no longer clearly adding to the meaning of the word, the form enters a linguistic twilight zone, still present but not productive. Examples abound in English. Consider the words "consult," "confer," "confraternity," "congratulate," "convocation," "cooperate," and "correlate." What does "co(n)–" mean and how is its pronunciation affected by the forms that it combines with? The person who has studied Latin or the history of English knows that "co(n)-" means 'with', and once it is pointed out to speakers of English, possible analyses can be suggested for each of the words just given. But do people really *know* that "co(n)-" means 'with' while they are using "correlate" or "confer"? What does "-sult" or "-fer" mean? They are present in other forms, such as "result," "insult," "refer," "infer," and "transfer." The same question can be raised for "re-" or "in-." These forms are part of the history of English; at one time, they freely combined to make new words, but now are much more restricted. Wilbur and Menn (1975) demonstrated that native speakers of English can still recognize the possible meanings of such forms, even though they are no longer separate morphemes.

A similar issue can be raised about the word families just discussed. As Frishberg and Gough (1973a) suggest, there are certain meanings associated with the handshapes, locations, direction of movements, or types of movements of these different groups of signs. With few exceptions, however, these are not productive forms that can freely combine with other constructions to make new words. The exceptions are those previously indicated, namely classifiers, numbers, and possibly the letters of the alphabet.

Even though the particular phonological pieces discussed here are not for the most part separate morphemes, it is clear that they still contribute to the meaning of the sign as a whole. Some of these contributions are direct: the movement upward of the signs APPEAR and IMPROVE contrasted with the movement downward of their opposites DISAPPEAR and GET-WORSE, the parallel fingers in AGREE compared to the opposing fingers in DISAGREE, the formation at the mouth of signs related to speech or communication such as SHOUT, TALK, PROMISE, TRUE, LIE, SECRET. Other contributions are more subtle, such as the closing of the hand for COPY, VIDEOTAPE, and LEARN, or the opening for INFORM, ADVISE, and CONTAGIOUS. It can be argued that these phonological pieces are contributing metaphorical information to the meaning of the sign. The upward direction of movement in IMPROVE and APPEAR is part of a more general assignment of positive connotations to "upwardness," with "downwardness' assigned a negative connotation (Lakoff and Johnson, 1980). The relevance of the notion of "parallel" versus "opposing" views (using the English terms) to the formation of the signs AGREE and DISAGREE is fairly obvious.

Less obvious is the meaning of the closing or opening hand in the signs just cited. There are (at least) two major metaphors for "understanding" in Western culture: "understanding is seeing" and "understanding is grasping" (Lakoff and Johnson, 1980). The "understanding is seeing" metaphor leads to English expressions such as "I see what you mean," "I don't see what he's getting at," or "It's not clear (= hard to see) what he means." The "understanding is grasping" metaphor yields "I had a hard time grasping what the lecture was all about" or "I didn't catch what that was all about." A statement such as "That stuff really went over my head" is consistent with both metaphors, as "over my head" can imply both "out of reach = cannot grasp" and "out of sight = cannot see." In the signs with closing hands (COPY, VIDEOTAPE, LEARN, to pick only a few), the contribution of the closing hand is the "grasping" or "holding" part; likewise, the opening hand implies "giving out (for others to grasp)" (INFORM, ADVISE, CONTAGIOUS = spreading around). What is being held or given out is *information*, except in the case of CONTAGIOUS, which is not a "communication" or "understanding" sign. There is considerably more to this story than is being explained here, as these are only a few examples. Boyes-Braem (1981), Gee and Kegl (1982), and others have approached the topic of metaphors in ASL with varying degrees of systematicity. Their purpose has been to show that the word families discussed are not accidents, that the phonological forms themselves may depend on which metaphor is being expressed, and that the often discussed iconicity of signed languages has a basis similar to what is found in spoken languages (as, for example, the illustration from English just given). Further discussion of this issue will be found in Chapter 7.

Families Related by Reduplication

This group has been separated from the others because the signs in it are related by a formational process (reduplication) that derives one from the other.

Frishberg and Gough (1973a) identified reduplication as a process that affects time nouns. Repetition of the sign WEEK with continuous brushing motion produces WEEKLY, similar reduplication of MONTH produces MONTHLY, and TOMORROW produces EVERYDAY/DAILY. The sign YEAR loses its circular motion (one s hand circles around the other and taps it) so that the brushing repetition of the top hand against the bottom one can produce YEARLY. Slow repetition (with concomitant wide circular path) indicates duration. Done this way, repetition of WEEK indicates "for weeks and weeks." Similarly, MONTH can be reduplicated to mean "for months and months," and DAY "for days and days." Other triplets include ONCE, reduplicated regularly for SOMETIMES, and slowly with circular motion for ONCE-IN-A-WHILE, and AGAIN, reduplicated regularly for OFTEN, and slowly for OVER-AND-OVER.

Kegl and Wilbur (1976) separated this type of reduplication, where the noun can be repeated several times, from reduplication that indicates augmentation (enlargement). For example, "big bowl" is produced by signing BOWL followed by a larger version. Only one repetition is possible for this type of reduplication. Fischer (1973a) discussed reduplication in its derivational function as it applies to verbs to indicate aspect. The use of reduplication is described in more detail in the next chapter.

SUMMARY

It should be clear from the discussion in this chapter that the number of ASL signs greatly exceeds what is usually found in the manuals used in sign classes. Merely listing the frozen signs leaves out all of the productive constructions discussed here: classifier and predicate combinations, noun/verb pairs, reduplicated forms, compounds, and derived forms, whether regular or idiomatic. Closer inspection of the classifier + predicate forms also reveals that they contain far more syntactic information than do single words in English; that is, they may contain the subject, direct object, indirect object, and/or locative phrase in addition to the verb. In English, these functions must be assigned to separate words, but in ASL, as in other languages, several morphemes may combine into one complex word/sign.

The brief discussion of the metaphorical underpinnings of many ASL signs (frozen or productive) is only the tip of the iceberg. Most speakers of English do not realize how extensive the metaphorical base is in spoken languages, including English, and as a result they tend to overreact to the occurrences in ASL merely because they are more obvious (in English, we say "What's up?" whereas in ASL, the sign with that meaning *actually* moves up). The discussion in Chapter 7 will elaborate on this topic in conjunction with the notion of iconicity. The next chapter will deal with modifications of signs for various morphological purposes; these modifications are accomplished in English by adverbs, prepositional phrases, adjectives, and other separate lexical items. In ASL, these modifications are made directly to the (predicate) signs.

CHAPTER 5

Sign Morphology: Inflection

Regardless of whether a sign is a frozen lexical item or constructed by the productive processes described in the previous chapter, there are further modifications that it can undergo. If it is a noun, there are only a few limited modifications, such as the plural. Verbs, however, are eligible for a variety of modifications, which would be translated into English with adverbs, prepositional phrases, aspectual verb markings (progressive "be" + "-ing," perfective "have" + past participle), and quantifiers ("each," "all"). The functions of inflectional processes in ASL greatly exceed those in English. Klima and Bellugi (1979) suggest at least eight categories of modifications, some with possible subcategories. They include modifications for indicating number, distributional aspect, temporal aspect, temporal focus, manner, and degree. Other researchers have added to the list. One particularly interesting feature of ASL is how several of these modifications can be used at the same time. This multiple marking is made possible by the fact that some of the modifications are spatial in nature, whereas others are represented by temporal rhythm and dynamic changes.

ADDITIONAL INFORMATION ABOUT
THE ARGUMENTS

Among the functions that can be indicated by particular spatial locations or arrangements are verb agreement (called indexic reference by Klima and Bellugi, 1979, among others), reciprocal, number agreement, and quantification (called distribution by Klima and Bellugi). Each of these functions provides information about the arguments (primary noun phrases) in the sentence. In addition to the preceding modifications, which are marked directly onto the predicate, pluralization of the nouns themselves will be considered at the end of this section.

Verb Agreement

There has already been considerable discussion of verb agreement, with respect to the specification of locations for the starting and ending points of path movement of particular verbs. In previous chapters, it was indicated that certain verbs could be specified for as many as two locations that could be filled in by combining the verb with agreement prefixes or suffixes (recall that these prefixes and suffixes do not make separate syllables). These two agreement locations are in addition to the possibility that the verb may also combine with a classifier handshape, which would provide agreement for a third argument (but not *location* agreement).

Looking at the formation of the predicate as a whole, it might be thought that changing the starting and ending locations of the predicate for agreement purposes is a modification of the predicate itself. However, the way the terms are being used here, the function of the changes in starting and ending location is to indicate additional information about the arguments (who is doing the action, what is undergoing the action). This contrasts with modifying the predicate by providing information about *how* the action is being performed, or for how long, or whether it is repeated. These latter modifications will be discussed in a later section.

In general, a predicate with path movement has only one starting point and one ending point (those without path movement will be discussed separately). It is predominantly single individuals or objects that are represented by these location points; plurals are treated differently. The majority of verbs that have two agreement points use the starting point to agree with the subject and the ending point to agree with the direct object (HIT, LOOK-AT, ASK) or what would be the indirect object in an English translation (in "give the

book to Mary," GIVE would agree in location with Mary, not with
BOOK, which would probably be represented as a classifier handshape). A smaller number of verbs display the reverse behavior, the
ending point agreeing with the subject and the starting point with
the surface object (e.g., TAKE). Recent extensive discussions of these
verb classes can be found in Padden (1983) and Meier (1982).

The agreeing verbs with path movement change their starting
and ending locations so that they indicate who is the subject and
who is the object. If John is at point a in Figure 5-1a, Mary is at
point b, and Bill is at point c, the sentence "John gave a book to
Mary" will start with the sign GIVE at point a and move it to point b,
while using the flat surface classifier (B hand) and "book." If Bill
gives the book to John, the sign starts at point c and moves to point
a. If TAKE is the main verb, the locations are reversed: for "John takes
the book from Mary," the sign for TAKE starts at point b and moves to
point a.

Verbs that have a contact specification for one of their two locations may only agree with one argument, using the location that is
not specified for contact. Thus, signs like TELL, which moves away
from contact at the mouth/chin, or INFORM, with contact at the forehead, may agree with their objects but not with their subjects (even
if they do not actually make the contact). Verbs that do not have path
movement may still indicate some agreement. Signs that have
a fixed location, either on the body or in space, may indicate agreement with the surface object by modifying the orientation rather
than a location specification (COUNSEL, WANT). These verbs orient in
the direction of the referent, but do not actually move to or toward it.
There are also some verbs that have no specific starting point indicated and their ending point is already specified as a location (e.g.,
E AT); these verbs do not have any opportunities for marking agreement with modifications of the starting or ending points of the path.

Not having an agreement specification does not mean that the
argument cannot be indicated. Usually, the noun phrases that indicate the subject and objects are produced before the predicate. These
noun phrases may be assigned to a particular point in space, either
by making the noun at that point or by using a POINT sign to the particular point in space (the POINT sign may precede or follow the noun,
and in the case of some one-handed nouns, may even be made at the
same time by using the other hand). It is these points in space that
are used by the verbs that inflect for agreement. The verbs that do
not inflect may simply not have any indication at all, or they may
have a POINT sign refer again to the point in space that has been assigned to the noun, or several nonmanual cues may indicate the par-

ticular point, including eye gaze directed at the point or a slight leaning of the shoulder, body, or head toward the point. Given that such indications are subtle, and that these points in space are made in the area that is perceived by the peripheral vision (cf. discussion in Chapter 2), it follows that points in space used to indicate different noun arguments must be far enough apart to be distinctive. Figure 5-1a illustrates one possible arrangement of these points, using left and right and the distance from the signer's body as the primary cues (Lacy, 1974). If only two referents are involved, a simple distinction of left versus right is sufficient. If more than two are involved, the distance from the signer's body also becomes important. Figure 5-1b illustrates another common arrangement, when only three referents are involved (three bears in Goldilocks, three little pigs, three different jobs). The referents may be people, objects, places, or events.

As a general observation, agreement with the object is required by many inflecting verbs, whereas agreement with the subject seems to be optional. In many cases, the subject is the agent of the action (the person who is doing the action) and the verbs are descriptions of actions that happen in sequence ("and then she did this, and then that, and then this happened"). In such cases, it is already clear that the subject of the verbs in sequence is the same as the subject of the first verb, thus once the subject has been indicated, it may be omitted until a new subject arises. These "subjectless verbs" are parallel to "serial verbs" or "chained verbs," which occur in many spoken languages (Kegl, 1977; Kegl and Farrington, 1985; Supalla, 1986).

The reciprocal inflection is a specific case in which two referents are both subject and object (direct or indirect) at the same time, usually translated in English as "each other." In order to be eligible for the reciprocal inflection, a predicate must have a meaning compatible with the notion "to each other" (a meaning such as "with each other," as in "they play golf with each other," would probably be translated by TOGETHER or BOTH). In addition, because the inflection is made with the two hands acting in opposition to each other (oriented toward each other, moving toward each other), the predicate must be able to be made with a single hand, so that one hand can represent one argument and the other hand can represent the other. "To look at each other" would be made with the sign LOOK-AT on both hands, facing each other. "To give to each other" would be made with the sign GIVE on both hands, the right hand starting at a distinctive point on the right (agreeing with one referent involved) and move toward the left (to agree with the other referent), while the left hand would simultaneously start at the left and move toward the right. If the hands moved alternately, first the right, then the left, the interpretation would not be reciprocal, but rather sequential: "first, the referent on the right gave the referent on the left, then the referent on the left gave the referent on the right." The reciprocal implies that the action is mutual and more or less at the same time, as in the exchange of gifts at Christmas.

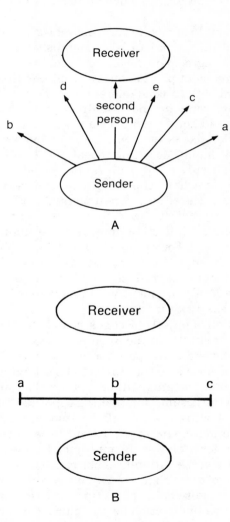

Figure 5-1. A common arrangement of referent points (A), and an arrangement for 3 referents (B).

Number Agreement

As indicated, each location for verb agreement refers to one referent at a time (singular). It is possible to indicate more than one, but the mechanisms are different. In Chapter 4, number substitutions were discussed: certain signs can replace their G handshape (= number 1, for example DAY, MONTH, WEEK) with another number handshape. A few predicates, such as MEET, can also take this type of substitution.

It is also possible to modify certain predicates to indicate two objects. This dual inflection can be accomplished in several ways. A sign that allows agreement for object, such as GIVE or INFORM, can move to the agreement point of one referent and then directly to the agreement point of the second referent. In this case, the two points in space for the referents are not usually very far apart, so that the move to the second point resembles a bounce more than a full path movement. A sign like INFORM, which also includes a local movement (opening of the hand), does not repeat the local movement as it moves from the first referent point to the second. An alternate form is possible: the right hand can move to one referent point while the left hand moves to the other referent point. Another possibility is to simply repeat the predicate twice, first to one point then to the other. In general, the dual inflection appears to be limited to signs that have path movement. For example, COUNSEL, which is made with an opening of the hand and contact with the back of the nonmoving hand, can be oriented toward the first referent point and then the second, but the local movement would have to be repeated and the construction seeks awkward at best.

The indication of plural object is accomplished by the addition of an affix to the predicate. In the majority of cases, which take object agreement at the end of the path movement, the affix will be a suffix, but for those few verbs that take the object agreement at the beginning (e.g., TAKE), the affix will be a prefix. The suffix case will be discussed, with the assumption that the opposite will be true for prefixes. The plural suffix is a smooth, horizontal arc ("sweep") that is added after the movement of the predicate is finished (Klima and Bellugi, 1979, refer to this as the multiple). Figure 5-2 diagrams the movement of two verbs with plural objects: TELL-THEM and BAWL-THEM-OUT. In the case of TELL (Figure 5-2a), its own movement away from the chin toward the referent point (in this case, unspecified) is followed by a change in direction for the plural (the actual production of this form may smooth the direction change so that no sharp corner exists). In the case of BAWL-OUT, the local movement (opening) is performed at the beginning, followed by the plural arc which takes its handshape from the second handshape in BAWL-OUT (after the hand has opened; Figure 5-2b). Smoothing of the two movements produces a single arc with the local movement finished before the halfway point of the arc (Figure 5-2c). This is a case where the underlying sequence is BAWL-OUT (local movement) followed by plural (arc), but the surface form is a phonetically assimilated construction with the local movement simultaneous to the first part of the arc path (this type of simultaneity, whereby the local movement is *not* spread out over the whole path, supports the notion discussed in Chapter 3 of internal pieces in the specification of movement; it also supports the contention that handshapes spread across morpheme boundaries but local movements do not, as suggested by Wilbur, Klima and Bellugi, 1983).

It is also possible for certain verbs to take a plural subject affix, giving for example the meaning "they gave to me." Conversationally, these do not occur frequently, in part because subject marking is less frequent than object marking (as discussed earlier, subject marking is optional).

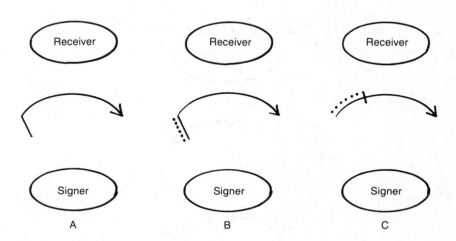

Figure 5-2. Movement paths for the plural of TELL and BAWL-OUT: (A) TELL-THEM, (B) BAWL-THEM-OUT, unassimilated, (C) BAWL-THEM-OUT, assimilated. © Brenda Schick, Purdue University.

Quantification

Quantifiers modify their nouns by indicating such information as "all," "each," "some," "any," "none," or "every." Linguists and philosophers have argued that certain of these forms are more basic than others (for discussion, see Wilbur and Goodhart, 1985). In the preceding discussion of the plural suffix, the translation used for the form with TELL meant "tell all of them." The implication of the plural form is that all of the referents are affected as a whole. If the desired interpretation is that each referent is affected individually, a different modification is used. Klima and Bellugi (1979) refer to this as the exhaustive modification; Anderson (1982) separates the forms into distributive (each) and collective (all). Figure 5-3 shows the pattern for the exhaustive of GIVE, meaning "give to each of them."

The plural inflection was described as a suffix added after the main verb movement. There is reason to believe that the exhaustive quantification is not just a suffix, but rather a complete reduplication of the verb. This is not obvious in a case like GIVE-TO-EACH-OF-THEM, where the movement seems to bounce from one point to the next, more or less as an extended version of the dual previously described. But in the case of verbs made with local movement, such as ASK (finger bending) or BAWL-OUT (hand opening), the exhaustive requires

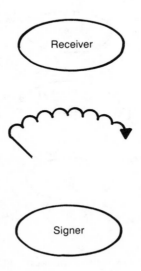

Figure 5-3. Movement pattern for the exhaustive of GIVE. © Brenda Schick, Purdue University.

that the local movement be repeated at individual points on the arc. It is probably appropriate to treat the exhaustive as a complex of verb plus the plural arc suffix plus the exhaustive reduplication at distinctive points. The minimum number of distinct points for these inflections is three, as only two would be interpreted as dual; signers rarely go beyond five, as there is a limit to the number of repetitions that can be meaningfully transmitted. In any case, three repetitions is usually sufficient to be interpreted as a general plural rather than as a specific three; specific three would be set up in the horizontal line described in Figure 5-1b.

Klima and Bellugi (1979) described several other inflections that add information about the arguments. These include the allocative, apportionative, and the seriated. The allocative has the meaning "certain, but not all." The repetitions of the movement are made at randomly varying points in space, rather than in a straight line or along a smooth arc, as with the exhaustive. Also, two hands are usually used to heighten the randomness. The apportionative inflection implies that the action of the verb is repeated to all the members of a group or to all the pieces of an object; the group or the object is the "whole," and the repetitions of the action are directed at the "parts." The apportionative is also a complex form, consisting of the reduplication of the verb movement, a circular path around the whole, and specification for either the horizontal or the vertical plane of formation. The horizontal plane indicates repetition around the different members of a group (for example, all the houses in a neighborhood; called the apportionative external by Klima and Bellugi, 1979), whereas the vertical plane indicates repetition around the parts of a single whole (for example, all the rooms in a house; called the apportionative internal by Klima and Bellugi, 1979).

Finally, the seriated inflection "specifies distribution of action with respect to objects of the same general class" (Klima and Bellugi, 1979). The repetition of movement is made in a straight line. This inflection also has an external and an internal form. The external form moves in a sideways straight line, whereas the internal form moves in a downward straight line. Thus, parallel to the apportionative, the seriated uses the horizontal plane for the external and the vertical plane for the internal.

These modifications allow specific aspects of spatial information, such as location, direction of movement, and contour of the movement path, to be used for adding information about the arguments of the verb. To translate this information into English would require many separate words from different parts of speech, sequenced appropriately. Here, a single sign can contain this information and still add information about the verb itself by undergoing modifications of the rhythm and temporal dynamics. These additional modifications will be discussed in a later section. Much research remains to be conducted on what restrictions exist on which verbs can take which inflections. Such restrictions include phonological factors, such as incompatibility of the verb movement with the inflection requirements, and semantic factors, such as the impossibility of a particular verb taking the meaning accompanying a particular inflection.

Noun Plurals

Jones and Mohr (1975) concentrated on the formation of noun plurals. They indicated that nearly all nouns can form a plural with the quantifier MANY. Many nouns also undergo reduplication and other modifications to form the plural. Jones and Mohr formalized several generalizations regarding these modifications, which are paraphrased here:

1. If a noun sign is made with one hand at a location on the face, its plural is generally made by repeating the sign alternately with both hands accompanied by a turning of the head from side to side. Exceptions to this generalization are GIRL (which follows the next rule) and FLOWER and APPLE (which require use of a quantifier).
2. If a noun sign is made with end contact, beginning contact, a double contact, continuous contact, or involves a change in orientation during its formation in the singular, the plural is made by reduplication and usually with a horizontal arc path movement. Exceptions seem to include OPERATIONS (surgical), which makes the subsequent repetitions slightly lower than the preceding ones, and YEARS, which involves only one repetition, is horizontal to begin with, and does not add the horizontal arc to its formation in the plural.
3. Noun signs that involve some type of wiggling movement or that have a holding contact with some other movement (opening or closing the hand, for example) are pluralized by continuing the movement while moving the hands horizontally. Nouns that have bending wrist movement or circular movement are pluralized by continuing their movement but without the horizontal sweep.
4. In general, any noun that involves repetition of movement in the singular does not undergo the above modifications, but takes the plural quantifier MANY instead (or a number — thus, MANY CHAIR or THREE CHAIR both indicate plural, even though the form of CHAIR is the same for singular and plural because it has repetition in the singular, being related to the verb SIT; see discussion in Chapter 4).

The pluralization of nouns depends in part on the type of move-ment that the noun sign has, the type of contact that it has, the loca-tion where it is made, and the orientation of the hand. There are probably many additional factors that enter into noun pluralization that would be uncovered by further research in this area, as the above generalizations have very limited applicability.

ADDITIONAL INFORMATION ABOUT THE PREDICATES

Unlike the spatial changes described above for arguments, the modifications discussed in this section change the rhythmic and dy-namic patterns of the movements themselves. These changes in-clude different rates of signing (fast, slow), degrees of tension (tense, lax), even or uneven rhythm, size of the path, and manner of the movement (restrained, continuous).

Aspect

Comrie (1976) suggests that "aspects are different ways of view-ing the internal temporal constituency of a situation," whereas Hop-per (1982) offers the definition "actions with a view to their comple-tion." The main issue dealt with by aspect is the way an event or situation is viewed as far as whether it is completed, ongoing, repeti-tive, not yet started, started but not yet finished, and so on. In addi-tion, these viewpoints are not merely expressed by phrases, as in English "I think he has started painting but has not finished yet," but rather by a modification to the predicate itself. In the English example just given, the main verb is "paint" and it is marked with the suffix "ing," which indicates ongoing activity (English progres-sive aspect). However, "paint" does not also indicate that the activ-ity has been started but is not yet completed (unaccomplished as-pect). Instead, that information is represented by a number of different words, including "has started" for the inception (begin-ning) part and "has not yet finished" for the unaccomplished (com-pletion) part.

Many languages have extensive aspectual systems that formally represent the different parts of an activity (inception, continuation, completion, repetition) by grammatical markers, usually added di-rectly to the verb. English has very little formal aspectual marking, with just the progressive and the perfective ("have" + past partici-ple). The progressive indicates ongoing activity and the perfective indicates completion. Langacker (1982) suggests that the perfective derives a *state* from a *process* by focusing on the point at which the activity is fully completed, whereas the progressive focuses attention on a single, arbitrarily selected internal point relative to a process. One way to think about this distinction is to consider the activity to be represented by a line that starts at the time the activity begins and ends at the time the activity is completed. If the time being discussed is between the beginning and the end points of the line, the activity is still ongoing and the progressive is used to describe the activity ("he is painting a picture"). If the time being discussed is after the end point of the line, the activity is completed and the perfective is used ("he has painted a picture"). If the time being discussed is before the activity starts, other constructions may be used ("he will paint a picture," "he may paint a picture," "he will start to paint a picture"). Notice that "he is starting to paint a picture" indicates that the activity of painting has started at the time the sentence is said.

In ASL, there are numerous morphological inflections for aspect. Different authors have used varying names for the aspects themselves. The list discussed here uses the terminology in Klima and Bellugi (1979) for those aspects that they discuss; readers are advised that a reanalysis of these aspects with different labels is presented in Anderson (1982), wherein the parallels between ASL aspect and that of various spoken languages are illustrated.

An activity that continues for a long time, whether an action such as eating or a changeable state such as being sick, can be modulated in ASL with a large, slow, elliptical path that has greater tension on the lexical part than it does on the return part (back to the starting point so that another cycle can be made). The large path and uneven rhythm of the continuative (Fig. 5–4A) contrasts with the small circular path with even rhythm that characterizes the durational (ongoing but not necessarily for a long time) (Fig. 5–4B). Tension and the size of the movement also distinguish the incessant (Fig. 5–4D) from the habitual (Fig. 5–4C). The incessant is made with short, tense, rapid repetitions, and carries the meaning of "constantly, incessantly." The habitual is made with rapid, nontense, and slightly larger repetitions, and carries the meaning "regularly, habitually." Another inflection is that of the iterative, which is made with a two part movement: first, a rapid, tense, straight line movement ending with a rapid deceleration (referred to in Chapter 3 as "short stop"); second, a slow, elliptical return to the starting position (Fig. 5–4E). The iterative carries the meaning of "over and over again."

Klima and Bellugi (1979) indicate that there are aspectual modifications for inceptive (beginning), resultative (end result), facilita-

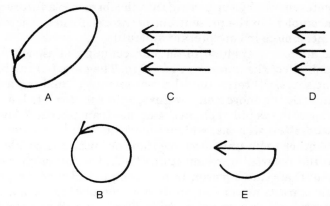

Figure 5-4. Movement patterns for several aspectual inflections: (A) Continuative, (B) Durational, (C) Habitual, (D) Incessant, (E) Iterative. © Brenda Schick, Purdue University.

tive (a manner modification meaning "with ease"), intensive (a degree modification meaning "very"), and approximative (also a degree modification meaning "sort of, not very"). These are associated directly with modifications of the manner of movement in the predicate. Thus, the approximative is made with lax movement, the intensive with tense movement, the facilitative with fast, elongated movement, and the resultative with a restrained beginning followed by a fast finish.

Liddell (1984b) describes another aspectual modulation, the unrealized-inceptive. This modulation carries the meaning "(just) about to begin" and its actual form depends on the phonological nature of the verb to which it is applying. Liddell divides verbs into three classes. The first class includes those verbs that keep their initial location segment and add a preceding movement that comes to a stop at the location where the verb would normally start. In this way, the meaning is indicated — about to start, but not yet started. The second class includes verbs also included in class I, but inflected for specific subject and object agreements that require changes in the phonological realization of the inflection. The third class includes those verbs that do not move to the starting location of the verb, but rather move away from the starting location to a location specified by the inflection (in other words, just the reverse of the first class).

Another aspect, the unaccomplished, was described by Jones (1978). Langacker (1972) separated "unaccomplished aspect" from "incomplete aspect" by suggesting that the former is a future action that is incomplete in the present but not in the future, whereas the latter is incomplete in both present and future.

There are four ways to form the unaccomplished aspect in ASL, all of which affect the movement of a sign. They are: (A) cutting the movement short. (B) retracting the movement, (C) making a "false start," and (D) the movement overextending its target. Unaccomplished aspect (A) would apply in a sentence translated as "My cat is dying" where the sign DIE, which requires both B hands (one palm down, the other palm up) to reverse their orientations, would never complete the reversal of orientation. Thus, the hands might stop part way in their turning over. In unaccomplished aspect type (B) a sign would start its movement, stop before completing its movement, and then return to its original position. Type (C) is illustrated by the sentence. "I am trying to do my homework," where the ASL FINISH MY HOMEWORK is made with the sign FINISH moving only slightly and hesitantly (and tensely) rather than its usual swift flicking of the wrists. Finally, type (D) is illustrated by the verb HIT made with the dominate A hand overshooting its normal ending position on the nondominant G hand (translated as "almost hit/tried to hit"). Jones (1978) pointed out that the verb MEET can undergo types (A), (B), and (D), an observation that is relevant to the discussion of grammatically constrained iconicity in Chapter 7.

All of the discussed modifications directly affect the formation of the movement of the verb sign. The functions served vary from adverbial comments about the activity (facilitative, intensive, approximative), to focus on the beginning or ending (inceptive, unrealized-inceptive, resultative, unaccomplished), to formal aspectual marking (continuative, durational, iterative, habitual, incessant). Additional information about time and tense can be added to an ASL sentence, but the mechanism for doing this is much simpler than those discussed — additional signs are merely added to the sentence.

Time and Tense

It has been noted by many sign language researchers that ASL does not provide tense marking on each verb in each sentence as, for example, English does, nor does it require a tense marking on each sentence as do Walbiri and Luiseño. Instead, ASL allows the time of the conversation to be marked at the beginning of that conversation and does not require further marking (although it *may* be) until the time reference is changed (as for example in Malay). Fischer and Gough (1972), Frishberg and Gough (1973b), Friedman (1975a), and

Cogen (1977) have all addressed aspects of the time marking system in ASL and modifications that may occur within that system.

Frishberg and Gough (1973b) describe the ASL "time line," a line that passes alongside the body from behind the head to a distance no greater than the full extent of the arm in front of the body, passing just below the ear. The space right in front of the body indicates the present, slightly more forward indicates near future, and greater distances forward reflect very distant future. The near past, of course, cannot be signed behind the body, so the space above the shoulder just about in line with the ear is near past, and distances farther back over the shoulder indicate distant past. Frishberg and Gough also indicate several signs which are used along this time line. For times in the past, there are (at least) four: PAST, BEFORE, LONG-TIME-AGO, and ONCE-UPON-A-TIME., They are differentiated by orientation of the hand (PAST and BEFORE face back over the shoulder and LONG-TIME-AGO and ONCE-UPON-A-TIME face the cheek), length of movement along the time line (BEFORE has a short movement, the others have a longer movement), and number of hands involved (PAST, BEFORE, and LONG-TIME-AGO are made with one hand, ONCE-UPON-A-TIME is made with two). The signs FUTURE, WILL, LATER, and IN-THE-FAR-FUTURE are similarly related, although none of them uses two hands (and many authors treat WILL and FUTURE as a single sign).

The signs TOMORROW and YESTERDAY are made on the cheek and move either forward or backward along the time line, respectively. Movement along the time line can become part of other time signs which are not normally made on the time line. The signs WEEK, MONTH, YEAR are made in neutral space in front of the signer's body, but can move forward or backward in space to indicate "a week from now/next week" or "a year ago/last year." With the incorporation of numbers, phrases such as "3 weeks from now" can be made with the handshape 3 making the movement of WEEK in its normal location across the nondominant palm followed by an added movement out past the palm and forward away from the signer. For the sign MONTH, movement in the past direction along the time line is permissible, but movement forward into the future direction is blocked by apparent structural constraints. Thus, "next month" is produced with a form of the sign NEXT and the sign MONTH.

If no time is marked at the beginning of a conversation, it is assumed to be the time of the speech act itself, the present. Time can be established by the time adverbials previously discussed (YESTER-DAY, NEXT THURSDAY, etc.), perfective markers (FINISH, NOT-YET), or the signs FUTURE, PAST, PAST-CONTINUOUS. The sign PAST-CONTINUOUS has been translated into English as "from then until now," "up to now," "ever since," and "have been." The use of one of the signs FUTURE, PAST, PAST-CONTINUOUS causes a shift in the interpretation of the timeline. For example, using the sign PAST causes that part of the time line previously interpreted as present to become past. Thus, within a conversation established in the past, the use of the sign TOMORROW might be interpreted as "the next day" (i.e., the day after the event that was just mentioned) rather than "tomorrow" (i.e., the day after the speech act itself). Thus, the base of time reference can be adjusted to permit time before and after a specified time in the past to be discussed in the present conversation.

Friedman (1975a) referred to FINISH and NOTYET as perfective markers, FINISH as positive and NOTYET as negative. She illustrated these with the sentences EAT YOU FINISH? 'Have you eaten?' and I NOT-YET SEE MOVIE 'I haven't seen the movie (yet).' Fischer and Gough (1972) concentrated primarily on FINISH. They indicated that there are "seven different meanings and at least four grammatical functions." The first use of FINISH is as a main verb that appears to make complements: WHEN YOU FINISH EAT, WE GO SHOPPING 'When you finish eating, we will go shopping.' Fischer and Gough do not provide an argument for this interpretation, leaving the above example open to interpretation as a perfective marker in the sense intended by Friedman, 'When you have finished eating/when you have eaten.' The important thing is that FINISH comes before the verb EAT.

Fischer and Gough (1972) noted several different uses of FINISH as an auxiliary. One may be restricted to adults' signing to children, however, in that the use of FINISH as a past tense marker is observed when signing to a very young child, but as the child matures linguistically, the parents resume use of the normal past indicators. As an auxiliary, FINISH follows the verb and functions as a marker of completed action, perfective aspect.

Two other uses of FINISH do not occur in the verb complex, but seem to be peripheral to the sentence itself. One is the use of FINISH to mean "that's all." It usually comes at the end of the sentence, and is often preceded by an intonation break (pause). It would be used in such instances as "you mean that's all he said?" or "That's all that's going to happen?" The other use of FINISH has the sense of "I've had enough" or "Have you had enough?" It is usually done in the direction of the subject or object of the activity and is often made with only one hand instead of the two used for the other instances discussed.

Structurally, Fischer and Gough note that FINISH most often occurs at the end of a clause, and tends to occur in the sequence Sentence FINISH Sentence, as in YOU EAT FINISH, WE GO SHOPPING, which can be viewed as YOU EAT (Sentence), FINISH, WE GO SHOPPING (Sentence). As a perfective marker, it almost always comes after the verb, and occasionally appears as an attachment to the verb with such verbs as SEE and READ. As a main verb, FINISH almost always precedes the verb of an embedded sentence. In those instances where it does not, an intonational pause usually occurs. When FINISH is used in the sense of "already," it generally precedes a verb or adjective.

When FINISH occurs as the main verb in a negative sentence, the negative precedes FINISH and cannot come between FINISH and the following verb. When FINISH is used in the sense of "already" or as a perfective marker (which comes after the verb), it cannot appear in the same sentence with a negative, and instead NOT-YET is used. Thus "John has not yet met Mary" must be signed JOHN NOT-YET MEET MARY and not *JOHN NOT FINISH MEET MARY.

MULTIPLY MARKED FORMS

Klima and Bellugi (1979) note that "the most salient formal characteristic of inflections for number and distributional aspect is spatial patterning, with displacement along lines, arcs, and circles in vertical and horizontal planes. By contrast, inflections for temporal aspect rely heavily on temporal patterning, making crucial use of dynamic qualities such as rate, tension, evenness, length, and manner in the movement of signs." Wilbur, Klima, and Bellugi (1983) argued that, in fact, the inflectional processes in ASL divide into basically two groups: those that affect the rhythmic and dynamic qualities of the movement and those that affect the spatial arrangement and/or location of the movement. This phonological split parallels a split in morphosyntactic functions: the modifications that result from the first group (rhythmic/dynamic changes) affect the meaning of the predicate itself, while those that result from the second group (spatial arrangement/location changes) affect the arguments of the predicate. As a result of this phonological split, it is possible to mark a single predicate with information from both groups.

Klima and Bellugi (1979) note that multiple marking can occur. They observe that with the sign GIVE (for example) the exhaustive inflection ("give to each") can be embedded in the durational inflection ("give continuously") to produce a form meaning "give to each, that action recurring over time" ([[exhaustive] durational]). They also note that the embedding of the durational into the exhaustive is allowable, creating a form that means "give continuously to each in turn" ([[durational] exhaustive]). Embedding of this latter form into the durational produces a form meaning "give continuously to each in turn, that action recurring over time," which can be represented as [[[durational] exhaustive] durational]. This embedding is possible, in part, because of the phonological separation that accompanies the morphological separation. That is, the phonological modifications required to indicate durational are different from those required for the exhaustive, and both can therefore be made at the same time without interfering with the production of the other.

Using data provided by Bellugi and Klima (1980), Wilbur, Klima, and Bellugi (1983) presented an analysis of possible multiple embeddings. The data contained permissibility judgments on various combinations of ten spatial inflections and four temporal inflections. Results show that 100 percent of the spatially indicated inflections may embed in the temporally indicated inflections, supporting the argument that the phonological and morphological separations allow multiple marking. For the alternative ordering, only 90 percent of the temporally indicated inflections can be embedded in the spatially indicated inflections. The reason for this is that one spatially indicated inflection, the plural suffix, does not permit certain embeddings, namely those that would destroy its phonological shape, the smooth, horizontal arc. Each of the four temporally indicated inflections (iterative, durational, habitual, and continuative) requires repetitions that would break up the smooth sweep that characterizes the plural, rendering it unrecognizable and defeating the entire purpose of selecting different phonological patterns for different morphological functions. Wilbur, Klima, and Bellugi (1983) referred to this as the morphological preservation principle. The plural, however, can embed in all of the temporally indicated inflections (as part of the 100 percent just mentioned); this is consistent with the morphological preservation principle, for the sweep can be made intact and repeated for those inflections that require repetition without obscuring the plural inflection itself.

Embeddings of temporally indicated inflections in temporally indicated inflections and of spatially indicated inflections in spatially indicated inflections involve other factors besides just phonological structure, although it is still an influence. Of the possible temporal inflections embedded into temporal inflections (e.g., iterative in iterative, continuative in durational), only 50 percent are considered acceptable. The habitual, made with rapid repetitions in a straight line with small, straight returns between repetitions, does not allow any of the temporally indicated inflections to embed (including itself). Once again, the morphological preservation principle appears to be involved, since such embedding would destroy the structure of the habitual. There are, however, other cases, such as embedding the continuative in the durational, which could occur phonologically, but do not. Similarly, only 35 percent to 67 percent of the possible embeddings of spatial inflections in spatial inflections occur (the acceptability of some cases is unclear; the lower figure assumes that unclear cases do not occur, while the higher figure assumes that they do). An investigation of the factors that affect such embeddings may reveal other patterns of phonological, morphological, or semantic constraints. The phonological separation that has been discussed here appears to be part of a more general phonological layering in ASL, discussed in the next section.

PRIMARILY FOR LINGUISTS

Phonological Layering for Morphological Purposes

Wilbur, Klima, and Bellugi (1983) argued explicitly that the phonology of ASL was layered in that certain phonological characteristics were used for lexical items, others for derivational processes, and others for inflectional processes. This layering distinguishes ASL (and probably other signed languages) from spoken languages, in that spoken languages do not reserve portions of their phonological inventory exclusively for morphological purposes. In English, for example, the phoneme /s/ may serve at least three morphological functions (noun plural, verb third person singular, possessive marker), but it may also occur as part of a lexical item where it serves no morphological function at all ("sell").

Linguists have found it useful to distinguish between "roots" and "words" (cf. Selkirk, 1982, for English). Affixes (prefixes or suffixes) are specified according to whether they attach to a root or a word and whether the resulting form is itself a root or a word. Root is considered to be the lower level, and root affixes may create a form that is still a root (that is, can add yet another root affix). Certain affixes can be added to a root and the resulting form will be a word; no further root affixes can be added but additional word level affixes can still be attached. If a root can stand alone with no added affixes, it is also a word. Wilbur, Klima, and Bellugi (1983) found this distinction to be useful for describing ASL. The frozen forms are simply *words*; they have no internal structure of root and affix. The productive forms are composed of roots and affixes.

Wilbur, Klima, and Bellugi (1983) argued that in ASL, derivational processes applied at both the root and the word level, but that inflectional processes applied only at the word level. They observed that root level derivational processes affect the local movement (either adding one or replacing one with another). A pivot at the wrist is added to the sign for QUIET to create a form meaning "acquiesce." The sign WRONG adds a twist of the wrist to obtain the meaning "suddenly, unexpectedly." An upwards twist of the wrist added to PARK-CAR creates "drive-in movie" (with appropriate modifications to account for the fact that the latter is a noun while the former is a verb). These derivations were referred to as "idiomatic derivations" by Bellugi and Newkirk (1981), who noted that they could not find "any consistent change in meaning correlated with consistent shifts in form." In other words, these derivational changes make new roots that have different but related meanings that are not predictable from the meaning of the form that serves as a base or from the change that is made. Other pairs that probably fall into this category are STUDY (wiggling fingers) and CRAM ("spritz," ballistic hand opening), DIRTY (wiggling) and FILTHY (spritz), and even FINGERSPELLING (wiggling) and TO-USE-SIGN-LANGUAGE-TO-COMMUNICATE (spritz). None of the observed modifications appear to be productive.

Supalla (1982) discusses productive root processes for the construction of verbs of motion in ASL. He takes the basic root to be linear path movement. To this basic root, several simultaneous root level morphemes may be added. These affixes include secondary movement affixes (which add manner of movement information, such as change of location, orientation, or shape parameters). Additional affixes specify noun agreement, noun placement, and noun classification (classifier handshapes). Of these, only noun classification is clearly simultaneous; the others must be represented sequentially, as was discussed in Chapter 3. All of Supalla's affixes are root level forms.

Gee and Kegl (1982) consider the linear path that Supalla takes as basic to be composed of two single argument predicates, FROM and TO. They suggest that FROM, which takes its argument in initial position, and TO, which takes its argument in final position, are concatenated to produce a morphologically complex, grammatically transitive form ____ FROM # TO ____ . The arguments are indicated by appropriate spatial locations. They argue that this form is the basis for all verbs of motion. The concatenation rule that they posit would be a root level derivational process. Shepard-Kegl (1985) modifies the details somewhat, but the resultant analysis still works primarily at the root level.

In contrast to the root level processes, whose meaning changes are unpredictable, derivational processes at the word level create predictable changes, primarily because they involve changes in lexical category. The derivation of "pious" from "church" involves the addition of a path movement to CHURCH. Similar derivations yield predicates from nouns, giving the meaning "to act like _____ " or "to appear like _____ ." The associated noun-verb pairs discussed by Supalla and Newport (1978) also differ in that the verb has a full path movement whereas the noun has reduced path (restrained, short, repeated movement). The inflectional processes described earlier in this chapter also involved modification of the path movement, whether of the starting and ending points or the rhythmic qualities. The argument made in Wilbur, Klima, and Bellugi (1983) was that all word level processes applied to path movement, whereas root level processes applied to local movement. The result of this split is that word level affixes do not obscure roots or root level affixes, or vice versa, thus allowing multimorphemic signs.

Not all linguists agree that only two levels are relevant. Shepard-Kegl (1985) argues that lexical items in ASL are composed of various affixes and nonaffixes that are combined by lexical X-bar rules. The nonaffixes include (from lowest level upward) the base form (what she calls MOVE), the root (base + terminator affix), the stem (root + locative argument marker), and the word (stem + classifier affix). The affixes are the terminators (IN, ON, AT, WARD), the locative argument markers (location specifications), and the classifier affixes (the handshape specification). There is a correspondence, then, between the various lexical formatives and phonological specifications: base = movement, terminators = spatial arrangement/direction/general location, locative argument markers = specific locations, and classifier = handshape. As each piece is added to the base, the level moves upward (from base to root to stem to word).

Noting the distinction between lexical (root) formations and modulations for morphological purposes, Klima and Bellugi (1979) observe "the properties of modulations appear to be different in kind from the properties of the movement components of lexical items. When we describe the movement components distinguishing lexical items of the language, we use terms like 'wrist rotation', 'nodding', 'contact', 'brushing', 'wiggling', 'joining', and 'grasping'," all of which are forms of local movement. Further, "when we consider the overall visual impression of the different modulatory processes, we use global terms such as the 'thrust', the 'marcato', the 'accelerando'. But when we describe the changes in movement imposed by these modulations on lexical signs, the terms we use are very different. Dynamic qualities and manners of movement characterize the modulatory processes. . . . , changes in rate, in tension, in acceleration, in length, in number of cycles, and so forth. In spoken languages the lexical items and the inflectional processes draw from the same phonemic inventory; in American Sign Language they appear not to" (p. 264).

Wilbur, Klima, and Bellugi (1983) made the following observations about lexical items, derivational processes, and inflectional processes in ASL:

1. In the lexicon, basic lexical entries do not make distinctive use of available modifications of *manner* of movement, that is, in the lexicon, there are no semantically unrelated pairs that differ only in that is tense and the other is lax. Similarly, there are no unrelated minimal pairs in the lexicon that differ only in that one of the pair is restrained in manner of production and the other is not. Also, there are no unrelated pairs in the lexicon that differ only in that one is reduplicated and the other is not (or that one is reduplicated twice and the other three times, or any combination of specific numbers of repetitions).

2. In the lexicon, lexical entries do not make distinctive use of particular points in space (as opposed to particular locations on the body). That is, whereas two signs, such as APPLE and ONION, may differ only in the location where they are made (ONION is closer to the eye, APPLE is lower on the cheek), there are no minimal pairs of basic lexical items that differ only in that they are made at two distinct points in space (whether it is starting point, ending point, or location where the entire sign is made).

3. In the lexicon, unrelated basic lexical entries do not make distinctive use of directions of movement in space (as opposed to those contacting the body). There are no signs that require a particular direction for production, except for paired opposites: IN/OUT, UP/DOWN, JOIN/QUIT, APPEAR/DISAPPEAR, IMPROVE/GET-WORSE. That is, if a sign has distinct meaningful direction (it would be judged incorrect by a native signer if made without that particular direction), then its opposite should be an existing meaningful sign.

4. Root level derivational processes affect local movement (or add local movement).

5. Word level derivational and inflectional processes affect the path movement (or add one). In addition, they can modify (or add) various rhythmic and spatial characteristics, such as features of manner of movement, spatial location, orientation, arrangement, and direction (which are apparently excluded from being distinctive in the lexicon).

Thus, much as consonants and vowels appear to be morphologically separated in Semitic (at least for the verb forms), various phonological characteristics (some segments, some features) in ASL are reserved for particular morphological functions. The combinations provide a seemingly endless source for creating new sign forms expressing both novel and conventional meanings, and indicating grammatical relations. The question remains of whether any spoken language restricts its phonological inventory to the extent that ASL does. It may well be that the phonological layering observed here is a result of a fundamental difference in the visual modality, in which case, similar layering should be found in the phonologies of other signed languages.

SUMMARY

This chapter has illustrated the variety of modifications that a single sign may undergo to carry additional information about the noun referents that serve as arguments and the manner in which the verb activity is performed. Spatial locations, changes in direction of movement, vertical and horizontal movement, and geometric contours (lines, arcs, circles) allow various information to be represented with respect to the noun referents that function as grammatical relations (subject, direct object, indirect object). Speed, rhythm, size, and tension all contribute information about the predicate itself. These modifications may apply to words whether they are frozen lexical items or productively formed by the processes discussed in the preceding chapter.

Given the number of morphemes that can be packed into a single sign, it is clearly inappropriate to treat the sign as the unit of analysis. This is not to say that specifications never make reference to the sign as a whole, as do for example some facial expressions, but rather that to treat signs as unanalyzable wholes is to miss numerous internal regularities that carry significant morphological information in ASL. Also, with all the grammatical information that can be carried by a single predicate, it should come as no surprise that word order is nowhere near as important to ASL sentence structure as it is to English, which must have almost every piece of information carried by a separate word sequenced in the right order. This will be pursued in detail in the next chapter.

CHAPTER 6

ASL Syntax

Native speakers of English equate proper word order with grammatical sentence structure. A survey of languages of the world quickly reveals that most languages do not rely primarily on word order for building sentences, especially not to the extent that English does. The situation may be thought of as a continuum: at one end are rigid word order languages like English, at the other end are languages with totally free word order. In fact, few languages are located at the extremes, as most languages have a combination of reserved word orders for certain structures or grammatical relations and freer word order for other situations. In order to allow (relatively) free word order and still permit the listener to understand the sentence, languages tend to use morphological markers to indicate information about the arguments (subject, direct object, and indirect object). A noun marked with the nominative case will most likely be interpreted as subject, whereas nouns in the accusative or dative cases will be interpreted as objects. English lacks this kind of marking (except in the pronoun system) and relies instead on word order.

As demonstrated in the previous chapters, a single sign may carry considerable information about the predicate and its arguments. Word order in an ASL sentence may therefore vary much more than in English. This fact was not well understood until certain types of inflections were identified and described. Early descriptions of ASL frequently compared the word order of ASL directly to English and, when the match was not very good, concluded that ASL was "ungrammatical." Of course, any other language compared to English would also be declared "ungrammatical," as only English has the syntax of English. Even close relatives, such as German, can be seen to have very different syntactic structures when compared to English.

Discussion of ASL syntax, then, should not be viewed as merely a matter of word order, but as an interaction of the word formation processes and morphological inflections discussed in the previous chapters with the few word order constraints that do exist. In order to provide some perspective on this interaction, some historical information about the study of ASL syntax is helpful as a starting point.

EARLY DESCRIPTIONS

There can be no doubt that the appendix on syntax from Stokoe, Casterline, and Croneberg (1976), which is derived from Stokoe's (1960) first outline of ASL structure, has been the foundation for nearly all of the topics of more recent descriptions. Stokoe and colleagues provide a functional definition for what they consider an utterance, that portion of linguistically meaningful body activity preceded and followed by nonlinguistic body activity. Defined this way, the signer may be seen to go from repose to signing to repose, and they note a high degree of consistency between the signer's position in repose before and after signing. They also discuss other clues to pauses and junctures (such as those presented in Covington, 1973a, b). Recent research by Baker (1977) on conversational turn-taking and regulators and by Grosjean and Lane (1977) on the relationship of pausing and syntax certainly derive their roots from Stokoe and colleagues.

The reason this early work was important is that it is difficult to define the notion of "sentence" in an unstudied language. Thus, Stokoe and colleagues began with the "utterance" as a unit of analysis, providing a principled way for dividing conversations. Whether each utterance is a sentence, more than one sentence, or a fragment of a sentence then becomes a linguistic question.

The discussion of "parts of speech" by Stokoe and colleagues (1976) covers such diverse topics as how to determine if a sign is a verb (discussed also by Fischer and Gough, 1978), the use of space for indicating grammatical information (the linguistic description of which has been the concern of nearly everyone since), the time line and its function, the use of various signs such as auxiliaries (CAN'T, CAN, FINISH, NOT-YET, which Stokoe and colleagues call "have not," MAY/ MIGHT, LET, SHOULD, MUST, and so on discussed by Fischer, 1978, and Fischer and Gough, 1972), the use of facial expression in a variety of structures (Baker, 1976; Baker and Padden, 1978), and the combination of directional preposition and verb (ASL ENTER compared to English "go in," where in English the particle "in" can stand as a separate word).

One interesting aspect of the discussion in Stokoe and colleagues (1976) is the suggestion that certain structures, such as GIVE (made from the addressee to the signer), which can be translated "you give me....," might better be translated in the passive, "I am given...." Such consideration of how a passive might be rendered in ASL in terms of ASL grammatical mechanisms is a far cry from those who determined that ASL does not have a passive simply by looking for markers comparable to those in English (form of the verb "be" plus past particle of the verb plus "by" phrase for agent). Thus although Stokoe and colleagues eventually decided that ASL did not have a passive, they did so by considering the structure of the language itself and not by comparison to English.

Another early description of ASL syntax was by McCall (1965). In her analysis, she noted the function of ASL auxiliary verbs, time adverbials, negatives, question markers, facial expression, reflexive and possessive pronouns, reduplication, and the use of space for reference to nouns. Fant (1972) also reviewed such aspects of sign modification as movement in space, number incorporation, inclusive (including the signer) and exclusive (not including the signer) pronoun interpretations, the time line, question formation, and facial expression. However, many more pieces were needed before the puzzle could be fitted together.

THE ISSUE OF WORD ORDER

The treatment of ASL word order in Fischer (1975) and Friedman (1976a) differed in part because of their different conception of how verbs behaved (whether they were inflected) and their conceptions of ASL pronominalization.

Fischer's (1975) paper basically argues that ASL has become a subject-verb-object (SVO) language like English, possibly through increasing influence from English itself. Fischer constructed sign sequences and presented them to native signers for interpretation. The presented sentences consisted of various permutations of two nouns and a verb: NVN, NNV, VNN. (When either of the two nouns can be interpreted as subject or object, the sentence is referred to as "reversible," e.g., "John kicked Bill," but if only one noun can logically or reasonably be considered the subject or object, the sentence is "nonreversible," e.g., "John kicked the chair.") Fischer reports that the interpretations provided by her informants were:

1. NVN was interpreted as SVO
2. NNV was interpreted as either (a) conjoined subject-verb (N and NV), or (b) OSV
3. VNN was interpreted as either (a) verb-conjoined object (VN and N), or (b) VOS

Fischer's conclusion from these interpretations was that ASL is an underlying SVO language. This does not mean that SVO is the only allowable surface word order: "Other orders are allowed under the circumstances that (1) something is topicalized, (2) the subject and object are non-reversible, and/or (3) the signer used space to indicate grammatical mechanisms" (Fischer, 1975). Variations from the basic SVO order can be signaled by "intonation breaks" which Fischer characterizes as consisting of pauses, head tilts, raised eyebrows and/or possibly other nonmanual cues. Thus NVN is interpreted as SVO, contains no breaks, and is considered the underlying order. N,NV may be interpreted as O,SV with the object topicalized and a break between it and the remainder of the sentence (an example of a topicalized object in English would be "as for the rhubarb, John ate it"). The sequence VN,N may be interpreted as VO,S with a topicalized verb phrase, followed by the subject with a break after the verb phrase (symbolized by the comma). (An example of a topicalized verb phrase in English is "As for doing the dishes, John will.") In discussing Fischer's data, Liddell (1977) notes that although these three orders include the subject in all three sentence positions, initial, medial, and final, this does not indicate random word order in ASL. Instead, he adds the observation that "if the subject or object accompanies the verb, the subject precedes the verb and the object follows the verb."

Friedman (1976a) takes issue with Fischer for basing her analysis on sentences that were presented to signers rather than on discourse excerpts and for not separating verbs into classes (body anchor, movable for subject and object, etc.). Based on her analysis of discourse samples, Friedman claims that "word order is relatively free, with the exception of the tendency for the verb to be last" and that "the vast majority of propositions in ASL discourse appear on the surface as either a verb alone, subject verb (SV) or conjoined subject plus verb (SSV, SSSV). Constructions like SVVV are common and can be analyzed as subject+verb, deleted subject+verb, etc." Friedman states that in the texts she analyzed, SVO order was present but relatively infrequent. She argues for basic underlying SOV by pointing out the relatively large number of OV constructions, which she argues results from deleted subjects. (Liddell, 1977, critically examines Friedman's claims at length and rejects this analysis.) Friedman's assumption that there are no grammatical inflections for verbs leads her to propose several strategies that signers use to identify subjects and objects in the absence of fixed word order (as in English) or case markings and inflections (which allow languages like Latin to have relatively free word order) (Friedman, 1976a):

1. With intransitive verbs (e.g., "sleep"), only one noun phrase (argument) may occur, namely, the subject (e.g., "John slept," but not *"John slept the bed").
2. With transitive verbs that can have two or more semantically nonreversible arguments, there is no problem since their roles are determined by the meaning (e.g., "John pushed the blanket," but *"The blanket pushed John").
3. For transitive verbs that allow the subject and object to be reversed, several possible strategies are presented:
   (a) the signing space is used to establish locations of referents and verbs are moved between them
   (b) the body and body space are used to distinguish referents
   (c) some ambiguous transitive constructions are avoided by choosing one-place verb constructions instead of two-place constructions (i.e., in English, "anger" is a two-place construction as seen in "John angered Mary," but "angry" is a one-place construction as seen in "Mary is angry"; Friedman is suggesting that ASL uses the latter but not the former to avoid ambiguity)
   (d) heavy reliance on context.

Friedman (1976a) summarizes the discourse situation in ASL as:

1. "Nominal signs are articulated and established in space, either by indexic or marker reference or by body position."

2. After this, "verb signs are then (a) manipulated between or among these previously established locations for nominal referents or (b) articulated on the body which is in the appropriate pre-established position for agent or experience."
3. The first verb is assumed to have first person subject unless an actual subject is indicated. Subsequent verbs that also appear without overt subjects are still interpreted as first person. Whenever a verb appears without a subject in connected discourse, the subject is "assumed to be the same as the last one given, until a new subject is mentioned."
4. As indicated earlier, word order appears relatively free, with a tendency for the verb to occur last.
5. The appearance or nonappearance of a noun sign after its initial establishment in the discourse seems to be in free variation, with its appearance functioning possibly as an indicator of emphasis, contrast, or clarification.
6. At most, four or five different referent locations may be used within a single discourse. These locations can then be used for later pronominal reference.

Friedman is suggesting that ASL has a series of avoidance strategies for processing and producing signed utterances that are necessary to compensate for constrained syntactic rules. Fundamental to her approach is the claim that the recognition of iconic representation in ASL requires abandonment of standard linguistic notation and concepts (see further discussion in Chapter 7). Other researchers have retained standard descriptions (Chinchor, 1978a; Kegl, 1976a, b; 1977, 1978a, b, c; Kegl and Wilbur, 1976; Lacy, 1974; Liddell, 1977, 1980), requiring whatever iconicity is present in the language to be constrained by linguistic rules for sign structure and syntax.

Kegl (1976b, 1977) identified a number of difficulties with Fischer's (1975) and Friedman's (1976a) approaches. She noted, as did Friedman, the risk involved in presenting sentences to signers for interpretations or judgments (as Fischer did) as opposed to more naturalistic data (as suggested by Friedman), but nonetheless, following Fischer's methodology, she presented similar sentences to signers, using both inflected and uninflected verbs.

When signers were presented with sentences in which the signs were in NVN order but the verb was not inflected, they interpreted the sentences as SVO. However, when asked when such a sentence would be used, they typically responded that an ASL signer would not sign the sentences that way, but that the sentences were understandable. They also suggested that hearing people might sign the sentences that way. One informant rejected all sentences that were presented without inflection on the verb.

When signers were presented with sentences in which the words were in the same order and the verb was inflected, the sentences were accepted as natural and were indicated as being preferred. If the verb was inflected and the words were in a non-SVO order, most signers accepted the sentences, but some indicated that they were stylistically awkward and that SVO order would be preferred.

The signers in Fischer's and Kegl's investigations were able to give consistent interpretations of sentences with uninflected verbs even though they are unacceptable in ASL. Kegl (1976b) attributes this to the bilingual nature of most signers. Although they may not be fluent readers and writers of English, they are nonetheless familiar with English in written and spoken form and in its signed equivalent, signed English (see Chapters 10 and 11). English has very little or no inflection of the verb (for person), no incorporation, no indexing (although there are pronouns and determiners which perform similar functions), and a fairly rigid fixed word order. Therefore, in cases where signers are presented with sentences that lack indexing and verb inflection, they may rely on English-related strategies (namely, word order) to determine grammatical relations. This bilingual phenomenon should be kept in mind.

Kegl's concept of the function of the point in space as part of an inflectional system in ASL also leads to a different interpretation of the data than Friedman's. Friedman seems to have advocated avoidance strategies rather than syntactic structure for ASL, and although Friedman was concerned with separating verbs into their classes, she did so according to the *number* of arguments they could have and whether those arguments were semantically reversible. Kegl separated verbs according to their *inflection,* and postulated the following solution to the word order controversy:

The Flexibility Condition: The more inflected the verb is, the freer the word order may be.

Thus, there is an interaction between verb inflection and word order. One may find that if a verb is fully inflected (for subject and object), that all word orders may occur (as Friedman suggested) and that signers may express word order preferences (as Kegl found). In addition, the types of intonation breaks reported by Fischer may be reflections of optional rules like topicalization for conversational focus or emphasis, rather than as markers of non-SVO word order.

Liddell (1977, 1980) provides an empirical analysis that supports Fischer's claim that ASL is underlying SVO; at the same time his discussion hints at the variability that led Kegl to the flexibility condition.

Liddell begins by demonstrating that, contrary to Friedman's claims, word order is significant in ASL, and that, for example, in a simple yes/no question "Did the woman forget her purse?", the *only* allowable order in ASL is $\overline{\text{WOMAN FORGET PURSE,}}^{q}$ SVO. Considering first NVN sequences, Fischer said that they were interpreted as SVO and that any other order must have intonation breaks in it. Liddell indicates that in fact SVO can have intonation breaks in it also, and that when such an intonation break occurs, the reading is S,VO with the subject topicalized. His measurements indicate that a noun sign that is in initial position but not a topic (i.e., SVO) is roughly 180 msec longer than the average duration of a noun sign in medial position (the shortest position). Signs in final position were approximately 280 msec longer than medial position, whereas noun signs that were topics (i.e., S,VO or O,SV) were held about 370 msec longer than medial position. Thus, his data indicate that part of the "intonation break" Fischer referred to is a result of longer duration of the topicalized sign. Liddell also identifies a particular facial expression and head position, which he calls "t," that marks topics. "t" is a combination of the head tilted backward slightly and the eyebrows raised. It co-occurs with the topicalized sign, then disappears for the remainder of the sentence. Thus, the change of facial expression and head position after the topic combined with the duration of the topicalized sign itself provides the cues that Fischer identified as intonation breaks.

Several other nonmanual markers were discussed in Chapter 2 and are relevant to the present discussion. One of them is the "q," shown in the previous example. "q" is defined by a leaning forward of the body, the head forward, and the eyebrows raised. It is used as a marker of yes/no questions, and, as indicated by the line above the entire sentence $\overline{\text{WOMAN FORGET PURSE,}}^{q}$ the nonmanual signal is held across all three manual signs (unlike "t," which is held only across the topic). Another nonmanual signal, "n," is a negating signal composed of a side-to-side headshake, and a special facial expression in which a primary feature is the turning down of the corners of the mouth. The sentence $\overline{\text{DOG CHASE CAT}}^{n}$ is translated as "The dog didn't chase the cat" or "It isn't the case that the dog chased the cat" (in other words, the whole proposition is negated). According to Liddell, when the topic marker "t" and the negative marker "n" are both present in the same sentence, the "n" does not co-occur with the "t," giving $\overline{\text{DOG}}^{t} \overline{\text{CHASE CAT}}^{n}$, "As for the dog, it didn't chase the cat." A third nonmanual signal is "hn," head nod. Liddell identifies "hn" as a slow, forward head nod which signals assertion and/or existence, and appears to be required in those syntactic structures in which the subject of the main clause is separated from its verb. Such cases include topicalized verb phrases VN, N, $\overline{\text{CHASE CAT}}^{\text{t}}$, $\overline{\text{DOG}}^{\text{hn}}$ "As for chasing the cat, the dog did it," where "hn" is required with DOG. Gapping sentences require "hn" on the second noun in each gapped construction. Similarly, the English sentence "John is a doctor" is signed in ASL as JOHN DOCTOR with no main verb. Liddell indicates that "hn" is required in JOHN $\overline{\text{DOCTOR}}^{\text{hn}}$ to distinguish it from JOHN DOCTOR "John's doctor." Finally, if a noun phrase and its pronoun (indicated by indexing with a deictic marker, not body shift or verb agreement) both occur in the same sentence (presumably for emphasis), then the pronoun is obligatorily accompanied by "hn." Liddell suggests that "hn" behaves as a parallel to English "be" and "do," especially in its function when the main verb is missing (environment for do-support in English) and for emphasis ("John *did* go to the movies").

With these nonmanual signals, Liddell can argue in favor of Fischer's contention that O,SV and VO,S are derived from underlying SVO by topicalization. He has shown ($\overline{\text{DOG}}^{\text{t}}\overline{\text{CHASE CAT}}^{\text{n}}$) that when a subject is topic, it does not fall within the scope of the "n" signal. He can also demonstrate that when the object occurs initially, it is accompanied by "t" and does not fall under the scope of "n," for example, $\overline{\text{CAT}}^{\text{t}}\overline{\text{DOG CHASE}}^{\text{n}}$ "As for the cat, the dog didn't chase it" but *$\overline{\text{CAT DOG CHASE}}^{\text{n}}$. This illustrates that certain changes in underlying word order must be accompanied by certain nonmanual signals. Failure to identify those nonmanual signals might lead to the belief that any word order is acceptable (e.g., Friedman, 1976a). Similar to the above example, when a verb phrase is topicalized, Liddell showed that "t" occurred on the verb phrase and that the subject was required to have "hn," $\overline{\text{CHASE CAT}}^{\text{t}}\overline{\text{DOG}}^{\text{hn}}$. In addition, when the verb phrase is topicalized, it does not fall within the scope of negation, for example, $\overline{\text{CHASE CAT}}^{\text{t}}\overline{\text{DOG}}^{\text{n}}$ "As for chasing the cat, the dog didn't."

The status of SOV sentences was also disputed by Fischer and Friedman. Although Friedman claimed that word order was free, she also contradicted herself by arguing that surface OV forms came from deleted underlying subjects, presumably SOV. Fischer noted that SOV may occur when the nouns involved are semantically nonreversible, for example, MAN BOOK READ can only mean "The man reads the book." However, Liddell found that some sentences that were interpretable in just this way nonetheless were considered unacceptable by his informants, and also that there are certain sentences which he claims must be SOV to be acceptable. Those that are unacceptable as SOV are just those that contain uninflected verbs, and in fact, one of his examples, MAN MOVIE SEE, was considered unacceptable without inflection, but acceptable when the verb was inflected by using eye gaze to establish an index for MOVIE and then orienting the verb SEE toward that index to agree with MOVIE. Those that must be signed SOV, Liddell claimed, involve iconicity and other mimetic devices. For example, he indicated that the sentence WOMAN PIE PUT-IN-OVEN "The woman put the pie in the oven" is acceptable only if the nondominant hand for PIE (B hand) is the one that is active for the verb PUT-IN-OVEN and that it is unacceptable if the other hand is used. Liddell (1977, 1980) considered this to be evidence that "the iconicity of the sequence is important for this SOV sequence." Viewed with the perspective of the preceding chapters, this example can be seen to contain a number of the possible parts of the verb complex. The sign PUT-IN-OVEN already consists of PUT and a locative phrase, "in the oven." Using the nondominant hand of PIE as the hand that does the putting involves the combination of the B hand classifier (object, flat (more or less), movable by outside source) and the verb PUT.

These data, then, are consistent with the formalism proposed by Kegl (1976b, 1977). Liddell's (1977, 1980) comments on variability, "judgments as to the grammaticality of these sentences would vary depending on where the sentence fell on the continuum (i.e., how well the relationship between the verb and the object is depicted)," is exactly what is predicted by the flexibility condition.

Finally, Liddell observed that when classifiers for location are involved, for example, "The cat is lying on the fence," the unmarked ASL order seems to be OSV, FENCE CAT LIE-ON-IT. In the articulation of this sentence, the sign FENCE is made, and then what Liddell calls the 4 classifier (4 hand, fingertips facing sideways, used for fence, wall, general erect rectangular objects) is made with the nondominant hand and held while the sign CAT is made, after which the V̌ classifier (bent legs) is made and placed in position with respect to the 4 classifier. The positioning of the two classifiers indicates whether the cat is on the fence, next to the fence, under the fence, etc., and Liddell considers the entire sentence to be composed of locative object-locative subject-locative predicate. He suggests, then, that although SVO is the general underlying order for ASL sentences, the order OSV is unmarked in the case of locatives (unmarked in the sense of there being no intonation breaks and no special nonmanual signals).

Subordination and Embedding

The issue of word order in ASL sentences revolved mainly around simple sentences. One reason for this is that linguists use the basic sentence types as the primary guide to a language's word order, with the assumption that more complicated sentences may contain deviations from the basic word order. When one sentence is included inside of another sentence, either by relative clause formation or any of the various types of subordination (complementation), the resulting complex sentence may or may not behave like a simple sentence. One of the problems that linguists have had to face with respect to ASL syntax is whether there are any complex sentences that have embedded clauses and, if so, what they look like and how they work.

Thompson (1977) claimed that ASL does not contain surface structures with subordinate clauses and that those sentences that look like they contain embedded sentences are really sequences of two sentences or coordinate sentences. Liddell (1978) indicates a number of problematic aspects of Thompson's argument, including contradictions between his claim and his data, which seem to arise from the way in which he translated the ASL sentences into English. Since Liddell (1978) reports several types of subordinate clauses and provides a nonmanual marker "r" for the relative clauses, his presentation, rather than the arguments against Thompson, are the major focus here.

In the discussion to follow, personal pronoun signs will be glossed as PT. First person will be indicated by 1, second person by 2, and third person by 3 (or 3a, 3b, etc., if needed).

One of Thompson's (1977) arguments is that ASL does not distinguish between direct speech ("John said, 'I...'") from indirect speech ("John$_1$ said that he$_1$ ...."). Liddell observes that just this distinction can be indicated by the presence or absence of body shifting. In the sentence with body shift, the verb SAY is not required, nor in many cases is the PT1 for "I." Thus, Liddell supplies the following examples (1977) renumbered for use here):

A. JOHN (SAY)^{shift} PT.1   "John said, I'm tired."

    TIRED

B. JOHN SAY PT.3 TIRED   "John said he (John) was tired."

In example A a direct report of what John said is given, whereas in B a report of the essential content of what John said is given, using pointing to indicate John. In example B there is a subordinate clause, PT.3 TIRED "he was tired."

Another of Thompson's arguments, with which Liddell appears to be in agreement, is that the verbs HAPPY, ANGRY, SURPRISED, RELIEVED, SORRY, and PROMISE do not take complements. However, neither Thompson nor Liddell indicates what alternative mechanism, if any, is used to report "Mary is sorry that she scared the cat away." One possibility is MARY SCARE-AWAY CAT, (PT.3) SORRY.

Liddell's (1978) most extensive discussion and analysis of subordinates is for restrictive relative clauses. He indicates that these clauses can occur in initial, medial, and final position within an ASL sentence. Furthermore, they are accompanied by a nonmanual signal "r," which is composed of raised brows, a backward tilt of the head, and raising of the cheek and upper lip muscles. In English, all relative clauses have what is known as an "external head," that is, the noun about which the relative clause is providing information is outside of the relative clause itself. Consider "The man who bought the yellow raincoat is John's father's best friend." The relative clause "who bought the yellow raincoat" provides information about "the man," which is the subject of the predicate "is John's father's best friend" and the outside head of the relative clause. Within the relative clause, the relative pronoun "who" is considered to have replaced an underlying "the man" so that the underlying form of the relative clause would be "the man bought the yellow raincoat." English does not allow "the man" to be repeated and substitutes "who" as subject of the relative clause in the surface structure.

Other languages do not work like English. They may have what is known as an "internal head," where the noun that is being modified occurs *within* the relative clause itself. Thus, in languages with "external heads," the noun that is the head of the relative clause appears in underlying structure twice, once in the main sentence and once in the embedded sentence, whereas in languages with "internal heads," the noun that is the head appears in underlying structure only once. The characteristics of an internal head relative clause that Liddell summarizes are that (1) it has the structure of a sentence, (2) it serves the same function that a simple noun phrase would in the main sentence, and (3) it is treated and interpreted as though the noun phrase in it that serves as the head is performing the function described in (2). Having established this, Liddell discussed several relative clause types in ASL that appear to have internal heads. For example, the sentence RECENTLY DOG CHASE CAT COME

HOME "The dog that recently chased the cat came home" has an internal head DOG which functions as the subject of COME HOME; at the same time RECENTLY DOG CHASE CAT is a sentence itself and is marked with the nonmanual signal "r" (which stops at the end of the embedded part). Interestingly, Liddell observes that RECENTLY, which co-occurs with the nonmanual adverb "cs," appears to have both "cs" and "r" at the same time. "It seems then that the nonmanual aspects of certain lexical items, expressions associated with individual signs or compounds, and non-manual grammatical markers are independent and additive" (Liddell, 1977).

Liddell considers the possibility that RECENTLY DOG CHASE CAT COME HOME is really two sentences concatenated temporally, but reports that when signers were asked to produce the two sentences separately, the nonmanual marker "r" was not used.

Liddell also made some measurements similar to those he used to support Fischer's (1975) claim of an intonation break in non-SVO ordered sentences. In this case, he used the sign CAT in a variety of positions in a relative clause. He reports that in medial position, the shortest duration, CAT lasted about 230 msec, in final position, 400 msec, and in initial position, 330 msec. When CAT occurred in initial position in the relative clause, it was always as the object of an OSV sequence. Looking at DOG when it occurred in relative clauses as the subject, he found that, in initial position and functioning as the head of the relative clause, DOG lasted 430 msec, but if not functioning as the head it lasted only 280 msec. In medial position, if DOG was the head, its duration was 370 msec, whereas if it was not the head, it lasted only 230 msec. Thus, the function of the head of a relative clause contributes to an increase in sign duration, as does final position (as reported by Grosjean and Lane, 1977) and initial position (as illustrated here).

Liddell (1977, 1980) covers a wide range of syntactic structures and markers in ASL. He also provides sophisticated linguistic argumentation for the description of many of these structures, and for topics not discussed here, such as determining the head of a relative clause. The serious student of syntax is advised to refer to the complete work and not to rely on the summary herein. Also relevant is Coulter's (1983) analysis of sentences containing relative clauses as conjoined structures.

Padden (1979, 1981, 1983) provides several syntactic arguments for determining whether a construction is a coordinate or subordinate structure. Coordinate structures can be joined with a signed conjunction (FINISH meaning "then," AND, BECAUSE, WHY used rhetorically) but subordinates cannot be. Thus, sentence C is gram-

matical and sentence D is not (recall that the subscripts indicate
verb agreement for the different referents involved and the "*"
means ungrammatical):

C. PT.3a $_{3a}$HIT$_{3b}$ FINISH, PT.3b TATTLE MOTHER
    "She hit him then he tattled to his mother."
D. * $_1$ PERMIT $_3$ AND USE C-A-R PT.3a
    "I let her and use the car."

Another difference between coordinate and subordinate structures
is that in a coordinate structure, the individual parts can stand
alone as sentences, whereas in subordinate structures they cannot.

Padden also argues that the sign NOTHING provides clues about internal structure. NOTHING generally occurs at the end of its phrase, as
in sentence E.

E. I SEE PEOPLE, $\overline{\text{NOTHING}}^n$.
    "I didn't see any people."

In coordinate sentences, NOTHING can be placed after either sentence:

F. PT.3a $_{3a}$HIT$_{3b}$ $\overline{\text{NOTHING}}^n$ (head nod) PT.3b TATTLE MOTHER PT.3b.
    "She didn't hit him but he told his mother."
G. PT.3a $_{3a}$HIT$_{3b}$ (head nod) PT.3b TATTLE MOTHER $\overline{\text{NOTHING PT.3b}}^n$.
    "She hit him but he didn't tell his mother."

The negated part includes only the verb in the clause containing
NOTHING. Padden notes that when NOTHING occurs at the end of a sentence containing an *embedded* clause, the negated part may be either the subordinate clause or the main clause. Theoretically, sentence H can have two meanings:

H. $_1$ TELL $_2$ $_2$ GIVE $_3$ BOOK $\overline{\text{NOTHING}}^n$.
    "I told you not to give him the book."
    "I didn't tell you to give him the book."

Perhaps the most interesting of Padden's syntactic tests for separating coordinates from subordinates is the one involving subject
pronoun copy. In simple sentences, a pronoun referring to the subject
(whether the subject is indicated by a noun, a pronoun, or verb
agreement) can be put on the end of the sentence, as in sentence I:

I. $_1$ TELL $_3$ $_3$ STAY PT.1.
    "I told her to stay, I did."

If the sentence is coordinate, such a structure is ungrammatical,
whereas if the sentence is subordinate, the structure is grammatical.

J. * PT.3a $_{3a}$HIT$_{3b}$ FINISH PT.2 TATTLE MOTHER PT.3a.
"She hit him then you told your mother, she did."

K. $_1$ TELL $_3$ SHOULD INFORM MOTHER PT.1.
"I told him he should tell his mother, I did."

Altogether, then, Padden has identified four separate techniques for distinguishing coordinates from subordinates: acceptability of the presence of a conjunction, ability of the individual clauses to stand alone as sentences, scope and acceptability of the negative NOTHING, and acceptability of subject pronoun copy.

PRIMARILY FOR LINGUISTS

Formalization of the Constituent Phrases

Several researchers have proposed structures for constituent phrases for nouns and verbs in ASL. Starting first with the noun phrase, recall that referents may be indicated by pronouns such as POINT signs, classifiers, verb agreement, or by a noun sign. If a noun sign is used and no further reference will be made to it, or if that noun will not participate in any of the verb-noun interactions previously discussed (e.g., the noun only occurs with body anchor verbs which do not agree with their object, or whatever), then no point in space need be established, and the production of the noun sign by itself is sufficient (e.g., "Where's the X?" requires only the production of the noun sign, WHERE, and question marker). For most other purposes, a point in space must be established. These points in space have been used here for descriptions of the verb behavior without explicit statement on how these points were established. The procedure for establishing the point in space is referred to by Kegl (1977) as "indexing," and the point in space to which the noun is related is part of the "index." The remainder of the index, called the "deictic marker," is dependent on how the point in space is established. In general, the deictic marker is a pointing gesture toward the point that is being established. It can take several handshapes: G hand for humans, ⊔ for general nonhumans, and A (or Å) for reflexive$_2$-intimate (intimate in the sense of an empathy hierarchy, reflexive in that it has the same handshape as the regular reflexive, reflexive$_1$, and in keeping with the general linguistic literature which refers to such intimate forms as types of reflexives). This pointing gesture may be made before, after, or simultaneously with the noun sign. Kegl (1977) illustrates this description with a tree for ASL noun phrases (NP):

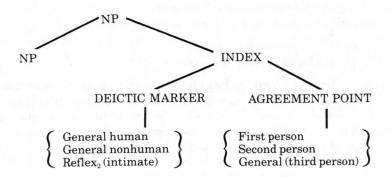

Since the index can precede, follow, or occur simultaneously with the noun, the tree must be considered to be unordered (that is, it can represent all three temporal possibilities). The allowability of unordered trees is critical to Kegl's analysis of ASL syntax.

Noun phrases that are not specifically assigned to an agreement point or otherwise indexed, perhaps because no further reference will be needed, are considered to have "null" indexes (Kegl, 1976a). The possibility exists that definite/indefinite distinctions which are reflected in English by the determiners "the" and "a(n)" are distinguished by whether a noun phrase has an index (definite) or not (indefinite).

In a further consideration of the structure of NPs in ASL, Chinchor (1978a, 1981) suggested that within a NP, there is a classifier phrase (CP) composed of a quantifier (Q) and a classifier (C). The order within the noun phrase and within the classifier phrase is variable (indicated by dotted lines in the tree) and is represented

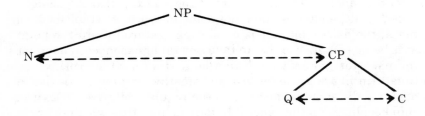

Chinchor argued that the ability of the quantifier and the classifier to blend (producing a single sign) is evidence of a stronger relationship between them than between the classifier phrase and the noun, which can assimilate (leaving two signs) but not blend. Chinchor

identified allowable blendings between the quantifiers ONE, TWO, THREE, and MANY with the person classifier in a variety of contexts. She also suggested that in ASL, measure phrases (MP; inch, mile, etc.) behave parallel to classifier phrases, with the quantifiers ONE through TEN blending with time measures and CENT. The time measures include WEEK, YEAR, MONTH, HOUR, MINUTE, and DAY, with each having a different set of allowable blendings with the numeral quantifiers. For example, Chinchor indicates that WEEK can blend with ONE through FIVE, but MONTH can blend only with ONE through THREE. Also, the allowable blendings change for each time measure when compounded for past and future along the time line. Finally, Chinchor noted that unit phrases (UP) also behave like classifier phrases within the NP. The numeral quantifiers ONE through NINE can blend with the unit HUNDRED to form ONE-HUNDRED, TWO-HUNDRED, and so on.

Although the order of occurrence is free within the NP, and within CP, MP, and UP (of course, order cannot be determined when blending has occurred, but we are referring here to order of unblended quantifier and classifier, measure, or unit sign), Chinchor notes additional support for her analysis from the fact that the noun cannot interrupt the CP, MP, or UP. For example, if there is an unblended numeral followed (or preceded) by a classifier, the noun cannot come between the numeral and classifier. This demonstrates the integrity of the classifier, measure, and unit phrases which Chinchor has proposed. Although the word order within these phrases may be free, Chinchor observes that different measures (time, weight, age, height, money, speed, length) appear to have different ordering preferences. For WEEK, YEAR, DAY, MONTH, HOUR, MINUTE, DOLLAR, MILE, TIMES, POUNDS, and OUNCES, the preference seems to be for the (unblended) numeral to precede the measure sign. For others, eg., CENT, TIME, AGE, WEIGHT, and HEIGHT, the quantifier generally follows the measure sign.

In ASL, then, the word order is relatively free at the level of major constituents; that is, the ordering of noun phrases with respect to each other and to the verb is free if the verb is inflected. The NP itself maintains integrity, in that it may not be broken up. Reference to "major constituents" brings up another facet of ASL that has not been explicitly discussed, namely, formalization of the verb behavior. Although Liddell (1977) utilized a formal node for verb phrase (VP), he did so without defending its use. Kegl (1977) indicated that no evidence is presently available for positing a VP constituent for ASL and suggested that until such time as a VP can be adequately demonstrated, the sentence can be characterized by a tree without a VP, but with a verb complex (VC):

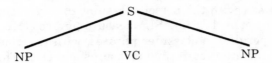

As long as the verb is inflected, constituents sharing the same node in the tree (i.e., connect to the same upper point) are ordered freely within that constituent. A full representation of an ASL sentence (from Kegl, 1977) might look like

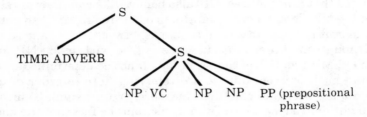

The verb carries much of the grammatical information in the ASL sentence. The unit that has been referred to as the "verb" may be viewed as a complex composed of agreement markers for the subject and object, the verb itself and NPs that can be incorporated by using classifiers. Also present in the verb complex is aspectual information, such as reduplication for habitual, durative, and so on, and changes in the movement of the verb for unaccomplished aspect. Except for the auxiliaries and unbound negative, the verb complex (VC) is a single unit (Figure 6–1).

Registration markers result from a process that Kegl (1977) treats as the blending of a verb and a preposition. Thus, a combination of the verb DRIVE and the preposition TO can be made if DRIVE loses its up and down alternation, but with a straight linear movement to location 4 ("the store"). With the VEHICLE classifier, we can get DRIVE-AROUND (3 hand moves around in circle), DRIVE-UNDER (3 hand moves underneath the nondominant hand), DRIVE-OVER (3 hand moves over nondominant hand), and so on, *without* using the separate preposition in the same sentence (this is the full meaning of incorporation). The effect of this process is to make what in English is the object of the preposition, for example, "to the store," the direct object of a verb in ASL, for example, DRIVE-TO STORE. As discussed in Chapter 5, Shepard-Kegl (1985) considers the combination of verb and preposition to be an integral part of lexical formation. If the preposition is what she calls a "terminator" (IN, ON, AT, WARD), the combination of base movement and terminator make a root, to which the location

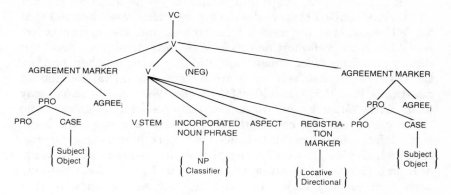

Figure 6-1. Kegl's (1977) representation of the verb complex.

specifications (such as those for AGREE$_i$ and AGREE$_j$) are added to make a stem. When the stem and the classifier (incorporated noun phrase in Figure 6–1) are combined, the result is a word level unit that can function as the verb complex.

The structure of the verb complex in Figure 6–1 is a full expansion of the possible forms. There are various rules that may neutralize agreement markings in some cases depending on the amount of redundancy in the sentence (Liddell, 1977, 1980, indicates that indirect quotes may be just such a case, whereas Kegl, 1976b, 1977 indicates topic chaining). In other words, the tree does not necessarily represent the surface form of the sentence. In addition, two further additions must be made to the VC tree, that of auxiliary (AUX) and the unbound (separate sign) negative (NEG). When all three are present, the ordering is AUX NEG VC. Therefore, we have:

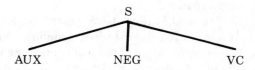

Other Syntactic Structures

The previous discussions have covered a wide range of syntactic structures, including negation, questions, topicalization, relative clauses, WH-complements, locative predicates, gapping, predicate nominatives, adverbs, verb agreement, pronouns, and word order. In contrast, this section is small.

As Liddell (1977, 1980) indicated, the yes/no question marker "q" includes raised brow and wide eyes. Others have observed that for WH-questions, the eyes are narrowed and the eyebrows are squished. ASL WH-questions have WH-words to signal them, but these words (WHO, WHEN, WHERE, WHAT, etc.) may occur in other than initial position (English WH-words are restricted to initial position for questions). Fant (1972) and Kegl (1977) observed that "bracing" may occur with WH-question words, for example, WHO GIVE₂ BOOK WHO "Who gave you a/the book?" (literally, "who gave you a/the book, who?"). Kegl considers this to be part of a more general bracing process in which a single word, entire phrase, or whole sentence can appear on both sides of a sentence (initially and finally). Kegl also suggests that bracing may serve as a test for constituency, in that whatever may brace a sentence must be a constituent (this is parallel to Liddell's use of the scope of the nonmanual markers to determine if some element was part of a phrase or not).

Fischer (1974) reports several rules which appear to operate in ASL. She notes that Ross's (1967) coordinate structure constraint is operative for ASL. She also notes that FOR is used to introduce purposive clauses (e.g., "for the purpose of") and that "unless" clauses are introduced by WITHOUT. She notes that auxiliaries in ASL include FINISH (perfective), BETTER (polite imperative), CAN, CAN'T, WILL, MUST, FROM-NOW-ON (future continuous marker), HAVE-BEEN (past continuous marker), NOT-YET (negative of FINISH), HAPPEN, SUCCEED, and possibly SEEM. These auxiliaries have the possibility of occurring at the beginning and/or end of a sentence without a change in meaning from their position in the middle of a sentence. In an embedded sentence, "the auxiliary can occur initially or preverbally, but not at the end" (Fischer, 1974). She postulates rules for auxiliary hopping (to move the auxiliary around), NP fronting (for topicalization), sentence topicalization, and VP topicalization. From the formalization of these last few rules, she concludes that Ross's (1967) complex NP constraint is also operative in ASL.

Both Kegl (1977) and O'Malley (1975) postulate deletion rules to handle those cases in which independent pronouns (such as pointing) do not occur in surface forms. Kegl postulates one relevant rule, copy drop. The rule of copy drop is dependent on the semantic notion of specificity, which refers to whether the NP or its copy (pronominal copy) indicates the narrowest set of possible references:

Copy Drop: Given NP and NP copy, NP deletes if NP is less than or equal to the copy with respect to specificity.

O'Malley posits several deletion rules that are very similar to Kegl's. He notes that the most deletable pronoun in ASL is first person singular, but only in subject position ("I"), and posits an optional rule of I-deletion. Another optional (and mirror image) rule is pronoun deletion, which deletes independent pronouns when the verb is inflected to convey the same information. He indicates that the function of these two rules is to "simplify sentence structure by removing redundant elements" (O'Malley, 1975) and that the information deleted by both rules is uniquely recoverable.

Fischer and Gough (1972) suggest that ASL might have a rule of EQUI-NP deletion (*equi*valent *NP deletion*). O'Malley argues that just such a rule can be postulated. A sentence like "I want John to go" is treated as though it comes from two underlying sentences, "I want" and "John go," through a process of complementation, whereby one sentence is modified to fit into the other (inserting the "to" in English). Consequently, a sentence like "I want to go" is treated as coming from two underlying sentences, "I want" and "I go," where the second occurrence of "I" is deleted by EQUI-NP deletion. O'Malley indicates that EQUI-NP deletion in ASL seems to be two rules, one that exactly parallels the English rule (the presence of which may be an ASL borrowing from English) and one that is restricted to avoid EQUI-NP application to sentences with auxiliaries, negatives, and modals.

SUMMARY

A variety of syntactic rules exist in ASL, many appreciably different from English. However, none of these rules indicates that ASL is extraordinary with respect to other languages of the world (except, of course, in how the output structure is constructed after application of the morphological and phonological rules). An adequate theory of ASL (morpho-)syntax would have to take into account the extensive system of inflections, verb agreement, classifiers, and nonmanual signals. Thus, an adequate theory would have to account for processes that do not depend primarily on word order or even on the sequential presentation of information (which is, after all, only the surface coding and therefore language specific). Such a theory should not be designed specifically for ASL, as there are many spoken languages that are similar to ASL as far as the small role that word order plays in basic sentence structure.

CHAPTER 7

Psycholinguistics and Neurolinguistics of Sign Usage

In Chapter 4, the fact that certain phonological pieces may contribute meaning to the construction of a sign, even if the sign is a frozen one, was discussed. Included were direction of movement (upward for APPEAR, downward for DISAPPEAR), spatial arrangement (parallel for AGREE, opposite for DISAGREE), location (talking signs at the mouth, thinking signs at the forehead), handshape change (opening for giving out information, closing for taking or catching), and handshape itself (the fingers as lines of information). In that discussion, it was pointed out that there is a fine line between saying that the phonological piece contributes to the meaning and saying that the phonological piece represents a separate morpheme. This problem is not unique to sign language and cannot be solved here. The discussion here will focus on the different perspectives that can be taken on the meaning of signs, including the role of iconicity and metaphor.

Research on perception, production, and memory of signs initially began as a way of testing whether sign language was really a language and/or whether iconicity had any role in the processing of sign language by fluent users of the language (in the beginning these two questions were treated together). Recent research has also addressed the question of whether linguists, who have proposed the various analyses presented in Chapters 2 to 6, are seeing things that are not really there. These studies have shown that inflections are in fact added to verbs, and that the linguistic use of space (for such things as verb agreement) is separate from the nonlinguistic use of space (for example, drawing a picture).

ICONICITY AND METAPHOR

Recent linguistic studies of English have focused on both metaphor and iconicity. Iconicity is supposed to be a reflection in language of the actual state of affairs in the real world (this is an informal definition). An example of how languages might be iconic is given by Haiman (1983, 1985), where he noted that languages tend to refer to direct causation with single lexical items and to less direct causation with multiword phrases. Thus in English, "Mary dropped the ball" reflects a direct causative relationship between Mary and the ball dropping. A less direct relationship would be indicated by "Mary caused the ball to drop," where Mary might have knocked over a glass on the table which hit the ball causing it to roll off the edge of the table. The contrast is between "drop" as a single word and "cause .... to drop" as a phrase. Whether such iconicity is systematic throughout languages awaits further investigation.

Perhaps the most controversial and misunderstood aspect of sign languages is their apparent iconicity. The possibility of relating the formation of a sign with some real world aspect of its meaning has led many to the erroneous assumption that sign languages are "pictures" in the air, and therefore unable to function or qualify as true languages. Often a sign will be presented to a new learner with a story attached to help "explain" the formational characteristics, for example, girl — the strings on a bonnet, boy — the visor on a cap. Such stories, whether true or not, provide memory aids to the learner. Significantly, such explanations are totally lacking in interactions between deaf parents and their sign language learning children (Moores, 1977).

In discussing iconicity, one can focus on several issues. How transparent are signs to people who are unfamiliar with signs? That is, can one tell what someone is signing without learning signs first? What are the factors involved in iconicity and what are the theoretical consequences of these factors?

Transparency for the Nonsigner

Several procedures have attempted to measure the degree of transparency that certain signs may have to the nonsigner (Bellugi and Klima, 1976; Hoemann, 1975). Bellugi and Klima (1976) presented 90 ASL signs and their English translations to a group of hearing nonsigners and asked them to describe the basis for the connection between the sign's meaning and its formation. They found that for over half of the signs, there was general agreement among the subjects as to the possible relationship. Thus, if the meaning is known, a relationship between the meaning and the formation can be determined for some signs. Bellugi and Klima termed this type of sign *translucent*. They also investigated the *transparency* of signs — what Lloyd and Fristoe (1978) have called *guessability*, namely, the likelihood of determining the correct meaning of a sign by a nonsigner. They used the same set of 90 signs with a different group of hearing nonsigners. They found that for 90 percent of the signs presented, not even one subject was able to determine the correct meaning. The remaining 10 percent (BED, BUTTON, EAR, EYES, MARBLE, MILK, OPERATION, PIE, and SURPRISE) were identifiable by some but not all subjects. Thus, most of the signs were not transparent to most of the subjects.

A third technique that Bellugi and Klima used was a multiple choice test constructed using the correct meaning and four alternatives chosen from the incorrect guesses of the preceding study. The correct response rate was no better than chance, indicating that under these more constrained conditions (choices given rather than free choice as before), the ASL signs were *opaque*. For 12 of the 90 signs, a majority of subjects guessed the correct meaning (BED, BUTTON, BODY, BOTH, BLOSSOM, DAY, EAR, EYES, ODOR, OPERATION, SURPRISE, and YEAR). For 36 of the 90 signs, no subject chose the correct meaning. Interestingly, a number of the signs that were never identified are ones that are commonly given stories when they are presented to people learning signs: BOY, CANADA, EARTH, GIRL, GRAVY, HOME, IDEA, SCIENCE, SUMMER, WEEK.

Bellugi and Klima (1976) also discussed the lack of evidence for a role of iconicity in memory, based on Bellugi, Klima, and Siple (1975), Bellugi and Siple (1974), and Klima and Bellugi (1975). They reviewed several grammatical modifications that signs can undergo, and pointed out that the identifiable iconic parts of certain signs are actually lost in grammatical contexts.

Possible Types of Iconic Representations

The results that Bellugi and Klima (1976) obtained are not surprising. There are many aspects of a real world action or object that might serve as the source for a sign. Although a spatial/visual language naturally takes advantage of its power to depict, each language seems to choose a different aspect to represent, thus providing an arbitrariness that renders the sign opaque to the nonsigner. Klima and Bellugi (1979), in their discussion of the formational differences in the signs for the concept "tree" in ASL, Danish Sign Language, and Chinese Sign Language, observe that the different sign languages choose different aspects of trees to represent. The ASL sign for TREE "shows" a trunk (with the arm) and tree branches (with the fingers and the hand); the Danish Sign Language sign for TREE depicts a round ball-shaped top and a columnar-shaped trunk by using both hands (in a c handshape) to outline first the top and then the trunk; and the Chinese Sign Language sign for TREE depicts only a thin, columnar trunk (as in "bamboo") using the bent thumb and index fingers of both hands. Similar differences can be seen in the signs for "cat" in ASL, Greek Sign Language, Spanish Sign Language, and Brazilian Sign Language (São Paulo; see Ferreira Brito, 1985, for two distinct Brazilian sign languages). The ASL sign for "cat" has "whiskers" as a base image, as does the sign in Brazilian Sign Language (Figure 7-1). Spanish Sign Language and Greek Sign Language use a different base image, that of petting or scratching the animal. Each can be related to aspects of cats (or trees, as discussed previously), but the different formations of the signs themselves are not predictable from knowledge of cats or tree structure and in this sense the signs are as arbitrary as spoken words (see also Boyes-Braem, 1981, for differences in signs for the same object among dialects of Swiss-German sign language). Furthermore, as Frishberg (1975, 1976) has shown, signs have historically changed away from iconic depictions and toward more arbitrary representations.

Mandel (1977) discussed several ways in which a sign can conceivably be iconic. He first distinguished *direct* representation, where the gesture is the thing being referred to, as for example the drawing of a house-like outline for the sign HOUSE or the pointing to the nose for NOSE. Nondirect representation, or *metonymy* (Battison, 1971; Schlesinger, Presser, Cohen, and Peled, 1970), refers to the use

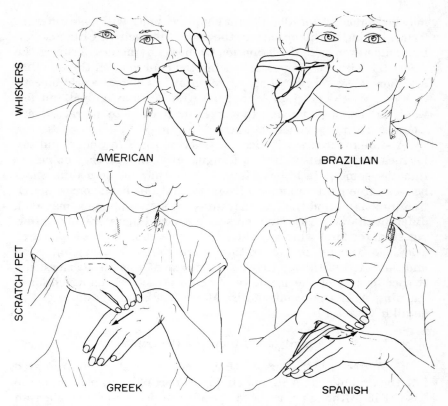

Figure 7-1. Signs for "cat" showing different formational bases. ©K.J. Graphics.

of *part* of an object or action as a reference for the whole, as for example when the grinding action is used for the sign COFFEE, even if the coffee being discussed is instant or drip (this is similar to the American English use of the word "blackboard" for boards that may be green, blue, or red). Mandel further distinguished *presentation* and *depiction. Presentation* refers to the use of a token of an object or activity, either by "mime" (BASEBALL) (Mandel does not separate sign from mime) or by indexing (NOSE). *Depiction,* on the other hand, may be either *substitutive,* as when the articulator is formed into the shape of an object (CUP), or *virtual,* in which the articulator is used to trace a picture in space (HOUSE).

The types of representations that Mandel identifies (and other subcategories included in them) provide a pool from which manual languages can pick and choose. Thus for any vocabulary item that may be iconically based, different sign languages will have different forms, adding to the opacity of the signs themselves. Chinese Sign Language even uses depiction for Chinese characters (forming the character with the fingers or tracing the character in the air) that are themselves former iconic representations of real world objects. One can see the original connection when it is explained, but few would be foolhardy enough to suggest that Chinese characters are iconic and can be read without actual training.

A similar discussion of iconicity is contained in Cohen and colleagues (1977) (on Israeli Sign Language). Although they do not go into the same detail that Mandel does, they do note differences between free pantomime and iconicity that has been conventionalized into signs, and the fact that different sign languages may pick different characteristics to represent and could therefore have different signs, each of which might still be guessable to the nonsigner. They, like Mandel, include in their discussion of iconicity inflection and classifiers (although they do not specifically name each as such). A specific test of the iconicity of these structures using children learning ASL was conducted by Meier (1982) and is discussed in detail in Chapter 8.

Iconicity and Linguistic Description

DeMatteo (1977) suggests that iconicity must be incorporated into the grammar of ASL, not simply as part of it, but rather as the base of it. Although unable to specify the details of how such an incorporation might be made, he does suggest that a visual analogue grammar that does not contain discrete units, such as NP, might be possible. He includes as part of his argument for the nondiscreteness of ASL many of the same things that Mandel (1977) and Cohen and colleagues (1977) do: verbs that agree with their arguments, signs that include location and direction, object-incorporating verbs (WASH as in WASH-DISHES, WASH-CAR), and classifiers (again, none of these are specifically named as such).

Much of DeMatteo's argument rests on surface similarities between the verb MEET (two G hands, each starting at its appropriate subject index point and both eventually coming together) and other verbs with different movement. For example, in "The boy and girl meet," the two hands start at their previously designated points and move together, usually in the middle of neutral space in front of the signer. In "The boy and the girl passed each other without stopping," the verb would be made without an end contact and of course the hands would pass each other going in opposite directions. In "The boy avoided meeting the girl," or "The boy avoided the girl," the hand that is co-referent with the boy would eventually turn in a different direction from the direction that the girl is moving in. DeMatteo provides other similar examples which he feels argue for a description in which each of these is seen as a modification of the movement of the verb MEET rather than as separate verbs. Furthermore, it is his contention that the modifications that do occur are visually based iconic changes that are potentially infinite, and therefore cannot be handled within current theoretical frameworks.

To say that iconicity is part of the structure of ASL is one thing; to say that it is the basis for the linguistic description of ASL is quite another. In one example, DeMatteo (1977) suggests that the signer's choice of the verb-locational preposition combination FLY-OVER rather than the sequence FLY OVER is "the more visually based representation, choosing descriptive signs or mimic signs in order to create an icon in the signing space". Such a statement overlooks the nonoccurrence of the preposition OVER in any kind of surface sequence of verb + preposition (possibly for the reason suggested by Shepard-Kegl, 1985, that verbs are really underlying prepositions) and that the citation form of OVER (and other prepositions, cf. AROUND, UNDER) only occur in citation environments ("What is the sign for X?") and signed English sequences. Suppose, however, that there existed a grammatical constraint in ASL that allowed OVER to occur in sequences only in stative, descriptive environments (e.g., "The lamp that hangs over the desk has a Tiffany shade"). If such a constraint existed, we would be primarily interested in determining (1) its existence, and (2) its domain of application (other locative prepositions? what counts as a stative verb in ASL?). To know that the signer produces a particular form, which to the listener seems to create a more appropriate visual image of the described event, does not necessarily indicate that he does so free from linguistic constraint. In order to investigate such constraints, and the phonological, morphological, and syntactic descriptions given elsewhere in this book, it is necessary to make a number of working assumptions:

1. ASL may be described in terms of discrete elements.
2. There are constraints on how these elements may be combined (Chapter 2). It is possible to violate these constraints, and native signers can make judgments of grammaticality using these constraints.
3. Elements near each other will affect each other. In other words, there are phonological modifications of signs in sequence (such as those discussed in Chapter 3).

4. There are derivational and inflectional morphological processes (Chapters 4 and 5).
5. There is an underlying level, a surface level, and a mapping from one to the other.
6. There are linguistic universals such as noun, verb, and the expression of grammatical relations in the base.
7. Any linguistic model that claims to provide a consistent description of language should be an appropriate framework in which to attempt an analysis of ASL (if it is good for other languages, then it should be valid for ASL as well). This framework should allow one to develop tests, arguments, and predictions. In other words, it should provide the linguistic mechanisms with which to work. (The progress in describing ASL word order, as outlined in Chapter 6, resulted from researchers developing specific tests and arguments, such as those presented by Padden, 1981, 1983, for distinguishing coordinate and subordinate structures.)
8. There will be variation that will occur which is not meaningful, either stylistically or sociolinguistically conditioned. Knowledge of the grammatical system as a whole will allow us to recognize points at which this nonmeaning-changing variation occurs.

These assumptions are essentially those that linguists work with when approaching a new language. In early papers on ASL, several authors, such as DeMatteo (1977), argued that the previous assumptions were not valid for ASL. By rejecting these assumptions and arguing for a visual analogue grammar, DeMatteo was, in essence, claiming that it was impossible to do current phonological, morphological, or syntactic analysis on ASL (or any other sign language). This viewpoint was taken despite the fact that, as discussed in Chapter 2 and the beginning of Chapter 6, much of the early description of ASL by Stokoe (1960) contained considerable linguistic sophistication (phonemic analysis, recognition of morphological functions, syntactic structures). It was in response to this viewpoint that Kegl and Wilbur (1976) felt compelled to state explicitly what the assumptions were. Most of the current progress stems from work conducted under these assumptions.

When iconicity does appear, it must obey the constraints on allowable signs. When visual analogue occurs (e.g., modifying the sign WALK-AROUND to include a slight hill or disturbance in the path), it is linguistically constrained such that (1) the resultant sign cannot violate the phonological conditions on allowable signs, (2) it cannot destroy the syntactic or morphological content of the sentence, and (3) it cannot be semantically distinct from the original meaning in the sense of a minimal pair. Thus, although DeMatteo (1977) argues strongly for visual analogue grammar based on the apparent continuity of modifications that the verb MEET can undergo, one must contend that because "The boy and the girl passed each other without stopping" is semantically distinct from "The boy and girl meet," which is distinct from "The boy avoided meeting the girl," and so on, they represent discrete semantic concepts, and therefore very likely discrete verbs (which may or may not be derivationally related to each other). If, in fact, there is a separate translation into English (or any other language) for each of the different meanings intended, it suggests that there is no apparent reason why ASL could not have separate and distinct verbs for each, at least at the semantic level. The internal complexity of the verb complex (Chapter 6) provides for a change in the direction, location, or manner of movement that could easily represent the kind of structures that DeMatteo (1977) feels are unable to be described. DeMatteo is concerned that this destroys the hope of "placing finite bounds on the number of lexical items", but if one views this as a complex of derivational and inflectional morphological and syntactic processes with regularities and constraints of application, then one can describe internal structure without being blinded by surface continuity.

All of this adds up to a single point: describing something as iconic may be true, but it is also linguistically insufficient.

Metaphor and Linguistic Description

The study of metaphor in language has recently left its exclusive domain in literature and come into linguistics and psychology. Among the suggestions that have been made is the idea that, even at the lexical level, systematic metaphors of Western culture underlie the interpretation of meaning. The notion of "metaphorical systematicity" is discussed extensively by Lakoff and Johnson (1980), where they extend its implications beyond words to cognitive systems and the philosophy of science. The present discussion will limit itself to the lexical level, however. In this regard, we are not concerned with metaphors of the nature of "The road was a ribbon of moonlight," but rather with common expressions such as:

A. "He woke *up* at ten"

B. "I came *down* with a cold"

C. "Around 3 o'clock in the afternoon, I *run out of steam*"

D. "He's really quite *brilliant,* you know"

In each of these expressions, the italicized words, although perfectly common, are not being used in a strictly literal sense, but nonetheless reflect the choice of underlying metaphors with which we describe the world. Lakoff and Johnson identify these corresponding metaphors as:

A'. The orientational metaphor "Conscious is up, unconscious is down"

B'. The orientational metaphor "Health and life are up, sickness and death are down"

C'. The ontological metaphor "The mind is an entity; the mind is a machine"

D'. The structural metaphor "Understanding is seeing; ideas are light-sources; discourse is a light medium."

Ontological metaphors treat activities, states, and events as entities and substances. "The mind is a machine" is one common metaphor, which contrasts with another "The mind is a fragile object." To say, "My algebra is rusty" is consistent with the former, whereas to say "His mind just snapped" is consistent with the latter. Structural metaphors structure one domain in terms of another; they may build on other metaphors.

Although the details of analysis may be unique to modern investigators, the observations concerning the role of metaphor in language structure are not. In an essay on natural language and the deaf, Roch-Ambroise Bébian (1827) argued the following:

Few people have an exact idea of the language of the deaf. Some assume that it is fingerspelling of words and sentences from spoken language; others recognize it as a genuine language, but think it is limited to the representation of concrete objects. In using it, will we constantly have to resort to metaphors that necessarily have the disadvantage of revealing the thought only through a partially transparent veil?

We shall not bother to combat this double error. Only the criticism concerning the need for metaphor warrants attention, but it is easy to demonstrate the contrary, that sign language has less need of metaphors than speech itself, for it is certain that all spoken languages contain not a single abstract word that did not originally designate a concrete object (Lane and Philip, 1984).

Bébian does not go on to document his claim. Nor will we be concerned here with which modality, speech or signing, has more or less need of metaphor. Rather we shall be concerned with the role of metaphor in the lexical construction of signs and how this compares to that identified for spoken languages.

The earliest work on sign morphology in modern times did not deal explicitly with metaphors, but rather with "sign families" (Frishberg and Gough 1973a; see Chapter 4). Although the notion of multimorphemic signs had not yet been formalized, Frishberg and Gough clearly intended to show morphological relatedness among groups of signs. Their families included signs related by motion similarities, by handshape similarities, by handshape changes during movement, and by location. They noted, for example, that the À handshape (fist with thumb extended) is used extensively (but not exclusively) in signs for negation and negative concepts: NOT, DENY, REFUSE, BLAME, ALCOHOLIC, SUFFER, STUPID. Another handshape observation was the use of the "open 8" (open hand, fingers spread, middle finger bent) in signs denoting emotions: EXCITE, DEPRESS, FEEL, LIKE, INTEREST(ING), PITY, SICK.

In perhaps the most extensive discussion to date of visual metaphor in sign language, Boyes-Braem (1981) argues for a lexical model with five stages:

1. Underlying concept

2. Visual metaphor

3. Morphophonemic-phonemic features of all parameters (location, orientation, handshape, movement, nonmanual components)

4. Underlying forms for each parameter

5. Surface forms

In support of her five stage model, she notes that the relationship between the underlying concept and the visual metaphor may take several forms: (1) the use of a part to stand for a whole (the use of the beak to stand for the concept "bird" as in the ASL sign BIRD) (2) the manner of manipulation of an object by the hand (HANDLE classifiers discussed in Chapter 4), (3) commonly made associations (the association of "cutting wool from sheep" for the ASL sign SHEEP which depicts cutting with scissors), and (4) one time associations (as in the creation of name signs for individuals). She views level 3 as the level where the aspects of the visual metaphor are associated with the formational features. The ASL sign FLOWER has the underlying visual metaphor "holding a small object to the nose for smelling." This metaphor is carried in part by the handshape which is specified as [+fingertip grasp] (this grasp is used only for small objects) and by the location at the side of the nose. At level 4, the various handshapes that are [+fingertip grasp] and that fit other specifications (such as the type of contact) are delineated, and only those that fit all requirements are available for actual use at the surface (level 5). In the case of FLOWER, 5 handshapes are possible at the surface; they are considered to be in free variation, unless dialect preferences intercede.

In her discussion, Boyes-Braem (1981) makes the following arguments: (1) the same underlying metaphor may be reflected by different handshapes on the surface, and (2) although several signs may have the same surface handshape, the fact that their underlying visual metaphors are different may be seen by the different allowable handshape variations that may occur. An example of the first argument is the base image of "whiskers," which surfaces in ASL with an F handshape but in Brazilian Sign Language with a babyo handshape (refer to Figure 7-1). Boyes-Braem documents her argument with examples of different lexical items for the same concepts in dialects of Swiss German Sign Language. The second argument, that the same surface handshape may represent different underlying metaphors, results from the interaction of the visual metaphors and the handshape, location, contact, and movement features. Boyes-Braem provides extensive argument for a system of handshape features that will allow this interaction and still predict the correct surface handshape variations. An example of the same handshape representing different base images from ASL is the S handshape, which can be said to represent a fist in HIT, a large spherical object in YEAR (earth going around the sun), and a HANDLE classifier in MOW-LAWN or SUITCASE.

One other recent discussion of metaphor in ASL is that contained in Gee and Kegl (1982) and, more recently, in Shepard-Kegl (1985). Gee and Kegl claim that the entire grammatical system of ASL is based on verbs of location/direction (the locative hypothesis in Shepard-Kegl, 1985), and that in order to be able to derive abstract verbs of emotion, perception, and cognition, ASL must have "metaphorical extension." They compare the formation of the sign IMPRESS ("His performance impressed me") with the ASL sign LETTER. The sign LETTER depicts a stamp being put on a flat surface by using a flat base hand (usually the left hand) into the palm of which the extended thumb of the moving A hand presses. They claim that in the sign LETTER, the flat surface represents an envelope, whereas in the sign IMPRESS, it represents a mental surface. The sign ENCOURAGE is formationally similar to the sign PUSH; they treat this as a metaphorical extension in which the hands orient "toward someone while pushing their spirit forward in a metaphorical sense." In the last set of examples they provide, "thought, sight, and sound are represented by the G classifier [long thin object]." That is, ASL uses the metaphor "lines of thought, lines of sight, and lines of sound." This accounts for the formation of the signs THINK, KNOW (plural lines of thought), LOOK-AT (lines from the eyes), and a parallel between "vehicle of perception" and the use of the VEHICLE classifier (the 3 hand) as part of the signs for PERCEIVE-BY-SIGHT and PERCEIVE-BY-EAR (recall the discussion of communication signs in Chapter 4).

Together, the sign families of Frishberg and Gough (1973a), the representation of visual metaphors by handshape features discussed by Boyes-Braem (1981), and the various examples of metaphorical extension by Gee and Kegl (1982) present a large group of interesting, but apparently unrelated examples. Using the framework provided by Lakoff and Johnson (1980), it can be seen that there is considerably more coherence to these examples than is immediately apparent.

Spatialization Metaphors

As might be predicted when discussing a language that is produced with movement in space, ASL uses space in a variety of ways to carry information, both literal and metaphorical. Some of these ways match spatializations that are present in spoken language. For example, Lakoff and Johnson's (1980) most basic metaphor system is what they call "orientational metaphors." Illustrated briefly were the use of "up-down" orientations for conscious/unconscious and health-life/sickness-death. Such up-down spatialization (Nagy, 1974) also includes happy/sad, having control or force/being subject to control or force, more/less, high status/low status (notice the terminology), good/bad, virtue/depravity, and rational/emotional. Other possible spatializations include in-out, front-back, on-off, deep-shallow, and central-peripheral. Hundreds of English expressions use nouns, verbs, and prepositions that reflect these orientations, including "*fall* ill," "*peak* of health," "dirty *low-down* no good," "wake *up*," "*drop* dead," "*climbing* the ladder of success," "six people work *under* her," "*high*-minded and *up*standing citizen," "*high* spirits," and "*under* hypnosis."

The fact that sign language utilizes these oppositions should come as no surprise; indeed, as Lakoff and Johnson (1980) argue, it is hard to imagine why a human language, signed or spoken, would not use these, given their universality in human experience. Consider the following lists:

"happy is up"
HAPPY
THRILL(ED)
EXCITE(D)
CHEERFUL
LAUGH

"sad is down"
SAD
CRY
DEPRESSED

"more is up"
RICH
EXPENSIVE

"less is down"
POOR
CHEAP

"positive value is up"
IMPORTANT
SUCCESS(FUL)
IMPROVE
BRILLIANT (mental)

"negative value is down"
LOUSY
FAIL
GET-WORSE
IGNORE
DON'T-CARE

In all of the previous examples, the direction of movement of the sign is upward for the "up" metaphors and downward for the "down" metaphors. Some pairs are actually formational opposites (IMPROVE and GET-WORSE differ only in direction of movement). Wilbur, Klima, and Bellugi (1983) argued that "in the lexicon, basic lexical entries do not make distinctive use of *directions* in space . . . except for paired opposites: IN/OUT, UP/DOWN, JOIN/QUIT, APPEAR/DISAPPEAR, IMPROVE/GET-WORSE." That is, distinctive use of direction of movement in the lexicon is reserved for meaningfully related pairs.

One interesting variation on the up/down spatialization is the pair GOOD/BAD, both of which move down from the chin. However, GOOD moves downward with the palm facing up, whereas BAD moves down with the palm facing down. Thus, it is not necessary for the up/down spatialization to be represented literally by movement up or down; orientation of the palm up or down is also acceptable.

Another pair of formational opposites, APPEAR and DISAPPEAR, are part of a general use of opposite movement as negation:

"up is unmarked"
APPEAR
WANT
HAVE
KNOW
LIKE
WITH

"down is negative"
DISAPPEAR
DON'T-WANT
DON'T-HAVE
DON'T-KNOW
DON'T-LIKE
WITHOUT

In these cases, the opposite movement for negation is always in the downward direction, while the unmarked form, or positive, does not necessarily have an upward movement (APPEAR moves up, but the others do not). This is accomplished because one component of the negative marking is movement *away* from wherever the sign is made (Gee & Kegl, 1982; Jones, 1978), and a downward component can be added to this "away" movement.

Another spatialization that is prominent in ASL is front/back. As has been noted, in ASL the future is forward and the past is behind. The dividing line is the signer's body. Signs that move forward for future include FUTURE, TOMORROW, NEXT-WEEK, NEXT-YEAR, SOON, POSTPONE ("put forward"), and BE-AHEAD-OF, and signs that move backward for past include PAST, YESTERDAY, LAST-WEEK, LAST-YEAR, LONG-TIME-AGO, ONCE-UPON-A-TIME, and RECENTLY. Some signs move from the back toward the front for continuity of time: HISTORY, GENERATION, SINCE (= FROM-THEN-UNTIL-NOW), and of course compounds built on these words (cf. Klima and Bellugi's discussion of the compound GENETIC-ENGINEERING, 1979)

English expressions such as "looking *forward* to next week's party" and "you can look *back* with pride at your accomplishments" show similar perspectives on future and past. H. Clark (1973) argues that time has properties that make one dimensional, linear terms appropriate, whereas two and three dimensional terms are not. That is, time can be treated as a point ("at that point in time"), or with positional or directional prepositions that deal with points (or intervals between points = lines). Thus, appropriate terms in English for time include "at" ("at three o'clock), "on" ("on time"), "in" ("in an hour"), "up to" ("up to an hour or more"), "from" ("from three to five p.m."), "between" ("between one and three") and "through" ("through next Tuesday"). Relational terms that do not presuppose more than one dimension can also be used: "front" and "back" ("move the meeting back an hour"), and the prepositions derived from them "before," "after," "ahead," "behind," "in front," "in back," and in special cases, "over" ("over the weekend").

Clark's (1973) observations that temporal terms in English are predominantly spatial metaphors have been extended to other domains besides time, most notably in Jackendoff (1983). Because any change can be viewed as going from one state to another, and "going" is a change from one *location* to another, states may be treated as though they were locations and changes may be treated as movement (the locative hypothesis in Shepard-Kegl, 1985). Thus, something that melts "goes" from solid to liquid, something that is given "goes" from one person to another, and so on. Similarly, something that stays does not go from one place to another. If John gives a book to Mary, the book goes from John to Mary, but if John merely has a book, the book remains with/at John. Some languages (cf. French) can code possession using the same preposition meaning "at"; "Le livre est à Jean," literally, 'the book is at Jean'. In a sentence used earlier in this section, the study of metaphor *left* literature and *came into* linguistics and psychology.

Things (events, states, activities, objects) that change are treated as *moving* and things that do not change are treated as *located* somewhere. (This fundamental split, dynamic versus static, mirrors the basic organization of ASL phonology, discussed in Chapter 3). Thus, in ASL, we can *see* the dynamic versus static nature of our conception of reality more directly than in spoken languages (Gee and Kegl, 1982; Jackendoff, 1983). This is part of what has been referred to as "iconicity."

Other spatializations that ASL can depict directly include parallel (parallel thinking = AGREE), opposite (DISAGREE, ARGUE, negatives discussed above), at (ARRIVE), on (sitting on the fence = UNDECIDED), in (put money in = SAVE and its related noun BANK), and the transfer of information from one place/person to another (to be discussed).

Ontological Metaphors — The Abstract as Concrete

Recall that in Lakoff and Johnson's framework, ontological metaphors treat activities, states, and events as entities and substances. They illustrated this type of metaphor with expressions using "the mind is a machine" and "the mind is a fragile object" metaphors. Activities, states, and events are abstract things that cannot be touched or held. Entities and substances are concrete things that can be touched or held. Nearly all the literature on metaphor and thought contains the observation that humans like/prefer/need to deal with intangible, abstract things in tangible, concrete ways. Viewing the mind alternately as a machine or as a fragile object allows different perspectives and comments about the mind to be expressed with reference to more familiar objects such as machines and breakable things.

ASL is able to express ontological metaphors with the help of classifiers. Recall the discussion of three different classifier types in Chapter 4. One type, the size-and-shape specifier (SASS), indicates information about the size and shape of an object. Another type, the semantic or abstract classifier, has a fixed shape and certain closely related objects associated with it (vehicles, for example). The third type, HANDLE classifiers, represents the object as it would be handled by a human. Each of these three types is available for expressing ontological metaphors in ASL, although the SASS and HANDLE classifiers are probably more common. The use of the semantic classifier for vehicle was mentioned earlier; Gee and Kegl (1982) noted its use in signs for visual and auditory perception. This use of the VEHICLE classifier is in keeping with expressions in English about metaphors themselves, such as "the meaning conveyed by the vehicle of the metaphor." In this case, the metaphor is a conveyance (vehicle) and the meaning is the thing conveyed. In the ASL example, information is conveyed into the eyes or ears by means of the vehicle of the fingers (literally for signing, figuratively for auditory perception).

Gee and Kegl (1982) interpret the fingers in these cases as lines of information, in which case the fingers are serving a double function, first as part of the VEHICLE classifier and second as SASSes representing lines ("long, thin things") of information themselves. Another ontological metaphor using SASS handshapes is "the mind is an expandable container." The sign CLEVER, for example, is made with the C handshape (the "container" handshape, cf. Wilbur et al., 1985) at the forehead. Presumably, this is a "full" container. Someone who suffers a momentary lapse in thought or an incomplete understanding of a topic may make the C handshape at the forehead and then collapse it, an "empty" container. Describing a situation in which thoughts come and go, one signer repeatedly collapsed and expanded the C handshape. One signer, when providing motherly advice on child development, told another signer that his daughter's mind would expand as she got older, using two C handshapes at the forehead which expanded and then increased the distance from each other, as one might describe a balloon being blown up. Another signer made up his own sign for "empty-headed," the left hand with a C handshape at the forehead (as for CLEVER) and the right hand making the movement used for NUDE/EMPTY (normally done on the back of the hand) with an open8 handshape inside the C handshape of the left hand. This invented sign contrasts with a frozen sign that means empty-headed, an O handshape at the forehead (meaning "zero/nothing in the head"). The frozen sign uses the head to mean the head/mind, a very direct and literal representation. But the invented sign uses the container classifier to metaphorically represent the head/mind, "the mind is a container."

With the mind as a container, things can be put into or taken out of it. The "things" are pieces of information, lines of information to be exact. The fingers serve as SASSes for lines of information, giving the basis for signs such as THINK, KNOW (plural lines of information), AGREE, DISAGREE, and ARGUE. The signs SEE and LOOK-AT made with the V handshape are perfectly suited to ASL on three counts: lines of information, the number two for two eyes, and the relationship between the V handshape used for them and for legs (STAND, WALK), leading to an ASL parallel to the English "the eyes are limbs," as in "keep an

eye on him" (Lakoff and Johnson, 1980). The v handshape in SEE and
LOOK-AT is reputed to have come from initialization of the old French
sign for "voir" meaning 'see'. Its fit with the above metaphors suggests one reason why it was adopted and kept (unlike others that
were modified).

The fingers serving as lines of information also appear in signs
that are not made in connection with the mind, but rather with communication in general. Some are made at the mouth, such as TELL,
ANSWER, and HEARING-PERSON (continuous line of information circling
out of the mouth). Others are involved with the hands, such as
FINGERSPELL (lines of information coming out continuously from
the hand), TO-USE-SIGN-LANGUAGE (alternating opening hands), and
COUNSEL (plural lines of information coming from the hand directed
toward someone). The sign for HEAR is made with a single line of information going into the ear. The Italian Sign Language sign for SPY
(remember, these are Western culture metaphors, according to Lakoff and Johnson, 1980, and will thus be found in other languages
besides English and ASL) is made with a fist at the mouth, all the
lines of information coming from the mouth covered up by the thumb
so that no one can see or hear them. The ASL sign for SECRET is similar except that the thumb covers the lips so that no lines of information can escape from them.

Taking these metaphors one step further, if the mind is a container and the fingers can represent lines of information, then communication is an entity that can be *handled.* In English, when we
understand someone, we can "grasp" or "catch" their meaning. In
ASL, the information can be held (here is where the HANDLE classifiers come in) and given or taken. The sign for INFORM takes information from the signer's mind (using the handshape for holding a flat
object, this being an alternate to the lines of information) and gives
it to the recipient by opening the hand (to make the lines of information visible or to present a flat surface from which information can
be obtained.) MEMORIZE takes lines of information into the mind,
where they are held (fist handshape). LEARN also takes information,
using the handshape for holding a flat object, and brings it to the
head. The sign for COPY also ends with the handshape for holding a
flat object, as does ACCEPT.

The ASL system, with mind as container, information as object
(whether line or flat), and the give/take transfer (from books to
minds, from one person to another) is an example of the "conduit"
metaphor elaborated in Reddy (1979), in which he suggested that
communication is talked about in English using the notions of the
mind as a container, ideas as objects, words as containers, and the
transfer of information through words as a conduit. People "take"

ideas (objects) from their minds (containers) and "put" their ideas into words (containers) to transfer them to others so that they can get out the meaning (remove the ideas from the words and put them into their own minds). The conduit may be written, spoken, or signed.

Structural Metaphors

The notion of a structural metaphor is to treat one concept, such as time, in terms of another, usually more tangible concept, such as money. The expression "time is money" implies that certain things that are true about money are also true about time, such as the fact that both can be saved, spent, wasted, counted, and limited. The expression "an argument is war" implies that in an argument, there will be a battle between two opposing sides, that there are tactics and strategies for winning, that there will eventually be a winner and a loser, and so on. In English, we talk about shooting holes in someone's argument, or blowing someone away, and other violent, warlike expressions. Lakoff and Johnson (1980) consider the differences in expressions when different metaphors are used for the same topic, such as "love is war" and "love is a mutual work of art."

Finding the structural metaphors in ASL is perhaps the hardest search. Giving a person the English equivalents and asking "how do you sign this?" will result in an ASL translation of an English expression, not the desired result. The means for expressing this type of metaphor are not as obvious as the preceding types, where there were clear correlations between spatializations, handshape types, and metaphorical concepts. Instead, internal patterns must be used as a guide.

Several times in the discussion, the expressions "understanding is seeing" and "understanding is grasping" have been mentioned. Many of the HANDLE expressions described above for communication and information are consistent with the "understanding is grasping" metaphor. One sign, GUESS, may be consistent with both metaphors, as the hands attempt to grasp something right in front of the eyes. The "understanding is seeing" metaphor leads to several related metaphors, such as "ideas are light sources" (so that they can be seen). This Western culture metaphor is pervasive; when Ford advertises that they "have a better idea", their lightbulb goes on. In cartoons for children, when a character gets an idea, the lightbulb goes on in the bubble. Someone who has lots of ideas has lots of light — is *brilliant*, in fact. In ASL, this same metaphor is used. The handshape and movement that is used for SHINY referring to a concrete object, like a new coat of paint on a car, is also used at the forehead for a sign that is interpreted into English as "brilliant." This is one illustration of a structural metaphor in ASL, the expression of information about understanding in terms of information about light.

There are many more metaphors in ASL than can be described here. The interested reader is referred to Boyes-Braem (1981) for one extensive discussion. It is important to emphasize that signers need not be aware at all of what these metaphors are, any more than speakers of English can explain why we say "wake *up*" or "*fall* asleep" One deaf consultant, when asked why certain signs were made the way they were, said "a long time ago, people decided how to make the signs; when we grew up, we just learned them that way." This same informant, when asked why the sign for BRILLIANT (in the mental sense) was made with the same handshape as the sign for SHINY/GLITTER, replied that a brilliant person had lots of ideas, which he signed by making the sign for "light-bulbs" on his head.

PRODUCTION AND PERCEPTION OF SIGNS

Many of the early linguistic and psycholinguistic studies of ASL were aimed at demonstrating that ASL was in fact a language in its own right. In the process of trying to make this point, psycholinguists were led into some of the less often studied aspects of language use. Thus, included in this section are aspects of pausing, rhythm, breathing, blinking, and the control of conversation. The information derived from these investigations supports the positions presented in Chapter 5 and 6 that there is structure to the ASL sentence, and that this structure affects aspects of the perception and production process. Without the benefit of a comprehensive grammatical description for ASL, psycholinguists began by observing measurable variables and then deriving syntactic information from their measurements. Word order was, of course, a prime target for investigation.

Using a memory paradigm, Hoemann and Florian (1976) found that random sequencing of signs produced less meaningful strings, as might be expected, based on the Chapter 6 discussion. Not only was meaningfulness reduced by random ordering, but apparently recall was also affected. This is in keeping with the findings of Miller and Isard (1963), who reported that, for English, random organization of words or correct organization but significant reduction in meaningfulness resulted in significantly poorer recall. Tweney and Heiman (1977), also using a memory paradigm, presented nonsense signs or a fingerspelled consonant-vowel-consonant (CVC) sequence embedded in either a grammatical sentence or a random string of signs. The number of nonsense signs and overall number of signs recalled were significantly greater in the grammatical strings than in the random strings. Such studies serve to demonstrate the role of grammatical structure in the processing of ASL and the similarity of sign language processing to spoken language processing.

Other studies, to be discussed, investigated particular consequences of ASL structure on processing.

Comparisons of Signing and Speaking

In a series of studies that investigated performance variables such as pausing, rate of signing, and breathing, Grosjean (1977, 1978; Grosjean and Lane, 1977) reported similarities and differences between the two language modes. Parallel to the studies of pausing and syntax in spoken languages (Grosjean and Deschamps, 1975), Grosjean and Lane (1977) found that the longest pauses in a signed story appeared at what might be considered the boundary between two sentences, that shorter pauses appeared between constituents that can be analyzed as parts of a conjoined sentence, and that the shortest pauses appeared between internal constituents of the sentence. Pauses that would not normally show up in conversational signing because of their brevity were elicited by asking signers to sign at half their normal rate and at a quarter of their normal rate. Grosjean and Collins (1978) reported that for English, pauses with durations of greater than 445 msec occurred at sentence boundaries; pauses between 245 and 445 msec occurred between conjoined sentences, between noun phrases and verb phrases, and between a complement and the following noun phrase; and pauses of less than 245 msec occurred within phrasal constituents. Grosjean and Lane's (1977) findings for ASL were that pauses between sentences had a mean of 229 msec, pauses between conjoined sentences had a mean of 134 msec, pauses between NP and VP had a mean of 106 msec, pauses within the NP had a mean of 6 msec, and pauses within the VP had a mean of 11 msec. These results are interpreted as clearly showing that sign sentences are organized hierarchically and that the signs are not strung together without internal constituents. This supports analyses such as Kegl's (1976b, 1977), Liddell's (1977, 1978, 1980), and Fischer's (1975) reviewed in Chapter 6 although it cannot be used to decide between conflicting claims about how the constituents are internally structured. Not specifically addressed in this study was an observation made by Grosjean (1979) that speakers when reading out loud tend to try and cut a sentence into two equal parts, possibly for rhythmic purposes, and that signers appeared to be doing some of the same (both signers and speakers are,

of course, constrained by the syntax of the sentence they are producing). This type of intonation and its interaction with that discussed
by Fischer (1975) and Liddell (1977) remains to be specifically
addressed.

The technique of asking signers to slow their rate of signing created some interesting questions. Grosjean (1977) investigated in detail the effects of rate change, again comparing signers to speakers.
If a speaker doubles his actual reading rate, he feels himself to have
increased by six times, whereas a listener perceives an increase of
three times (Lane and Grosjean, 1973). Thus, produced rates and
perceived rates differ in spoken language. Similarly, if a signer increases his signing rate by two, he perceives an increase by six,
whereas an observer (signer or nonsigner) perceives an increase by
three (Grosjean, 1977). However, unlike Lane and Grosjean (1973),
Grosjean (1977) found that when readers double their rate of reading, listeners perceive an increase by four. Regardless of which listener rate is used, the overall effect seems to be that judgments of
self-production of speech or signing rates are equivalent for speakers
and signers, but that judgments of perceived speech rates tend to be
overestimated more than perceived rates of signing. Grosjean suggested that the similarity in judgments on the part of the producers
(speaker or signer) may be attributable to similar muscle feedback
(despite the different articulation in the two modalities), whereas
the differences in the perceivers may be attributable to the different
perception systems in use, visual versus auditory.

Grosjean (1978) looked at the differences in how signers and
speakers were able to accomplish these changes in rate. Speakers
tend to change the amount of time they pause, whereas signers tend
to adjust the time they spend articulating. Grosjean showed that the
time spent articulating a sign is modified directly by changes in
movement as opposed to any other parameter (e.g., addition of extra
location, modification of handshape, etc.). If a signer does modify his
pause time, it generally affects both the number of pauses and the
length of the pause. On the other hand, speakers primarily alter the
number of pauses but not the pause durations, which have a minimum duration of the time needed for a breath. Interestingly, although speakers, because of the very nature of the speech process,
must breathe between words, primarily at syntactic breaks, signers
maintain normal breathing rhythm while signing, although breathing rate may be affected by the physical effort required to sign at, for
instance, three times the normal rate. Grosjean also found that signs
tend to be longer in sentence final position than within sentences,
and that the first occurrence of a sign within a single conversation is
longer than the second or subsequent occurrences of that same sign
(controlling for syntactic position).

One further aspect of speaking and signing rate is the comparison done by Bellugi and Fischer (1972) of the time needed to relate a story in both modalities. The same story produced in both modalities contained the same number of propositions, covered the same semantic ground, and took about the same amount of time to produce. However, the modality made a difference: 50 percent more spoken words than signs were needed (as a result of the differences in ASL and English syntax) but were nonetheless produced in the same amount of time, since spoken words take considerably less time to produce than signs. Although the duration of syllables in English and ASL are roughly comparable (Wilbur and Nolen, 1986), some signs will have additional syllables due to reduplication for inflection and affixation (e.g., plural). One implication of this study is that, at some level of processing, there is an optimum time or rate for transmission of information regardless of modality (supported by the similarity of syllable duration reported by Wilbur and Nolen, 1986). The finding that signed English sentences for this same story increased the story time (but not the number of propositions) by almost 50 percent can be interpreted as a potential problem for signed English usage, in terms of perception, production, and memory processing.

Pause duration may serve as a marker for sentence boundaries. Conversations, of course, must have beginnings and ends. Eye contact, among other variables, plays a significant role in the marking of conversational turns. A conversation cannot begin without direct eye contact between the signer and the receiver. During the conversation, the addressee must continue to watch the signer, but the signer need not maintain eye contact with the addressee. As in spoken conversation, the sender is free to look away, for purposes of organizing thought or to maintain the floor, but must check back with the addressee every so often to be certain that the addressee is following the conversation. A signer can ignore an interruption by not establishing eye contact with the person attempting to interrupt (Baker, 1976, 1977).

Covington (1973a, b) and Baker (1977) have reported on junctures that mark turns within the conversation. For example, Baker (1977) reported on several hand positions that are part of the regulators of turn-taking. When a signer is listening and not intending to take a turn, the hands remain at full extension. When a signer is preparing to sign, perhaps to interrupt or simply waiting for a turn but wanting the present signer to acknowledge that he is waiting, the hands assume half-rest position, generally at waist level and with increased body tension (possibly a slight lean forward). Hands higher than this are in quarter-rest position, a strong indication to the current signer to yield the floor. Of course, a signer can simply

begin to sign and hope that the other signer will yield the floor (doing this too forcefully or too often is as rude as it is in speech).
The floor is yielded by returning hands to full-rest position or maybe
half-rest as an indication of wanting the floor back as soon
as possible.

In a study of ASL discourse, Wilbur and Petitto (1981, 1983) investigated devices used to initiate, maintain, and terminate topics in
conversations. They noted that one frequent way to introduce a new
topic is to accompany the statement of the new topic with a head
nod. Head nods were also used to maintain topics that were already
established, as were lexical items such as RIGHT, SAME, WOW, and WELL.
Another device used to maintain topics is lexical copy, using one or
more of the signs that the conversational partner has just used.
Wilbur and Petitto argued that signers, like speakers, maintain
a conversational contract between them that keeps the flow of
topics going.

Baker and Padden (1978) investigated the blinking behavior of
deaf signers engaged in conversation. As Grosjean and Lane (1977)
indicated, speakers do not breathe in the middle of a spoken word
but signers may breathe anywhere they please. Baker and Padden
(1978) reported that speakers may blink anywhere they please
whereas signers do not blink in the middle of a sign. Signers appear
to blink at phrase boundaries, such as between subject and predicate, or setting off a direct object, or after a time indicator (e.g., YES-
TERDAY, TOMORROW, etc.). In conditional sentences, signers tend to blink
between the first and second clauses if the conditional is a statement
but not if it is a question. Finally, the addressee does not take his cue
of when to blink from the signer (as evidenced by signer blinks not
followed by addressee blinks, as well as addressee blinks that immediately precede signer blinks) but nonetheless blinks at grammatical boundaries, indicating that the addressee is anticipating when
these boundaries will occur. Baker and Padden (1978) suggested
that this may be an aid to the linguistic processing of incoming
information.

MEMORY FOR ASL

Studies of memory with hearing adults have indicated that
adults tend to make mistakes in recall based on the phonological
properties of the words they hear, particularly if the possibility of using semantic information has been eliminated by the task design.
Such studies have determined that several features in a sound seg-

ment are crucial to memory coding and recall, even when the material to be remembered is presented visually (e.g., printed word lists) (Conrad, 1962; Wickelgren, 1965). There is considerable evidence that memory for signs is affected by formational similarity of the signs. Lists of signs with formational similarities (such as the same handshape) are recalled more poorly than lists of signs with semantic similarities (such as color terms or names of animals or activities). Bellugi and Siple (1974) conducted a study to investigate memory for signs in deaf adults. They found that the deaf subjects' performance was similar to that of the hearing in that they made mistakes based on the formational characteristics of the signs themselves. For example, given the word "tea," a hearing person might mistakenly recall it as *key* because of the similar phonological properties. However, a deaf person might mistakenly recall the sign TEA as the sign VOTE, which differs from TEA only in motion. Bellugi and Siple (1974) and Bellugi, Klima, and Siple (1975) reported that mistakes were made according to handshape, place of formation, and motion (orientation and other features like contact were not investigated). Whether there exists a hierarchy of these features is an intriguing question. From the Bellugi memory studies and some acquisition studies (Kantor, 1977; Wilbur and Jones, 1974) it might be inferred that location would be best remembered, motion next, and handshape and orientation worst remembered, but no studies have explicitly tested this hypothesis.

In a direct test of the effects of formational similarity on memory for lists of signs, Mills and Weldon (1983) compared semantically similar signs with formationally similar signs and reported that, in all cases, the signs that were semantically similar were better remembered than those that were formationally similar. Fuller and Wilbur (in press) attempted to modify memory for lists of formationally similar signs by providing subjects with the metaphorical or iconic meanings associated with the signs used, such as "this handshape means holding something" for signs like MOW-LAWN or COPY. The meaning cues could have provided semantic coherence to the lists, given the design of the study, but they did not. Instead, memory for formationally similar lists with cues did not differ from memory for formationally similar lists without cues, and both were significantly worse than semantically similar lists, confirming the findings of Mills and Weldon (1983).

In Chapter 5, inflections that are added to signs, whether frozen or productive, were discussed. A study by Poizner, Newkirk, Bellugi, and Klima (1981) demonstrated that the inflections are in fact separable pieces in memory. Given lists of signs composed of verbs and inflections, signers frequently made mistakes and recalled the wrong verb with the wrong inflection. The authors noted two patterns of errors, (1) remembering the verbs in the right order but confusing the inflections, and (2) remembering the inflections in the right order but confusing the verbs. Given a list of signs containing the sequence TAKE-ADVANTAGE-OF-THEM (which has the plural suffix) and PAY-ME (which has first person singular object), the signer might recall TAKE-ADVANTAGE-OF-ME and PAY-THEM. A similar finding was reported by Hanson and Bellugi (1982), who found that sentence processing studies revealed that signers decompose signs into their verb and inflection parts and remember the meanings associated with each rather than the exact structure (thus, signers readily accepted paraphrases that preserved the meaning of the original while rejecting forms that had the same structure but different meanings). The separability of verb and inflection supports the analysis presented in Chapter 5 of inflections being morphologically added to signs.

Other studies with deaf subjects (Conrad, 1970, 1971, 1972, 1973; Conrad and Rush, 1965; Locke, 1970; Locke and Locke, 1971; Siple and Brewer, 1985) have investigated the roles of English phonemics, visual graphemes, and dactylic (fingerspelling) coding in memory processing but have not specifically attended to the possible role of sign features. These studies were primarily concerned with how the deaf person as a bilingual would handle memory processing for English. This question still remains unanswered and is of primary concern for the development of appropriate educational technology, as well as for the theoretical implications for memory (and possibly cerebral) organization. Wilbur (1976) suggested that, as hearing people seem to convert visually presented written material into its corresponding phonological representation for coding and storage, perhaps deaf people who know ASL utilize it for the coding and recall of written English, converting the English to a sign representation much as a compound bilingual might do. (This hypothesis would still presume the absence of the possibility of using a semantic representation strategy, as one would normally do in more real world situations, e.g., a conversation.) Some support for this hypothesis comes from a study done by Odom, Blanton, and McIntyre (1970). They compared recall accuracy of deaf signers and hearing nonsigners on two lists of English words — those for which there exists an appropriate ASL equivalent and those for which there is no exact convenient simple sign, thus necessitating fingerspelling. The results were as hypothesized: the deaf subjects performed significantly better on the list of signable words; the hearing subjects, of course, showed no difference between the two lists. Also interesting was the fact that the performance of the deaf subjects on the list of signable words was significantly superior to the performance of the hearing subjects on both lists. In a study with a similar design, Bonvillian (1983) found that for deaf subjects, both the availability of a sign language equivalent and a high imagery value assisted word recall. For hearing subjects, high imagery value improved recall but availability of sign equivalent (of which the hearing subjects would have had no knowledge) had no effect. Unlike Odom and colleagues (1970), Bonvillian found that the hearing subjects recalled significantly more words than the deaf subjects in both immediate and delayed recall conditions. In addition, Bonvillian found that deaf subjects who had deaf parents (half of his deaf sample) recalled significantly more than the deaf subjects who had hearing parents in the immediate recall condition. A similar pattern was found for the delayed recall condition, although the difference was not significant.

Shand (1982) tested speech-based and sign-based coding for English words. As expected, he found that when the English words in a list had signs that were formationally similar, the recall was poorer than when the English words had signs that were not similar in formation. This is consistent with the findings of sign-based coding in Odom and colleagues (1970). Significantly, Shand did not find evidence for phonetic coding in the deaf subjects, as lists of phonetically similar words were *not* recalled more poorly than lists of phonetically dissimilar words, supporting the notion that subjects were not using speech-based coding. Pursuing this line of investigation, Hanson (1982) reported that in fact deaf subjects did use speech-based coding, specifically for ordered recall rather than for free recall (that is, when the order of recall of the items is important for the task as opposed to when it is not). Furthermore, she reported that the greater the reliance on speech-coding, the more accurate the recall was.

Further research is obviously needed here also. One aspect that must constantly be kept in mind is the interaction of the bilingual nature of many deaf people with the task requirements. Harlan Lane (personal communication) has emphasized the need to avoid creating a "set" for English processing, perhaps by requiring English output, or by giving instructions in English, or by inviting English processing by presenting obviously rhyming English words. Great care must be taken to avoid contaminating memory study results, particularly when potential cross-lingual processing is the desired target of investigation.

Another factor that must be kept in mind is that not all deaf signers learn to sign from birth; the age of acquisition and the number of years of experience with signing are both potential concerns when studying memory. In a series of papers, Mayberry has investigated the effects of the number of years of experience that a person has with signing and the age of acquisition of signing on sign processing in sentences and memory. Mayberry and Fischer (1985) reported that a signer's performance on sentence recall and shadowing tasks was directly related to the number of years of experience a signer has with signing (from 2 to 20 years). Mayberry and Tuchman (1985) and Mayberry and Eichen (1985) both report that truly proficient signers (one group learned to sign before age 5, the other group learned to sign between 5 and 8) discard language form after they process it (as suggested previously by Hanson and Bellugi, 1982). Thus, in a memory task containing several pointing signs per sentence, proficient signers actually produced *fewer* points in their recall than less proficient signers, presumably because the proficient signers interpreted the meaning of the sentences and then produced an equivalent ASL version, which may have contained an inflected verb rather than individual pointing signs. The less proficient signers relied more heavily on the surface coding of the sentences, and were thus more likely to reproduce the stimulus sentence with separate pointing signs. In general, these and other studies show that even with 20 or 30 years of experience of signing, the age of acquisition plays an important role in performance on memory and sentence processing for ASL. In particular, people who learned signing before the age of 5 can be distinguished from those who learned between 5 and 8, who in turn can be distinguished from adolescent and adult learners (see also Newport, 1986).

CEREBRAL LATERALIZATION AND APHASIA

Research from neuropathology and neuropsychology studies has documented an apparent separation of specialization of the cerebral hemispheres for linguistic or nonlinguistic processing. These reports include the disruption of language and other functions (orienting oneself in space, etc.) from brain damage as well as controlled experimentation on dichotic and visual half-field tasks with normal hearing adults. From these studies, one can infer that in the majority of right-handed hearing adults, the left hemisphere seems to be specialized for language processing and other types of temporal sequencing and analytic tasks, whereas the right hemisphere seems to be more involved in holistic visual-spatial tasks (this statement is greatly simplified, but suffices for purposes at present).

Because of this apparent hemispheric dichotomy, the relationship between cerebral dominance and sign language has recently commanded greater attention. The central issue of concern is how the brain would treat a language that is visual/spatial in modality. The left hemisphere might be supposed to specialize for ASL because it is a language, or the right hemisphere might be supposed to specialize for ASL because it is visual/spatial. It might also be supposed that determining the answer to this question should be an easy matter. Recent literature (reviewed in both Poizner and Lane, 1977, and Neville and Bellugi 1978) and a caveat from Obler (1980) reveal why this is not so.

Empirical Investigations

As background for the methodology of a study by McKeever, Hoemann, Florian, and Van Deventer (1976), consider how a standard dichotic listening test is conducted with hearing adults. Two messages are presented simultaneously through earphones to the left and right ears of the listener. The listener is required to report what he heard. The accuracy of report for each ear, as well as the order of report, the latency or response time of report, and in some cases the evoked electrical potential in each hemisphere, may be of relevance in determining the lateralization or dominance of the listener. In most cases, material presented to the right ear (left hemisphere) is reported better (faster, more accurately, with higher evoked potential and quicker peaking of the electric signal) than that presented to the left ear (right hemisphere) when the material is linguistic in nature; this is possibly reversed for nonlinguistic material. To translate this task for deaf people and for ASL is complicated by two major factors: (1) the eyes are not connected to the brain in the same way that the ears are (each ear "connects" primarily to the opposite hemisphere, and each eye is "connected" equally to both hemispheres, thus requiring a division of each eye's field of sight into hemifields, one connected to the ipsilateral hemisphere, the other connected to the contralateral hemisphere), and (2) ASL moves in space as well as in time, thereby rendering traditional tachistoscopic presentation either difficult or unsuitable. To avoid this latter difficulty, McKeever and colleagues (and several of the next studies also) used only line drawings of ASL signs, line drawings of manual alphabet handshapes, and English letters and words. Material was presented appropriately to the visual hemifields. Hearing subjects showed significant left hemispheric advantage to two of the three tasks involving English words or letters, but the deaf subjects showed left hemispheric advantage in only one of the tasks involving English stimuli. On the other two English tasks, they showed no hemispheric difference; however both the nonhearing and the hearing subjects showed right hemispheric advantages for the manual alphabet handshapes and the ASL signs. Poizner and Lane (1977) indicate that this study contains several methodological problems, among which are the failure to present nonlinguistic materials to determine what, if any, lateralization exists (needed to compare with linguistic results), the fact that the hearing and deaf subjects used different response modes, making their results not directly comparable, and most importantly, the data analysis which pooled the high recognition scores for the manual alphabet tasks with the comparably lower scores for the ASL tasks, thus skewing the analysis toward the manual alphabet stimuli.

In their initial study, Manning, Goble, Markman, and LaBreche (1977) presented English words and line drawings, but also included random geometrical shapes (presumably right hemispheric) to deaf subjects and the words and geometric shapes to the hearing subjects. As expected, the hearing subjects displayed a significant left hemispheric advantage for the English words; the deaf subjects showed only a trend in that direction. For the remaining conditions (signs and geometric shapes for the deaf, shapes for the hearing) no hemispheric differences were recorded.

A second study by Manning and colleagues presented photographs of signs, signs and their corresponding English translation together, and English words alone to deaf subjects and English words alone to the hearing subjects. Unlike their initial study, in this one the response modes for both groups of subjects were the same, with the subjects required to indicate the appropriate picture on a response board. Again, as expected, the hearing subjects showed a significant left hemispheric advantage for the English words, whereas the deaf subjects showed a trend toward left advantage for the words alone and a trend toward right advantage for the signs alone. The combined sign and English word stimuli revealed little or no hemispheric differences.

Among the methodological problems in the Manning and colleagues study discussed by Poizner and Lane (1977) are the lack of clear indication of subjects' knowledge and fluency of ASL, a definite concern of cerebral dominance studies with any language (Obler, 1980), and the fact that some signs used were not bilaterally symmetric (two-handed signs that have the same handshape and the same or mirror image movement are bilaterally symmetrical around the axis from head to foot down the center of the front of the body, whereas all one-handed signs, and two-handed signs where only one hand moves, are not bilaterally symmetric). This latter factor creates difficulty with respect to visual acuity in terms of the stimuli distance from the fixation point (cf. Siple, 1973).

Phippard's (1977) study included two groups of deaf subjects, one group of orally trained deaf students, the other group trained in both oral and manual communication. English letters, variously oriented lines, and faces were presented to the hearing controls; English letters and lines were presented to the orally trained deaf; English letters, lines, manual alphabet handshapes, and faces were presented to the deaf subjects with combined manual and oral communication. The hearing subjects performed as expected, with left hemispheric advantage for the English letters and right hemispheric advantage for the lines and faces. The orally trained deaf adults showed right hemispheric advantages for both the English letters and the lines, whereas the subjects with familiarity in manual communication showed no visual field preferences for the four stimuli types. Poizner and Lane (1977) suggested that interpretation problems for lateralization of ASL were confounded again by lack of indication of knowledge of ASL as a native language, and also by the presentation of manual alphabet handshapes but no signs.

Lubert's (1975) study is similar in nature to the preceding studies, in that materials were presented tachistoscopically with English letters, photographs of ASL signs that did not require movement to be identified, photographs of manual alphabet handshapes, and a dot enumeration task. Unlike the previous studies, the hearing subjects did not show the expected left hemispheric advantage for the English letters, thereby complicating the interpretation of all the other results. Both deaf and hearing subjects showed right hemispheric advantage to the photographs of ASL signs, and no preferences for the dots or the manual handshapes.

Neville and Bellugi (1978) presented to deaf subjects line drawings of a person making signs, 22 of which were bilaterally symmetrical and 20 of which were not (these latter were made on the face, using the right hand for presentation in the right visual field and the left hand for the left visual field). In addition, a dot localization task was used for deaf and hearing subjects (a dot was presented in one of 20 possible positions in a rectangle, and subjects were required to indicate on a response grid where the dot had been). Subjects were tested in both unilateral and bilateral presentation conditions, although hearing subjects found bilateral presentation of the dot localization condition too difficult for it to be continued.

No difference was found in the deaf subjects' performance on the symmetrical and asymmetrical signs, and they were therefore collapsed, yielding a left hemispheric advantage for the unilateral presentation but no differences for the bilateral presentations. Similarly, the deaf subjects showed left hemispheric advantage for the dot localization task when presented unilaterally, but no differences when presented bilaterally. As expected, the hearing subjects showed right hemispheric advantages for the dot localization task.

Neville and Bellugi's discussion of these results adds an interesting dimension to the original alternatives presented in the introduction to this section. First, the fact that there is hemispheric preference for unilateral presentation but not bilateral presentation seems to be partially explicable by a strategy adopted by the deaf subjects to handle the task requirements, namely, to focus their attention (but not their eye gaze) on one visual field for several items, then switch back, giving a net effect of no preference. Second, the left hemispheric advantage for signs is an indication of cerebral lateralization for language developing independently from language modality. However, they interpret the left hemispheric advantage for the dot localization task as evidence that because the language modality is visual/spatial, and because the left hemisphere is handling the language, it is also handling the visual/ spatial components which would be right hemispherically lateralized in the person who learns a spoken language. They suggest that this is analogous to the findings that hearing people show left hemispheric advantage for judgments of temporally sequenced nonlinguistic material, presumably because temporal processing is a major function of the left hemisphere (participating, for example, in processing fine distinctions in speech perception).

Poizner and Lane (1977) tachistoscopically presented adult deaf native signers and hearing nonsigners with photographs of the ASL numbers SIX, SEVEN, EIGHT, and NINE (none of which requires movement); photographs of nonoccurring handshapes; Arabic numbers 6, 7, 8, and 9 in print; and four randomly shaped geometric forms. For the hearing subjects, a left hemispheric preference was found for the Arabic digits and a right hemispheric advantage for the ASL signed numbers and the non-ASL handshapes. The deaf subjects showed a right hemispheric advantage for the ASL signed numbers and the non-ASL handshapes. Neither group showed hemispheric advantage for the randomly shaped geometric forms.

Poizner and Lane argued that the right hemispheric advantage arose from processing the "complex spatial properties of the static signs." They suggested that their results are incompatible with theories that assign language to the left hemisphere and visual/spatial processing to the right. They also suggested, but did not discuss, the possibility that ASL may be bilaterally processed. They suggested that their results indicate that language processing of ASL "engages" the left hemisphere, and that the visual/spatial processing of ASL "engages" the right hemisphere, and that the visual/spatial processing in the right hemisphere predominates.

In reviewing the literature, Poizner and Lane (1977) put forth as their major criticism the fact that all previous studies were performed with statically presented signs and that one cannot really know how processing of moving language is done until a more real world experimental condition is constructed. Poizner, Battison, and Lane (1978) presented three types of stimuli — English words, static signs, and signs portrayed with movement — to deaf native signers. Hearing controls viewed only the English words. For the moving presentation, three frames displayed the beginning, middle, and end points of the sign for a total exposure of time of 167 msec: for the static signs, the total exposure time was also 167 msec and consisted of three identical frames of the same sign. As expected, the hearing subjects showed a left hemispheric advantage to the English words. The deaf subjects also showed a left hemispheric advantage to the English words, but a right hemispheric advantage to the static signs. Most importantly, the deaf subjects showed no hemispheric advantage for the moving signs. Poizner and colleagues interpreted this as possible evidence that ASL requires more bilateral participation than spoken English. However, this interpretation may require further modification in light of the spoken language results reported by Obler (1980).

A Caveat on Interpretation

Obler's (1980) investigation is not a study of cerebral dominance in sign language users, nor is it concerned with deaf subjects at all. Instead it is concerned with the development of cerebral dominance in bilingual hearing adults, with the factors that can affect how this dominance is established, and is thus directly relevant to the interpretation of the results of the preceding experiments. Obler indicates that a review of the experimental and aphasiological literature reveals a generally greater right hemispheric participation (or less pronounced left lateralization) in bilinguals than in monolinguals. She also indicates that the development of dominance may be influenced by such factors as "language-specific effects" (e.g., direction of reading scan, such as right-to-left for Hebrew versus left-to-right for English), cognitive strategies used in teaching the second language (so-called deductive teaching where traditional drilling is used versus inductive teaching where conversational approaches are used).

All of these may be relevant to the deaf signer even if native, since no deaf adults in the United States have escaped some exposure to the second language teaching of English. They are therefore to some degree (some obviously more than others) bilinguals, and thus the possibility of a greater right hemispheric contribution to the processing of ASL regardless of its visual/spatial properties cannot be dismissed out of hand. This does not mean that ASL will be "in" the right hemisphere or that the left hemisphere is not involved, only that any bilingual situation seems to be confounded by a greater general right hemispheric participation.

Insights from Aphasia in Deaf Signers

Interest in the effects of aphasia on deaf people's signing, fingerspelling, spoken English, and written English goes back to the 1970s (Battison, 1971; Battison and Markowicz, 1974; Battison and Padden, 1974; Chinchor, 1977), but has only recently received systematic and extensive attention. One result of this attention is additional support for the previous findings, namely, that hearing and speech are not necessary for lateralization, as lesion sites in different hemispheres produce different types of linguistic and nonlinguistic impairments (Klima, Bellugi, and Poizner, 1985; Poizner, Klima, and Bellugi, in press).

A second result is the finding that damage to the brain may differentially affect linguistic and nonlinguistic visual-spatial tasks. In general, left-hemisphere damaged deaf signers perform similarly to left-hemisphere damaged hearing patients on tasks that are spatial but nonlinguistic in nature (Poizner, Kaplan, Bellugi, and Padden, 1984). Such tasks include the WAIS block design (where patients have to assemble a group of blocks to match the design of a model), drawing tasks (with and without a model), tests of unilateral vision, facial recognition, judgment of line orientation (choosing the one that matches the orientation of the model), and dot localization (pointing to the location in a response display to indicate where on the screen a dot was seen). The patients with left-hemisphere damage were able to process the spatial relations in an appropriate manner (reflecting an intact right hemisphere), as opposed to the right-hemisphere damaged signers who displayed substantial visual-spatial difficulty (as would be predicted on the basis of right-hemisphere damaged hearing patients).

On linguistic tasks, the left-hemisphere damaged deaf signers all showed impairments, but of different types. One patient showed agrammatic signing similar to Broca's aphasia in hearing patients.

Syntactic and morphological markings on signs were absent and the signing was reduced to primarily referential signs (e.g., nouns, pointing). Another left-hemisphere damaged patient showed lexical difficulties within otherwise fluent signing; lexical difficulties included handshape, movement, and location substitutions. Yet another left-hemisphere damaged deaf signer displayed extensive grammatical impairment. Inflections were frequently confused, and occasionally combinations of sign and inflection were produced that were ungrammatical (not possible combinations in ASL). This same patient also showed extensive difficulty with the use of space for syntactic purposes (verb agreement, setting up spatial locations for later reference to nouns), even though no significant impairment in spatial ability was apparent on the nonlinguistic visual-spatial tasks (Bellugi, Poizner, and Klima, 1983). Such findings provide additional support for the treatment of spatial processes in ASL as specific parts of the language itself, and not as general spatial abilities that are available to both signers and nonsigners. General spatial abilities may remain intact while specifically linguistic abilities, required for the grammar of ASL, may be impaired by aphasia.

SUMMARY

This chapter has dealt with a variety of ways in which the processing of ASL grammar may be viewed as distinct from general abilities available to signers and nonsigners alike. Beginning with the observation that even though signers and nonsigners share Western culture metaphors that are reflected in sign formation, only signers know what a sign means (most signs are opaque to nonsigners, whereas some are translucent). Furthermore, the formation of a particular sign cannot be predicted even if the sign is iconic (recall the different signs for "tree" in ASL, Chinese Sign Language, and Danish Sign Language).

Production of signing reflects modality differences: signers breathe and blink differently than speakers during linguistic activity. Memory, on the other hand, functions similarly in both modalities, with formational similarity causing interference in recall of lists. Memory studies also support the analysis of complex signs, with inflections as separable pieces that are added to the basic form. Age of acquisition and number of years of experience with signing affect the performance of signers on memory and sentence processing tasks; these findings have considerable importance for educational decisions about when to start signing with deaf children.

Finally, lateralization studies and difficulties resulting from aphasia indicate that ASL is lateralized in ways that are similar to spoken language and that the use of space for linguistic purposes is lateralized separately from the use of space for nonlinguistic functions.

CHAPTER 8

Sign Language Acquisition

THE ACQUISITION OF ASL COMPARED
TO SPOKEN ENGLISH

Studies of the acquisition of ASL (Ashbrook, 1977; Bellugi and Klima, 1972; Boyes-Braem, 1973; Hoffmeister, 1977, 1978; Kantor, 1977; Lacy, 1972a, b; McIntire, 1974, 1977; Wilbur and Jones, 1974) indicate that children learning ASL pass through developmental stages similar to those reported for children learning spoken languages. For example, Ashbrook (1977), Bellugi and Klima (1972), and Hoffmeister (1977) report that the full range of semantic relations found in children learning English (Bloom, 1970) is expressed by children in the early stages of ASL acquisition. Wilbur and Jones (1974) report similar findings for hearing children of deaf parents who are learning both ASL and English.

It seems that a deaf child's first sign may emerge two to three months earlier than a hearing child's first spoken word (Boyes-Braem, 1973; McIntire, 1974; Wilbur and Jones, 1974). Similarly, in hearing children of deaf parents, the child's first sign may emerge several months before the same child's first spoken words (Wilbur and Jones, 1974). In addition, the child's spoken vocabulary complements his sign vocabulary, with only a small overlap of words that are spoken and signed (Wilbur and Jones, 1974). This indicates that the child is not simply learning spoken words to correspond to signs already known, nor signs to correspond to spoken words already known, at least not in the initial stages (the opportunity for differential usage of signs and speech is probably substantially involved in this difference). (For other studies of hearing children of deaf parents, which are not specifically sign studies but both sign and speech, see Bard and Sachs, 1977; Jackson, 1984; Jones, 1976; Mayberry, 1976b; Sachs and Johnson, 1976; Todd, 1972, 1975; for studies of invented home-signs of deaf children with hearing parents, see Goldin-Meadow, 1975; Goldin-Meadow and Feldman, 1975; Goldin-Meadow and Mylander, 1984).

One further comparison that has been made is that of vocabulary size. McIntire (1974) reports a vocabulary of about 20 signs at age 10 months, the age at which a hearing child is likely to produce his first spoken word. McIntire also reports two-sign utterances at 10 months (two spoken word utterances generally begin at about 18 months) and three-sign utterances at 18 months.

The accelerated rate of development, both in terms of onset and number of vocabulary items at given ages, is supported in studies of 13 children reported by Bonvillian and his colleagues (Bonvillian, Orlansky, and Novack, 1983; Bonvillian, Orlansky, Novack, Folven, and Holley-Wilcox, 1985; Orlansky and Bonvillian, 1985). Bonvillian and colleagues (1985) do caution that there is wide variation in the rate of development over the first two years among the different children that they are studying. They also note that the accelerated development is established for production but that no information is available on the development of comprehension.

These comparisons of the "first" sign to the "first" spoken word must be considered with caution. There is, of course, considerable difficulty in determining when a child produces his first spoken word, because what may be intelligible to parents who are with the child constantly may not be intelligible to an outside observer. Another problem is that a deaf child learning to sign is often credited for many of his gestures as "baby signs" and for his pointing behavior, whereas a hearing child is only given credit for his spoken items.

If a hearing child says "kitty" (even if it is only partially intelligible) and points in the direction of a cat, only one word is counted. However, if the signing child makes the sign for CAT and points to the cat (either simultaneously or sequentially), two signs will be counted. Although there are perfectly legitimate reasons for counting pointing as part of ASL structure at the adult level, it is not clear that a young deaf child's early pointing can be separated from a young hearing child's early pointing. Although there may be other gestures that are common to children that may also be treated as "baby signs" (Petitto, 1986), pointing seems to be the major concern because of its frequency. There have been several studies that have dealt directly with the acquisition of pointing; these will be discussed in a later section.

The previous comparisons should be approached with caution for another reason: the number of children studied to date is extremely small. Considerably more documentation is needed for all of these comparisons, but should the differences noted above be confirmed, the earlier emergence of signs is of considerable interest. It is possible that the earlier emergence and growth of signs is attributable to greater control of the hand muscles as compared to the oral muscles (Bonvillian, Orlansky, and Novack, 1983).

DETAILS OF SIGN LANGUAGE ACQUISITION

Phonological Acquisition

The study of the acquisition of phonology in ASL has been limited primarily to the acquisition of handshape. Boyes-Braem (1973) presented a model of handshape complexity based on anatomical considerations of the hands and their motor development sequence. Within this model, A is considered the unmarked handshape, and the others are described in terms of the addition of features. Thus, s represents the addition of "opposition of the thumb," 5 is the addition of "extension away from the initial axis of one or more digits," K illustrates the addition of "contact of the knuckle with the thumb," and so on. She also provided a number of secondary factors that may be involved: pantomime, anticipation and retention of adjacent handshapes, preference for fingertip contact, nature of the feedback, and nature of the movement of the sign.

McIntire (1974, 1977) modified the Boyes-Braem model, eliminating the distinctions that seem irrelevant to early development (such as the distinction between A and s). She reported four stages of handshape development which are affected by (1) opposition of the thumb, (2) extension of one or more fingers, and (3) contact of a finger with the thumb. In the first stage, only one of the handshapes requires a finger to make contact with the thumb. At this initial stage, the child can produce the following handshapes: 5, s, L, A, G, C, and baby O, in which an O handshape is made with only the thumb and index finger rather than with all the fingers. The second, third, and fourth stages include handshapes that involve touching a finger to the thumb, or more than one of the factors previously mentioned. Stage 2 includes B, F, and adult O. Stage 3 includes I, Y, D, P, 3, V, H, and W, some of which include extension of the weaker fingers (ring finger and pinkie). The fourth stage includes 8, 7, X, R, T, M, N, and E, some of which involve crossing fingers.

Initial analyses of the acquisition of phonology in spoken languages focused on the sequence of acquisition of segments (cf. Jakobson, 1968), similar in many respects to McIntire and Boyes-Braem. Further investigation (Moskowitz, 1970) indicated a crucial interaction between word position and order of acquisition. Thus, Moskowitz found that the word initial position tended to be more stable for consonant pronunciation than either medial or final position. This interaction was also found at the distinctive feature level — when the child learned a distinction, for example, voiced/voiceless, that distinction may have appeared in initial position, but not in similar segments that occurred in final position (i.e., the child may be able to correctly pronounce "pill" and "bill" but not "cup" and "cub"). The interaction of context in the acquisition of segments has been pursued in other studies of spoken phonological development (Ingram, 1974, 1976; Menn, 1976; Smith, 1973). The dominance of initial position does not hold up across children; instead, individual strategies seem to characterize different children. In addition to the importance of context, these studies also emphasize the relevance of function. Smith (1973) reported the child's ability to pronounce [v] perfectly in the English word "very," but at the same time, the child failed to produce it in the remaining words that should have it. Thus, other words that begin with [v] in the adult form were pronounced with [w], [β] or [v] in free variation (not consistently one or the other). Smith emphasized that [v] does not function in the child's system in the same way that it does in the adult's despite its apparently correct articulation in the one word in which it consistently appears. For spoken segment acquisition, it has become necessary to distinguish between (1) discriminating sounds perceptually, (2) pronouncing sounds correctly, and (3) using sounds appropriately.

These distinctions are undoubtedly relevant to the study of manual language. We might expect to find modification of a handshape depending on the environment in which it occurs (type of motion, orientation, location). For example, a child who can produce the 3 handshape for the number 3 might not be able to produce that same handshape in the sign for DEVIL, which requires thumbtip contact and bending of the fingers. Thus, McIntire's stages are relevant primarily to the acquisition of handshapes within single signs, usually simple lexical items, although an interaction in complex forms does occur (to be discussed).

The previous studies dealt primarily with handshape development. What little information is known about acquisition of location and movement comes from a study of 13 children of deaf parents (12 hearing and 1 deaf), with 10 of them first observed when they were under the age of one year (Bonvillian, et al., 1985). The frequency of different locations used by the children was significantly correlated with the frequency of use in their parents' signing. The children made many errors in locational usage, including greater difficulties with elbow locations, pronated wrist, face or whole head, and the forehead. Similarly, the frequency of usage of different movements by the children was highly correlated with that of their parents, and many errors were apparent. Many movements were simply omitted in the children's productions, and certain favorites, such as up-and-down movement, were inappropriately substituted for the correct movement. The children had particular difficulty with handshape changes, such as bending or extending fingers, or opening and closing handshapes. Bonvillian and colleagues provide information on the relative frequencies of various handshapes, locations, and movements in children's signing; information such as this has proved useful in the past for educators who are concerned with using signs with hearing people who need alternative or augmentative communication systems and who may have physical difficulty producing signs (see Chapter 12).

Morphological and Syntactic Acquisition

Studies of morphological and syntactic acquisition, like those of phonological acquisition, are few in number. Many of them focus on the complexity of what the child has to learn, as well as on the role that iconicity might play in sign language acquisition.

Negation

Lacy (1972a, b) and Ellenberger, Moores, and Hoffmeister (1975) investigated the beginning stages of acquisition of negation by deaf children of deaf parents. Lacy (1972b) reported from his longitudinal investigation that the earliest forms of negation were #NO (a sign derived from the fingerspelled n-o) and the negative headshake (which is more frequent). The negative headshake could occur either in linear order with manual signs, or simultaneously with a sign or sign sequence. In a later stage, the use of #NO decreased, and the two signs NOT and CAN'T (not a contraction of CAN NOT) were used in sentences. As in the acquisition of spoken English, the form for "can't" was acquired before "can." These developmental stages parallel those reported by Bellugi (1967) in her study of the acquisition of negation by hearing children learning English. Bellugi (1967) reported that children tend to use "can't" and "don't" before they use any other auxiliaries, even "can" and "do." Early negation tends to be outside the sentence, in the form of "no." Later negatives appear inside the sentence, before the verb.

Classifiers

Kantor (1980) investigated the acquisition of classifiers in young deaf children. The description of classifiers described in Kegl and Wilbur (1976) and investigated in Wilbur, Bernstein, and Kantor (1985) was treated as the form to be learned. Within this model of classifiers, classifier signs are linguistically complex, requiring syntactic, semantic, and phonological information for appropriate choice and function. If they are linguistically complex, and if there is any relationship between linguistic complexity and ease/order/age of acquisition, then one might expect that classifiers would take longer than other signs for deaf children to learn, although this relationship is not necessarily so direct (Wilbur, 1981). They may also require different strategies because of the interaction of phonological, syntactic, and semantic components for their use.

Kantor conducted a cross-sectional study, using nine children, ages 3 to 11 years. All children were congenitally, profoundly deaf with deaf parents. They were presented with a story specifically designed for elicitation of classifiers, signed by a native user of ASL on videotape, after which they were asked to retell and discuss the story with a deaf houseparent. This interaction was videotaped for later analysis. The children also were given imitation and comprehension tasks to provide a complete picture of their abilities.

The results of this investigation can be more easily discussed in light of a model of classifier usage modified from a more general model of development suggested by M. Bernstein (cited in Kantor, 1980). "The use of a classifier in any utterance can be illustrated in the following way":

1) There is a proposition to express.
2) If the environment requires a classifier, substitute one and attach it to the verb.

Does require substitution   Does not require substitution

Use citation form

3) What is the appropriate form?
   a) semantically (What are the properties of the noun; i.e., is it taller than it is wide, etc.?)
   b) phonologically (What are the parameters of the actual sign?)
   c) syntactically (Where does it move; What are the agreement points?)

The first step in classifier usage, then, is the syntactic recognition that one is needed. Kantor found that even the youngest children in the study were making this recognition, and only one or two real violations of the environments for classifier usage occurred. If a classifier was not actually used, then either (1) deletion occurred such that no form was used, or (2) the citation form of the verb was used without the element that would have required the classifier (e.g., without verb agreement or without the directional preposition, this information simply being omitted). If a classifier did occur, it was likely that other modifications would occur.

The remaining steps that are required for total mastery of the classifier system do not come until much later, in the sense that proper substitution of a classifier in one environment did not ensure that the same classifier would be substituted in another environment, and phonological modifications occurred as a result of the differences in syntactic environments. Handshapes that were used appropriately in simple signs (such as 3 in the numeral, or v in the sign SEE) were not used correctly in the classifier forms in a consistent manner. These developmental discrepancies within each child parallel the findings in spoken language acquisition discussed previously with respect to function and linguistic complexity. It is also significant that, whatever modifications of handshape, orientation, or motion the children made, the resulting sign did not violate the phonological constraints of ASL.

Looking at Kantor's data group by group reveals developmental stages and details of the children's strategies and patterns. The youngest group (3 years to 3 years 11 months) had limited control over classifier usage. They were able to demonstrate recognition of the classifier forms, as evidenced, for example, by substituting the citation form WALK in an imitation task where the PERSON-BY-LEGS classifier was presented. In terms of what control the children did have, the VEHICLE classifier seems to be the most advanced, the tall-upright object classifier next, and the PERSON-BY-LEGS classifier the least developed. The children's errors consisted mostly of deletions (simply not using the form at all) and modifications of handshape, orientation, and, for the PERSON-BY-LEGS classifier, motion. One common substitution was the use of the 5 hand in place of the 3 hand for the VEHICLE classifier and in place of the V hand in the PERSON-BY-LEGS classifier. This substitution of 5 for 3 and V is in keeping with McIntire's suggestion that 5 is developmentally easier. The complexity of V is increased when it occurs in signs like PERSON-BY-LEGS-WALK, which involves a combination of linear movement ("to") and finger wiggling movement ("walk"). Very few signs actually involve this combination; most other signs have linear movement or some type of angular movement (twisting, wiggling, flicking, etc.) but not both. However, the motoric simplicity of 5 is interacting with the other requirements on classifier usage: 5 is not used solely because it is motorically simpler, as evidenced by these same children using 3 and V correctly in nonclassifier forms. This is further illustrated by another example. In an imitation task, Kantor found that a child who could imitate VEHICLE correctly in a sentence with only one classifier nonetheless modified the handshape of that same classifier in a sentence that contained four classifiers and verb agreement. Similar effects of additional complexity within the sentence on children's performance are also reported by Supalla (1982) and Schick and Wilbur (1985).

The middle group (5 years 8 months to 6 years) expanded the semantic domain of their VEHICLE classifier to allow its use for "trains" (the younger group used it for "car" and "motorcycle"), while still using tall-upright object classifier with a restricted subset of nouns (e.g., "tree" but not "building"). In the VEHICLE classifier, a variant handshape (B hand with extended thumb) was more frequent (again, this handshape is simpler than 3 within the McIntire/Boyes-Braem model). Finally, use of PERSON-BY-LEGS increased, but still with modifications of orientation and motion.

In the next older group (6 years to 7 years), the 3 hand VEHICLE classifier was used in a wide variety of contexts and expanded semantically to include "trucks" and "parked cars." The tall-upright object classifier was used more consistently, and a fourth classifier, the stationary surface (B hand, palm down) was spontaneously used. PERSON-BY-LEGS classifiers were still being deleted or modified.

The oldest group (10 years to 11 years) used all classifiers correctly and productively (see Table 8–1).

From the types of errors that the children made, their relative performance on the three different tasks, and the changes in abilities over age, Kantor made these conclusions:

Table 8-1. *Percent correct and error types in combined comprehension, imitation, and production tasks*

	Modifications	Deletions	Substitutions	Correct usage
Youngest	45%	20%	12.5%	22.5%
Middle	6.4%	17%	10.6%	66%
Older	3.3%	9.8%	3.3%	83.6%
Oldest	0	0	0	100%

Adapted from Kantor (1980).

1. The late acquisition of classifiers confirms the description of them as a system of great complexity.
2. Classifiers are not acquired as lexical items per se but rather as a complex process. This is evidenced by several instances of appropriate classifier usage in some environments and inappropriate usage in others.
3. Classifiers begin to emerge around age 3, but are not completely mastered until 8 or 9 years of age.
4. The deaf child's acquisition of segments is not simply a matter of incremental ability to control the weaker digits of the hand. Rather, it is a complex interaction of the various components of the language.
5. There is an influence of syntactic and phonological environments operating on the acquisition of rules in ASL similar to the effect of environment on spoken language rule acquisition as described by Smith (1973) and Menyuk (1977).
6. The notion of function as described by Smith (1973), Ingram (1976), and Menn (1976) is applicable to the acquisition of segments in ASL.
7. The domain of application for a rule widens as the child matures in much the same way as it does in hearing children as described by Menyuk (1977).
8. The earliest handshapes correspond to the stages of development suggested by Boyes-Braem (1973) and McIntire (1977).
9. The order of feature acquisition corresponds to the hierarchy suggested by Wilbur and Jones (1974) with the addition of orientation. On the basis of developmental stages within the acquisition of simple single signs, Wilbur and Jones (1974) suggested that the order of acquisition of parameters would be location, movement, and handshape. Kantor found that orientation seems to share the final stage with handshape, resulting in location, movement, handshape/orientation.

Thus Kantor's study confirms a number of important issues regarding the adult description of ASL (such as the complexity of classifiers). The role that classifiers play in the acquisition of sign language will be addressed again in connection with complex morphology.

Verb Agreement

Given the difficulty that young deaf children have with forms containing classifiers, it should not be surprising that there is strong evidence that young deaf children are sensitive to the presence of the various inflections that may occur on verbs. This means that when they learn verb forms that are inflected, they do not simply imitate what the adults are doing, but instead produce simplified forms in which parts of the complex morphology have been omitted. These findings demonstrate that the acquisition of sign language is not merely a matter of copying or "apeing" the adult forms. One of the studies of verb inflection, Meier (1982), addresses this question directly and will be discussed later.

As a general observation, it should be noted that Fischer (1973b), Hoffmeister (1977), and Meier (1982) agree remarkably well that the beginning of productive verb inflection emerges before age 3. In the first study of the acquisition of verb agreement, Fischer (1973b) reported on the acquisition of verb inflection by two deaf children of deaf parents, Shirley and Cory. Fischer divided the data into arbitrary 6-month stages. For Cory, she analyzed five stages, Stage Zero (age 2 years), Stage I (age 2 years 6 months), Stage II (age 3 years), stage III (age 3 years 6 months), Stage IV (age 4 years). For Shirley, there were four stages, from Stage I (same age) on up. Fischer included in her study aspects of verb inflection related to the phonological realization of verb agreement. She divided the verbs into three classes: (1) locational (verbs that can be made at an agreement point other than the body, (2) "reversing" verbs (those that reverse or modify hand orientation toward an agreement point), and (3) directional verbs (those that move between two agreement points). Looking at the phonological realizations, Fischer reported that at Stage Zero, Cory showed no inflections at all, and that verbs that should have been inflected were modified to an uninflected form. At Stage I for both children, Fischer observed only locational verbs, with nonlocational verbs incorrectly modified to be locational (i.e., directional verbs became locational). At Stage II, the children indicated regular overgeneralization of the verb inflection rule (parallel to hearing children first correctly producing "came," then later incorrectly producing "camed"). Body anchor verbs that were not in any of the previous three classes and were correctly produced at Stage I were now incorrectly made into locational verbs. Reversal also appeared at this stage and was overgeneralized. The beginning of directional verbs was also observed at this stage. By Stage III, both girls clearly knew which verbs inflected in which ways, although at Stage IV, Cory was still making occasional overgeneralizations.

Meier (1982) compared three models that make predictions about how deaf children might acquire verb agreement. Two of the three models were in some part based on iconicity, whereas the third used notions of theoretical linguistic complexity. Meier's observations that deaf children of deaf parents produce uninflected verb forms that are actually *countericonic* and incorrect by adult standards confirmed previous reports by Fischer (1973b), Newport and Ashbrook (1977), and Supalla (1982). That is, Meier found that children produced incorrect verb forms that were less obviously related to their meanings because by omitting the verb agreements the verbs moved between arbitrary points rather than between the proper referents, which were present in the experimental situation. Thus, to leave out the inflections, the children had to *ignore* the presence of the real-world referents (for example, two dolls seated on a table) and produce a form that did not match the actual situation.

In addition, Meier found that verbs that agreed with only one argument were produced correctly before verbs that agreed with two arguments. Furthermore, in verbs with two arguments, the agreement for subject was most frequently omitted, in part because there are many situations in ASL where it is acceptable to do so. Thus, the children adopt a general principle that subject agreement may be omitted, leading to incorrect results in many cases. Meier concluded that the model based on linguistic complexity best predicted the results that he observed. The literature on deaf children's early acquisition of sign language repeatedly demonstrates that the presence of iconicity in ASL contributes little if anything to the overall development of sign morphology, although there may be an effect for individual lexical items (Bellugi and Klima, 1982; Bernstein, 1980; Fischer, 1973b; Goodhart, 1984; Hoffmeister, 1977, 1978; Kantor, 1977, 1982; Launer, 1982; Loew, 1983; Meier, 1982; Orlansky and Bonvillian, 1984; Schick and Wilbur, 1985; Supalla, 1982).

Pronominal Reference

Although both classifiers and verb agreement can serve to indicate a previously mentioned person or object, this section will deal primarily with the role of pointing as a pronominal indicator. Hoffmeister (1977, 1978) identified various functions that the pointing gesture can serve in adult language: as the demonstrative pronoun, as a determiner, as part of the possessive system (with the B hand), or as a reflexive (with the Á hand), as well as to indicate the plural and specific reference. Hoffmeister named the pointing gesture POINT, and this notation is used for this discussion. His observations indicate that the POINT forms the basis for several developmental stages. For example, the early two-sign productions consist of two POINTS: if a child wishes to indicate that a particular toy is his, this possessor-possessed relationship might be a sequence of two POINTS, one to the toy, the other to the child himself. He also found that the first three-sign utterances consisted of three POINTS: "let's you and me go downstairs" POINT (to addressee) POINT (to self) POINT (down). Subsequent developments in the three-sign stage included one sign and two POINTS, two signs and one POINT, and finally three non-POINT signs.

Hoffmeister's intention was to show that the POINT was part of the developmental sequence of ASL and that the child learning ASL used pointing gestures in a manner that was linguistically constrained and functional within a system, which a hearing child's pointing gestures would not be. This observation and his documentation of it should have a profound effect on how nonsigners view all the pointing that a signer uses. Often this pointing is interpreted as limiting a signer to talking about only those objects that are present in the room, "concretely-bound language." As we have seen, agreement points can be established in space for reference to nonpresent objects and persons, which represents a greater linguistic abstraction than pointing to visibly present objects. In fact, Hoffmeister found that a developmental sequence was present, such that the "concrete" pointing was acquired earlier than the abstract pointing. The significance for child language studies is easy to demonstrate. In Wilbur and Jones (1974), there occurred sequences of a noun sign followed by or preceded by a pointing gesture, which one might naïvely assume was there because the child lacked the linguistic ability to say what he wanted and chose to point instead, hoping to be understood. Locative POINTS were not separated from object reference POINTS, nor was it considered that such a distinction might exist. It was incorrectly decided that POINTS did not count. In looking back at the data, it is quite clear that for the subjects in Wilbur and Jones (1974), the earliest two-sign utterances were combinations of sign and POINT, and that such sequences occurred at least a month earlier than two non-POINT signs together. The POINT signs of these subjects obeyed the same type of constraints that Hoffmeister observed.

Hoffmeister's study was part of a larger study. In all, some 500 hours of videotape were collected on about 10 deaf children of deaf parents for periods ranging up to about 5 years duration. For his investigation of the role of pointing, Hoffmeister chose one child, named Alice, and backed up his findings by selectively sampling the data of other children. Alice's productions were divided into arbitrary units of 1000 utterances each, giving the following stages and ages: Stage I (29 months), Stage II (38 months), Stage III (45 months), Stage IV (50 months), and Stage V (52 months). Stages I through IV are remarkably similar in age to those reported by Fischer (1973b): Stage I (30 months), Stage II (36 months), Stage III (42 months), and Stage IV (48 months). Bear in mind that Fischer decided on her stages by 6-month age intervals (not developmental sequences) and Hoffmeister arrived at his by total output of utterances. Neither of these reports is intended to convey the concept of developmental stage (i.e., they do not mean stage in the same sense that Brown, 1973, uses it to refer to a range of linguistic development from MLU 1.0 to MLU 2.0).

In the expression of semantic relations, Hoffmeister reported that at Stage I, the use of a POINT and a noun for demonstrative+entity ("that book") or POINT and an adjective for demonstrative+attribute ("that (is) red") constituted 56.3 percent of all semantic relations expressed. By Stage II, this had decreased to 24.3 percent, by Stage III to 12.8 percent, and by Stages IV and V, to about 5 percent.

At Stage I, the POINT was used to indicate agent, patient, locative, object-possessed, and possessor, and was used syntactically as a demonstrative. All these POINTs had to be directed at a real world object or person visibly present in the environment. In the initial stage, these pointing gestures were constrained to the signer, the addressee, and objects present in the room. Also in the early part of Stage I, the possessor-possessed relationship was represented by a POINT to the object followed by a POINT to self, using the G hand for pointing. Later in Stage I, the B hand began to replace the G hand when referring to the possessor (but with considerable alternation between G and B). The possessed object again had to be present in the room. When using the B hand to indicate the possessor, the child might "back up" this production with an additional G hand POINT, just to be sure the message was correctly received. Also present in Stage I was the possessive construction N+N (as in "Mommy sock"). Plurals at this stage were indicated by repeated POINTs to the same object (i.e., "lamps" might be represented by pointing several times to a lamp), also sometimes accompanied by the sign MANY/MUCH or a numeral.

In Stage II, the POINT might now be made with a Y hand (herein glossed as THAT, even though it was not produced with the nondominant B hand, which is used in the citation form). Sometimes the POINT with G hand would be used as a backup for THAT. Occasionally, THAT would actually touch the real world object it was referring to, and then the POINT would be aimed at the object (but not contacted). In the possessive construction at this stage, the possessor could not be a third person (not just signer and addressee), and a new development, the use of HAVE, was seen: CAT HAVE LEG "The cat has a leg." For plurals, a continuous POINT to many pictures was used to mean "all"; pointing to two objects, each with a different hand, was used to mean "both of them"; and two fingers on one hand were used also to mean "both of these" (this latter is not necessarily the V hand, but is the precursor of the adult dual pronoun). In Stage II, Hoffmeister also observed that the POINT was used to establish a particular index, after which the verb was inflected to agree. (Stage II was also when Fischer (1973b) first observed verb inflections.) In contrast to Kantor's (1980) findings of late acquisition of the PERSON-BY-LEGS classifier, Hoffmeister reported a single use at this stage, but did not indicate if its usage was completely correct. Also present was the use of the signer's body as a pronoun, as when Alice designated herself to be Goldilocks. In general, at this stage, the use of POINT to indicate reference was frequent.

In Stage III, Hoffmeister reported that developments were primarily in areas other than the POINT, with complex and conjoined sentences appearing. The signed English possessive affix 'S appeared in Alice's signing, correctly from the beginning, reflecting the influence of her schooling on her signing. In this stage, the requirement of real world referent started to fade. Alice set up her G hand as a substitute for SUN (definitely the wrong classifier) and then referred to her finger with the other hand. Hoffmeister commented that the G hand, which had performed so many functions for the child already, was now adapted for yet one more purpose.

In Stage IV, full control of all two- and three-unit semantic relations was observed. All possible forms of the possessive were correctly produced. The reflexive (Å hand) was begun, with the POINT again used as a backup. In the development of the use of the reflexive, one could see the entire developmental sequence reflected again. Aside from the initial backup of the POINT, the reflexive was also initially confined to reference within the conversational dyad (signer and addressee), after which outside third persons could be referenced. In addition, third person reference was at first restricted to real world objects, and then extended to objects that were not present. It is exceptional that this developmental sequence for reflexive was manifested in Stage IV, when control of the other pronominal and possessive POINTS had already been established for reference outside the dyad and to nonpresent objects. In Stage IV, the adult dual pronoun made with the v hand appeared. Finally, although Alice began to use reference to nonpresent objects in Stage III, the remaining control was established here in two ways. In one form, a real world object that was present in the room was used to substitute for another object that was not present. Thus, Alice pointed to a lamp near her while referring in her conversation to another lamp in her room which she had broken. In the other form, arbitrary points in space were established, and the verb was moved between them, with some usage of classifiers if needed, and with the backup of the familiar POINT just in case.

By Stage V, Alice had mastered adult use of the POINT, possessive, plural, reflexive, and verb agreement in terms of establishing arbitrary points in space.

Hoffmeister (1977) demonstrated that, while hearing children's parents are busy teaching them that "it's not nice to point at people," deaf children learning to sign are busy acquiring constraints on the use of pointing for person reference. Among nonsigners, popular opinion views pointing as a fundamental gesture, so basic that its use in ASL was overlooked for a long time and, when it finally was recognized, treated as evidence that ASL was concrete and context-bound. Bellugi and Klima (1985) remarked that before beginning the study of the pronominal system, they "had fully expected that the learning of the equivalent of pronominal reference in ASL would be easy and early ('trivial' is the way we expressed it)." If pointing is as basic, iconic, and concrete as is commonly thought, they reasoned that there should be no developmental progression in its acquisition by young deaf children. As discussed previously, Hoffmeister reported a number of stages in the development of the proper use of pointing. In another study of earlier pointing behavior, Petitto (1985) reported other developments in the acquisition of pointing.

Petitto reported that a young deaf child, aged 10 months, used pointing to refer to herself and to others for pronominal reference, and pointed also to objects and locations. What Petitto observed was that for a period of nearly one year, the child stopped using pointing for pronominal reference, substituting instead lexical items (primarily people's names), but continued to use pointing for other functions (establishing joint attention, answering questions such as "Where's X?"). At about 1 year 10 months, she began using pointing for pronominal reference again, but much to everyone's surprise, she made pronominal reversal errors. For example, she pointed to herself when she meant "you" and pointed to her mother when she meant "me."

Over the next few months, she continued to use these reversed forms and appeared to be unaffected by her mother's efforts to correct them. The errors disappeared by age 2 years 3 months. Bellugi and Klima (1985) noted that this child's errors parallel hearing children learning English in terms of the emergence and disappearance of these reversal errors. Thus, although adults view pointing as a basic and trivial gesture, it is clear that, to the child learning pointing as part of the ASL linguistic system, the matter is far more complex. Petitto suggests that the child incorrectly concluded that POINT signs were like other signs, in that they had a relatively constant shape associated with their meaning. When an adult makes the sign for CAT, the child has to put the same handshape at the same place on the face with the same orientation of the palm and fingers and make the same movement. With pointing, whenever the mother referred to the child, the POINT faced away from the mother and toward the child. Apparently, the child assumed that to refer to herself, she should make a sign that pointed *away* from herself and toward the other person. That is, she apparently assumed that the index finger pointed away from the body was a (name) sign referring to her. A later development is the realization that pointing signs used for pronominal reference *change* their orientation according to which person is being referred to. After this realization, the later stages described by Hoffmeister (1977) can emerge.

The finding that there are developmental stages for something as basic as pointing has significant implications for theories of language acquisition. Petitto (1985) discusses at length how her findings run counter to those theories that claim that language acquisition derives from more general communicative and cognitive behaviors. She notes that these theories would not be able to explain why the child, who had pointing behaviors apparently correct at age 10 months, would then drop certain types of pointing and re-emerge one year later with incorrect pointing behaviors. Readers interested in this area should refer directly to Petitto (1985) and supporting discussion in Bonvillian and Orlansky (1984), and Orlansky and Bonvillian (1985).

Complex Morphology

In the previous studies of classifiers, verb agreement, and pointing for pronominal reference, the investigators have tried to isolate the pieces of interest for closer investigation. This is difficult to do, as the pieces interact with each other. Several of the researchers have reported that the more complex the situation (specific forms or entire sentences), the more difficulty children had with the particular pieces being investigated. Further investigation reveals interesting strategies that children may adopt to deal with a complexity overload.

In addition to the presence of classifiers, locations and directions of movement for verb agreement, and modifications to movement discussed in Chapter 5 for morphological inflections, there are several other morphemes that may contribute to the complexity of a particular form (see Supalla, 1982, for an analysis containing over a dozen possible morphemes associated with the verb; Shepard-Kegl, 1985; and the verb complex formulated in Chapter 6). One of these additional morphemes is the use of the second hand for a reference object: the dominant hand indicates what Supalla (1982) called the "central object" which may be located with respect to, or move with respect to, a "secondary object." The base hand may also represent the "ground," against which the central object is highlighted (that is, the ground may be a place rather than an object). Supalla notes that there are constraints on the allowable combinations of central object, secondary object, and ground depending on how many hands are involved in the formation of each. For example, if the central object is one-handed, the secondary object may be marked by the base hand simultaneously with the central object. However, if it takes two hands to make the sign containing the central object, then the ground is made as part of a separate verb of location, which precedes the formation of the sign containing the central object. Similar constraints hold for indicating the ground. As an example, consider the sentence (from Liddell, 1977), "the cat is on the fence." In this case, the fence is the secondary object, and the central object "cat" is located with reference to the fence, namely "on" it. To produce this sentence, the sign for FENCE (which is two-handed) is made first at a particular location to be used for future reference, after which the base hand is made at that location with the classifier for flat surface extended in horizontal direction and oriented in upright direction (B with palm facing sideways) and held there while the sign CAT is made with the dominant hand. The dominant hand then takes the classifier form for ANIMAL-BY-LEGS (bent V) and moves to contact with the top edge of the base hand (ON). Supalla's analysis of this sequence would be (1) FENCE, (2) here is a pronoun referring to the fence, (3) CAT, (4) here is a pronoun referring to the cat, and (5) here is the cat-pronoun located on top of the fence-pronoun. The secondary object is established first, followed by the central object, and then the locative predicate (TO-BE-LOCATED-ON). If a ground were also present ("the cat is on the fence in the neighbor's yard"), it would have to be established before the secondary object. That is, with verb constructions such as this, the ground is indicated first, the secondary object next, and the central object last. (Supalla notes that the reverse order occurs with verbs of motion.)

Supalla (1982) reports that young deaf children learning ASL demonstrate mastery of the central object very early. However, when a secondary object is added to the predicate, children do not produce a complex form containing both central and secondary objects. Instead, secondary objects are frequently omitted, or put in separate predicates of location even though they should not be. The difficulty with secondary objects is attributed to the fact that they are not required in all predicate constructions but rather only those predicate constructions referring to a situation where a secondary object is relevant. This contrasts with the central object, which is required with these types of predicates because it is impossible to sign these forms without a handshape; the child must therefore choose which handshape to use for the central object, but the child does not have to decide *if* the central object should be used. For the secondary object, the child must decide if an indication of secondary object should be made, and if so, which handshape and how many hands to use, from which the decision to produce it simultaneously or sequentially should follow using the mentioned constraints. Thus, the production of a secondary object requires considerably more sophistication than the central object. Supalla reports similar difficulty with the development of indicators for the ground, as they are also constrained in various ways and not required in all predicates, and furthermore can only be included in a single complex predicate (as opposed to being used in a sequence of predicates) when there is no secondary object.

Schick and Wilbur (1985) reported similar difficulties with respect to the secondary object. Their older deaf subjects tended to make more handshape substitution errors with secondary object references than with central object references. Furthermore, when the secondary object and central object morphemes were the same (*car* passing *car; person* standing next to *person*), the children were more likely to put everything together into a single complex predicate; when the morphemes were different (*car* passing *person*), they were more likely to break the production into two (or more) separate predicates.

When a construction has both a central and a secondary object, they are located in some kind of relationship with respect to each other. They may be facing each other, or away; one may be in, on, under, over, next to, above, in front of, or behind the other (to name but a few). These relationships form part of what Supalla (1982) called the "base grid system," the arrangement of objects in space. The acquisition of the spatial grid is another part of the acquisition of the overall use of space for linguistic purposes in ASL. Schick and

Wilbur (1985) observed that children may have difficulty maintaining the proper grid when they break a complex predicate into smaller sequential predicates. To produce "the truck drove between the two fences," two classifiers for fence-pronouns must be located parallel to each other in space; the right hand then makes the VEHICLE handshape for truck and moves it parallel to the left hand, which has remained stationary as a secondary referent object. In this adult form, the right hand representation for fence is replaced by the reference to the truck. One child, aged 6 years, placed both fences in their appropriate positions using the classifiers, then removed both hands (deleted both references). She then used her right hand to make the truck incorrectly drive *through* where the fences had been, instead of *between* where they had been. One may speculate that if she had left her left hand in place, she would have realized that the truck would crash into the fence given the orientation she was using.

The relationships among the objects themselves are also acquired in sequence. Schick and Wilbur (1985) reported that "on" was acquired before "back," which was acquired before "between." This order parallels that given by Johnston and Slobin (1977) for children learning locatives in Italian, Serbo-Croatian, Turkish, and English. Schick (1985b) also reported that complex predicates with moving verbs were acquired earlier than those with stative verbs. She speculates that a moving figure in the figure/ground relationship makes the objects more salient to the children than in nonmoving situations.

Noun/Verb Pair Distinctions

In her study of the acquisition of related noun and verb pairs (cf. AIRPLANE and FLY), Launer (1982) observed that her findings seemed to "support the theory of the prominence of *object motion,* use or function in early word acquisition (cf. Nelson, 1974) as opposed to form or perceptual features (cf. E. Clark, 1973; Gentner, 1977)" [emphasis added]. The children displayed knowledge of the signs for nouns that represented movable concrete objects more frequently in their early lexicons than nouns representing large, static objects or abstract nouns. Also, very young children made no formal distinctions between nouns and verbs, and when such distinctions did emerge, they were frequently made with features other than the ones used by adult signers (recall that AIRPLANE is made with a restrained, repeated, short movement, whereas FLY is made with a smooth, larger path movement). In their early attempts to mark such distinctions, the children sometimes used only one of the several required features (movement shape, manner of offset, face/body movements). Launer (1982) also observed that children overgeneralized the noun/verb distinction to create new forms that do not exist in adult ASL. One noun sign, JAIL, is made with a smooth, path movement to contact; it has no associated verb form. One child mistook the sign JAIL to mean "to put in jail," that is, she treated JAIL as a verb, and created a novel noun form with short, repeated movements. In this case, the child had incorrectly generalized the verb form of smooth large movement to the noun JAIL and then produced a corresponding but nonexistent noun form to go with it.

It should be clear from the previous reports that the surface has only been scratched as far as the development of morphology in ASL is concerned. Presumably, each of the many morphemes that are involved in the construction of complex predicates contributes to the difficulty of learning, with some morphemes being more difficult than others. To properly study ASL acquisition, the investigator must be familiar with the literature on the acquisition of languages with complex morphologies; knowledge of the acquisition of English, which lacks morphological complexity, provides very little insight into the processes involved in ASL.

The Use of Space in Discourse

Up to this point, the discussion of the use of space in signing has concentrated on the question of whether the child can use different locations in space for morphological functions such as verb agreement. A separate and interesting question is whether the child knows how to assign different referents to different locations in the first place. In order to move a verb between two verb agreement points, the verb agreement points have to be associated with particular referents to which the signer will subsequently refer. Recall from Chapter 5 that there are several possible arrangements in space for referents, depending on how many will be needed. Two referents are usually located with one on the signer's right and the other on the signer's left; three referents may be located evenly spaced on a straight line in front of the signer; three or more referents may be alternately located on the signer's left and right with increasing distance away from the signer's body (to a limit — the signer should never have to straighten the bent elbows to reach a location point in the signing space and there is also a limit to how many referents can be easily located, remembered, and discussed at one time); finally, if the conversation includes a description of a place (room with furniture, accident scene) where the relative locations are determined by the referents themselves, the location points will mirror the real world situation rather than the arbitrary alternation of points in space.

Hoffmeister's (1977) study reported that children begin by referencing themselves, the person they are signing with, and objects that are present in the room. Only later do they begin to reference people or objects that are not present. At least in one case, the child used a lamp in the room to refer to another lamp that she had broken. The process of acquiring pronominal reference is fairly complicated.

When children tell stories, it is often difficult to follow who is doing what to whom. Frequently, verbs that should be marked with verb agreement are incorrectly made without it. Sometimes, the verbs are inflected between different points in space, but the child has not indicated who or what the referents of those points are. Loew (1983) reported that children did not properly combine the verb agreement markers with the establishment of nouns at particular locations in space. Loew (1983) and Pettito (1980) observed that when children do begin to use points in space as grammatical markers (around age 3 years 6 months), they may start by putting all of their referents at a single point, essentially stacking them one on the other. In one story observed by Petitto, a child stacked 11 characters in the same place. Loew further observed that even when children began to use different points in space in verb agreement for referents, they frequently failed to indicate who or what was located at each point. As late as 4 years 9 months, the child Loew observed still made numerous errors in the use of space, frequently omitting verb agreement and not indicating which referents were at which locations. These findings reinforce the notion that ASL has several complex morphological systems (verb agreement, noun indexing, pronominal reference) that interact, creating a formidable challenge to the child learning the language. To put this in perspective, it should be pointed out that the Egyptian noun plurals are supposed to be so complex that they are not fully mastered until around age 15.

PARENTS SIGNING TO CHILDREN

In addition to the recent interest in the acquisition of sign language by young deaf children, several researchers have investigated the modifications that parents make when signing to their children. Thus, in accordance with Hoffmeister's (1977) observation that many of the early two-sign and three-sign combinations produced by the deaf children he studied consisted in whole or in part of pointing, Kantor (1982) reported that the deaf mothers she observed used extensive amounts of pointing with their young deaf children. This occasionally involved replacing the normal handshapes associated with signs such as MOTHER, EAT, and DRINK with the pointing handshape. This form of "baby sign" was later paired with the appropriate adult form of the sign, so that the child could see both together. Thus, the mother might sign EAT with the G handshape at the mouth followed by EAT with the proper O handshape.

Launer (1982) also reports extensive modifications made by the mothers she studied. Launer noted that the mothers modified the movement of related noun and verb pairs, such as AIRPLANE and FLY. The modifications the mothers made resulted in forms that were neither nouns nor verbs; in fact, the result might not even be an ASL sign at all, but rather an unacceptable distortion. The modifications allowed the parents to highlight certain of the signs' formational features without concern for morphological distinctions that the children were unable to handle.

Launer also noted that the mothers' signing to children contained the same features of simplicity and redundancy that have been reported for spoken language "motherese." Both Launer (1982) and Maestas y Moores (1980) reported that parents positioned their bodies and those of their children to maximize attention, interspersed nonvocal affective acts with language interactions, used alternate or simultaneous modalities to communicate with the child, and repeated signs many times. Launer noted that mothers repeated the sign movement, occasionally as many as 12 times, even when the sign would not be repeated in the adult form.

Launer also observed that exaggerated size appears to be the signing counterpart of exaggerated intonation reported for spoken language motherese. To this end, mothers were observed to exaggerate their productions of certain signs, so as to highlight the form for the child, while producing a countericonic sign that would be unacceptable in adult signing. Launer (1982), Maestas y Moores (1980), and Petitto (1984) also observed several other important aspects of mothers' signing to deaf children: (1) the tendency to sign on the child's face and body rather than on the mother's; (2) the tendency to produce certain signs, in particular the names of objects, but also adjectives, on the object itself, highlighting the association between the object and the sign; and (3) the tendency of parents to move or mold the child's hand to form a particular sign. Parents apparently go to great lengths in order to maximize the visual attention and message reception of their children.

DEAF CHILDREN OF HEARING PARENTS —
THE ACQUISITION OF SIGNED ENGLISH

There are few studies of sign acquisition by deaf children of hearing parents. Hoffmeister and Wilbur (1980) outlined a number of these studies and noted that one of the reasons why there are so few studies is that until recently, hearing parents did not have extensive access to sign language when their child was first identified as deaf. Currently, more hearing parents have had the opportunity to learn some kind of signing, thus providing a signing environment for their deaf child. For a variety of reasons, most hearing parents have opted for a manual coding of English rather than for ASL. The study of sign acquisition by deaf children who have hearing parents can then take two directions, one being the study of the acquisition of manually coded or signed English, and the other being the actual acquisition of ASL, if and when children learning the latter are identified. Those readers who are not familiar with manually coded English and sign systems used in educational settings should refer to Chapter 10.

Schlesinger and Meadow (1972) reported the early sign development in two deaf children of hearing parents. One child's parents began using a sign system when she was age 17 months, whereas the other child's parents began when she was age 36 months. After 19 months of exposure to sign for the first child and only 6 months for the second, the test of comprehension described in Fraser, Bellugi, and Brown (1963) was administered. Both children were able to comprehend the contrasts of subject/object, present progressive/past, singular/plural, and affirmative/negative. In addition, subsequent observation indicated that the second child could also use appropriately the -s sign inflection for plural, present progressive, and possessive. Schlesinger (1978) indicates in a follow-up report that five other deaf children of hearing parents were obtaining similar success in acquiring signs. All the children she studied appeared to follow Slobin's (1973) operating principles of "pay attention to the order of words" and "to the ends of words." These are important in learning manually coded English because inflections are separate sign segments attached to signs (designed to parallel English morphology). All of the children appeared to acquire the appropriate inflections by the age of six.

In another report, a young deaf child whose mother and teacher began using signs when he was 12 months old displayed the early emergence of signs also seen in deaf children of deaf parents (Stoloff and Dennis, 1978). At one year 6 months, this child was combining signs and was rapidly expanding his vocabulary. Hoffmeister and Wilbur (1980) suggested that this child's success with signed English underscores the potential of a visual language when presented to young deaf children. They also noted that in the various reports by Schlesinger and Meadow (1972), Schlesinger (1978), and Stoloff and Dennis (1978), the child's natural tendency to vocalize does not decrease as the child acquires signs, but rather that all of the authors observed that the children may use some speech when no sign exists or when they have not yet learned the sign equivalent.

One detailed longitudinal study that described a deaf child of hearing parents was reported by Hoffmeister and his colleagues (Goodhart, 1978; Hoffmeister and Goodhart, 1978; Hoffmeister, Goodhart, and Dworski, 1978). At 2 years 5 months, the child had only 9 months of sign exposure; he was nonetheless capable of expressing two and three sign semantic relations expected of hearing children at that same age. In addition, he expanded references to nouns using adjectives and/or determiners as part of the expanded noun phrase. Because his mother was presenting a combination of ASL and signed English, the child produced a number of signed sequences that are common to both systems. For example, at 2 years 5 months, he used verb modulations similar to those found in ASL, as in one sequence where he inflected the sign FLY toward the ceiling for "those bugs flew to the ceiling." He also used repetition for indicating plurals on nouns, and pointing to indicate reference to present objects. One novel construction that he created was a simultaneous compound, using features of two signs simultaneously. To refer to a toy boat in the shape of fish, he used the handshape and orientation of FISH with the movement and direction of motion of BOAT. In another case, he combined YELLOW and BUG by using the handshape and movement from YELLOW at the location (on the nose) of BUG.

By age 3, this child was equivalent to the deaf child of deaf parents reported by Hoffmeister (1977) in terms of complexity, quantity, and quality of linguistic knowledge. The fact that this was accomplished in less than one year of exposure to signing with parents who were just beginning to learn sign language supports the notion that language presented to children during the critical early years will be rapidly acquired, thus paving the way for later linguistic and cognitive development.

In a major study of the acquisition of both signed English and ASL by six older deaf children (ages ranging from 6 to 16 years) whose parents did not sign, Livingston (1981) reports the emergence of ASL structures similar to those discussed in preceding sections and the development of signed English structures such as those just discussed, albeit at a much later age. Livingston's study is of interest to those concerned with sign learning in an educational environment, but because the children in it were learning sign only in school, only 6 hours a day, and were past the normal age for language acquisition (they had oral education prior to being placed in the total communication classrooms), their development of sign skills is not strictly comparable to those reported for younger deaf children who learn ASL or signed English as their initial language. The detail and scope of Livingston's study make it an important resource for those readers specifically interested in the acquisition of educational signing.

In a related report, Livingston (1985) focused on the development of sign meaning in the previously mentioned children. She noted that as with hearing children, these deaf children tended to make mistakes in the semantic domain of words, using a sign to mean either something too narrow or something too broad. These errors tend to be based on shared features between the actual referent of the sign and the referent to which the child has incorrectly applied the sign. For example, MOTHER might be used to refer to a wife or to a witch in a story, the overlapping feature being female. Similarly, FATHER is extended to a husband, a giant, and a hunter, all having in common the feature male. The sign MARRY was incorrectly used to mean husband, whereas PEOPLE was incorrectly used to mean girls sometimes and boys at other times. Livingston suggests that deaf children only partially learn sign meanings and use under and over extensions to test hypotheses about the domain of a sign's usage. In this way, they parallel what has been reported about the acquisition of word meaning by hearing children.

One study (Swisher, 1985) focused on the signing of the mothers themselves. Swisher reports extensive deletions, both of major content words and minor function words. At the same time, they tend not to use contractions, saying "What is he doing?" rather than "What's he doing?" Thus, their communication with the children sounds stilted, with many hesitations and slower speech, while their signing tends to be brief, simple, and far from complete. Other studies of simultaneous speaking and signing indicate that this is a very complex area requiring considerable further study (Bernstein, Maxwell, and Matthews, 1985; Maxwell, 1983; Maxwell and Bernstein, 1985; Stokoe, 1985).

THE ACQUISITION OF FINGERSPELLING

Fingerspelling is a manual coding for the spelling of a spoken language; in the United States, the language is English. Many fluent users of ASL include fingerspelling as part of their conversations, and the process by which fingerspelled words become loan signs has been studied extensively (Battison, 1978). The mastery of fingerspelling will in general be a later development than signing (for those children learning both) because of the complexity involved in the detailed handshapes, sequencing of handshapes, and number of syllables involved per word. Nonetheless, children do learn to fingerspell, frequently treating it as though it were a variant form of signing (Akamatsu, 1982, 1985). That is, they frequently make the same handshape substitutions in the development of signing observed by McIntire (1977), using developmentally simpler handshapes in place of more complex ones. Akamatsu (1982, 1985) suggests that the neuromuscular constraints that are relevant to sign forms (reported by Mandel, 1979; see Chapter 2) operate also on the children's productions, making certain forms more likely than others. These constraints result in modifications of transition movements between handshapes so that they better resemble the movements in regular signs. Akamatsu argues strongly that it is incorrect to view fluent fingerspelling as merely the sequencing of individual handshapes (what she calls " the cipher model"). She provides evidence that neither adults nor children treat fingerspelling as simply sequences of handshapes. Rather, she argues, the perceptual impression of fluent fingerspelling is one of wiggly fingers; the movement is a critical part of the fingerspelled form and the shape of the movement (what she calls "the movement envelope") is a primary factor in adult perception and child production of fingerspelling. She notes several anecdotes in which various signers demonstrate that although they are using a fingerspelled form, they are not actually aware of the spelling itself. This can result from the fact that in fluent fingerspelling, initial and final handshapes are more salient than those in the middle, which may be blurred, omitted, or even incorrect. Instead, the signer concentrates or producing a sequence that approximates a certain overall movement shape. One adult signer, for example, after an extended discussion of mortgages in which a fingerspelled sign for "mortgage" had been used over and over, asked HOW SPELL *mortgage*? Another signer had been using a fingerspelled form for years, learned from his mother, when he realized that it decomposed into "s+a+f+e+w+a+y" (the supermarket "Safeway"). In some respects, this parallels the situation in spoken English where people use the word "breakfast" for many years, not knowing its components, then finally learning the word "fast" and realizing that "breakfast" means "to break the (overnight) fast."

Akamatsu (1982) noted that adult signers, when asked about the best way to read fingerspelling, stated "pay attention to the shape."

Apparently, this is serious advice. She reported that many instances of adult usage of fingerspelling were unintelligible when decomposed into their individual parts (due to omissions, substitutions, and blurring), while at the same time perfectly intelligible when taken as whole. In this regard, Hanson (1980) showed that deaf adults can judge whether a rapidly presented sequence of hand-shapes forms a word or not, but at the same time are frequently unable to write down the actual sequence of letters. For example, when presented with the sequence FTERNAPS, the subjects were able to judge it as a nonword, but when they were asked to write it down, they tended to regularize the spelling in accordance with English spelling and word formation rules, creating forms like AFTERNAPS.

That adults treat fluent fingerspelling as a movement envelope containing handshape changes, rather than as a sequence of hand-shapes with transitions between them, has important implications for the acquisition of fingerspelling by young children. Akamatsu (1982) observed three hearing children of deaf parents, aged 3 years 8 months to 5 years 3 months. The children's fingerspelled forms showed a strong tendency to match the adult's movement envelopes, even though the individual handshapes were frequently incorrect, omitted, in the wrong order, or simply unintelligible. Figure 8–1 shows some of the adult envelopes compared with the children's productions. Open handshapes (with fingers extended) are represented by rectangles that are higher than they are wide; closed handshapes (such as the fist handshapes S, A, T and so on) are represented by squares; handshapes that require an orientation where the wrist twists to the side, such as fingerspelled G, are represented by rectangles that are wider than they are high; and handshapes that require the wrist to bend down so that the fingers extend below the hand, such as Q, are represented with a rectangle that drops below the bottom line of the other handshape rectangles.

Padden and Le Master (1985) reported a study of the acquisition of fingerspelling by six deaf children aged 2 years 3 months to 7 years 11 months. They noted that at very early ages, children seemed unaware of what was involved in fingerspelling and would move their fingers to comply with a request to name certain objects, but that older children showed increasing agitation with requests for fingerspelled productions, in part, they argue, because the older children realized that there was something more involved in finger-spelling than they fully understood. This accords with Akamatsu's (1982, 1985) argument that early acquisition of fingerspelling is heavily movement-shape dependent, rather than handshape-sequence dependent; the younger children are happy to make a movement envelope without further analysis, whereas the older chil-

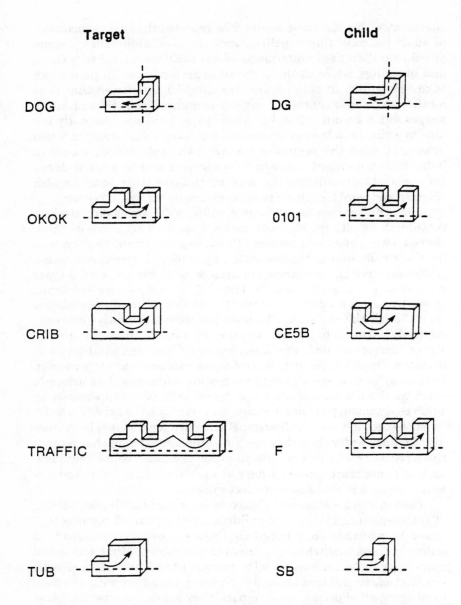

Figure 8-1. A comparison of adult (target) and child movement envelopes, reprinted from Akamatsu (1982).

dren are beginning to be aware of spelling and print and thus are somewhat concerned about whether they have all the pieces correct.

Padden and Le Master (1985) also noted that the children's early fingerspelling productions consisted of fingers moved in a manner mimicking fingerspelling, with only the first letter distinct; "these forms only resembled the general appearance of adult fingerspelled items enough to be recognized by parents for what was intended." In addition, they report that as young as age 2 years 9 months, the children are able to distinguish contexts for fingerspelling and contexts for signs. When asked WHAT THAT?, the children would respond with a sign, but when asked WHAT NAME THAT?, they would attempt a fingerspelled response. Padden and Le Master suggest that this behavior is similar to that reported by Ferreiro (1978) for hearing children learning about spoken and printed English, in that hearing children treat printed words as "names." The young deaf children in this study are treating the fingerspelled words as appropriate for "something else," the question of exactly what remaining unanswered.

SUMMARY

The studies of sign language acquisition provide evidence that there are developmental sequences in the acquisition of ASL, even for basic gestures like pointing. The timetable for acquisition of ASL is similar to that for spoken language, with the possibility that ASL acquisition may be initially accelerated. The acquisition of ASL, like that of spoken language, is affected by motor complexity, morphological complexity, syntactic complexity, and semantic complexity. By contrast, iconicity appears to be of minimal importance, although not totally irrelevant. Parents signing to children tend to pay more attention to overall form, such that when they try to highlight a sign's formational features for the children, the resultant form may actually be countericonic and possibly ungrammatical by adult standards. When children reach the age where they can handle more complexity, parents' signing tends to become more complex, as evidenced by the initial use of pointing handshapes for certain signs, followed later by a pairing of the pointing form with the adult form containing the correct handshape.

Deaf children of hearing parents represent a separate population, which researchers have only begun to investigate. Those who learn signing from the beginning appear to be parallel to young deaf children of deaf parents, whereas those who learn signing at later ages (such as those investigated by Livingston, 1981) display emerging knowledge of both ASL and signed English, albeit not fluency.

The acquisition of fingerspelling represents a separate issue also. The different repertoire of handshapes and movements, compared to ASL, provide different challenges to young children, and the relationship that fingerspelling bears to English words is a late realization for them. Whether there are important differences in the acquisition of fingerspelling by deaf children of deaf parents, deaf children of hearing parents, and hearing children of deaf parents awaits investigation.

CHAPTER 9

Sociolinguistic Aspects of Sign Language and Deaf Culture

In Chapter 1, ASL and its nearest relatives were discussed. This chapter examines Woodward's (1978) argument that ASL was not "invented" or "started" in France, but that it developed naturally over time, and that it absorbed French signs when they were introduced in 1817, much the way English absorbed many French words after the Norman conquest in 1066. As a natural language, ASL has considerable variation; it is affected by factors such as geography, age and education of the signer, and formality of the situation in which the conversation is taking place. Interaction between deaf and hearing people is greatly affected by the hearing person's general unfamiliarity with ASL and the degree of familiarity with English possessed by the deaf person. In such situations, the use of pidgin (neither group's daily language) has developed (Pidgin Sign English). A signer's fluency in ASL may make him eligible for membership in the deaf community, bound together by linguistic factors rather than just deafness (some members may be hard of hearing or even hearing). This situation contributes significantly to the difficulty of obtaining unbiased information on the structure of ASL and its role in the lives of deaf people. No matter what level of fluency a hearing signer attains, it should never be assumed that conversations with native deaf ASL users are actually being conducted in ASL rather than in Pidgin Sign English. The educational implications of the existence of the deaf community and the variation in sign language will be discussed at the end of the chapter.

IN THE BEGINNING

One frequently asked question about ASL is "Where did it come from and when did it start?" One approach to answering the question is to point out the parallel difficulty of answering the question "Where did spoken language come from?" Many theories of the origin of spoken language still compete—the Tower of Babel, a gift from beings from outer space, even that the first languages may have been manual languages which became spoken as man needed his hands for other tasks. Whatever the origins, one thing is clear—where there are humans, there is language.

Nonetheless, one may read in the literature on deaf education or on sign language that ASL began when Thomas Hopkins Gallaudet returned from studying signs in France, bringing with him Laurent Clerc, a deaf teacher. The two established the American Asylum for the Education and Instruction of the Deaf and Dumb in 1817 (now the American School for the Deaf in Hartford, Connecticut), which used signs modified from French Sign Language (FSL). Woodward (1978) argues that it is inappropriate to treat the origin of ASL as resulting from this source, citing a number of factors that make it highly improbable that these two men were responsible for the establishment of an entire language. There is evidence that signs existed in the United States before 1817 and both Gallaudet and Clerc, one hearing and the other a foreigner, were unlikely role models for the American deaf.

Woodward carries his argument through by showing that the similarities between modern FSL and ASL are too small for them to have separated as previously suggested. If ASL was indeed a direct descendant of FSL and started in 1817 as suggested, one would expect modern ASL and modern FSL to have many similar signs (what we call cognates). Using the same statistical techniques that are used to calculate such differences with spoken languages (Gudschinsky, 1964), Woodward compared modern ASL signs with those listed in a dictionary of modern FSL (Oleron, 1974). Only 61 percent were cognates. This percentage would place the split between ASL and FSL at between 504 A.D. and 1172 A.D., long before Gallaudet and Clerc. Two other comparisons yielded data supporting Woodward's argument. Although not all reseachers agree on the validity of using these techniques, the resulting figures are so far off the 1817 date that one must question either the statistics or the historical story. Woodward was able to show, with the help of Russian Sign Language and ASL, that sign languages change over the years at about the same rate as spoken languages, or even slightly slower. Thus if the figures are in error, it is in the direction of underestimating how long ago the two languages would have had to split apart. Woodward argues instead that it would be more appropriate to assume that there were signers using an older form of ASL when Gallaudet and Clerc brought over the modified French signs, and that when the modified signs were introduced at the school, the deaf pupils changed them to make them fit into the rules for allowable signs in ASL. This creolization process would also account for the fact that most of the changes seem to have occurred in the early to mid-1800s, when the FSL signs were introduced. Separate data show that there is nearly 90 percent agreement between modern ASL signs and signs recorded from 1913 to 1918. Thus, very little of the change has occurred in the twentieth century (the changes that have occurred are the ones described by Frishberg, 1975, and discussed in Chapter 2). So much new information about the history of signs and deaf people in America is now available that some programs have begun teaching separate courses in Deaf History (cf. books by Lane, 1984; Lane and Philip, 1984; Panara and Panara, 1983).

VARIATION WITHIN ASL

Phonological Variation

Frishberg (1975, 1976) reported a number of changes in how signs were made in 1918 compared to the present (discussed in Chapter 2). Extensive investigations of a number of ASL dialects by Woodward (1972, 1973a, b, c, 1974b, c, 1975, 1976a) and Woodward and Erting (1975) revealed that (1) these dialects provide additional support for the historical changes described by Frishberg, (2) these dialects indicate that some of those changes are still in progress, and (3) other changes not observed by Frishberg also seemed to occur. For example, Frishberg (1975, 1976a) reported that signs tended to move up from the waist as part of the centralization trend, but Woodward and Erting (1975) found that signs like YOUNG were still made on the waist for some signers. Similarly, Frishberg reported the tendency toward symmetry which often resulted in a one-handed sign becoming two-handed. Woodward and Erting found that in some black Louisiana signers, DIE/DEAD/KILL was still made with only one hand.

Woodward continued his investigation into the relationship between FSL and ASL as it is reflected in the historical changes that have occurred and in the sociolinguistic variation that exists. Frishberg reported that two-handed signs made on or in front of the face tended to become one-handed. Thus, the two-handed versions are older. Woodward and DeSantis (1977a) found that users of modern FSL tended to use more two-handed versions than users of ASL, and that white Americans over the age of 47 tended to use older forms more than whites under the age of 47. These demographic variables illustrate the widespread systematic variation that can occur.

Woodward (1976b) extensively discussed handshape changes that have occurred. He illustrated four basic types of changes: thumb extension (known as the "rule of thumb," Battison et al., 1975), simplification, metathesis, and maximal differentiation (keeping the handshapes as distinct as possible). Variation in location, motion (Woodward, 1976b), and use of face (Woodward, Erting, and Oliver, 1976) have been documented.

Battison and colleagues (1975) reported on the tendency in some dialects for the thumb to be extended in the formation of G and H handshapes. They suggested that this change might be attributable to naturalness of articulation. Several FSL signs have undergone this change to produce modern ASL signs: PLAY, made in FSL with I handshape, now made with Y (I plus extended thumb) in ASL; ACCIDENT, made in FSL with S handshape, made in ASL with A handshape (S plus extended thumb).

Lexical Variation

The different signs that exist in different dialects in the United States are legendary among signers. It is quite common for a conversation to come to a temporary halt while two signers compare notes on the use or meaning of a particular sign that one of them has just used. There are at least three different ways to sign the numbers from 16 to 19, depending on whether one makes a 10 fist (A hand with wrist twist) followed by the number 6, 7, 8, or 9, or whether one makes the handshape for the number and then either shakes the wrist (actually a reduced repeated elbow rotate) or rubs the thumb against the side of the relevant finger. A recent book, Shroyer and Shroyer (1984), addresses this question directly; it contains dialect variations for 130 signs illustrated by states. For example, there are 12 signs for "early," the first one of which is used in 10 states, the second of which is used in four states, and so on, with occasional multiple listings for the same state (Florida and North Carolina both use the first and second versions of "early," whereas Illinois uses the first version and the fifth version). These differences are no more disruptive than those experienced by New Yorkers living in Los Angeles (wanting what is called "soft drink" in Indiana and "tonic" in New England, the New Yorker asks for "soda" and the stockboy in the supermarket responds "Washing or baking?"; in Los Angeles, it is "pop.")

Grammatical Variation

Just as the handshapes of signs and the signs themselves vary from dialect to dialect, so do the grammatical rules. Woodward (1973a) found that investigating three rules allowed him to determine variation and then to correlate that variation with characteristics of the signers themselves, such as age, education, and when they learned to sign. As with spoken languages, sign dialects are affected by characteristics of the users as well as geographical separation. The three rules that Woodward investigated are negative incorporation, verb reduplication, and what he called "agent-beneficiary incorporation" (our verb agreement).

In his investigation of reduplication, Woodward (1973a) investigated the question of whether all signers would be willing to produce and judge acceptable reduplicated forms of all nine stimulus verbs: MEET, MEMORIZE, SEE, WANT, STUDY, READ, KNOW, RUN, and DRIVE. He found that the variation that existed among signers allowed him to construct an "implicational ordering," an ordering in which the form at the bottom is the most commonly used, the form at the top is the least commonly used, and the ones in the middle are ordered so that if a signer uses reduplication of a verb that is in the middle, it means that he will also reduplicate all the signs listed below it, but not necessarily all or any of the signs listed above it. In the implicational ordering that Woodward found for verb reduplication, MEET was at the top, DRIVE was at the bottom, and the others were ordered exactly as listed in the first sentence of this paragraph. Thus, a signer who produces and accepts reduplication of MEET will produce and accept reduplication of all of the other verbs, but a signer who reduplicates KNOW can only be predicted with certainty to reduplicate RUN and DRIVE. Theoretically, then, a simple test for general re-

duplication preferences is to present MEET; if the signer produces and
accepts the reduplicated form readily, he most likely will reduplicate
all of the others. If he does not readily accept reduplication of MEET,
then the next item to try is MEMORIZE, and so on. In Table 9–1, the
verb reduplication implication reported by Woodward (1973a) is presented in a table format. Each "+" indicates that the signer produced and accepted reduplication. The term "lect" refers to groups of
signers who share common characteristics, in this case with respect
to verb reduplication. Lect 1 is the group (which may have as few as
one signer in it) that most readily uses and accepts reduplication;
lect 10 is the group that uses no reduplication at all (at least not on
this scale). Each lect differs from the one above or below it by the
presence or absence of one "+"; this is both an ideal and a classic example. Woodward found signers who fell into each of the 10 lects,
supporting the idea that this is not just a theoretical division. Lects
1 to 5, which allow the wider range of reduplication, are considered
to be more ASL-like, whereas lects 6 to 10 are considered to be less
ASL-like.

Woodward (1974a) found a similar implicational theory in his
investigation of negative incorporation. Several verbs may add a
negative affix, which is an outward twisting movement of the hands.
Before discussing the implicational hierarchy that Woodward found
and its eventual implication for sign language research, some relevant history of the process of negative incorporation is appropriate.

Woodward and DeSantis (1977b) discussed this history in detail.
According to them, negative incorporation is a purely phonological
process in FSL, where the verb is traditionally followed by NOT. The
FSL NOT is made with a G hand, facing outward, pointing upward,
and shaking repeatedly from side to side. In general then the hand
must twist to an outward orientation for NOT after forming the verb.

Table 9-1. *Verb reduplication implication*

Lects	MEET	MEMORIZE	SEE	WANT	STUDY	READ	KNOW	RUN	DRIVE
1	+	+	+	+	+	+	+	+	+
2	–	+	+	+	+	+	+	+	+
3	–	–	+	+	+	+	+	+	+
4	–	–	–	+	+	+	+	+	+
5	–	–	–	–	+	+	+	+	+
6	–	–	–	–	–	+	+	+	+
7	–	–	–	–	–	–	+	+	+
8	–	–	–	–	–	–	–	+	+
9	–	–	–	–	–	–	–	–	+
10	–	–	–	–	–	–	–	–	–

Assimilation of handshape then affected FSL verbs KNOW, WANT, LIKE, and HAVE, so that they were restructured into single units in ASL (bear in mind that ASL NOT is formationally unrelated to FSL NOT, and that ASL NOT cannot be the source of negative incorporation). These lexical units (DON'T-KNOW, DON'T-WANT, DON'T-LIKE, DON'T-HAVE) were the basis for a generalization of a grammatical process of negative formation which extended to ASL GOOD to form ASL BAD (GOOD-NOT). Although the actual scope of this process is extremely limited, its salience as a generalization (in the sense of Wilbur and Menn, 1975) is demonstrated by overgeneralizations made by hearing people (*DON'T-THINK) and children learning ASL (*DON'T-LOVE).

Using signers from areas in the northeast and northwest of the United States, Woodward (1974a) found an implicational ordering for negative incorporation, presented in Table 9–2; the number of signers from each geographical area who fell into the different lects is also given. Here lects 1 to 3 were considered most ASL-like and 4 to 6 least ASL-like.

Finally, Woodward also found an implicational ordering for the use of agent-beneficiary incorporation (verb agreement). Then, putting the results from the three rules together, he found an implicational ordering for them also, given in Table 9–3, with agent-beneficiary incorporation at the top and verb reduplication at the bottom. Again, a lect with all three rules (lect 1) can be considered more ASL-like than a lect with just two of the rules (lect 2), which in turn is more ASL-like than a lect with just one rule (lect 3) or a lect with none of the rules (lect 4).

Aside from geographical factors, Woodward and his associates found that variation in lects is significantly correlated with four variables: (1) whether or not the signer is deaf, (2) whether or not the signer has deaf parents, (3) whether or not the signer learned signs before age 6, and (4) whether or not the signer has had some college experience (for deaf signers only). Using the lects from Table 9–3, these factors are illustrated in Table 9–4, showing the distribution of signers according to lects and variables. "One is more likely to find a deaf person, a person with deaf parents, and a person who learned signing before age six in lects that approach ASL; one is more likely to find a hearing person, a person with hearing parents, and a person who learned signing after six in lects that do not approach ASL closely" (Woodward, 1973c). Further analysis of these data revealed that for deaf people with deaf parents, college (usually Gallaudet) tends to inhibit the use of ASL; the person tends to increase usage of signed English. For deaf people with hearing parents, college experience tends to encourage and expand use of ASL rather than signed English.

Table 9-2. *Negative incorporation implication*

Lects	HAVE	LIKE	WANT	KNOW	GOOD	Northeastern	Northwestern
1	+	+	+	+	+	17	12
2	−	+	+	+	+	23	14
3	−	−	+	+	+	50	7
4	−	−	−	+	+	10	1
5	−	−	−	−	+	8	2
6	−	−	−	−	−	0	0
Total						108	36

From Woodward and DeSantis (1979b).

Table 9-3. *Implicational hierarchy for all three rules*

Lects	Agent beneficiary incorporation lects 1-5	Negative incorporation lects 1-3	Verb reduplication lects 1-5	N
1	+	+	+	84
2	−	+	+	27
3	−	−	+	12
4	−	−	−	18

Table 9-4. *Factors responsible for variation in lects (n = 141)*

Variable	Lects 1,2	Lects 3,4
A. Deaf	97	11
Hearing	14	19
B. Deaf parents	34	2
Hearing parents	77	28
C. ASL 0-6 years	60	5
ASL after 6 years	51	25
D. College	42	2
No college	55	9

PIDGIN SIGN ENGLISH

The widespread dialect variation discussed in the preceding section is coupled with another type of variation, the stylistic variation that occurs when individuals are in different situations. Informal situations tend to favor use of ASL, whereas more formal situations require more English-like signing. Thus, even a single signer will have a range of signing styles within the dialect that he or she generally uses. Pidgin Sign English (PSE) refers to a signing variety that is neither ASL nor signed English, but shares features in common with both (Friedman, 1975a; Stokoe, 1970; Woodward, 1972, 1973a; Woodward and Markowicz, 1975).

Roughly put, a pidgin is characterized by (1) a mixture of structures from two or more languages, (2) structures that do not belong to either or any of the languages from which they are derived, (3) reduction in structure compared to other languages, (4) not being the native language of any of the people who use it, (5) restricted social situations, such as between employer and employee, but not personally expressive situations, such as between family members, and (6) accompanying negative attitudes toward the pidgin (Woodward, 1973d). Creoles are often described as pidgins that have become someone's native language, although a previous pidgin state is not absolutely necessary for creolization to occur (Hymes, 1971).

Woodward (1973d) described PSE as having the following linguistic characteristics (he emphasizes that much more remains to be investigated).

ARTICLES. English uses the articles *a/n* and *the*, whereas ASL uses pointing and specific locations in space to make the distinction between definite ("the") and indefinite ("a"). PSE has a sign for "a" and fingerspells "the."

PLURALITY. English adds –*s* to most nouns, whereas ASL may use reduplication or signs like MANY. PSE uses some noun reduplication and does not generally have an equivalent for –*s*. If the plurality is to be emphasized, the plural noun may be fingerspelled.

COPULA. Like Russian, ASL does not have a separate word for the copula "be" in present tense sentences such as "John is a teacher" (except for the required head nod, Liddell, 1977). However, Russian does have copula forms in the other tenses, but ASL does not. English has many copula forms (*be, is, am, are, was, were*, plus complex forms *will be, would be, could be*, etc.). PSE as used by older persons tends to use the ASL sign TRUE/REALLY, whereas newer signs that have been created for educational purposes (primarily initialized forms of TRUE, FUTURE, and PAST) have worked their way into PSE usage for some signers.

PROGRESSIVE ASPECT. The progressive aspect is represented in English by a combination of *be* + *verb* + *ing* ("is going," "was running"). In ASL, it is represented by various types of reduplication as discussed earlier. PSE uses verb reduplication in some environments, but also uses copula + verb (without –*ing*), illustrating the reduced structure characteristic of pidgins.

PERFECTIVE ASPECT. In English, the perfective aspect is indicated by a combination of *have* + *verb* + *en* ("have broken," irregular "have gone"). ASL uses the sign FINISH. Woodward noted that a variant of FINISH is used in PSE, followed by the verb (without +*en*).

INCORPORATIONS. In general, PSE tends to use fewer incorporations than ASL. Woodward and Markowicz (1975) indicated that PSE includes lects 4-6 for negative incorporation (Table 9–2), lects 6-10 for agent-beneficiary incorporation, and only the numbers 1 and 2 for number incorporation in pronouns.

In addition, Woodward and Markowicz (1975) also noted that PSE tends to be signed in a more restricted, centralized signing space than that observed for ASL. Facial expression is also more restricted.

The characteristics described for PSE are similar to those of other pidgins. In most pidgins, articles are deleted; the copula is usually uninflected; inflections such as English plural are lost and most derivations are lost, just as they are in PSE. Perfective aspect in pidgins is often expressed through FINISH or a similar verb like DONE (Woodward, 1973b).

LANGUAGE AND THE COMMUNITY

The inability to hear is treated by most people, particularly the educational community, as a handicapping condition. The concept of the deaf community as a linguistic minority (Charrow and Wilbur, 1975) bound together by a common language provides a perspective that is foreign to most people. "Members of the deaf community include the profoundly deaf, the hard of hearing, the prelingually and the postlingually deaf, those who have intelligible speech as well as those who don't" (Markowicz and Woodward, 1978), and occasional hearing people with deaf parents may be included. Membership in this minority group seems to be based on two important criteria: "1) attendance in a residential school for the deaf, and 2) communicative competence in ASL (Stokoe et al., 1965)" (Markowicz and Woodward, 1978). According to Meadow (1977), about half of the 90 percent of deaf children who have hearing parents attend residential schools, where they are enculturated into the deaf community by older children and those who have deaf parents. Although the situation is gradually improving, most deaf children have little or no contact with deaf adults. The use of ASL-like signing (as opposed to signed English) serves to solidify people within the deaf community while excluding outsiders. PSE serves as a buffer between the hearing and deaf communities (Markowicz and Woodward, 1978).

Who's In and Who's Out: An Empirical Study

Kantor (1978) pursued Markowicz and Woodward's (1978) report of the linguistic criteria for membership in the deaf community by investigating the identifiability of signers as native or nonnative, hearing or deaf. She conducted a study aimed at determining the ability of signers (native deaf, nonnative deaf, native hearing, nonnative hearing) to identify other signers (presented on videotape) as native deaf, nonnative deaf, native hearing, or nonnative hearing, and to determine what factors influenced these decisions. The nonnative signers were all second-language (L2) signers (deaf or hearing) who had learned to sign after puberty; native signers had all learned ASL from birth. She reported her results in terms of the accuracy of the judges and the identifiability of the signers being judged.

IDENTIFIABILITY OF THE SIGNERS. The native deaf signers and the L2 hearing signers were the most easily identified groups (50 percent and 60 percent, respectively). In contrast, overall judgments on native hearing signers and L2 deaf signers were extremely inaccurate (10 percent and 8 percent correct, respectively). Instead, the L2 signers were correctly identified as deaf (73 percent) but rarely as L2 (15 percent) whereas the L2 hearing signers were correctly recognized as L2 (79 percent) and hearing (66 percent). What these data show clearly is that the prototypical member of the deaf community, the native deaf signer, is easily distinguished as "in," whereas the prototypical nonmember, the hearing person who has learned signing as a second language, is easily identified as "out." Native signers who are hearing and deaf signers who learned signing later in life are the "in between" group. Comments given later support this interpretation.

CHARACTERISTICS THAT INFLUENCED DECISIONS. Raters were given several characteristics to check off or describe if they felt it was relevant to their decision regarding the signers to be judged, and were also asked to provide additional characteristics or comments which might be helpful to the experimenter. Table 9–5 presents the percentages of judgments that were influenced by the various characteristics according to the group being judged.

The hands, face, body, and kinds of signs were the primary telltale characteristics. For the native deaf signers, comments included: "facial expression dominates," "affirmative nodding of head while telling a story," "incomplete mouthing of words," use of mime, use of particular signs ("deaf signs," "expressive signs"), and rhythm of signing, including speed, fluency, and use of space. For the L2 deaf,

Table 9-5. *Percentages of judgments influenced by characteristics*

Characteristics	Native deaf	L2 Deaf	Native hearing	L2 Hearing
Hands	100%	65%	33%	81%
Rhythm	100%	54%	23%	49%
Kinds of signs	92%	50%	9%	57%
Face	100%	58%	21%	77%
Body	95%	31%	13%	53%
Location of signs	81%	19%	7%	38%
Finger size	9%	0	0	7%

comments included: "exaggerated mouth movements indicates early oral training," "hesitant speech with the signing," "the speed is halting," and "deaf facial expressions." For the native hearing, comments included: "good use of body emphasis," "fluent use of signs, but pattern of words seems hearing," and "signs are very fluid." Finally, for the L2 hearing, comments included: "way hands shaped while signing too stiff and formal," "body too stiff," "too much false facial expression," "face kind of blah," "facial expression not deafy," "used all easy basic signs," "used same sign too often," "used signs that hearing people use," "sign for 'just right' was the giveaway," "excessive fingerspelling," "fingerspelling too quick," and "slow fingerspelling."

ACCURACY OF THE RATERS. The native signers (both deaf and hearing) were most accurate in determining the proper category for the signers being judged. With a 25 percent chance of making a completely correct judgment (50 percent probability of getting deaf or hearing correct, 50 percent chance for getting native or L2 correct, but only 25 percent chance for getting both characteristics correct for any particular signer), the native deaf and native hearing groups scored 40 percent and 41 percent correct, respectively, whereas the L2 deaf and L2 hearing performed less accurately (21 percent and 34 percent, respectively). Interestingly, both hearing groups were better able to accurately identify a signer as deaf or hearing, and both deaf groups were more accurate in determining whether signers were native or L2.

Native deaf signers were most accurate at identifying native deaf signers (70 percent) and L2 hearing signers (68 percent correct), supporting Markowicz and Woodward's (1978) contention that the linguistic abilities helped bind the community together. Similarly, native hearing signers were highly accurate in identifying native deaf (67 percent) and L2 hearing (73 percent) signers. The L2 deaf and hearing judges performed considerably below the native groups, suggesting that they were less attuned to the salient characteristics.

Between Two Worlds:
Hearing Children of Deaf Parents

Kantor's (1978) study of the identifiability of signers included native hearing signers, a group that has been largely ignored in the research on sign language or sociolinguistic factors related to deafness. The result of many of the marriages between deaf people is hearing offspring. Hearing children who have deaf parents (HCDP) grow up bilingually, learning the spoken language in their community and the signed language of their parents. However, specific studies of their sign language abilities have not been conducted (several studies of their sign language acquisition are cited in Chapter 8). It may be that their signing falls into the "more English-like" group identified by Woodward (1974a), because their knowledge of spoken English affects their signing, or it may be that if they learned ASL natively, they could maintain two separate languages and use their ASL just like native deaf signers. Kantor's (1978) study does not help resolve this question. On one hand, the native hearing signers were most frequently mistaken as deaf native signers, indicating that their signing was good enough to fool the judges, even the deaf native signers. On the other hand, some of the comments, especially "fluent use of signs, but pattern of words seems hearing," suggest that there may be crossover between the two languages, but the experimental situation used in Kantor's study was not "pure" enough to really judge what the signing style might have been like in actual conversation with other native signers.

With the increase in general attention paid to the sociology and sociolinguistics of deafness, there has been an increase in attention to hearing children of deaf parents (Bunde, 1979; Wilbur and Fristoe, 1986). Prior to this, the focus of research on hearing children of deaf parents has been on the question of whether there would be language or speech problems for those children as a result of the communicative situation in the home or, occasionally, on the question of how the sign language acquisition of these children compares to their spoken language. The general findings so far suggest that these children are no more at risk for extensive language problems than if their parents had been hearing (Bard and Sachs, 1977; Brejle, 1971; Griffith, 1980; Johnson, 1980; Jones and Quigley, 1979; Mayberry, 1976b; Prinz and Prinz, 1979, 1981; Sachs and Johnson, 1976; Sachs, Bard, and Johnson, 1981; Schiff, 1979; Schiff-Meyers, 1982; Schiff and Ventry, 1976; Todd, 1975; Wilbur and Jones, 1974).

A recent extensive survey of adult hearing children of deaf parents (AHDCP) investigated aspects of sign language learning, interpreting, other responsibilities of the children, occupational choice, and other aspects of the effects of having deaf parents on the lives and personalities of AHCDP (Wilbur and Fristoe, 1986). The survey found that most of them learned to sign at home and that a large majority of them use their signing in deafness-related occupations (interpreter; teacher of the deaf; sign language teacher; counselor; social worker; faculty in deaf education programs; or faculty at Gallaudet, California State University, Northridge, National Technical Institute for the Deaf, and others). Many others use their signing on the job even though they are not in occupations specifically related to deafness (lawyers who have deaf clients, administrative and clerical personnel in companies with deaf employees or deaf customers, and psychologists and social workers who see deaf clients). Many of the people surveyed felt lucky to be members of both the deaf and the hearing worlds, although others felt that they did not really fit into either the deaf or the hearing worlds. As a group, they tended to be much better educated than a random sample of the American public would indicate, perhaps because their parents' heightened sensitivity to the benefits of education led them to place even greater emphasis on getting an education than is usually the case.

The overwhelming majority (above 80 percent) served as interpreter for their parents. As might be expected from a large survey, the feelings of the people responding were mixed, both within an individual and across the group as a whole. For some, interpreting for their parents led to a feeling of resentment because they were always on call for their parents' needs and their parents were more dependent on them than in the average hearing family. For others, this additional responsibility was seen as a benefit for the development of maturity and a skill for future employment. Many felt responsible for their parents and had trouble establishing their own independence. Many also indicated that they felt that they had missed out on being a child, and that having to help out in the family had forced them to grow up earlier than other people. At the same time, they also developed high standards of performance for themselves and for others, and tended to be more critical of themselves than they felt other people were of them.

There are groups of children other than HCDP who are thrust into assuming various adult responsibilities at an early age. Some of these are children of physically impaired parents, children of recent immigrants, children with single parents, and children with handicapped siblings. One interesting parallel is that between the AHCDP as a group and children from alcoholic families. Such children are also called upon to take extra responsibilities at an early age; the effects of these experiences on their personalities have been well-documented (Black, 1981; Woititz, 1983). In both cases, the impact of early responsibility and maturity are evident in mixed ways, positive for some and negative for others.

There is a second reason for being interested in the parallels between AHCDP and children from alcoholic families. Steitler, Cassell, and Webster (1982) suggested that some hearing-impaired people were at risk for developing alcoholism or other drug abuse, although no data are available to determine the prevalence of such problems among deaf people. Four personality components — submissiveness, dependency, rigidity, and antisocial behavior — are associated with increased risk for substance abuse. Deaf people's communication difficulties, such as letting hearing people make decisions, depending on hearing people to interpret, or being unable to express their feelings and form close relationships, may predispose deaf individuals to drug or alcohol abuse. To the extent that deaf people might develop these personality traits, *even if they do not in fact drink or use drugs too much,* their children may be growing up in an environment similar to that of children from alcoholic families and may therefore have similar experiences.

The finding that there are similarities between adult hearing children of deaf parents and children from alcoholic families does not mean that there is something *wrong* with these children, anymore than there is something wrong with a child who grows up in a single parent family. Rather, there are similar experiences that children from these kinds of families have that children from other kinds of families may not have. Just as the New Yorker living in the midwest may seek out other New Yorkers for a feeling of familiarity and comfort, given their shared cultural heritage, AHCDP may be interested in sharing their experiences with others who understand first-hand what their families were like. Indeed, the announcement for the first conference of hearing children from deaf families calls itself a "celebration and exploration of our heritage." Children from alcoholic families have formed discussion groups all over the country for similar purposes (as well as to help them cope with their own and their parents' problems). Thus, it would be incorrect to conclude that similarities between AHCDP and children from alcoholic families imply something negative about these groups. Investigations of their similarities (and other types of families) highlight the importance of communication in the lives of everyone, and place an extra responsibility on the educational system to ensure that deaf people will have *all* the communication skills they will need to live healthy and happy lives. The importance of training professional people who are sensitive to the special needs of deaf people and their families, and who have good signing skills so that an interpreter is not needed during a sensitive or emotional discussion, cannot be overstated.

THE INTERACTION OF DEAF AND HEARING PEOPLE

Communicative interaction between deaf and hearing people was addressed in several articles in a recent Gallaudet series on social aspects of deafness (Boros and Stuckless, 1982; Culhane and Williams, 1982; Erting and Meisegeier, 1982; Hoemann and Wilbur, 1982). McIntire and Groode (1982) describe differences between hearing culture and deaf culture in terms of what is considered polite and the conventions surrounding proper conversational routine. Hearing people who are not familiar with the conventions of deaf society frequently may think that a deaf person is being abrupt, blunt, or rude. They note that the deaf community is more like a small town than a large city. It is difficult to keep secrets, and topics not normally discussed in "polite" hearing society such as the cost of someone's new car, their salaries, or their appearance, are acceptable among members of the deaf community. Manners are different; it is possible and acceptable to "talk" with one's mouth full. Banging on the table is an acceptable way of getting someone's attention, as is tapping them on the arm or shoulder, or flashing the lights (for a group).

Deaf people tend to treat facility with speech as hearing people treat an excellent pianist, that is, as a talent, not an achievement. Thus, the frequently heard praise "Good language" from teacher to student may not carry the same import to the student that the teacher intends. On the other side, the highest compliment that a deaf person can bestow on a hearing person is SIGN LIKE DEAF.

One of the very first questions asked by deaf people of a newly introduced acquaintance concerns the hearing status. Hearing people can tell easily if someone is deaf or hearing, but deaf people must ask this information explicitly, and it is considered extremely rude to play games or be untruthful concerning this information. McIntire and Groode (1982) also described the rules for communication using TDDs (telecommunication devices for the deaf, formerly called TTYs). Both deaf and hearing people must learn to identify themselves (deaf people cannot identify someone by the sound of his or her voice, or the speed of their typing on the TDD), to indicate "GA" for "go ahead" when their turn is finished, and to follow the etiquette of typing "GA to SK" when starting to end a conversation, then "SKSK" after the other person has typed "SK" indicating that it is okay to end the conversation. In between the first "GA to SK" and the final "SKSK," there will be a variety of turns consisting of such statements as "guess that's all for now," "thanks for calling," "see you next Saturday," and the nearly mandatory "have a nice day."

In a general book that deals with sign language and the deaf community, Neisser (1983) highlights the importance of TDDs, sign language interpreters, and captioned television to the deaf community. All three have in common their function as a means of transferring information, which deaf people crave as much as hearing people do. The deaf community has had to lobby long and hard to achieve equal access to information, and there is still much more that needs to be done. Deaf people need to be able to call the fire department, ambulance, hospital, and the poison hotline, among others, using their TDDs. Only a few cities currently offer these services. Deaf people need to be able to call people who do not have TDDs; in some cities, an operator service is available so that deaf people can place their calls using a TDD and then the operator can continue the call to the third party by voice.

As for interpreters, in addition to the childhood internship served by hearing children of deaf parents discussed previously, interpreter programs around the country seem to be expanding. Certification of interpreting skills is provided by the Registry of Interpreters for the Deaf (RID) to individuals passing the evaluation exams. A small amount of research has been started on the interpreting process itself. This research will eventually provide insights into the psycholinguistic processes of listening to a language, storing it in memory while converting to sign language, and then producing the sign language while still listening to new information coming in, and the reverse — going from signing to a spoken translation.

Another aspect of the interaction of deaf and hearing people that has been generally overlooked is how deaf people feel about their educational experiences, especially the attempts of hearing people to teach them English. Meath-Lang, Caccamise, and Albertini (1982) asked deaf students enrolled as college students at NTID (National Technical Institute for the Deaf) to write a description of their English language learning and communication experiences. This paper, which should be required reading for anyone interested in teaching deaf students, provides extra impact by quoting liberally from the deaf students themselves, giving a good sample of the type of written English that can be expected from many deaf college students. Responses from the students indicate that they do not see their education in English as being intended to provide them with a communication tool that they can use everyday, but rather with an academic skill parallel perhaps to learning to bisect a triangle or solve an algebraic equation. Meath-Lang and colleagues (1982) also note that students tended to write about "learning about English" rather than "learning English." Such comments as "I learned grammar and also English," "I learn a lot about diagram," and "I learn to write noun and verbs, subject, and write composition and have vocabulary word," reflect this sense of lack of purpose. Also supporting the idea that deaf students have dissociated learning English from its daily function for communication was one student's entire written essay: "I speak the words — then get candy for the right way." Students also don't understand the relationship of written and spoken language, as evidenced by one student who wrote, "I can use good English language when I talk. I can't use good english [sic] when I write." Reading is also considered a separate academic skill: "I learned English combined with reading."

Deaf students' perceptions of their teachers and parents are also enlightening. Students wrote about teachers who talked with their backs to the students while writing on the board, "a blammermouth that won't let me have a chance to ask questions," and "floppy sign languages, too." One student who was failing in public school and transferred into a school for the deaf made the following observation "The English class I was in for three years in that deaf school sucks because the level wasn't as high enough as I was in public school." This student cited boredom as the reason for not studying harder. One student noted, "My mom wanted me to grow up like a hearing person," and another wrote, "My father slapped my face that he don't want me to go to school for the deaf."

Meath-Lang and colleagues (1982) note that the students in their study do not fully understand the purpose of English education, that they see themselves as *being taught* rather than as *learning* English skills, that they view hearing people in general as smarter, that they feel badly about their own weak language abilities, and that they are generally not internally motivated to do better because of the overall lack of function of English in their personal lives. In a general consideration of the role of mainstreaming as part of the educational process, Rodda (1982) considers the effects of placing a student in a school for the deaf as opposed to placing him in a mainstreamed public classroom. Rodda argues that the detachment many deaf students feel from their education is related to their being isolated even while in a mainstreamed classroom. Contrary to popular belief, the "least restrictive environment," which is frequently translated as a hearing classroom, can actually be more restrictive for deaf students by depriving them of adequate communication, giving them a feeling of being different and not quite as good, and not giving them the cultural support that they would have when surrounded by peers who are like them. Rodda argues that the crucial concerns should include not only the educational setting, but also the support services, the contact with the deaf community, the attitude and stability of the family, and the emotional maturity of the child. The prerequisites for successful education seem to be good communication skills, someone interesting to communicate with, and something interesting to communicate about. As Meath-Lang and colleagues (1982) point out, the papers on "how I spent my summer vacation," which students mentioned frequently in their essays, are not likely to motivate deaf students to bridge the gap between their weak skills in English and those desired by the educational community and hearing society around them.

SUMMARY

The implications of this chapter for linguistic research on ASL and for the educational community are profound. As suggested several times in this and other chapters, the influence of English can never be ignored or underestimated when studying ASL; here, the effect of hearing, particularly of the researcher, is added to the list of cautions. Educators, in addition, must remember that deaf children will eventually be faced with the choice of joining the deaf community after they leave school, and their decision to do so will be greatly facilitated by knowledge of ASL (not instead of, but in addition to, English). The sign system currently in vogue in educational programs for deaf children do not resemble ASL or English as much as their creators and advocates think they do (see discussion next chapter). One can also question the effect on deaf children learning the different sign systems when they attempt to enter the deaf community and have (1) different lexical items, and (2) little or no knowledge of ASL syntax. As more of the linguistic information on ASL becomes available, it will be harder for teachers and others in contact with deaf children to use the difficulty of obtaining real ASL as their excuse to know only signed English. Meanwhile, the existence of the deaf community places deaf people in a category apart from those with other sensory, cognitive, or physical disabilities. Although retarded or physically disabled people may eventually leave a sheltered environment, marry, and raise families, they are not bound together in the same way by a separate, communal language. In fact, Charrow and Wilbur (1975) and others have argued for treating deaf children as a linguistic minority rather than as a handicapped population. Such a perspective raises the importance of bilingual approaches to educating deaf children, and suggests that teachers of deaf students might benefit from academic programs in bilingual education and teaching English as a second language.

Part II

Applied Dimensions

CHAPTER 10

Sign Systems Used in Educational Settings

Linguists frequently need to make the distinction between "language" as a system of organized rules for word and sentence structure and "code" as a means of transmitting language. Common codes include speech, writing, Morse code, and Braille. In each case, the code must be deciphered in order for the message contained in the language to be obtained. To understand a message, one must know both the language and the code. If one is illiterate, one knows the English language and the speech code, but not the written code. Occasionally, one may know the written code (because the alphabet is the same as ours) but not decipher the message because the language is unknown. Actually, this is more common than it seems; knowledge of the code allows us to recognize and even attempt to pronounce languages like French, Spanish, Italian, Portuguese, Dutch, German, and so on, even though we may not know anything about the languages themselves.

There are direct parallels in the manual modality. Two different types of manual language codes are (1) fingerspelling (one hand-shape for each letter of the alphabet) and (2) sign for word (one sign for each word of the spoken language). A third form, which is discussed at the end of the chapter, is Cued Speech, which is neither a language nor a complete language code, but which is included here because of its relevance to the education of deaf children.

It does not make sense to try to fingerspell to someone who does not know fingerspelling; it also does not make sense to fingerspell to someone who does not know how to spell; and finally, it does not make sense to fingerspell English to someone who does not know English. As in the spoken modality, the code and the language being transmitted must be known by both sender and receiver.

The linguistic structure of ASL is sufficiently different from English that true simultaneous communication in ASL and spoken English is very difficult, if not impossible, to accomplish. Nonetheless, English is the predominant language in American education and society. For this reason, manual systems have been created in order to permit simultaneous signing and speaking using English syntax. That these systems are considerably different from ASL is clear; that they are also different from English (which they are intended to represent faithfully) presents problems.

The term "systems" designates those manual methods that have been developed for educational purposes but are not currently used as the home language by large groups of deaf people (Wilbur, 1976, 1979). A manual system is formally different from both ASL and English, and for many reasons cannot be considered "language" in the same sense that ASL and English are.

It should be clear that the systems do not simply take "the signs of ASL and put them in English word order." They also drastically alter the morphological and phonological processes that users of ASL are accustomed to producing and perceiving (e.g., reduplication, blending, assimilations). The systems were designed to parallel English based on the assumption that signing English would be more effective in teaching written English syntax than signing ASL.

Deaf children's problems with English syntax are discussed in greater detail in Chapter 11. Given what we now know about deaf children's English difficulties, we cannot rule out the possibility that the same problems that are seen in written English will not also occur in their acquisition of signed English, regardless of which system is used. In particular, many of the problems that deaf children have learning English are related to their inability to determine what the correct rules for English sentence structure are or their inability to determine which English structure to use in different circumstances. These problems may be traced to two primary sources, one being the complexity of the English syntactic system itself and the other being the approaches used to teach English to deaf children. To the extent that both of these are independent of modality (are not dependent on whether one is speaking, signing, writing, fingerspelling), the sentence structure used in a signed version may show the same syntactic problems that we see in deaf children's writing. These points will be elaborated in Chapter 11.

HISTORY OF SIGN SYSTEMS

The first constructed signing system undoubtedly was that of the Abbé de l'Epée, who modified the signs used by the deaf community in France to create a system of signed French. The history of deaf education in France and the decisions that various educators made about how (or if) to sign with their students is documented in two fascinating books by Harlan Lane (1984; Lane and Philip, 1984). The "methodical" signs that the Abbé created (as opposed to the natural signs that deaf people actually used) were of two types — lexical and grammatical. The grammatical signs were created to parallel French syntax, whereas the lexical signs were created to label things that did not already have signs or to make distinctions between French words that might share the same sign. Many of de l'Epée's signs were demonstrated first with a series of pantomimes to convey the meaning to the deaf students, after which the invented sign was presented. These "methodical" signs were among the signs that were brought to the United States by Laurent Clerc and Thomas Gallaudet, where they were adapted to teach English.

The first English-based system was developed by Sir Richard Paget (1951) in England. He called his system "A New Sign Language." After his death, Lady Grace Paget and Dr. Pierre Gorman continued his work, revising the system and calling it "A Systematic Sign Language" (Paget and Gorman, 1968). This name was abandoned in 1971 (Paget, 1971) in recognition of the fact that it is not a language (as distinguished in Wilbur, 1976, 1979), and the system is now known as the "Paget-Gorman Sign System" (PGSS) (Craig, 1976).

The first system in the United States was developed by David Anthony, who was interested in producing a simplified system to use with multihandicapped deaf children. Anthony's (1966, 1971) original system eventually became known as Seeing Essential English (SEE 1), from which Linguistics of Visual English (Wampler, 1971, 1972) and Signing Exact English (SEE 2) (Gustason, Pfetzing, and Zawolkow, 1972, 1973, 1974) subsequently were derived. Another system, called Manual English, was developed at the Washington State School for the Deaf (1972), utilizing many of the principles and basic assumptions of the other systems, with differences that are noted in subsequent sections. Another system whose use has become quite widespread is Signed English. In discussing this, a distinction must be made between Signed English as a developed system (Bornstein, Hamilton, Kannapell, Roy, and Saulnier, 1973, 1975) and signed English as a loosely defined means of using ASL signs in English word order without invented endings or separate grammatical signs; this would allow use of ASL syntactic devices such as reduplication and spatialization (as discussed in Part I). The phrase signed English can also refer to the signing that is used by hearing people who have learned signs but have not learned ASL syntax and thus put the signs together in English order and fingerspell whatever signs they do not know. Thus, signed English may be the most widely used of all the systems, but it is the least well defined.

The final system included in this discussion is also not a formal system, but rather a synthesis of several other systems. The *Perkins Sign Language Dictionary* (Robbins et al., 1975) was originally developed to meet the needs of those working with visually impaired deaf students. The dictionary includes entries from 11 sign text sources, chosen according to criteria that are discussed later. The issue of syntax is discussed at length in the Introduction to the dictionary, where it is suggested that several levels of grammatical markers might be needed and that their use should be governed by the level of functioning of each child rather than by absolute principles based on English syntax.

COMPARISON OF THE SYSTEMS TO ENGLISH

In looking at the relationship between the several systems and English, three major questions can be addressed: (1) What are the basic guidelines that have been established for each system? (2) How do these guidelines compare to the structure of English or to the structure of ASL? (3) When do these guidelines break down (when are they inconsistent, counterintuitive) and how serious is this problem?

The creators of each system believe that their system faithfully reflects the structure of English in a visual mode. Because English is a spoken language, many arbitrary decisions have to be made about how to represent spoken English in signs. It may be said of all the systems as a group that they follow English word order. However, several of the systems have made different decisions regarding the formation and use of new signs (see Table 10–1) and the amount of fingerspelling permitted.

The formation of past tense verbs provides an illustration of these arbitrary decisions. In English, verbs can be divided into those that form their past tense by a regular rule and those that are in some way irregular. The regular past tense rule is to add the suffix "ed" to the verb ("talk"-"talked"). The irregular verbs can be subdivided into several groups. There are those for which the past tense is the same as the present, for example, "hit"-"hit"; those that display internal vowel changes, for example, "meet"-"met"; those that have vowel changes in both the past tense and the past participle, for example, "ring"-"rang"-"rung"; others that use "-ought" or "-aught," for example, "fight"-"fought," "catch"-"caught"; and a few for which the past tense does not resemble the present tense at all, for example, "go"-"went." The differences are all reflections of processes that occurred earlier in the history of the English language.

There are many ways in which a sign system can code the past tenses of English verbs. One possibility is to represent English past tenses by signing all the verbs in the same way. For example, one could sign the verb followed by the ASL PAST sign ("talked" = TALK + PAST, "came" = COME + PAST), or one could sign the verb followed by another past tense marker such as fingerspelled "d" ("talked" = TALK + d, "came" = COME + d). Another approach is to divide the verbs into regular and irregular, and use one past tense marking for the regular verbs and another for the irregular verbs: (1) sign the verb plus the ASL PAST for the regular verbs and another marker, perhaps fingerspelled "d" for the irregular verbs ("talked = TALK + PAST, "came" = COME + d), (2) the opposite of (1) ("talked" = TALK + d, "came" = COME + PAST), (3) sign the verb plus PAST marker for the regular verbs and use new signs for the irregular verbs ("talked" = TALK + PAST, "came" = CAME), (4) sign the verb plus PAST for the regular verbs and fingerspell the irregular verbs ("talked" = TALK + PAST, "came" = c + a + m + e). Two more might be like (3) or (4), but using "d" for the regular verbs. Other possibilities include subdividing the irregular verbs into smaller groups, along the same lines that they are divided in English. All of these approaches can be used in various combinations with initialized signs to create even more possibilities.

The logical possibilities have not been exhausted, but it should be clear from the previous examples that the manner of treating past tenses is more or less an arbitrary decision made by the creator of the system. There is nothing about the structure of English that

Table 10-1. *Characteristics of manual systems*

System	Author(s)	ASL signs?	Fingerspelling?	Basic morphological principle(s)
Paget-Gorman Sign System (PGSS)	Paget (1951) Paget and Gorman (1968, 1971)	No	Only for proper names	One meaning-one sign
Seeing Essential English (SEE 1)	Anthony (1966, 1971)	For the most part	Some	Two out of three: sound, meaning, and spelling
Signing Exact English (SEE 2)	Gustason, Pfetzing, and Zawolkow (1972)	Same as SEE 1	Same as SEE 1	Same as SEE 1
Linguistics of Visual English	Wampler (1971, 1972)	Same as SEE 1	Same as SEE 1	Same as SEE 1
Manual English	Washington State School for the Deaf (1972)	Yes	More than SEE 1	Variable – one meaning-one sign Some same as SEE 1
Signed English	Bornstein et al. (1973, 1975)	Yes	Yes Variable amounts	To string together ASL signs with 14 markers and fingerspelling
signed English Siglish Ameslish	Riekehof (1963) Fant (1964, 1972) Watson (1964) Bragg (1973) O'Rourke (1973)	Yes	Yes	Pidginization of ASL signs and English markers and word order

From Fristoe and Lloyd (1978) (modified from Wilbur, 1976)

would force any particular combination of the outlined possibilities. Since English irregular verbs are subdivided into groups, perhaps a manual system that also subdivided them would be preferable to one that did not. However, the number of ways in which the verbs can be subdivided, and the way they are treated once they have been subdivided, is largely a matter of preference. Consider how the past tenses are actually treated.

As indicated earlier, time is indicated in ASL by the use of the time line. The time is generally established by the use of a time adverbial (YESTERDAY, TOMORROW, LAST-WEEK), after which if no time indication is given, it is assumed to be at that time. "Time . . . seems to be in sign language a sentence or utterance rather than a verb matter. Unlike an English finite verb, which must indicate tense, a sign verb will remain uninflected for time. Instead, the sentence or utterance as a whole will have whatever time reference the situation or a general or specific time sign has indicated until a change is signalled" (Stokoe and colleagues, 1976). In fact, Stokoe and colleagues' description is not strictly speaking correct. For those readers unfamiliar with time and aspectual systems in other languages, it should be pointed out that spoken languages do not all require a tense marker added to the verb the way English does. Some require even more elaborate systems (for example, French and other Romance languages), but many do not mark the verbs at all. Other options include having a single marker in each sentence or having a single marker on the conversation itself. ASL frequently uses one conversational time marker, as Stokoe and colleagues have described, but use other signs, such as FINISH, to help sequence the order of events (in general, languages prefer to put the description of events in the same order as they actually happen in the real world, this order being changed for dramatic purposes like storytelling). Languages that use a single marker for every sentence frequently put that marker in the second position (as the second word) in the sentence, but linguists do not really know why the second position is special. ASL does not use the second position marker strategy, and seems to use the sentence marking strategy much less frequently than the primary strategy of just marking the conversation itself. In this way, ASL differs dramatically from English, but not from other spoken languages.

In the PGSS system, verbs are divided into two groups, those made with one hand and those made with two hands. The one-handed signs form their past tense by simultaneously signing the verb with one hand and the sign PAST with the other. The two-handed signs form their past tense by sequentially signing first the verb and then the PAST sign (PGSS does not use ASL signs).

In general, the past tense in SEE 2 is formed by signing the verb followed by the ASL sign PAST. The past participle is formed by signing the verb plus FINISH.

In Manual English, all verbs form their past tense by using the sign PAST after the verb. However, verbs are divided into regular and irregular for purposes of forming the past participle. For regular verbs, the past participle is the same as the past tense (VERB + PAST). For irregular past participles, the sequence VERB + PAST + FINISH is used.

In Bornstein and colleagues' (1973, 1975) version of Signed English, two past tense markers are used, one for regular verbs and one for irregular verbs.

It should now be clear that each system has its own "systematic principle." Each principle is arbitrary in terms of the structure of English. However, as far as the child is concerned, each system has its own set of signs to correspond to different concepts. Since the child does not yet know English, it makes little difference linguistically whether he learns TEAR (with an E hand) as the sign for "tore," or TEAR + PAST, or TEAR + d, or t + o + r + e. The creators of the sign systems hope, however, that the basic principles of their system will somehow become real and meaningful to the child, that the child will learn that all verbs signed one way have something in common. However, there are no data as yet to indicate whether a child realizes that what those signs have in common is that their English equivalents correspond to the regular rule of English past tense formation. Children are most likely to look only for generalizations about the system that they are learning, in order to organize their memory more efficiently and to make their task of comprehension and production easier. It remains to be experimentally demonstrated that these generalizations carry over into their use of English.

GENERAL COMMENTS ON THE SYSTEMS

Before giving a description of each of the systems, several major differences should be pointed out. In the area of sign usage and sign formation, the systems have different principles which serve as guidelines for determining what signs should be used (particularly for the many words not listed in the system's dictionary or manual of usage). For example, the PGSS system utilizes a combination of basic sign + modifier sign to form most of its words. The basic sign is a category, like PERSON or ANIMAL. The modifier sign specifies the nature of the particular intended referent. One hand forms the sign

PERSON and the other forms the sign TOOTH ("dentist"), TEACH ("teacher"), FIRE ("fireman"), or STETHOSCOPE ("doctor"). For every meaning there is a separate sign. (Interestingly, Craig, 1976, reports that "in practice it has been found that with the possible exception of the ANIMAL signs, children are not aware of the derivation of the signs any more than hearing children are aware of the derivation of words until they have acquired considerable linguistic sophistication," thus supporting skepticism concerning the supposed benefits of the sign systems.)

On the other hand, SEE 2 has as a basic principle that if two of the following three criteria are identical for two English words, the same sign is used for both of them: (1) pronunciation, (2) spelling, and (3) meaning. For example, "wind" (breeze) and "wind" (what you do to a clock or watch) are spelled the same but are pronounced differently and have different meanings; therefore they have different signs. On the other hand, "sock," which can mean both "stocking" and "to hit," is spelled and pronounced the same for both of its two meanings and is thus represented by one sign despite widely divergent meanings.

Manual English, like PGSS, generally has one sign for each meaning. The English word "call" is represented with four separate ASL signs in Manual English: NAME, SUMMONS, PHONE, and SHOUT. (SEE 2 would use one sign based on pronunciation and spelling). Bornstein (1973) does not believe that an "altered form of the sign word will facilitate the learning of the English word form" and hence Signed English uses ASL signs for all types of English words. These rules are summarized in Table 10–1.

The systems also differ in their expressed attitude toward the use of fingerspelling. In PGSS, fingerspelling is used only for proper names. In SEE 2, fingerspelling is generally avoided. Manual English, on the other hand, is not opposed to the use of fingerspelling and would permit it, for example, as an alternate form of the past tense formation. In Signed English, whenever an English word cannot be represented by one sign word and one sign marker, fingerspelling is recommended. The amount of fingerspelling in signed English varies, the actual amount depending greatly on the person's fluency in English and whom the person is signing with.

Where possible, the following discussion will be organized so that the general principles are outlined first, followed by examples from pronouns and verbs, then followed by discussion of the rules for creating new words and compounds. In each case, problems with these will be identified as they occur.

PAGET-GORMAN SYSTEMATIC SIGN (PGSS)

General Principles

PGSS was developed in England with the intention that the system be discarded by the child when he no longer needed it for communication (i.e., when the child had mastered English). Craig (1976) lists the following aims for PGSS:

1. To provide correct patterns of English to enable the deaf child to learn language at an age which is more commensurate with the natural optimum age of language learning in normally hearing children.
2. To increase the deaf child's comprehension by giving clearer patterns of correct language than those which are available to him by speechreading alone.
3. To enable the deaf child to build up an understanding of correct language in conjunction with speech and speechreading. It should provide a sound foundation for the future use of speech and speechreading to be used by themselves where possible or for correct fingerspelling to be used where this form of communication is considered to be most appropriate for the individual child.
4. To encourage in the deaf child a desire to communicate verbally.
5. To accelerate his learning of all school subjects by providing clear, unambiguous patterns of correct language.
6. To encourage the deaf child to express English which would be considered acceptable for his age and environment.
7. To increase the probability of the deaf child's reaching a reading level which would enable him to read with facility, and so benefit him educationally and socially.
8. To offer a method of remedial teaching for those deaf children or young adults whose language has not been adequately developed by other methods of teaching.

Since PGSS was developed in England it does not use signs from ASL. The system is based on pantomimic signs which include 21 standard hand positions and 39 basic signs used in different combinations. Each basic sign serves to group together signs with a common concept. Basic signs exist for FOOD, INSECT, PERSON, ANIMAL, and so on. The standard hand configurations serve to differentiate specific lexical items in each group, although a basic sign is not necessary for every sign. As indicated earlier, this internal sign structure seems to be opaque to the children. Craig (1976) points out that "although the Basic Signs are not functioning in the way that the authors originally intended they are by no means a useless feature of the system.... They are of considerable value to hearing adults learning to use the system since they form the basis of a fairly logical pattern to which the system largely conforms. Because of this relatively logical pattern to the system, most of the signs can be learned with comparative ease, though not without some effort."

Aside from the lexical signs described, there are also grammatical signs in PGSS. The following affixes are listed in Craig (1976):

1. Plural of nouns (regular or irregular)
2. Possessive
3. Comparative and superlative of adjectives (-ER, -EST). (Those that would be said with "more" or "most" in English are signed with MORE or MOST.)
4. Present progressive (-ING)
5. Past tense of verbs (regular or irregular)
6. Past participle
7. Third person singular -S in present tense verbs
8. Adverb (-LY)
9. Adjective (-Y)

Pronouns

The PGSS pronoun system follows the pattern of English pronouns. There are separate signs for first, second, and third person singular pronouns: I, YOU, and IT. The other pronouns are variations of the main sign. For example, the pronoun "he" is signed by combining the pronoun IT on one hand with the sign MALE on the other. Reflexive pronouns are formed by signing the possessive form (formed on the nominative) and then the pronoun SELF. Thus "myself" is MY + SELF. (Implication: the reflexive "himself" is signed as HIS + SELF, a common mistake made by young hearing children, second language learners, and deaf children). Plurals in PGSS are formed by signing the functional sign PLURAL after the noun: NOUN + PLURAL (for both regular and irregular nouns). Possessives are formed by signing the noun and then the functional sign POSSESSIVE (NOUN + POSSESSIVE). Plural possessives have the form NOUN + PLURAL + POSSESSIVE.

Verbs

All verbs are treated alike in PGSS except the verb "to be." "Be" has six distinct signs: BE, AM, IS, ARE, WAS, and WERE. The other verbs are all used unmarked in the present tense, except third person singular. That is, there are no endings or modifications to indicate first or second person singular or plural, third person plural, or regular versus irregular verb. The future tense is formed by using a separate sign TIME-FORWARD before each verb (analogous to English "will" + verb). As mentioned earlier, the past tense involves a division of verbs into one-handed and two-handed signs (rather than the English regular versus irregular), with one-handed signs simultaneously signing the verb and TIME-BACKWARD and two-handed signs sequentially signing the verb and then TIME-BACKWARD. The present participle is formed by a functional sign -ING which follows the verb. The sign PAST PARTICIPLE (PAST PART) is used to form participles from the past tense, that is, VERB + TIME-BACKWARD + PAST PART, where TIME-BACKWARD follows the rule for past tense formation.

New Word Formation

The formation of compound and complex signs is the area in which most of the systems run into trouble. They end up being either internally inconsistent, cumbersome, or counterintuitive. The PGSS system has attempted to avoid the complexities inherent in paralleling English word formation by establishing its own morphological rules, although a few still parallel English. The -ING functional sign can be used to derive nouns from verbs, and the -LY suffix is used to derive some adjectives and adverbs. For the most part, however, the signs are formed on productive combinations of the 39 basic signs and the 21 standard hand configurations. Examples of human signs ("dentist," "fireman," "doctor") were given earlier. Others include "elephant" = ANIMAL + LONG-NOSE, "leopard" = ANIMAL + SPOTS, "lion" = ANIMAL + ROAR. Compound signs are made by combining two or more basic signs: "bedroom" = BED + SLEEP, "scent" = GOOD + SMELL, "contract" = PAPER + LAW, "breakfast" = MORNING + FOOD.

The signs of PGSS are pantomimic in some sense, but could not be taken as universal. For example, the sign for "frog" is ANIMAL + JUMP, which could be taken to refer to a kangaroo in Australia. Furthermore, PGSS violates an American cultural taboo on extended middle finger by using this hand configuration in some of its signs (this hand configuration is allowable in British Sign Language).

PGSS does not exist alone in England. In an article on the role of sign language in the British Deaf community, Lawson (1983) discussed another system — a signed version of the Makaton vocabulary — and British Sign Language, and the attitudes of deaf people toward them. Further descriptions of British Sign Language are available in Woll, Kyle, and Deuchar (1981), Brennan, Colville, and Lawson (1980), and Kyle and Woll (1983). The British sign language researchers have been among the most active outside the United States.

SIGNING EXACT ENGLISH (SEE 2)

General Principles

SEE 2 is an outgrowth of David Anthony's original work on Seeing Essential English (SEE 1). Bornstein (1973) reports an overlap between SEE 2 and SEE 1 of 75 percent (general vocabulary only) to 80 percent (affixes, pronouns, and "be"-verbs included). SEE 2 was developed by Gustason, Pfetzing, and Zawolkow (1972). The manual and a supplement are currently available from the National Association of the Deaf. The SEE 2 manual includes 2100 words and 70 affixes, with 7 contractions. Words are divided into basic words, complex words, and compound words. The system uses the two-out-of-three principle described previously, namely, that the same sign is used for two English words if those two words are alike in two of the three features — pronunciation, spelling, and meaning. One of the ASL signs may be chosen to represent the two words, or a new sign may be invented. The ASL sign would be used if it is "clear, unambiguous, and has only one English translation" (Gustason, Pfetzing, and Zawolkow, 1974). The exception to the basic two-out-of-three principle is that inflected basic forms cannot be used as new basic words. For example, the past tense of "see," "saw," cannot be used as the sign for the verb "to saw."

Pronouns

SEE 2 retains some of the ASL pronoun signs — ME, YOU, and YOUR. Initialized signs have been invented for the other pronouns, using, for example, the E hand for "he," the M hand for "him," and the S hand for "his." Possessive pronouns are formed by adding -S to the possessive adjectives; for example, "yours" is signed as YOUR + S. The exception to this is "mine," which is MY + EN. The reflexives are formed by the same principles as in PGSS (only using some ASL signs) with the possessive adjective (MY, YOUR, HIS, etc.) followed by SELF for the singular and SELF + s for the plural. Regular plural nouns are formed by signing s after the noun. Irregular nouns are divided — nouns in which the final consonant is a voiceless fricative in the singular and a voiced fricative in the plural ("leaf"-"leaves") are treated as ASL plurals and pluralized by reduplication. Possessives are formed using the contraction 's (an s hand that moves in the shape of an apostrophe), added directly to singular nouns and after the plural marker s in plural nouns (the plural marker is also an s hand, but it does not move).

Verbs

Regular and irregular verbs are treated similarly in SEE 2. In the present tense, the third person singular is inflected with -s (same s as the plural marker). The ASL sign PAST is used after the verb to indicate past tense. The future is formed with the ASL sign FUTURE which has been initialized with a w handshape to stand for "will." For the present participle, the suffix -ING is used, and for the past participle the ASL sign FINISH is used after the verb. Auxiliary verbs are differentiated, however. The past tense is formed using the past participle sign FINISH, so "could" = CAN + FINISH. Also, the verb "to be" has several signs associated with it. Some are derived from the ASL sign TRULY, which is initialized with A for "am," R for "are," I for "is," B for "be." To indicate past tense, the ASL sign PAST has been initialized with s for "was," R for "were." Some of these signs for "be" have been accepted into ASL and are now being used by deaf adults in formal situations in many parts of the country.

New Word Formation

In every language, words are created by combining one or more morphemes. For example, the word "farmers" is composed of the morphemes "farm" + "er" + "s," where "farm" is a verb stem, "er" is an agentive suffix (one who does), and "s" is a plural marker. The PGSS system does not attempt to parallel English morphology, but the SEE 2 system does. It uses morphemes that are productive and have constant semantic value (thus the meaning of a word composed of morphemes A + B + C should be predictable from the meaning of the individual morphemes themselves. An example of an English word that does not have the meaning of its composite morphemes is "carpet," which has a meaning unrelated to either "car" or "pet"). As with SEE 1, the two-out-of-three principle holds for choice of signs. Since the affix "-ship" (as in "relationship") has the same spelling and pronunciation as the noun "ship," one sign is used for both, even though the meanings are radically different. Complex words are formed by adding an affix if there is one in English, regardless of meaning. For example, the pair "red"-"redden" follows an English rule for deriving verbs from adjectives ("light"-"lighten," "white"-"whiten") and an -EN suffix is used in SEE 2 for these forms. However, the same -EN suffix is used in SEE 2 for words that in English mean something entirely different as a result of an "-en" ending, such as "chick"-"chicken," "mitt"-"mitten," "my"-"mine." (In addition, the -EN sign is actually the past participle FINISH sign, so "chicken" is really signed as CHICK + FINISH. The "chick"-"chicken" pair is particularly disturbing, since it seems that the sign should instead indicate that "chick" is a "little chicken.") Whether or not these system deviances have any effect on children's acquisition of English remains to be seen.

Despite the fact that SEE 2 holds to the two-out-of-three principle even in some very strange situations (as in "-ship," "ship"), it nonetheless includes a number of words that are not formed along this principle at all. Some forms are actually broken down into archaic morpheme divisions ("height" = HIGH + T), or syllable divisions ("sorrow" = SORRY + W, "jewelry" = JEWEL + R + Y, "nursery" = NURSE + ER + Y, "any" = AN + Y). This is not done systematically, however, since, for example, "although," "also," "already" are signed as two signs, namely, AL + THOUGH, whereas "almost," which could easily be divided like the others, is nonetheless one sign.

With respect to compound signs, SEE 2 uses two signs if the word retains the meaning of the two words that compose it ("babysit," "shepherd") and uses a single sign (ASL or invented) for words that have nonpredictable meanings ("carpet" has its own sign because it has nothing to do with either "cars" or "pets"). Words like "yesterday" and "today" are treated as two signs each, ignoring available ASL signs for both of them. "Hot dog" is also treated as two signs even though the relationship between its meaning and that of "a hot dog" is fairly obscure. Again, it should be pointed out that these are purely arbitrary decisions and that most of the systems have this kind of problem with English morphology, so SEE 2 alone cannot be faulted.

MANUAL ENGLISH

General Principles

Manual English was developed by the Total Communication Program at the Washington State School for the Deaf in order to provide a system that would parallel English sufficiently well that it could be used in conjunction with normal speech. The system is taught to adults who are in contact with the child so that English structure can be reinforced through signs at all times. Again, it must be noted that English syntax can be presented this way, but that English morphology causes difficulty. Manual English uses more fingerspelling than does SEE 2. A signer also has several options, such as forming a verb tense as VERB + TENSE or of partially spelling the word, for example, VERB + e + d.

Pronouns and Verbs

Manual English uses many of the ASL signs. If an English word has more than one meaning, and each of those meanings has a separate ASL sign, then ASL signs are retained. A large number of initialized signs are used. The pronouns in Manual English are the same as those in SEE 2, except that "mine" = MY + e whereas SEE 2 uses MY + EN. The contractions, plurals, and possessives are the same as in SEE 2. Manual English handles the verb "to be" in the same manner as SEE 2 but differs in its treatment of main verbs, notably in its handling of the past participle. The ASL sign FINISH is used as a suffix marker for the past participle, but, unlike SEE 2, Manual English divides the verbs into regular and irregular. Those irregular verbs that have a distinct word for present, past, and past participle forms, as "speak-spoke-spoken," use the past participle form VERB + PAST + FINISH. (One should bear in mind that distinctions such as this are opaque to all but the most knowledgeable students, for whom this division, as most of the others, is purely an arbitrary one requiring special memorization. That is, the student must learn the list of signs that take FINISH in their past participles as exceptions to the otherwise regular rule of having simply VERB + PAST.) Other irregular verbs, such as "hit-hit-hit" and "come-came-come," are not discussed in the manual. The auxiliary verbs in Manual English are derived from English, ASL, and SEE 2. The auxiliary verb "have to" has its own sign from ASL. Initialized versions of this sign are used for NEED, MUST, and OUGHT TO. "Would," "should," and "could" are treated as the past tenses of "will," "shall," and "can," respectively — WOULD = WILL + d, SHOULD = SHALL + d, COULD = CAN + d. Thus, in Manual English, "I would have been given . . ." would be signed I WILL + d HAVE BE + PAST PART GIVE + PAST + FINISH.

New Word Formation

In compound and complex sign formation, Manual English has borrowed some signs from SEE 2, eliminated others, and altered others. Some nonproductive affixes like -NEATH, and YESTER- have been eliminated because of their limited use ("beneath," "underneath," "yesterday," "yesteryear"). Unlike SEE 2, which uses the same -ER suffix for most occurrences of English "-er," Manual English has three -ER signs, one for the agentive "-er" (one who does) using the ASL sign PERSON, one for the comparative "-er" ("bigger," "smaller"), and one for everything else ("prayer," "eraser," "dryer"). Note that in this last category, an eraser is that which erases, and a dryer is that which dries, but a prayer is not that which prays, nor one who prays (one who prays would be agentive and would use PERSON), so that the third group is an arbitrary collection of leftovers.

The principles for complex word formation vary. The basic rule is supposed to be that if no ASL sign exists for a complex word, then an affix may be used to form a sign. However, there are cases where this principle is overlooked, as seen by the use of NEAR + PERSON for "neighbor." The same principle is supposed to hold for compound words, so that "oversight," "grandmother," "gentleman," and "workshop" use the ASL signs, whereas two signs are put together when needed, for example, "houseparent" = HOUSE + PARENT.

SIGNED ENGLISH

General Principles

Bornstein and his colleagues (Bornstein, 1973, 1978; Bornstein and Hamilton, 1972; Bornstein et al., 1973, 1975; Bornstein and Saulnier, 1981; Bornstein, Saulnier, and Hamilton, 1980) constructed Signed English for use with preschool and elementary school children. The intention is to provide "a semantic approximation to the usual language environment of the hearing child" (Bornstein, 1973). The 2500-word vocabulary is chosen for use with the young child and includes sign words and sign markers. Of these 2500 signs, 1700 are from ASL and the rest are either invented or borrowed from other systems. The 12 sign markers function for basic English structures. The plural is marked by fingerspelling "-s" after the sign for regular nouns, and by reduplication for irregular nouns (again, an arbitrary choice of divisions). The 's sign for possessive, which has been somewhat accepted into ASL, is used in Signed English. Unlike the other systems, contractions are treated as separate words and have their own signs. Thus, there is a separate sign for "don't," which is not an alteration of "do not." The evidence from early language acquisition in hearing children supports the view that children learn contractions as separate entities ("don't" and "can't" appear in utterances in an earlier developmental stage than "can" and "do" or the other modals, which suggests that they are learned as whole units, rather than as contractions of their component words). Four sign markers are used with the verbs, one for the past tense of regular verbs, one for the past tense of irregular verbs, one for the third person singular present, and one for the past participle. The possible combinations of signs and markers are limited, so anything not covered by these principles is fingerspelled. In all probability, the system is sufficient for the young child and many retarded individuals.

PERKINS SIGN LANGUAGE DICTIONARY

General Principles

The *Perkins Sign Language Dictionary* represents a synthesis from 11 other sources compiled by the Department for Deaf-Blind Children of the Perkins School for the Blind in Massachusetts. The sources that are included are Babbini (1974), Bornstein and colleagues (1973), Fant (1972), Gustason, Pfetzing, and Zawolkow (1972, 1973, 1974), Huffman et al. (1974), Kannapell, Hamilton, and Bornstein (1969), Madsen (1972), O'Rourke (1973), Riekehof (1963), Sanders (1968), and Watson (1964). Thus, this dictionary includes signs from several systems (SEE 1, SEE 2, Signed English) as well as ASL signs. The population for which this dictionary was originally constructed and the objectives that the authors set for their language instruction are discussed in greater detail in Chapter 12. The discussion here is confined to the structure of the system as it might concern those who are teaching normal deaf children. The authors do not see their primary goal as teaching English to the children, thus the dictionary is aimed first at "communication, expressiveness, language for learning, language for thinking, communication skills to enhance a sense of personal worth and relationship to others" (Robbins et al., 1975). They see the "acquisition of English as an important secondary goal" for those students who are likely to go on to learn to read, at which time they suggest an attempt at "a reasonably good match between English and the sign system used *but* while maintaining 'meaning', not phonetic or written word, as the basic unit to be respected." Thus, the dictionary is not a system in the same sense as SEE 2, for example, in that it does not provide a series of guidelines based on English spelling, meaning, and pronunciation for choosing signs, but instead has laid out a totally different set of criteria for sign choice.

To begin with, the Perkins group recognizes the need for more than one "system" for a varied population and that the best approach for an individual child may change as the child matures. They are concerned with systems that are "expressive, focusing on intended meaning and feeling, *not* on stringing together of surface structure words." The systems should be easy for parents and teachers to learn, "relating to English but not to the point of becoming overly self-conscious and burdened with affixes and rules." After learning the system, students should also be able to communicate with ASL users and signed English users. For more complex markers, rather than develop a separate set of special signs for English affixes and function words, the use of fingerspelling is preferred.

The vocabulary itself is chosen from several sources. The Lexington *Vocabulary Norms for Deaf Children* aided in choosing word categories. Once the vocabulary was determined, signs were chosen to represent them. The 11 previously named sources were consulted, as were deaf adults. If more than one sign was available for a given word or concept, the following criteria were used for making a decision (Robbins et al., 1975):

1. The preferred sign was that seeming to be most descriptive of *meaning* rather than of English surface or phonological structure.
2. An attempt was made to choose signs that had a high consensus of usage among 11 sources.
3. If there was no consensus, signs advocated by Riekehof and ABC [O'Rourke] were given first priority; those from Bornstein and Watson were given second priority; the other sources were then considered.
4. Occasionally, a sign was chosen because it was motorically easiest, after the first three criteria above had been met.

The use of these types of criteria, rather than the two-out-of-three principle, or the rigid one sign-one meaning approach, provides a reasonable perspective on using signs to teach children. Of particular importance is the fact that the users of such a system are not misled into thinking that they are providing a perfect parallel for English, and are thus not disturbed when deaf children do not produce the type of sentences that the other systems imply that they should.

A major advantage to the use of the *Perkins Sign Language Dictionary* as a system for teaching deaf children is its flexibility in the area of syntax. Although ASL syntax is not used, neither is strict English syntax. Instead, the dictionary recognizes levels of competence that might require different forms of syntactic expression. Three levels are described (Manual English, Basic Signed English, and Perkins Signed English) which move toward increasing use of fingerspelling, more emphasis on English written structure, and a closer approximation of English syntax.

The first level, Manual English, consists of the Perkins Sign Vocabulary, English word order, and facial and body expressiveness with mime when needed. This is the starting level, and the child may be presented with the second level only when he begins to spontaneously use three or more signs together.

The second level, Basic Signed English, includes the Perkins Sign Vocabulary, English word order, facial and body expressiveness, four sign markers (PAST, PLURAL, POSSESSIVE, and PERSON), and increased fingerspelling for more complicated English structures. A child may be presented with the third level of complexity only after he:

a) is reading stories *not* relating to his own personal experiences and of more than two or three paragraphs, and b) *spontaneously* and *consistently* expressing the following structures in his everyday language:
(1) Use of PAST MARKER
(2) Use of POSSESSIVE MARKER
(3) Use of PLURAL MARKER
(4) Use of PERSON MARKER
(5) Use of range of TIME INDICATOR WORDS
(6) Formulates questions using WHO, WHAT, WHEN, and WHERE (Robbins et al., 1975)

The third level of complexity, Perkins Signed English, includes the Perkins Sign Vocabulary, English word order, facial and body expressiveness, the sign markers COMPARATIVE and SUPERLATIVE, and expansion of fingerspelling. During reading or grammar lessons, four other markers may also be used — adverb marker -LY, adjective marker -Y, contraction marker -N'T, and gerund marker -ING. Robbins and colleagues (1975) offer some guidelines for the use of markers and the different levels:

1. Importance is placed on evaluating the child's *own* expressive everyday performance in language as a cue to how enthusiastic one should be about the use of English markers.
2. If the essentials of language (an agent, an action, a time indication, and so on) are not expressed in the simplest forms, by the student, then to push for or expect further differentiation of structure is unrealistic; conversely, if the elements of language structure *are* expressed readily one can assume a reasonable language learning capacity and explore for the possibility of added differentiated structures related to English.

signed ENGLISH

The system of signed English is an outgrowth of the ASL-English pidginization process (Fant, 1964; O'Rourke, 1973; Watson, 1964; see also Chapter 9). It includes a great deal of variation.

signed English uses ASL signs strung together in English word order by the use of fingerspelling and some conjunction words. The degree of English word order may vary, however, depending on the amount of fingerspelling used. Thus, the signer may use T+h+e TWO MAN w+e+r+e s+e+a+r+c+h+i+n+g QUIET for "The two men were searching quietly" in a formal situation and in a less formal situation use TWO MAN SEARCH++ QUIET SEARCH++, using ASL reduplication to indicate the present progressive. This variability closely approximates the situation in spoken languages, where each person has several styles corresponding to the formality of the situation and the people involved. Consider for example the difference between everyday speech and formal letter writing, or telephone calls to a friend, or to the boss, or to a client, or to a stranger. What varies is not just the content, but also the linguistic structure, the carefulness of articulation, and the choice of vocabulary items. In signed English this is reflected in the amount of fingerspelling used and the number of rules chosen from English or ASL (see discussion in Chapter 9 on Pidgin Sign English). It provides for greater fluency, since if one does not know a sign, communication can continue uninterrupted by fingerspelling the word as long as the deaf person knows the English word that is spelled. In addition, the need for arbitrary sign formation rules is eliminated, since words for which no sign exists can be fingerspelled. Situations such as these test new or invented signs. Some catch on and become accepted (particularly some initialized signs as, for example, the different signs for the verb "to be") whereas others are rejected and drop from usage. Dialects develop (a natural situation for any language) and historical changes take place. Furthermore, the teacher can legitimately insist on grammatical signed English in the classroom and still condone the manual communication that goes on outside the classroom as a reflection of these different linguistic styles (nobody really speaks the way English teachers would like them to, but many people expect deaf children to use classroom language outside the classroom, a highly artificial situation). Furthermore, differences in sign usage, such as might occur between users of SEE 2 and users of Manual English, do not occur here.

FINGERSPELLING AND CUED SPEECH

Fingerspelling and cued speech have been separated from the other systems because their relationship with English and speech is different. They are treated individually here.

Fingerspelling

Fingerspelling (dactylology) is a procedure whereby each letter of the spelling of a word is represented by a handshape. There are 26 distinct handshapes that correspond to the 26 letters of the alphabet (see Figure 2–2), although two letters, "j" and "z," require movement as well. Because the hand configurations correspond to the letters of the alphabet, fingerspelling in the United States is a manual representation of written English; other countries have their own fingerspelling alphabets (for illustrations of alphabets from 45 countries, see Carmel, 1982). In England, although the spoken language is also English, the fingerspelling alphabet is two-handed. The fingerspelling alphabets used in France, Italy, and other European countries are similar to that used in the United States. This similarity led to the adoption of the International Fingerspelling Alphabet by the Fourth Congress of the World Federation of the Deaf in Stockholm in 1963 (this is also illustrated in Carmel, 1982). The International Fingerspelling Alphabet, although not really universal, has gained some acceptance in Europe.

Because fingerspelling is a manual representation of the spoken language, it has no separate syntax, morphology, phonology, or semantics, but instead is entirely dependent on the linguistic structure of the language it is representing. In this sense, it is similar to Morse code, which translates each letter of the alphabet into dots and dashes. The consistent pairing of fingerspelling with speech as a means of communication is known as the Rochester Method in the United States and as Neo-oralism in the Soviet Union (Moores, 1974, 1977).

Fingerspelling presents several obvious advantages and disadvantages. Skilled fingerspelling can provide rapid transmission of a message. Another advantage is the fact that anyone who can spell can quickly learn to produce the 26 handshapes. Thus teachers, parents, and clinicians are provided with a quick and easy way to begin communication with deaf people, although teachers of sign language do *not* recommend learning fingerspelling as a first step (too easy to fall into the bad habit of spelling everything rather than remembering the actual sign; for more on this topic, see Baker and Cokely, 1980). On the other hand, even though the average adult can learn to fingerspell in short order, learning to perceive and read fingerspelling is another matter. A skilled fingerspeller learns to form words as units, rather than as sequences of letters. In natural conversation, familiarity with the context allows some letters to be slurred or omitted without loss of intelligibility. The center letters of a word may be assimilated to the surrounding letters, blurring the formation of the letters and creating a perception problem. In fact, rapid fingerspelling appears to be perceived as a movement envelope inside of which there are rapid handshape changes. A fingerspelled word can still be accurately understood even if some of the handshape changes within the envelope are slurred or omitted because the envelope is what the skilled fingerspelling reader is expecting (Akamatsu, 1982, 1985; see Chapter 8). In rapid fingerspelling reading, one has to make successive guesses as to what is being spelled, in which case a thorough knowledge of the grammar of English (which determines what possible words can follow the words already read) is absolutely essential. In this respect, reading fingerspelling parallels speechreading. The problem of fingerspelling reading can be eased if the fingerspeller slows down considerably. This enables the reader to follow the fingers, but destroys the normal rate of conversation, and interrupts the normal flow of speech and intonation.

The reading of fingerspelling is not the only problem associated with it, the other problems being related to the use of fingerspelling with very young children (below age 5). The movements of the fingers are not large, and are usually rapid. Fingerspelling requires a considerably greater degree of manual motor coordination than does signing. Although a child may put two or three signs together into an utterance at about 1 year 6 months, fingerspelling does not emerge until much later. Wilbur and Jones (1974) observed nearly none at age 3 years 6 months. In fact, the only spelling seen was the child's own name, which was not done correctly, as a double consonant in the name was improperly formed by the child. In addition to the motor problem, very young children have difficulty learning to fingerspell because the ability to spell is important to fingerspelling. Hearing children do not usually learn to spell until they have had considerable experience with reading and spelling practice. Therefore, one cannot expect a very young child to acquire fingerspelling without a great deal of effort (drill, patience, practice) and formal training. Language is not learned by means of formal training by hearing children, and consequently the learning of fingerspelling should not be viewed as a normal language learning situation.

This is not to say that children *cannot* learn to fingerspell. Akamatsu (1982) has shown that young deaf children learn fingerspelling by learning the movement envelopes that deaf adults use to perceive fingerspelling. Fingerspelling has also been shown to be an effective aid in educational settings. Moores (1974, 1977) reviewed several Russian studies that reported success with fingerspelling combined with speech. Moores, Weiss, and Goodwin (1977) followed seven preschool programs for several years. They found that in one program, children taught with the Rochester Method seemed to lag at the early ages, but that by the time the children were about 8 years, their academic performance was significantly superior to children in the oral-only program. The total communication programs fell between the oral and the Rochester methods. In a study specifically designed to assess the effectiveness of fingerspelling as an educational tool, Quigley (1969) compared two preschool programs, one using the Rochester Method (simultaneous fingerspelling and speech) and the other using a traditional oral approach. He followed the two programs for 4 years. At the end, he found that the Rochester Method students were superior in one of two measures of speechreading, five of seven measures of reading, and in three of five measures of written language. The oral group was superior in only one measure of written language. Quigley also compared three residential schools using the Rochester Method with three comparable schools using simultaneous signs, fingerspelling, and speech (probably signed English). No differences in speech or speechreading were found between the two groups. Quigley (1969) concluded that "1) The use of fingerspelling in combination with speech as practiced in the Rochester Method can lead to improved achievement in deaf students particularly on those variables where meaningful language is involved. 2) When good oral techniques are used in conjunction with fingerspelling there need be no detrimental effects on the acquisition of oral skills. 3) Fingerspelling is likely to produce greater benefits when used with younger rather than older children. It was used successfully in the experimental study with children as young as three and a half years of age. 4) Fingerspelling is a useful tool for instructing deaf children, but it is not a panacea."

Children of deaf parents who sign and fingerspell have considerable opportunity to observe their parents and to learn from them. In this situation, (1) signing is the primary language that is learned according to developmental stages and without formal instruction and (2) the fingerspelling that is acquired emerges much later and only as an auxiliary. The adult problem of perceiving and comprehending rapid fingerspelling is magnified with the very young child, both in terms of small hand movements and speed. Finally, fingerspelling is slow when compared to signing or speech. To get a feel for what it must be like, have someone read you the last paragraph letter by letter.

Cued Speech

Cornet (1967, 1969) described Cued Speech as a system designed "to enable the deaf child to learn language through exposure to a visible phonetic analog of speech supplied by the lip movements and supplementing hand cues." As Moores (1969) pointed out, the components ("cues") have no meaning independent of their association with those lip movements. (One cue may represent three consonants. The lip movements are needed in order to determine which of the three is intended.) Thus, the system is most appropriately viewed as an *auxiliary* to speech and not as a separate communication channel for language. In addition to the system of Cued Speech developed by Cornett, several other similar systems were developed in Europe. In the mid-nineteenth century, a French monk, Friar Bernard of Saint Gabriel, developed a system that cued only consonants. Several years later, another Frenchman, Monsieur Fourcade, developed a similar system. Another system was developed by Dr. Georg Forchhammer of the Boarding School for Deaf and Hard-of-Hearing Children at Frederica. Forchhammer's doctoral dissertation reported that the system had a beneficial effect on communication. His system employs hand movements to demonstrate the movement of the mouth organs that cannot be observed during normal speech (glottis, palate, etc.) rather than cueing particular phonetic segments (Børrild, 1972).

In Cornett's system, there are 36 cues for the 44 phonemes of English. The vowel cues are represented by hand locations and the consonant cues are represented by hand configurations. It is therefore possible to represent consonant-vowel pairs by combining the consonant hand configuration on the vowel location. Diphthongs are represented by a sequence of the first vowel location followed by the second vowel location. Some of the handshapes are similar to those of ASL. The 5-hand configuration of ASL is identical to the cue for /m/, /f/, and /t/. The F hand of the fingerspelling alphabet is the cue for /h/, /s/, and /r/. The B hand clues /n/, /b/, and /ʍ/ ('wh'). The L hand cues /l/, /ʃ/ ('sh'), and /w/. The G hand (upright) cues /d/, /p/, and /ʒ/. Vowel locations are to the right side of the face near the ear, lower on the face by the cheek, below the chin and slightly to the right, and on the right side of the lips. In other words, the cues are made near the face so that they may be easily seen in the perceptual field while the eyes are on the lips, but so that they never come in front of the lips where they would obscure the lip movement.

Like fingerspelling, Cued Speech has its advantages and disadvantages. To its credit, it can be useful for conveying fine phonetic distinctions of either standard or dialect pronunciation to the already knowledgeable speaker. Success with Cued Speech, in the form of increased accuracy in speechreading, greater vocabulary, greater relaxation among the children, shortening of delay time between learning something receptively and producing expressively, increased communication among the children, and increased intelligibility of the children, has been reported (Rupert, 1969).

Moores (1969) has critically reviewed Cued Speech. Objections to the use of Cued Speech can be divided into those that deal with the general assumptions and rationale of the system and those that deal specifically with the system's phonetic base.

ASSUMPTIONS. In fact, the first objection is not to an explicit assumption, but to the lack of an explicit distinction, namely, the failure of Cornett to distinguish between language and speech. As indicated previously, such distinction is crucial to understanding the nature of language and how language is acquired. Not having made this distinction leads to another assumption, quite commonly held, that language is learned by imitation. It is Cornett's belief that the child will copy the adult cues and thus make himself better understood by the cues even though his speech may not be accurate. This will reduce frustration between adult and child and create a better atmosphere for learning. The problem is that the considerable body of research that exists on the acquisition of language indicates that the role of imitation is nowhere near as central to language acquisition as was previously thought. In investigating imitation, Bloom (1973a) was able to sort children into those who do imitate and those who do not. Clearly, those who do not imitate stand as evidence to the contrary of a theory of acquisition by imitation.

PHONETIC PROBLEMS. Moores (1969) pointed out that Cued Speech is intrinsically tied to the sound system and has little or no transfer potential to reading. It is the nature of English orthography that *phonemic* distinctions are indicated, but predictable *phonetic* ones are not. For example, in English /d/ and /t/ are pronounced as flaps when they come between two vowels. No one actually says [rayter] for "writer" and [ryder] for "rider." This flapping process is a general process which holds true for all the words of English for all the speakers. The written forms of the words do not indicate this process, yet it is a phonetic distinction. Likewise, certain unstressed vowels are reduced to a more central, less distinct vowel. This is also not indicated by the orthography. In addition, dialect pronunciation is of course not indicated by the orthography. One does not write "Cuber" for the New Englanders' "Cuba," although certainly such a major mark of New England pronunciation would have to be cued, otherwise the child would end up missing a major feature of the dialect. The reason for the discrepancy between the written forms and the types of phonetic processes just indicated is that certain phonetic distinctions do not make a difference, even though they are perfectly regular. For example, every voiceless consonant is aspirated at the beginning of an English word. If it were left out, however, its absence might not even be noticed. Cornett's system does not differentiate between those phonetic processes that are dialectal (the fine distinctions mentioned earlier) and those that are redundant, regular, not indicated in the writing systems, and consequently not crucial. It is a far more serious error for the vowel in "bat" to be mispronounced, since it could come out as "beat," "bit," "bait," "boat," "bought," "but," "bet," "bite," "beaut," and so on. The system does not set guidelines for the adult as to which phonetic distinctions are important and which are not. In fact, one could suggest that rather than maintain a phonetic base, a phonemic base would be preferable, but then the benefit of indicating fine dialectal distinctions would be lost. This leads to the next point, namely, the competence of the average adult with respect to phonetics. Berko and Brown (1966) remarked, "The untrained adult cannot even approximate an accurate phonetic record." Casual observation reveals that the untrained adult tends to resort to the *spelling* of the word, rather than its phonetic form. Thus we have the situation of an untrained adult trying to indicate phonetic distinctions which may or may not be important in a manner which may or may not be accurate to a child who may or may not imitate the cues, who may or may not produce them spontaneously on his own, but who is highly unlikely to understand what they indicate, and cannot utilize that information in learning to read. Børrild (1972) reported that a cued speech system has been in use in most Danish schools for nearly 70 years, and that "it is pretty obvious that most pupils having been trained in the mouth-hand system to accompany speech are rather helpless when they have to face pure lipreading. And in spite of the past 70 years, a very small minority only of the population will be acquainted with the mouth-hand system, and a far smaller minority will really master it." Again it should be emphasized that the entire system is geared toward speech and not toward language. Børrild concurred: "It is an indisputable fact that the mouth-hand system is an excellent medium in the articulation training, and that in many cases it is indispensable for adult persons with acquired deafness without any hearing residue but with a normal language...."

SUMMARY

The variety of approaches to the goal of representing English in a visual mode demonstrates the arbitrary nature of the choices that are made. Long-term evaluations of the relative effectiveness of the different systems must be conducted. The need for such comparisons should not be confused with the many comparisons of oral mode versus manual mode versus combined mode versus fingerspelling versus cued speech which have been conducted to demonstrate that the use of one or more manual modes is superior to the use of oral input only (cf. Beckmeyer, 1976, and Moores, 1974). Comparisons of methodology are addressed in more detail in Chapter 11. For purposes of interpreting the problems raised in this chapter with respect to questionable choices and assumptions involving various sign systems, the general trend indicated by most of the methodology studies is that signs, in any form, seem to be more preferable educationally than no signs at all. It remains to be determined if signs in an English-based system are preferable to ASL or even PSE.

CHAPTER 11

Sign Language and the Education of Deaf Children

All of the preceding information presented in this book would be, to many people, only an interesting academic exercise if it were not for the considerable educational, sociological and psychological implications that result from the use of ASL and the several sign systems. Jordan, Gustason, and Rosen (1976) found that 510 programs reported using total communication, some 333 of which (about 65 percent) had changed between 1968 and 1975. Children in these programs are learning some form of signed English. Included in this chapter is the research available on the feasibility and effectiveness of using manual communication with deaf children. In Chapter 12, similar research is reviewed on the use of sign langauge with non-deaf populations.

GENERAL COMMENTS ON READING AND WRITING

Deaf people who have lost their hearing before learning English have considerable difficulty with reading and writing. It is unusual for a deaf person to read at or above the fifth grade level at age 18. In the discussion that follows, it will be argued that this poor performance results from at least three sources: (1) inadequate language skills resulting from the reduced language input due to the hearing loss (2) inadequate methods of teaching deaf children, in part due to excessive concerns over modality (signing or speech) and in part due to a lack of appreciation of the complexities of language and language acquisition, and (3) reading instruction that focuses on one aspect, sentence interpretation, to the virtual exclusion of other aspects, such as decoding, inferencing, and paragraph structure.

By the time hearing children begin to learn to read, they already have conversational fluency in their native language and they can transfer this knowledge to the reading task. Deaf children who have lost their hearing at an early age do not have this knowledge. Thus, they do not come to the reading task with the same skills in sentence formation, vocabulary, and world knowledge as hearing children. Deaf children who have deaf parents (less than 10 percent of all deaf children) who use sign language at home are an apparent exception. These children are more similar to hearing children who must learn to read and write in a second language, and their performance on such tasks tends to be better than deaf children who have hearing parents and who did not use signing from an early age. In fact, deaf children with deaf parents are four times more likely to go to college than deaf children with hearing parents (this will be discussed in a later section).

Reading

The process by which hearing children learn to read is still not completely understood. Many levels of processing are involved: (1) decoding or word recognition, (2) acquiring, storing, and retrieving word meanings, (3) extracting sentence meaning from words and syntactic structures, (4) realizing what is not stated but implied (inferencing), and (5) using the structure of the text to organize, store, and recall information.

CODING.   One approach to teaching hearing children to read involves the association of written letters (graphemes) with sounds, so that they can sound out the word and possibly recognize it when they hear it. Another approach teaches whole word recognition, rather than letter by letter. Once recognized, the child can pronounce the word. These approaches both assume that the child already knows the vocabulary word. In both cases, the major goal is the association of the printed word with speech. Fluent readers report that they have an "inner voice" when they read silently. The translation from print to speech, whether silently or out loud, is called phonological or sound recoding.

In spite of the fact that deaf students may not have developed spoken language, techniques for teaching them reading do not differ significantly from those used for hearing children. Students are taught to make letter-sound or whole word-sound associations, using whatever residual hearing and speech skills may be available. Beginning readers are expected to be able to read out loud, not only as a means of teaching reading but also as a way of working on speech skills. This is true in both oral and total communication programs. In total communication programs, the children may also sign the sentences "out loud," but the primary strategies focus on some form of sound recoding. Studies of deaf readers show that sound recoding is used by some for reading and memory purposes, but that other strategies are also present. These other strategies include recoding to signs, to fingerspelling, and to an internal representation of the printed letters ("graphemic recoding"). Sound recoding seems to be used more by deaf people whose hearing loss is not as severe, who have better speech skills, who score higher on intelligence tests, and who have higher educational achievement (these latter both contribute to and result from better reading ability). Sign recoding is used more frequently by native signers and individuals who do not meet the above-mentioned characteristics. Most deaf people show indications of using more than one strategy. However, the benefits of these other strategies are not systematically called upon in current programs for the teaching of reading.

VOCABULARY. The advantage of speech coding for hearing children lies in the possibility that they will recognize the vocabulary word once they can sound it out. Estimates of hearing children's vocabulary at the time they begin to learn to read range from 3000 to 5000 words. Estimates of deaf children's vocabularies are not available. One problem in making such an estimate is the fact that the student might know many signs but not know the corresponding English word in print, speechreading, or fingerspelling. Another problem is the method for testing word meaning in print; in one study the student has to correctly choose "time between sunrise and sunset" to demonstrate understanding of the word "day." This task probably underestimates the student's word knowledge because the student may know "day" but not "sunrise," "sunset," or the time concept involved.

It has been estimated that as much as two-thirds of written and spoken English involves some type of figurative language. There is a surprising amount of evidence (discussed later) that deaf readers can in fact understand various idioms, metaphors, and similes, although their abilities still lag far behind their hearing counterparts.

SYNTAX. Overall, the deaf student at age 18 does not have the facility with English syntax that a 10 year old hearing child has. Teachers expend much of their energy in the teaching of the particular rules for English sentence structure. In addition to the direct teaching of English syntax, teachers and materials developers have also modified the syntax of reading materials to make them less complex so that other learning (content) can take place. This has led to the development of "linguistically controlled" reading materials (see, for example, Quigley and King, 1985; Shulman and Decker, 1980). Details of some of the particularly difficult structures will be given in the more specific discussion that follows, along with some suggestions as to what causes these difficulties.

TEXT PROCESSING AND STORY GRAMMARS. Recent research on teaching reading to deaf children reflects an increasing awareness that there is more to the comprehension of text than word recognition and processing syntax. Current models of reading stress that it is a process that not only involves text-based, or "bottom-up," processing but also reader-based, or "top-down," processing. Top-down processing refers to the reader's ability to use prior knowledge of the topic, the story, the characters, similar situations, pictures in the text, and the like to make and test hypotheses about the text. The processing of a potentially ambiguous sentence "The chickens were too hot to eat" might depend on whether the story were titled "A Hot Day on the Farm" or the next sentence was "We sat in the dining room, sipping our lemonade, and waiting for them to cool." The reader's ability to use these cues affects the interpretation of the sentence and the larger context in which it occurs. Current comprehension theory suggests that readers attempt to construct a coherent mental representation of a passage based on both textual information and the reader's prior knowledge. The syntactic structure is but one clue to the correct meaning (Kretschmer, 1982; Wilbur and Nolen, in press).

Writing

The skilled writer, like the skilled reader, must be able to perform several tasks: (1) determine the structure of the text to be produced, (2) construct paragraphs that convey the major points, (3) construct and sequence grammatical sentences, (4) choose the correct vocabulary, (5) spell the words correctly, and (6) produce legible handwriting. All of this must be done while keeping in mind what the intended reader already knows and must know in order to understand what is written.

In many respects, deaf people's problems with writing are parallel to their problems with reading, and reflect the same general deficiency with English. They tend to display the same concern with the structure of individual sentences that their teachers do, and approach the task of writing a paragraph or letter as a matter of stringing "good" sentences together. Their paragraphs are stilted, and do not contain the connecting words that skilled writers use, such as "then," "so," "after a while." These words allow the thoughts or events to be framed with reference to other thoughts, events, or time frames. Deaf writers tend to omit these words and order their description of events in the same order that they actually happened. The resulting story structures lack complexity and creativity in terms of temporal sequence. The practice of teaching sentence by sentence certainly contributes to this problem.

There are two trends that may have future influence on deaf people's writing. One is the increasing use of telecommunications devices (TDDs) for phone calls. The conversation must be typed on a keyboard (from which it is transmitted over the phone lines to the TDD at the other end). This can provide a powerful motivation to learn more about English sentence structure and discourse structure (see discussion in Chapter 9). The other trend is the increasing presence of computers in the classroom. Some of the programs provide direct instruction in writing grammatical sentences, whereas others focus on larger contexts such as paragraphs and stories. Both types of technology require greater interaction with written material and cannot but help deaf people's abilities with reading and writing.

ACQUISITION OF ENGLISH

Learning English Syntax

The general difficulty that deaf children have learning English has been very well documented (Quigley and Kretschmer, 1982; Quigley and Paul, 1984; Wilbur, 1979; see Table 11-1). With respect to reading, Furth (1966a) reported that less than 12 percent of deaf students between the ages of 15 years 6 months and 16 years 6 months can read at a fourth-grade reading level or above (as meas-

Table 11-1. *Studies on specific literal and figurative structures*

Structure	Reference	Journal*
Passives	Power and Quigley (1973)	JSHR
	Nolen and Wilbur (1985)	AAD
Relative Clauses	Quigley, Smith, and Wilbur (1974)	JSHR
	Nolen and Wilbur (1985)	AAD
Questions		
(General)	Quigley, Wilbur, and Montanelli (1974)	JSHR
(Why)	Wilbur, Goodhart, and Montandon (1983)	The Volta Review
Pronouns		
(General)	Wilbur, Montanelli, and Quigley (1976)	JSHR
(Indefinite)	Wilbur, Goodhart, and Montandon (1983)	The Volta Review
(Indefinite)	Wilbur and Goodhart (1985)	Applied Psycholinguistics
(Reciprocal)	Wilbur, Goodhart, and Montandon (1983)	The Volta Review
Conjunctions	Wilbur, Quigley, and Montanelli (1975)	JSHR
Verbs		
(Complements)	Quigley, Wilbur, and Montanelli (1976)	JSHR
(Auxiliary)	Quigley, Montanelli and Wilbur (1976)	JSHR
(Modals)	Wilbur, Goodhart, and Montandon (1983)	The Volta Review
Determiners	Wilbur (1977)	The Volta Review
Quantifiers	Wilbur, Goodhart, and Montandon (1983)	The Volta Review
Conditionals	Wilbur, Goodhart, and Montandon (1983)	The Volta Review
Comparatives	Wilbur, Goodhart, and Montandon (1983)	The Volta Review
Prepositions	Wilbur, Goodhart, and Montandon (1983)	The Volta Review
Elliptical Phrases	Wilbur, Goodhart, and Montandon (1983)	The Volta Review
Temporal Sequence	Jarvella and Lubinsky (1975)	JSHR

Table 11-1 *(continued).*

Structure	Reference	Journal*
Idioms	Conley (1976)	AAD
	Fruchter, Wilbur, and Fraser (1984)	The Volta Review
Metaphors	Iran-Nejad, Ortony, and Rittenhouse (1981)	JSHR
	Rittenhouse, Morreau, and Iran-Nejad (1981)	AAD
	Rittenhouse and Stearns (1982)	AAD
Similes	Iran-Nejad, Ortony, and Rittenhouse (1981)	JSHR

* JSHR = Journal of Speech and Hearing Research
AAD = American Annals of the Deaf

ured on the Metropolitan Reading Achievement Test). This result was confirmed by the Office of Demographic Studies at Gallaudet College (1972).

Older studies of specific problems have focused on the errors, counting the number of omissions, substitutions, redundancies, and word order errors (Myklebust, 1964). These categories tend to obscure the causes for the errors and do not provide much guidance to teachers. Research on language deficits often reflects current linguistic frameworks and the area of deaf students' difficulties with English syntax is no exception. Earlier studies reflected older linguistic approaches that stressed either parts of speech or word order within a sentence. Recent advances in syntax and pragmatics have added considerably to our knowledge of deaf students' problems.

The major question is What causes the problems that deaf students have learning English? Several answers are available from the research studies, and they are all probably correct. One reason is that deaf students have learned general strategies for understanding sentences. These general strategies are based on the students' familiarity with basic English sentences that have a subject, verb, and direct object. From such familiarity, the students learn that the understanding of a sentence involves interpreting the first noun as the agent, the verb as the action, and the second noun as the recipient of the action. This strategy is referred to as reading surface order (RSO) and works very well for many English sentences, especially the simple ones presented to very young children. Unfortunately for the deaf students, there are many structures where this strategy produces exactly the opposite of the desired results. This can be seen in the discussion of passives and relative clauses below. There are probably other strategies that they use which have yet to be identified. The reading surface order strategy is also seen in young hearing children learning English, but appears to be used by deaf students beyond the age when a hearing child would have abandoned it. As a general observation, even by age 18, deaf students do not have the linguistic competence of 10 year old hearing children in many syntactic structures of English.

Contributing also is the fact that deaf students receive only a limited amount of input (all modalities combined); as a result, when deaf students do begin to learn English syntactic rules, they simply learn some of the details incorrectly and do not have enough experiences with the structures to realize their mistakes. In several of the structures to be reviewed in the next section, relative clauses, questions, and conjunctions, these incorrect rules can be readily seen.

Another reason that deaf students do not learn English correctly is that they are frequently taught structures in isolated sentences that do not provide enough information for them to learn all of the situations in which a structure is used and all of the constraints on its usage. This problem can be seen in the discussion of deaf students' problems with determiners and pronouns. In a specific test of this hypothesis, Nolen and Wilbur (1985) found that for difficult structures, such as relative clauses, deaf students' comprehension was much better when the structure was presented in a meaningful context than when it was presented in an isolated sentence. For other difficult structures, such as passives, context did not help, apparently because it made it more difficult for the students to find the specific cues that marked the sentence as passive.

Still another reason is related to teaching techniques — because it is impossible to teach deaf students everything there is to know about English all at once, the structures must be spread out over several years of school. In any given year, certain structures will be covered and others will not be (this is also true for vocabulary). If a particular structure is tested, the students can only be expected to know it if it has already been taught (preferably not too long ago). In two studies of deaf students' knowledge of English structures, Wilbur and Goodhart (1983, 1985) compared the students' actual performance with predictions made from either the order of acquisition of the structures by hearing children or the theoretical linguistic complexity. In both cases, the theoretical complexity was a better predictor of the deaf students' performance, in part because as teachers spread the structures out over the years, they intuitively feel that certain structures are more difficult than others, and their intuitions appear to reflect linguistic complexity. Hearing children, on the other hand, learn language in a nonsystematic way, acquiring whatever structures might happen to occur in a particular situation. Thus, although there is a certain overall developmental trend to hearing children's acquisition of English syntax, this trend is as much influenced by frequency of occurrence in daily interactions as by linguistic complexity. It is possible, then, that a hearing child could learn a more complex form earlier than would be predicted primarily because it occurs more frequently in his or her environment. Deaf students are much less influenced by general environmental effects and much more influenced by what is presented in class.

Finally, there is one glaring absence in the list of possible causes for problems with syntax, and that is knowledge of ASL. Many people have claimed that knowledge of ASL interferes with deaf students' ability to learn English. They have even claimed that "deaf students write in ASL syntax." There is no evidence among all of the studies of deaf students learning English syntax to support his statement. There really are two issues hidden here. One is that when deaf children do not write in grammatical English, ASL interference is assumed. People unfamiliar with ASL structure believe that the ungrammatical forms that deaf students produce must be another language because it is not English. The other is that the patterns in deaf students' errors and the fact that these errors are made by deaf children regardless of the type of educational program they are in do not support an ASL interference explanation. The similarity between deaf students' error patterns and those of hearing people learning English as a second language also indicates that the problems are related to English structure itself (which is why signing English does not automatically solve the problem, as discussed in Chapter 10) and to the techniques used to teach English as a second language.

Specific Syntactic Structures of English

Passive

In an initial study that tested deaf students' ability to match sentences to their appropriate pictures, Schmitt (1968) found that even by age 17 many deaf students had not mastered comprehension of the passive voice. Power and Quigley (1973) investigated this further. They found steady improvement with age, but by age 18, almost 40 percent of the students still did not understand the passive. If the sentence given was "The truck was hit by the car," the students would interpret this according to the surface word order, that is, the RSO, for example, "The truck hit the car." The strength of this RSO strategy is affected by the type of sentence. For example, if the sentence is "nonreversible," (the subject and object cannot be readily interchanged), such as "The books were destroyed by the children," comprehension was better than when the sentences were "reversible," as in the truck/car sentence given earlier. One significant concern that this information raises is related to the fact that passive sentences occur as early as the first grade readers for children (hearing or deaf), yet clearly they are not being read properly, even at the oldest ages. It should also be mentioned that only slightly over 40 percent of the oldest students were able to *produce* a correct passive.

Relative Clauses

Relative clauses were studied as part of a larger study of deaf students' problems with English syntax (Quigley, Wilbur, Power, Montanelli, and Steinkamp, 1976). Quigley, Smith, and Wilbur (1974) reported that deaf students aged 10 to 18 performed considerably worse when compared with 8 to 10 year old hearing children. The RSO strategy is not restricted to passives, but is also found in the processing of relative clauses. Given a sentence such as "The boy who hit the girl went home," and a multiple choice, yes/no task, the deaf students frequently responded "yes" to the "The girl went home." This shows the use of surface reading, connecting the verb "go" to the closest possible noun "the girl." In terms of correct comprehension of the whole sentence, relative clauses that do not interrupt the main sentence (final relative clauses) are easier for deaf students to understand than embedded relative clauses that do separate the main sentence subject noun phrase from its corresponding verb.

Another interesting example that illustrates incomplete learning of the English rules is the deaf students' production of sentences such as "The dog *which the dog* bit the cat ran away," instead of "The dog which bit the cat ran away." According to standard models of transformational grammar, this complex sentence is formed by combining two simpler sentences "The dog ran away" and "The dog bit the cat." Theoretically, a rule replaces the repeated noun phrase "the dog" in the sentence to be embedded with the appropriate WH-word (who, what, which), giving the correct sentence. Deaf students appear to insert the WH-word in the proper place, but incorrectly keep the word(s) that the WH-word is supposed to replace. This gives the redundant result "which the dog bit the cat." The detail that the students are missing is the fact that the WH-word *replaces* the redundant word(s). Otherwise, their rule is correct (correct WH-word, correct place in the sentence for both the WH-word and the entire embedded clause). Although the occurrence of this incorrect structure is relatively infrequent in deaf students' writing, over 30 percent of the oldest deaf students in Quigley and colleagues' sample considered these sentences to be grammatical when they were asked for such judgments (for details of the sample and its generalizability, see Quigley, Wilbur, Power, Montanelli, and Steinkamp 1976).

Questions

This same error is also found in WH-questions (who, what, when, where, why, which, how), confirming that it is closely connected to the function and usage of WH-words. An example of a WH-question with this error is a sentence such as "*Who* did the dog bite *the cat?*"

The study of questions in general (Quigley, Wilbur, and Montanelli, 1974) indicated that, in terms of general comprehension, yes/no questions ("Is the earth flat?") were easier than WH-questions, which in turn were easier than tag questions ("John didn't come to school today, *did he?*"). Stages of development for the deaf students were found to be parallel to those reported in the literature for young hearing children (Brown and Hanlon, 1970; Ervin-Tripp, 1970; Klima and Bellugi-Klima, 1966). The difference, of course, is the age difference.

In a separate study, Wilbur, Goodhart, and Montandon (1983) found that comprehension of questions with "why" developed early in comparison to other complex structures, with lower reading levels (1 and 2) performing poorly (below 75 percent) and higher reading levels performing quite well (80 percent correct at reading level 3 to 98 percent at reading level 8). The difficulty with "why" questions lies not in the structure itself, but with the student's ability to formulate an appropriate "because" answer. In other words, it is the concept of "why" and the understanding of various kinds of causation that contribute to the difficulty, rather than the syntactic structure itself, which is parallel to other WH-questions.

Conjunctions

The rules for conjoining sentences in English seem to cause less difficulty for deaf students than relative clauses, passives, and various verb constructions. Wilbur and colleagues (1975) found developmental trends similar to those reported by Menyuk (1963, 1964). The easiest type of conjunction for deaf students is the conjoined sentence, especially when the sentences do not share common elements. In this general case, the child need only put an "and" between two separate sentences to produce a conjoined sentence. Deaf students correctly produced this kind of conjoined sentences ranging from less than half the time (46 percent) at age 10 to 76 percent at age 18.

A more difficult conjoined structure is the conjoined noun phrase, with subject noun phrases being easier than object noun phrases. Thus, from two sentences, "Ann went to school" and "John went to school," one sentence, "Ann and John went to school," can be produced with the subject conjoined noun phrase "Ann and John." With this type of structure, deaf students did less well than with conjoined sentences, producing 34 percent correct at age 10 but increasing to 81 percent at age 18. Object conjoined noun phrases ("the boy spilled the milk and the cookie box") were even harder, with only 7 percent correct at age 10 but increasing dramatically to 77 percent at age 18. In both the subject noun phrase and object noun phrase situations, the largest "error" response was to produce a fully conjoined sentence without reduction to conjoined noun phrases (e.g., "Ann went to school and John went to school," "The boy spilled the milk and the boy [or he] spilled the cookie box."). Because conjoined sentences are an earlier stage of development than conjoined noun phrases, the source of this error is easily understood.

Conjoined verb phrases are the most difficult type of major conjoined phrase. From two full sentences, "John washed the car" and "John waxed the car," a conjoined verb phrase, "John washed the car and waxed it," is the expected form. At age 10, deaf students produced only 3 percent correct conjoined verb phrases, improving to only 62 percent by age 18. The fully conjoined sentence "John washed the car and he waxed it" was the most common "error" response. From these data, we can see the same overall pattern (from easiest to hardest) reported by Menyuk (1963, 1964): conjoined sentences (easiest), conjoined subject noun phrases, conjoined object noun phrases, conjoined verb phrases (hardest). This pattern, if it were the only one we had, might suggest a mere delay in deaf students' development. Other data, however, suggested that something more than a mere delay is occurring.

As indicated previously, conjoined sentences were the easiest form for deaf students to handle because they are mastered at an early developmental stage. However, the restriction "in the general case" was placed on this discussion because of problems that arise with two more specific cases. If the two sentences were related in such a way that they shared similar subjects or objects, a number of unusual omissions occurred. For example, two sentences, "John washed the car" and "Mary waxed the car," might be rewritten as "John washed the car and Mary waxed," where the object of the second sentence has been deleted. This has been referred to as object-object deletion; the second object was deleted because it is identical to the first object. Likewise, "The boy hit the girl" and "The girl hit him back," might be rewritten as "The boy hit the girl and hit him back" where the second subject has been deleted because it is identical to the first object (object-subject deletion). Wilbur and colleagues (1975) reported reduced performance on sentence rewrite items when deaf students were presented with object-object deletion environments (25 percent correct at age 10 to 68 percent at age 18) or object-subject deletion items (44 percent at age 10 to 45 percent at age 18) when compared to the general case sentences (again, 46 percent at age 10 to 76 percent at age 18). In the written language samples, both object-object deletion and object-subject deletion occurred. Interestingly, object-object deletion declined with age (from a small 6 percent at age 10 down to 1 percent at age 18), whereas object-subject deletion *increased* from 12 percent at age 10 to 32 percent at age 18. The production data are consistent with the test results, in that object-object deletion seems to disappear with age in both cases, but object-subject deletion does not.

The first step in providing an explanation for these two rules is to notice that they are not simply random deletions, but that they occur in the second sentence of two conjoined sentences, and that in fact this is one of the environments in which English normally puts in pronouns. Thus, one begins by hypothesizing that deaf children are aware of the need for reducing redundancy, which is what pronominalizing does, but instead of pronominalizing, they simply delete. Indeed, this initial hypothesis still seems valid, but requires further discussion. Why does object-subject deletion increase in use but object-object deletion decrease? This question is especially important, given that the above hypothesis attempts to explain both rules as a single process, when they clearly do not behave as a single process. One important implication of the decline of object-object deletion is that it provides evidence that deaf students are still revising and refining their hypotheses about the structure of English even at the oldest ages tested in this study. Furthermore, it is possible to explain the nature of these revisions and refinements within a framework based solely on the structure of English, that is, without resorting to an "ASL interference" hypothesis. There are environments in English in which it *is* possible to delete the subject of the second sentence in a conjoined structure. The result of this process is a conjoined verb phrase, such as "The elephant crushed the roots and ate them," which comes from "the elephant crushed the roots" and "The elephant ate them (the roots)." The general rule for English is that the subject of the second sentence may be deleted if it is identical to the *subject* of the first sentence. The deaf students who use object-subject deletion are deleting the second subject when it is identical to the first *object.* Together with object-object deletion, their generalization is probably to "delete a noun phrase in the second sentence if it occurs in the first sentence." This generalization gives correct forms (conjoined verb phrases) as well as incorrect forms. As the deaf students get older, they seem to come to realize that objects are not deleted in English. However, their increasing mastery and use of conjoined verb phrases reinforces the deletion of subjects. Thus, as they mature, a new generalization is formulated — "Delete the subject in the second sentence if it occurs in the first sentence." This generalization produces correct conjoined verb phrases and incorrect object-subject deletion, accounting for the failure of object-subject deletion to disappear. Because there is no similar parallel for objects, the loss of object-object deletion is predictable. This situation suggests that deaf students' problems with English syntax reflect their attempts at coping with increasing, but still limited, data.

Pronouns

The investigation of pronouns (Wilbur et al., 1976) focused on two aspects of English pronouns — which ones to use and when to use them. The study presented students with two sentences, the second one containing a blank where a pronoun should go. The first sentence, then, provided the antecedent to the second sentence. The student was required to choose the correct pronoun from three or four choices given beneath the item sentences. Essentially, then, the students were told, "A pronoun goes in this slot — which one is it?" In this situation, even the youngest students (age 10 years) did quite well. The mean percent correct across all age levels was 72 percent for subject pronouns (I, we, you, he, she, it, they), 74 percent for object pronouns (me, us, you, him, her, it, them), 63 percent for possessive adjectives (my, our, your, his, her, its, their), 50 percent for possessive pronouns (mine, ours, yours, his, hers, its, theirs), and 55 percent for reflexives (myself, ourselves, yourself, yourselves, himself, herself, itself, themselves).

In addition to the syntactic tests, written language samples were collected from each student in the study, using a sequence of four pictures that "told a story." These written samples were analyzed for correct pronoun usage. Two analyses were done. The first examined pronoun usage when the antecedent of the pronoun was in the same sentence as the pronoun itself. In this case, the students did well, with scores ranging from 75 percent at age 10 to a high of 93 percent at age 17. The other analysis examined pronoun usage when the referent did not occur in the same sentence as the pronoun, but rather appeared in an earlier sentence. The difference in performance was striking — correct usage ranged from only 40 percent at age 10 to 80 percent at age 18. These data indicate that deaf students' problems with pronouns are related to when to use them, not which ones to use.

Determiners

An analysis of determiner usage in the written language sample (Wilbur, 1977) revealed a pattern opposite to that discussed for the pronouns. Determiners were correctly placed before the noun 61 percent of the time at age 10, increasing to 76 percent of the time at age 18. However, of the correctly placed determiners, 25 percent (mean across all ages) were incorrect in terms of their usage, either being definite ("the") when they should be indefinite, or, indefinite ("a") when they should be definite. Thus, although deaf students seem to know when to use determiners (unlike pronouns), they do not seem to know which ones to use (also unlike pronouns).

Possible Explanations

The above data, together with data on negation (Quigley, Wilbur, Power, Montanelli, and Steinkamp, 1976), verbal auxiliaries (Quigley, Montanelli, and Wilbur, 1976), and verbal complements (Quigley, Wilbur, and Montanelli, 1976), indicate the considerable difficulty deaf students have with English. It has been suggested that deaf children's difficulty in acquiring English is not limited to linguistic processing but extends to their general cognitive ability to form generalizations. Furth (1966b) has demonstrated that the general cognitive ability of deaf people is not greatly different from hearing people in nonlinguistic tasks. Given this information, it has been suggested that deaf people do not develop the ability to apply their nonlinguistic cognitive skills to linguistic tasks. This suggestion ignores the fact that the acquisition of ASL is a linguistic task that many deaf children accomplish easily. However, it is still suggested by some that the difficulty is specific to English but not specific to syntax.

In a study directly relevant to this issue, Wilbur (1982b) investigated nonsyntactic generalizations made by deaf students. The task required recognition of English constraints on the structure of allowable words. For example, *blick* could be a word of English, although it actually is not. However, *bnick* could not be a word of English because of the structure of the initial consonant cluster *bn* (compare with Russian which allows initial clusters *zd* and *gd*). One need not know what these words might mean in order to decide which is acceptable to English and which is not. Furthermore, these constraints, unlike spelling rules and "proper" grammatical rules, are not specifically taught to either deaf or hearing children in school. Therefore, any knowledge that deaf children have of these constraints must have been extracted entirely on their own, thus giving an indication of their processing ability relative to English. First-, third-, fifth-, and seventh-grade deaf and third/fourth- and seventh-grade hearing children were tested on their ability to reject incorrectly formed words such as *bnick*. Although the deaf students' scores were quantitatively below those of the hearing children until the seventh grade, the scores were not qualitatively different. That is, violations of English word structure constraints that were easy for the hearing children to spot were also easy for the deaf students, and those that were hard for the hearing children were also hard for the deaf children. It was concluded that deaf students' difficulty in learning the proper rules for the more complex syntactic patterns is not attributable to a disturbance of general linguistic or cognitive processing (see Furth, 1966b), but rather to difficulty in learning the specific rules of English. This is strengthened by the fact that by seventh grade, the deaf and the hearing students performed equally well.

Wilbur (1977) provided an explanation of this difficulty by considering the larger pragmatic environment in which these structures must be used and comparing it with the manner in which they are taught. The study of language within a pragmatic framework includes contextual environments larger than a sentence, such as a paragraph (in writing) or a conversation (in speaking). The context interacts with the syntax in such a way as to allow certain syntactic structures and prohibit others. Consider the two syntactically and semantically related sentences "The car hit the truck" and "The truck was hit by the car." The difference in meaning or function between these two sentences is not at all obvious without the benefit of context. Although they are similar in meaning, their use in context reflects a difference in function. For example, the passive may be appropriate and the active inappropriate in a given context, or vice versa. An appropriate response to "What hit the truck?" may be either 'The car hit the truck" or "The truck was hit by the car." However, if the question is "What did the car hit?" it would be inappropriate to respond with "The truck was hit by the car." The pragmatic domain, then, is concerned with messages intended, sent, and received, in terms of shared knowledge between sender and receiver, expectations of both based on world knowledge, conversational content, and linguistic structure, and the effects of these on choice of syntactic structure.

A primary pragmatic consideration is the separation of old and new information. If information has already been presented, repeated reference to it may become redundant, and thus deletion rules or pronominal rules may apply. One may wish to refer to a specific piece of information already introduced, in which case a definite determiner ("the") would be used. Old information may be put in a relative clause ("The boy whom I told you about"). Within a pragmatic perspective, then, several of the syntactic structures that deaf students have difficulty with seem to form a group in that they are involved in separating old from new information. Three of the structures — pronominalization, conjunctions, and determiners — illustrate the problem. As indicated above, deaf students were able to handle the choice of pronouns when presented with pronoun environments, but experienced difficulty in deciding when to use pronouns. In particular, pronoun usage was easier within a sentence than across two sentences. This was interpreted as evidence that deaf students perform better with single sentences than sentences in sequence. The problem with sentences in sequence is that the first one introduces new information ("This is my friend John") which immediately after presentation is considered *old* information. Thus the second sentence, if it refers back to the first, must use a pronoun ("He goes to school with me"). This situation is further complicated in the case of pronouns by the lack of a fixed rule for pronoun usage in English. A pronoun should be used to avoid redundancy when information is referred to several times in succession, but at the same time ambiguity of reference must be avoided. The same general tendency of reducing redundancy is apparent in the deletions that produce conjoined structures, and deaf students' confusion is similarly reflected in their overgeneralization of the deletion process. In fact, the deletions that occur may be alternately viewed as further difficulty with the use or nonuse of pronouns in their function of referring to old information.

Deaf students' difficulty with determiners is also an old versus new problem. The use of "the" when introducing *new* material is severely constrained ("This is the woman I mentioned to you," where "the woman" must be further modified by a relative clause). In general, "the" is reserved for reference to old information.

As indicated previously, deaf students' problem with determiners is not the placement of determiners before nouns, but rather the distinction of definite/indefinite. Determiner usage constraints, and the other pragmatic constraints, must be applied to each individual conversational situation, making the acquisition of such constraints a complicated task.

Wilbur (1977) argues that part of the problem, particularly that part which is pragmatically controlled, may be attributable to the heavy emphasis placed on the proper structure of the single sentence in the language training programs for deaf children. Older approaches (Fitzgerald, 1929; Wing, 1887) were primarily concerned with the order of words within a sentence. More recent programs, especially those based on transformational grammar, emphasize the function of words in a sentence (grammatical relations such as subject and object) and relationships between sentences (active-passive, declarative-question-imperative, positive-negative). Even so, the emphasis may still be on the structure of the sentence alone, rather than on the use of the sentence within its larger environment. Obviously, both types of study, pragmatic and syntactic, are needed, indeed are crucial, for the development of deaf individuals with high degrees of competence and flexibility in English use.

Figurative Language

There are many different types of figurative language. The best known forms are idioms, metaphors, similes, personification, allusion, proverbs, and hyperbole. Still other nonliteral forms include puns, sarcasm, understatement, quotations, indirect requests, jokes, teasing, and conversational routines (for example, "How do you do?"). Of these, the three most commonly investigated forms are idioms, metaphors, and similes.

Similes are easy for people to spot because of the typical presence of "like," as in "He acted like a chicken without a head." Metaphors and idioms are more difficult to separate, in part because idioms may have their origins in metaphorical expressions that become fixed over time. Discussing the difference between idioms and metaphors, Strand and Fraser (1979) noted that "for a metaphor, the intended meaning must be figured out, calculated from factors of context and cultural beliefs; for an idiom, the meaning is fixed by convention." They consider idioms to be "linguistic unit(s) consisting of one or more constituents, the meaning of which cannot be fully determined from the knowledge of the individual word meanings and the particular syntactic structure"; in other words, they must be semantic "big words."

Conventional wisdom has always said that deaf students could not understand nonliteral language. The argument was basically that there was overwhelming evidence that they did not understand straightforward literal language, thus "more complicated" figurative language must be beyond their grasp. Nonetheless, attention has recently been turned to determining not only what deaf students can and cannot understand when presented with figurative language, but also where their problems lie. This increase in research parallels an increased interest in studying figurative language development in hearing children.

One study with hearing children suggested that children under the age of 9 could not handle the semantic duality or ambiguity necessary to understand idioms (Lodge and Leach, 1975). By contrast, other researchers argued that hearing children as young as age 2 could understand some aspects of metaphorical expressions (Winner, McCarthy, Kleinman, and Gardner, 1979). Furthermore, there is evidence that 5 year old hearing children not only understand many idioms, as demonstrated by a picture selection task, but that they can provide some explanation of the idiomatic meanings (Strand and Fraser, 1979). Other studies have followed up on these findings in more detail (Boynton and Kossan, 1981; Dixon and Collins, 1981; Godwin, Boyce, and Larson, 1980; Nippold, 1982).

With deaf students, the studies that do exist have been primarily exploratory in nature. Investigations of idiom comprehension have revealed a surprisingly high level of performance, although still far below much younger hearing children (Conley, 1976; Fruchter, 1986; Fruchter et al., 1984; Giorcelli, 1982). The evidence is clear that idiom acquisition is approached as a "big word" learning task. Fruchter and colleagues (1984) reported that figurative comprehension averaged 53.7 percent across 20 idioms for deaf students at reading levels 1 to 10, whereas literal comprehension of the same expressions averaged 92.8 percent. Students at the lowest reading levels (1 and 2) performed at chance levels on the idiom comprehension portion in this study, confirming that figurative language ability is a later development in deaf children. Again, this may be attributed to insufficient input and teachers' choices of what to teach first; there is no evidence of a cognitive deficit related to processing figurative language (Quigley and Paul, 1984).

Metaphors and similes have also recently been investigated. Hamacher (1980) demonstrated that deaf students' performance on tests of metaphorical comprehension is strongly affected by what the choices are in multiple choice tasks. When the literal interpretation is offered as an option, the students will most likely choose it. If the literal option is not offered, then deaf students are more likely to select the correct figurative response. Iran-Nejad and colleagues (1981) investigated both metaphors and similes. Using a task that required the student to choose the sentence that best completed the paragraph, they found that deaf students were better able to choose the correct response from a set of four similes than from a set of four equivalent metaphors. In this case, the presence of "like" provides an additional cue to the reader that a comparison is being made and that nonliteral processing may be appropriate.

There are many aspects of figurative language that remain to be investigated. Aside from all the other types of figurative forms that have never been studied, there are still many questions about the factors that affect figurative comprehension in idioms, metaphors, and similes (such as frequency of occurrence, syntactic structure, likelihood of literal interpretation in the real world). But now that substantial progress has been made in identifying the problems with literal language and providing materials for solving those problems, it seems reasonable to expect that more attention will be turned to figurative comprehension and production.

CODING AND MEMORY

Two questions related to memory and sign language may be profitably asked: (1) What is the effect of knowledge of sign language on the organizations of memory, particularly with respect to the coding of English? (2) What is the effect of early acquisition of sign language on the development of memory itself?

Organization of Memory and English

The reader should recall at this point the earlier research on memory (Chapter 7), where Bellugi and Siple's (1974) investigation of the parameters of ASL is discussed. Their study dealt specifically with the organization of memory for ASL. It was briefly pointed out that when deprived of an opportunity to use semantic information in the recall of words, hearing people tend to make mistakes based on the phonological properties of the words they hear or see; phonological properties of signs produce similar errors in deaf persons. In order to better consider the research that has been done on memory process of deaf individuals, the research on hearing people is now briefly overviewed.

The recall of lists of unrelated words is heavily influenced by the sounds that constitute those words. Conrad (1962) demonstrated that hearing people have greater difficulty recalling lists of unrelated words that sound alike. Wickelgren (1965) investigated the contributions to memory of the major phonetic distinctive features of which sounds are composed (place of articulation: bilabial, dental, velar, etc.; and manner of articulation: voiced/voiceless, nasal/oral, aspirated/unaspirated, etc.). The use of phonological information for memory coding was shown to be effective regardless of whether the lists were presented in an auditory or visual manner. However, research has also demonstrated that, if at all possible, people will attempt to organize the words to be recalled according to some semantic or syntactic relationship. If a person can relate five words in a list by a sentence, or by remembering that they were all four-legged animals, this information will aid in recall. The use of semantic information provides a greater benefit to memory than syntactic information. In fact, Sachs (1967) found that the actual syntax of a sentence is discarded very shortly after the sentence is seen or heard, because once the meaning of a sentence has been extracted, the syntax is no longer useful information. Thus, for hearing people, one can expect that memory for unrelated word lists will be coded on a phonological basis unless semantic clustering can be accomplished, and that memory for sentences will be coded on a semantic basis and not on the form (syntax) of the sentence (Bransford, Barclay, and Franks, 1972; Bransford and Franks, 1971; Crowder, 1972; Franks and Bransford, 1972; LaBerge, 1972; Norman, 1972; Paris and Carter, 1973). Although there are considerable problems with their method, assumptions, and conclusions, Moulton and Beasley's (1975) results do indicate that deaf subjects (like hearing subjects) will take advantage of the semantics of stimulus items when possible, but that they resort to signed-based coding when the meaning cannot be of assistance.

To determine the role of phonological features in deaf people's memory, Conrad and Rush (1965) investigated recall of lists of consonants presented visually (presuming that the same strategies are at work with lists of letters as with lists of unrelated words). Some of the nine consonants used were phonetically similar (B, P, T, C), others were visually similar (A, H, T, I). The recorded error patterns did not support either a phonological or a visual encoding strategy. Locke (1970) investigated the same consonants to determine whether the fingerspelling alphabet was responsible for the errors (and would thus be a coding strategy for deaf persons), but found little support for this hypothesis.

Conrad (1970, 1971, 1972, 1973) determined that it was possible for prelingually, profoundly deaf people to use an auditory encoding strategy. In a school in which the method of instruction was predominantly oral, he compared two groups of deaf students: those for whom the phonological properties of the consonant letters provided at least some support to coding and recall (this group was subsequently rated "above average" in speech quality by independent judges) and those for whom the auditory features seemed to be largely irrelevant (this group was subsequently rated as "average" in speech quality). Conrad inferred that the above average group articulated while reading (not necessarily overtly) whereas the average group did not. He then compared the two groups on recall of visually presented material in two conditions, one in which they silently read the presented material, and the other in which they read out loud the presented material. Recall was not greatly improved by vocalization for the "articulating" group but was significantly hampered for the "nonarticulating" group. The inference is that the articulating group had acquired some form of a phonological code so that actually articulating the material while reading did not either help or hinder them. However, the nonarticulating group had acquired a nonphonological coding system, and reading out loud actually interfered with their normal coding process.

A further study by Locke and Locke (1971) determined that the type of linguistic coding strategy correlated to some extent with the deaf person's articulatory skills. Unintelligible deaf subjects made more errors in recall of visually similar letter pairs than did the intelligible deaf subjects and hearing controls. Furthermore, unintelligible deaf subjects made more dactylically similar confusions (based on the fingerspelling alphabet) than did the other two groups.

The implications of the above studies are: (1) coding strategies are learned, not innate; (2) deaf people have a choice of coding language either by phonological, visual, or manual means; (3) oral training methods do not guarantee phonological coding strategies; (4) deaf people who do not have phonological coding strategies and do not use sign do not give clear evidence of reliance on only one of the other possible strategies.

There is at this point one further clarification that needs to be made with respect to the notion of strategies in memory. One strategy is to use a *code*, and the lack of clear strategies as to what code to use has been discussed herein. This does not imply that deaf people's use of other memory strategies is also necessarily impaired. There is evidence that deaf students do not have good memory strategy techniques but that when they are given instructions (for example, to use fingerspelling during rehearsal, or different rehearsal strategies), their performance improves to nearly 100 percent (Belmont, Karchmer, and Pilkonis, 1976; Karchmer and Belmont, 1976). As Belmont and colleagues concluded, "deaf people's deficiency reflects in large measure a failure to develop spontaneous use of cognitive processes" for memory efficiency. Also, when deaf students' performance on memory for English words is compared to their performance on memory for nonverbal information such as pictures, it is clear that the problem is specific to the linguistic task (English words) and not to memory in general (Karchmer and Belmont, 1976).

Several questions can be raised here which unfortunately cannot be answered. One major question pertains to the normal, daily treatment of English input in memory processing in persons who are native or near-native deaf signers. Is English translated into ASL and then coded in memory? Is it simply processed in English to get the meaning, the syntax discarded as suggested by Sachs (1967), and constructed from storage in whatever response mode is required? If semantics is unavailable to help in memory processing, is the English processed using auditory phonological processing, while the ASL is separately treated using sign-based phonology? Is there one memory processing system or two? One relevant study is that of Odom, Blanton, and McIntyre (1970), which indicates that English words that have direct equivalents in ASL are recalled significantly better than words that do not. What happens with whole sentences is not yet known. The answers to these questions are of particular importance to the use of total communication (TC) in educational settings where the child may be asked to process separate systems (the signs, the lips, and whatever auditory information is available) simultaneously and to the teaching of reading. If the child is attempting to process the signs using sign phonology and the speech using speech phonology (or its equivalent, whatever that is for speech reading), he is obviously trying to do two different tasks at once. Although parallel processing of incoming information has been suggested as a necessary part of input analysis (Neisser, 1967), it is not clear how such a model would be reconciled with multiple modality linguistic input of the type we have discussed here. If in fact such parallel processing exists, it remains to be determined whether the information from the speechreading is competing with the information from the sign reading for processing by the parallel processors, or whether separate parallel processors would be assigned to handle each type of input (all simultaneously). In any case, the processing demands that TC places on the perceptual and cognitive systems is a critical concern for the psychological development of children being exposed to it.

Development of Memory

Related to the preceding discussion is the obvious question: How does learning ASL as a native language affect the eventual organization of the memory process? Put another way, will someone who learns ASL as a first language as an infant have a more effective memory, and thus greater learning potential, than someone who learns ASL when he enters school at age 5? Than someone who learns ASL in high school? Than someone who learns ASL as an adult? Than someone who never learns ASL?

Because the deaf students are not grossly deficient in their memory processing, and yet are significantly behind in their acquisition of English, the focus should be shifted from "how much" memory to "what kind" of memory. If, as the Conrad and Locke studies indicate, many deaf people are using a variety of strategies, will early ASL usage provide a more efficient strategy, which can facilitate later learning of English? Again, the Odom and colleagues (1970) study is suggestive. The deaf subjects' recall of English words with ASL equivalents is significantly better than the hearing subjects' recall of both lists of English words (those with ASL equivalents and those without). Unfortunately, the central question being raised here — how does early learning of ASL or other manual coding systems affect memory — has not been specifically studied.

Memory and Reading

Aside from the direct implication that the Odom and colleagues (1970) study has for memory, it also has another important implication for the teaching of reading. Research on hearing children indicates that children who learn letter-sound association, and then use these associations in reading (by sounding out the word), experience superior reading achievement (Chall, 1967). Consequently, reading materials intended for hearing children rely heavily on the phonological properties of the words to serve as recognition cues to the beginning reader. Such materials would seem to be inappropriate for use with deaf children, even aside from syntactic difficulties (Quigley et al., 1976). Instead, the study suggested that memory for English words can be strongly affected by associations with signs. Perhaps reading materials written to reflect correspondences between English and ASL would avoid the frustration involved in initial reading attempts. At present, several primary level readers are available that contain a story in English and in Signed English (Bornstein et al., 1973, 1975) where the Signed English is drawn in, usually parallel to the printed English. This type of reader presents the child with a choice of codes and does not have the possible draw-back of TC, which requires real-time processing of both signals (signs and speechreading). Although presentation of static pictures is not the same as presentation of actual signs, it will be interesting to observe the results with these readers (assuming their use is maintained) over the next few years.

COMPARATIVE STUDIES

Implications for the Acquisition of English Syntax

As indicated earlier, there is no research support for the notion that knowledge of ASL interferes with the acquisition of English syntax. One study (Brasel and Quigley, 1977) addressed this question directly. They defined four groups on the basis of the educational approach of the parents with respect to the child. The parents of the first group used Manual English (ME), the parents of the second group used ASL (referred to as the Average Manual (AM) group), the parents of the third group began intensive oral (IO) training with the child at an early age, and the parents of the fourth group used oral communication but did not use any kind of special early training (referred to as the Average Oral (AO) group). The groups themselves each contained 18 deaf students, with a mean age for each group of 14.8 years. It should be pointed out that the groups were confounded in the same way that many other such studies are, namely, that the parents of the deaf students in the manual groups were deaf and the parents of the deaf students in the oral group were hearing. This entails sociological and emotional interaction in addition to the language variable being studied.

The groups were compared on the same tests of English syntax, the Test of Syntactic Ability (TSA), that were used in the previously mentioned studies (Quigley et al., 1976) and on four subtests of the Stanford Achievement Test (Language, Paragraph Meaning, Word Meaning, and Spelling). The results of the Brasel and Quigley study showed "that the two Manual groups were significantly better than the two Oral groups on every test measure employed." On the Stanford Achievement Test subtests, the ME group was significantly superior to the other three groups on all four subtests, with the ME group being from one to nearly four grades ahead with its nearest competitor being the AM group. Brasel and Quigley (1977) concluded that "the greatest advantage appears to come when the parents are competent in Standard English and use Manual English with and around the child, as witness the marked superiority of the ME group over both Oral groups on nearly every test measure employed and that some advantage is found where early Manual communication exists regardless of degree of deviation from Standard English syntax."

Bonvillian, Charrow, and Nelson (1973), Bonvillian, Nelson, and Charrow (1976), and Moores (1974, 1977) also reviewed several studies that have been conducted on differences between groups of deaf students trained orally and manually. These studies cover a wide range of areas (social adjustment and mathematics, for example) not directly related to the topic of English syntax. These studies will be reviewed subsequently.

Implications for Early Language Learning

There is another implication of manual communication for language acquisition that bears discussion. It has been well documented that the brain develops rapidly until puberty, at which time establishment of synaptic patterns ceases (Lenneberg, 1967). At the same time, it has been observed that language acquisition before puberty happens more or less naturally, with children being able to acquire any language(s) to which they are exposed, whereas language acquisition after puberty becomes more of a process of conscious learning (as opposed to more or less spontaneous acquisition). It has been hypothesized that the high correlation between these two events, brain development and language acquisition, is in fact a causal relationship, such that the acquisition of a first language after puberty should be virtually impossible (referred to as the critical age hypothesis in Lenneberg, 1967). Furthermore, it has been observed that the most rapid rate of brain development and organization occurs before 5 or 6 years, which is also the time of the most rapid development of language in normal children. As the child grows toward puberty, the establishment of neural synaptic networks and language development slows down. There is, then, a time in the life of a child from birth to about 6 years that is undoubtedly the most critical with respect to the proper acquisition of language.

Consider this with respect to some data from the Brasel and Quigley (1977) study. For the ME and AM groups, the children were confirmed deaf at 7 months of age or younger. For the IO and AO groups, the children were confirmed deaf at about 1 year, 2 months. With the exception of the IO group, the children did not begin formal schooling until they were at least 4 years old. The IO group began

formal training at around 2 years (recall that the subjects were selected *because* of the so-called early intensive training which they received). In the 4 years from birth until they began schooling, the deaf
children in the ME and AM groups had an opportunity to observe
the use of language in the visual mode, a mode that functions normally for them. Through this mode they were able to perceive language and use their normal linguistic processes (whatever those
might be) to acquire language from their environment, utilizing the
same types of early acquisition strategies as young hearing children, and passing through similar developmental stages (one-word
stage, two-word stage, the several different semantic relationship
stages, etc.).

The deaf child in the AO group received minimal language input
(English or otherwise) until he started school at age 4, at which
point nearly two-thirds of those crucial years were gone. He had
missed the developmental stages that a child normally passes
through in language acquisition and had to compensate for them
with formal training. The deaf child in the IO group was given a partial opportunity at age 2 to begin the developmental sequence, but
this was done in such a way that the child was formally presented
with input, based on what the adults thought the child should be
learning, in a mode that requires considerably greater effort from
the child because of his auditory deficit. Furthermore, the mode and
the formal presentation distract from other aspects of language acquisition, primarily syntax and pragmatics. The deaf child has considerable difficulty in mastering English syntax. This can be explained partially by the specific methodology used to teach it,
namely, concentrating on the single sentence. Just as the teacher's
overemphasis on sentences can lead to incorrect assumptions about
how such sentences should be constructed and used in contexts, over-
emphasizing articulation leads to overlooking both syntax and pragmatics. Research on hearing infants (Donahue, 1977a b; Donahue
and Watson, 1976; Watson, 1977) indicates that the child partici-
pates actively in conversations with adults (primarily the mother)
through a variety of means before the child can talk intelligibly.
These include responding to a mother's questioning intonation with
a statement intonation (spread across a babbled sequence), mother's
imitation of the child followed by the child's imitation of the mother
(indicating some knowledge on the child's part of turn-taking cues),
and in later developments, the child's use of back-channel communication to the mother (head nods, "uh-huh," "mm," "yea"). These
early conversations provide the child with important social and linguistic information. A child learns strategies for dealing with situa-

tions in which he has not been understood properly (e.g., repeating himself louder, phrasing himself differently). Other information, such as phrase structure, may come from conversational clues, such as adult pausing and intonation. All of these provide the very young hearing child with help in decoding the language he hears. The language acquisition process is similar in deaf children of deaf parents who learn ASL as a first language. The deaf child's problem arises in the acquisition of English. Heavy emphasis on one particular aspect to the (partial) exclusion of all others is detrimental to the child by depriving him of clues to the decoding of English and the appropriate use of it. The reader should recall also the discussion of parental modifications of signs for the child's benefit (Chapter 8); the inability of speakers to make similar modifications of speech places the young deaf child at a great disadvantage for early language learning.

Implications for Development of Speech Skills

If the deaf individual is to function in a hearing world, speech is clearly a useful tool. It is a common belief that the use of manual communication hinders the development of speech. Moores (1971) summarized several studies that directly compared early oral preschool children with children who had no preschool. None of the studies cited reported any difference in oral skills (speech and speechreading) between the two groups. One of the studies (Vernon and Koh, 1970) compared deaf children of hearing parents with early intensive oral training to deaf children of deaf parents with no preschool (i.e., ASL users). Again, no differences in oral skills were found between the two groups, but the students with deaf parents were found to be superior in reading and general achievement.

Several studies have compared deaf children of deaf parents to deaf children of hearing parents. Four of these studies included results that are relevant here (Meadow, 1966; Quigley and Frisina, 1961; Stevenson, 1964; Stuckless and Birch, 1966; for a description of these, see Bonvillian, Charrow, and Nelson, 1973; Moores, 1971, 1974). The four studies reported that the deaf children of deaf parents were superior on some or all of the English skills and general measures of ability. Three of these studies reported no difference between the two groups on measures of speech production, but the fourth reported that the deaf children of hearing parents were better. One of the studies also reported that the deaf children of deaf parents were better on measures of speechreading ability, whereas the other three reported no differences between the two groups.

Direct studies of the effects of manual communication on speech are rare. Quigley (1969) reported no difference in speech or speech-reading for students using the Rochester Method (simultaneous fingerspelling) when compared with those using simultaneous signing and speech. A study of children using Swedish Sign (Ahlström, 1972) reported that "speech was not adversely affected by knowledge of signs" (Power, 1974).

What is striking about the studies summarized in Power (1974) and Moores (1971, 1974) is the lack of any direct evidence that the use of manual communication is in fact detrimental to the development of speech skills. If such an interference relationship existed, one would expect to see it reported in study after study. Its absence is thus noteworthy.

Researchers investigating the use of manual communication with other populations with normal hearing (retarded, autistic, language delayed) have reported beneficial effects of manual communication on speech skills (discussed in Chapter 12).

The development of speech skills is offered as the primary concern of those people who do not choose to use manual communication with deaf children. Children's competence with speech and speechreading has come to represent (whether appropriately or not) a measure of the effectiveness of educational programs, particularly those using manual communication. The use of simultaneous communication (Sim-com) (meaning here signing and speaking English) is a sensitive issue. Many people have equated the use of Sim-com with the use of signs themselves. Thus, a negative comment against Sim-com is often wrongly interpreted as a negative comment against the use of any manual communication.

One assumption that underlies the use of Sim-com as part of total communication is that by simultaneously signing and speaking with the child, the child is receiving speech input and speechreading practice, which will lead to the child's own speech production. Put another way, the responsibility for intensive speech instruction may have been given up because one assumes that the child is being presented with sufficient practice as a consequence of the continuous use of Sim-com. The expectation then is that the child's speech skills will not decline, and may even grow, with the use of Sim-com (other skills, such as language, other academic subjects, and social interactions, are also expected to improve). If such an expectation is not met, Sim-com and by extension TC, may be faulted and might well be abandoned. The caution raised here challenges these assumptions and expectations. First, the child's attention must be split between the two visual systems, manual (sign and/or fingerspelling) reading and speechreading. One should not expect this to be as effective for speech skills as intensive speech training. If speech is the skill being taught, there is no substitute for intensive speech training. If English, history, math, or science are being taught, Sim-com should be used if desired, or ASL only if possible and appropriate; one should not pretend to be fulfilling responsibilities in the area of speech skills. Moores (1980) indicates that there are two schools of thought: (1) the bilingual school, with the child learning to sign first, and using sign to learn everything else (English, speech, etc.) later, and (2) the school that says we all know English so let's use it with these children. He points out that the second school predominates. The first position, suggested here for further consideration, is often viewed as a radical perspective, but may turn out to be more viable in the long run. The potential role of bilingualism in the education of deaf children is discussed extensively in a recent book by Quigley and Paul (1984). They consider a variety of issues related to the fields of ESL (English as a Second Language) and bilingualism (such as the relationship between the two languages being learned, whether the child learns them together or sequentially). Their discussion is marred, however, by their lack of familiarity with ASL structure and its similarity to the structure of spoken languages other than English. Thus, while they suggest bilingualism as a possibility for educating deaf students, they also appear ready with explanations if such an effort should fail.

Socialization, Achievement, and Emotional Development

The relationship of the use of manual communication to the well-being of the deaf person interacts with the relationship of a deaf person to his parents. Several of the earlier cited studies that compared deaf students of deaf parents to deaf students of hearing parents to determine the relationship of manual communication to the acquisition of English or of speech skills are relevant here (see Table 11-2). These studies overwhelmingly reported better overall achievement for the deaf students of deaf parents, even though there were differences on some measures, and, in some cases, no differences at all. It is probable that much of this achievement depends directly on better parent-child relations, which in turn are a function of better communication channels.

Moores (1974) summarized several studies comparing deaf students of deaf parents to deaf students of hearing parents. Relevant portions are discussed here, but the reader is advised that these are

Table 11-2. *Studies of deaf children of deaf parents receiving manual communication*

Investigator	Comparison	Programs	Results
Stevenson (1964)	134 deaf students of deaf parents to 134 deaf students of hearing parents	California School for Deaf, Berkeley	Those with deaf parents were educationally superior in 90% of pair matchings, 38% of students with deaf parents went to college, 9% of those with hearing parents.
Stuckless and Birch (1966)	38 deaf students of deaf parents matched to 38 deaf students of hearing parents	American School for Deaf, Pennsylvania School for Deaf, West. Pa. School for Deaf, Martin School for Deaf, Indiana School for Deaf	Children with deaf parents superior in reading, speechreading and written language. No differences in speech or psychosocial development.
Meadow (1966)	59 deaf students of deaf parents matched to 59 deaf students of hearing parents	California School for Deaf, Berkeley	Children with deaf parents ahead 1.25 years in arithmetic, 2.1 years in reading, 1.28 years in achievement. Superior in written language, fingerspelling, signs, willingness to communicate with strangers. More mature, responsible, sociable. No differences in speech or speechreading.

(continued)

Table 11-2. *(continued)*

Investigator	Comparison	Programs	Results
Quigley and Frisina (1961)	16 deaf students with deaf parents out of a population of 120 deaf students	Kansas School for Deaf, Michigan School for Deaf, Pennsylvania School for Deaf, Texas School for Deaf, Rochester School for Deaf, California School for Deaf, Riverside	Children with deaf parents superior in fingerspelling and vocabulary. No differences in speechreading and achievement. Children with hearing parents superior in speech.
Vernon and Koh (1970)	32 deaf students with deaf parents matched with 32 recessively deaf students with hearing parents	California School for Deaf, Riverside	Children with deaf parents — an average of 1.44 years superior on academic achievement and superior in reading vocabulary and written language. No differences in speech and speechreading.

From Moores (1971).

only summaries. Stevenson (1964) compared 134 deaf students of hearing parents, and reported higher educational achievement for the deaf students of deaf parents in 90 percent of the comparisons, with 38 percent of the students with deaf parents going on to college, compared to only 9 percent of the students with hearing parents. Stuckless and Birch (1966) reported superior reading, speechreading, and written language for the deaf students of deaf parents, with no differences noted in speech or psychosocial development.

Meadow (1966) reported higher self-image and academic achievement in deaf children of deaf parents. She reported a superiority of 1.25 years in arithmetic, 2.1 years in reading, and 1.28 years overall for these students. In addition, teachers' ratings of the students were in favor of the deaf students of deaf parents on maturity, responsibility, independence, sociability, appropriate sex role, popularity, appropriate responses to situations, fingerspelling ability, written language, signing ability, absence of communicative frustration, and willingness to communicate with strangers. No difference was noted in speech or speechreading.

Vernon and Koh (1970) likewise found that deaf students of deaf parents were superior in reading, vocabulary, and written language, with an overall achievement of 1.44 years higher than the students of hearing parents (and no manual communication). No differences were found in speech, speechreading, or psychosocial adjustment. Quigley and Frisina (1961) found higher vocabulary levels for the deaf students of deaf parents, no differences in speechreading or educational achievement, and better speech for the deaf students of hearing parents. Vernon and Koh (1970) compared the academic achievement of deaf students of deaf parents with early manual communication to deaf students of hearing parents with early intensive oral training (John Tracy Clinic program). They found that the students of deaf parents were one full grade ahead in all areas and had superior reading skills. No differences were found in speech or speechreading.

Comparisons of deaf students of deaf parents with deaf students of hearing parents revealed that 60 percent of the deaf students of deaf parents did not have preschool education, whereas only 18 percent of the deaf students of hearing parents had not attended preschool. The hearing parents had a significantly higher socioeconomic status than the deaf parents, and nearly 90 percent of the hearing parents had some contact with the John Tracy Clinic program.

These studies do not tell the whole story, however. The existence of a deaf community (Chapter 9) that is bound together by a common language has a profound effect on the perspective from which one views the relationship between socioemotional development and use of manual communication. The deaf person, unlike other language-disrupted persons, has the deaf community to enjoy while growing up and as an adult. Social functions, religious groups, educational seminars, and political lobbying are all part of the activities within the deaf community. Markowicz and Woodward (1978) report that "ASL serves as the primary linguistic criterion for identification of self and others as members of the deaf subculture, and for the promotion of solidarity within the group." The deaf community may include the profoundly deaf and the hard of hearing, both prelingually and postlingually deaf individuals, those with good speech and those without, and occasional hearing people (usually with deaf parents). At the same time, there are hearing-impaired people who are not members of the deaf community and who have little or no contact with its members. Two criteria that seem to determine membership in the deaf community are (1) attendance at a residential school for the deaf (where deaf children of hearing parents are socialized into the community by older children and peers who have deaf parents) and (2) competence in ASL (Stokoe et al., 1976).

Charrow and Wilbur (1975) discussed the parallels between the minority deaf culture and other minority groups in the United States. Of particular sociolinguistic interest are the different social conventions and politeness rules for signers than for speakers/listeners. For example, Baker (1977) has described turn-taking signals in ASL conversations (see Chapter 7) that are different from those in English, and has identified different conventions for eye contact, distance between signer and addressee, and other such cultural differences.

Information is scarce concerning the relationship between manual communication and vocational success, although it is known that good speech skills are highly correlated with employment opportunities and financial rewards (Boatner, Stuckless, and Moores, 1964). Information of psychosocial aspects of manual communication usage continues to be gathered (Bolton, 1976; see especially Bornstein, Woodward, and Tully, 1976; Meadow, 1976). One study (Rainer, Altshuler, and Kallmann, 1963) reported on the marital patterns of deaf women, indicating that 95 percent of marriages of women born deaf and 91 percent of marriages of women adventitiously deafened at an early age are to deaf men. They also reported that the better the communication skills (oral or manual), the higher the probability of marriage. However, ironically, once married, the better the communication skills, the higher the incidence of marital discord. Such information, although interesting, does not directly pertain to the use of manual communication itself as much as to the need for greater understanding of the dynamics of communication in marriage and the additional effects that deafness contributes.

SUMMARY

The studies reviewed in this chapter suggest that deaf children's problems learning English are not primarily the result of their knowledge of sign language, and similarly that their acquisition of speech is not hindered by their knowledge of sign language. It is also clear that early use of sign language has a beneficial effect on performance in English and may substantially contribute to the better overall performance of deaf children of deaf parents when compared to deaf children of hearing parents. Although the data does not argue convincingly in favor of signed English forms as opposed to ASL, they do argue that signs in any form are preferable to no signs at all. This conclusion is qualified by the cautions that have been raised, particularly that children should be treated individually, that it should not be assumed that one system is best for all, and that attempts to teach deaf children to speak should not be lessened by the assumption that the children will "pick up" what they need from the TC input.

CHAPTER 12

Signs and Communicatively Handicapped People Who Are Not Deaf

In many respects, the current popularity of signing with deaf children traces its origins to the observations of many clinicians and educators that sign usage was effective with various kinds of children who had communication problems but no hearing loss, especially the minimally verbal autistic and intellectually handicapped populations, although sign training with chimpanzees also had an effect on attitudes toward signs (Mayberry, 1976a; Neisser, 1983). Although results varied widely, signs when used alone or in conjunction with speech (simultaneous communication) helped to establish communication beyond whatever the child previously had. For some children, the comprehension and production of a few signs may have been all they were able to accomplish. Other children, however, acquired many more signs, although it would probably not be correct to say that any of them actually learned "sign language" (that is, learned enough vocabulary and syntax to be considered fluent users of either signed English or ASL. One of the more puzzling observations was that certain children who received sign intervention began to use (more) spoken output; sometimes the output was unintelligible vocalization, but sometimes the verbalization was recognizable speech. These same children had not previously profited from speech training. Although few in number, there have also been reports of children who decreased their use of signs as their speech increased and even occasions when new words have been acquired incidentally from the environment without being specifically taught. The end of this sequence is an arduous achievement and is not to be expected as an inevitable outcome of the use of sign intervention. As Moores (1980) indicated, "it is unrealistic to believe that children with severe cognitive, physical, or emotional handicaps would benefit from exposure to the Rochester Method [simultaneous fingerspelling and speech], with its demands on perceptual and motor integration, with the complete, sophisticated American Sign Language, or with one of its variants [sign systems]." Some studies have used signs alone (that is, not speaking at the same time) while others have used simultaneous signing and speech. Frequently, the simultaneous signing and speech is limited to single signs rather than phrases or sentences, as phrase structure and syntax are usually reserved for more sophisticated communication situations than are possible with these populations. In some cases, however, simultaneous signing and speaking is done in a "key word" format, where the speech is more or less unchanged compared to a speech only condition, and the key or major words in the sentence are also signed.

There has been much discussion and speculation as to why sign intervention has proved successful where prior speech training has not in the various reviews that have surveyed the research literature (Bonvillian, Nelson, and Rhyne, 1981; Carr, 1979; Layton, Leslie, and Helmer, 1983). Some of the considerations involved in using sign intervention and in determining reasonable expectations are discussed at the end of this chapter. Before approaching those issues, some reports of sign intervention with autistic, intellectually handicapped, and other populations are presented. The reader is referred to Kiernan (1977), Poulton and Algozzine (1980), and Schiefelbusch (1980) for discussions of sign intervention along with other forms of "nonspeech" language strategies (Blissymbolics, rebus, Premack symbols) with these same populations.

AUTISTIC CHILDREN

Early reports (Rutter, 1968; Webster, McPherson, Sloman, Evans, and Kaucher, 1973) of autistic children's responsiveness to the use of gestures (not signs) suggested that manual communication might be a successful approach. Miller and Miller (1973) used ASL signs along with body awareness training with 19 autistic children, using signs limited to particular goals or activities, and reported the development of speech in two of the children. Creedon (1973, 1975) has reported on the success of a TC program with autistic children, indicating improvement in socialization and decrease in self-stimulatory behavior (often noted by other reports, e.g., Benaroya, Wesley, Ogilvie, Klein, and Meaney, 1977; Bonvillian and Nelson, 1978; Casey, 1978). One limitation of studies in this area has been that sign training programs are frequently accompanied by training in play skills and attending behavior. Thus, it is not always possible to determine which part of the program is responsible for the reported improvement; this topic is discussed in depth in Bonvillian and Blackburn (1986).

Creedon (1976) reported that about two-thirds of the children receiving manual communication intervention initiated some form of speech, including fluent speech for a small number of children. Fulwiler and Fouts (1976) worked with a single autistic boy and reported the development of some speech accompanying the signs. Schaeffer, Kollinzas, Musil, and McDowell, (1977) and Schaeffer (1980) reported progress with three autistic boys ages 4 years, 6 months, 5 years, and 5 years, 6 months. The children were presented with what Schaeffer calls "signed speech," which is the simultaneous presentation of signs and speech. The children progressed from using signs only spontaneously to using signs and speech simultaneously in about 4 to 5 months. After 5 months, all three children began to use speech spontaneously without signs, at which point signing was faded for those structures the child could produce in speech. Schaeffer suggested several advantages that contributed to the children's success in attaining spontaneous speech: (1) the children's constant exposure to signs and speech may have provided important clues to the relationship between signs and speech; (2) when the children were still using only signs in the sessions, the instructor spoke the word while the child signed to encourage the child to imitate it; (3) as soon as the children had developed necessary sound production skills, specific speech instruction was aimed at teaching them to pronounce the words they could already sign; (4) the children were taught to imitate after the instructor rather than to shadow the instructor's voice, forcing them to rely more heavily on their own memory for sounds; (5) when the children began to spontaneously combine speech and signs, they were thereafter required to do so; and (6) the children were taught to coordinate their sign movements and their speech syllables precisely. The necessity and efficiency of each technique for general instruction remain to be determined.

Several studies have compared the effectiveness of signs, speech, and combinations of the two with autistic children. Webster, Konstantareas, and Oxman (1976) compared the abilities of four autistic children to follow commands, name actions or objects, and imitate as a function of the presentation mode of the instructions. They reported that for all four children, signs were at least as effective as speech, and there was no significant difference between signs only and combined signs and speech. Baron and Isensee (1977) compared comprehension of instructions presented in signs only with instructions presented in speech only and found a definite advantage to the signs (83.5 percent) compared to the speech (56.2 percent) over a variety of linguistic variables and contexts (pictures versus real objects) for a single girl aged 12 years 6 months. Barrera, Lobato-Barrera, and Sulzer-Azaroff (1980) used operant conditioning techniques to train words in all three conditions (signs only, speech only, combination of signs and speech) and concluded that the combination of signs and speech was most effective. However, they used only a single subject, they attempted to train 30 words in each condition in five hours of training for each condition, and the number of words learned in each condition was very small — seven for the combination condition and four each for the signs only and the speech only condition. (Additional training for three hours with simultaneous speaking and signing did provide further progress, with another 11 words learned.)

Other studies have not found a significant difference between sign-only conditions and simultaneous speaking and signing conditions. Remington and Clarke (1983), for example, found that in the simultaneous condition two autistic adolescents needed more trials to criterion than in the sign-only condition, although the difference was not significant. In another study, Layton and Stutts (1985) compared the number of communicative functions (requests, descriptions, etc.) used by children assigned to one of four treatment groups (the fourth condition was an alternating treatment of sometimes signing and sometimes speaking). No differences were found among the four treatments. Along with other studies (Brady and Smouse, 1978; Liebovitz, 1976, cited in Konstantareas and Liebovitz, 1981), the general consensus seems to be that simultaneous speaking and signing is as effective as sign-only training, and in some instances, more so.

Among the main issues that confront those who are involved in planning language intervention with the autistic population is the question of whether to use sign training and, if so, how to proceed. In fact, the first decision is usually not whether to use signs themselves, but rather whether to use any kind of augmentative communication at all. The literature on augmentative communication contains several excellent overviews of the available options (Carlson, 1982; Cohen and Shane, 1982; Lloyd and Karlan, 1984; Rabush, Lloyd, and Gerdes, 1982a, b, c; Reichle and Karlan, 1985; Schiefelbusch, 1980; Vanderheiden and Grilley, 1976; and Yoder and Kraat, 1982). To make an objective decision concerning the use of signs or other techniques, familiarity with these different options is necessary. Several articles (Shane, 1980; Shane and Bashir, 1980; Yoder and Porter, 1984) help in the planning stages by providing decision-making flowcharts and criteria for adopting different available systems.

The decision to use signs with an autistic person requires consideration of a number of characteristics of the individual. Bonvillian and colleagues (1981) surveyed the literature on sign usage with autistic children and reported that nearly all of the 100 children learned some receptive and expressive signs. They also noted that several researchers reported that individuals who could indicate their desires through pointing before the beginning of sign training seemed to do well when presented with signs. Howlin (1981) found that neither age nor IQ was a good indicator of potential language learning for autistic individuals, but that prior language abilities and social skills were important predictors.

The most extensive investigation of which autistic children are likely to learn signs was conducted by Helmer, Layton, and Wolfe (1982). They attempted to determine groups of autistic children aged 3 to 9 on the basis of language skills and to investigate which of them would be good candidates for sign training. They identified five groups on the basis of the Sequenced Inventory of Communication Development (Hedrick, Prather, and Tobin, 1975). The first group had better expressive skills than receptive skills, tended to use a few spoken words spontaneously, but had poor imitation skills and did not speak when requested. These children had some gestures and vocalizations in their attempts to communicate, and the authors suggested that this group may include the children most likely to benefit from a simultaneous communication approach, with the probability that they might eventually develop usable speech from it. Helmer and colleagues' second group was identified by overall better receptive skills than expressive skills, a better response to words alone as compared to words and gestures combined, and infrequent attempts to initiate communication. This group actually had two subgroups, one with nearly normal nonverbal IQs and echolalic tendencies and the other with the lowest IQs in their survey (below 30) and muteness. The authors suggested that, for both subgroups, significant amounts of prelingual training in general communication skills would be necessary before language training, and that some alternative means of communication would probably be required, given the poor speech capabilities of the children. The children in the third group had good receptive skills and poor expressive skills, responded well to gestured directions, appeared to understand speech well without additional cues, but had poor vocal imitation skills and no functional speech. Helmer and colleagues suggested that this group would profit from a sign program. Group four included children who were echolalic, had good vocal and verbal imitation skills, and were highly interactive. They differed from the echolalic children in group two in that they had low IQs (around 50) and that they scored higher on the expressive scale because of their interaction with others. Helmer and colleagues suggested that children in group four would need special training on speech comprehension, whereas group two would need training in communication itself. They suggested that sign intervention appeared to be detrimental to the children in group four, but did not provide further details. Finally, the fifth group contained children who had generally low receptive skills and expressive skills, were aided in comprehension by the presence of gestures in addition to spoken words, had poor vocal and verbal imitation skills, and were relatively noncommunicative. They suggested that this group also would benefit from training on prelingual communication skills before the start of language training and that signs or other alternative communication would be appropriate.

INTELLECTUALLY HANDICAPPED
CHILDREN

There are numerous reports of sign intervention with intellectually handicapped individuals, including Bricker (1972), Kahn (1981), Kiernan and Jones (1985), Kotkin, Simpson, and Desanto (1978), Levitt (1972), Owens and Harper (1971), Shaffer and Goehl

(1974), Stohr and Van Hook (1973), Sutherland and Becket (1969), Wilson (1974), Van Biervliet (1977), and Wagenen, Jenson, Worsham, and Petersen (1985). Many of these have reported results similar to those in Stremel-Campbell, Cantrell, and Halle (1977), who found that six of nine trainable children began production of speech as a result of manual communication training.

The previous reports represent only a small number of the programs that are using sign communication with intellectually handicapped individuals (Fristoe and Lloyd, 1977a). In a nationwide survey of speech, hearing, and language services for the retarded, Fristoe (1975) reported that over 10 percent of those responding were using manual communication or other nonvocal communication systems (including Blissymbols, rebuses, and communication boards; see Lloyd, 1976, and Schiefelbusch, 1980, for discussion of these systems). The results of the survey, and a follow-up (Fristoe and Lloyd, 1977b), indicated a widespread proliferation of the use of manual communication but, at the same time, a minimal awareness on the part of the program of what other teachers, clinicians, and researchers were doing. In many cases, respondents indicated a lack of understanding regarding the difference between using the signs from ASL (usually in English word order) from using ASL itself.

One of the major concerns of those initiating manual communication programs with retarded individuals is where to start. Because of the concern over what signs to teach, Fristoe and Lloyd (1980) suggested a first sign lexicon based on their analysis of the signs that are currently being used with retarded individuals (including some of the signs in the *Perkins Sign Language Dictionary*, see Chapter 10) and principles for selection from a variety of sources. Of primary concern are the first sign(s) to be taught: those that are functional and give the child some control over his environment, such as EAT, DRINK, and TOILET, or important to the child like COOKIE or TICKLE. Furthermore, Fouts (1973) indicated that teaching the chimpanzee Washoe signs that involved contact was easier than teaching signs that were made in neutral space and involved no contact. Fouts' observations are supported by other studies with children (Kohl, 1981; Stremel-Campbell, Cantrell, and Halle, 1977; Thrasher and Bray, 1984), although there are other factors that may interact with this generalization (Doherty, 1985). Doherty notes that the ambiguity of contact as both as feature of location and a movement type (as discussed in Chapter 3) creates problems for the interpretation of the studies of the effect of contact versus no contact. Several other characteristics of signs have been suggested as relevant to their acquisition, including symmetry, one versus two hands, location (referred to by some as "visibility"), reduplication (by which the authors have apparently meant "repetition" rather than morphological reduplication, as discussed in Chapter 5), complexity (one versus two movements per sign), and whether the sign has a handshape change (referred to as "fluidity" by Dennis, Reichle, Williams, and Vogelsberg, 1982). As discussed in the chapter on sign language acquisition (Chapter 8), no single component of a sign can be learned in isolation from the other components; thus it is not surprising that these sign characteristics interact with each other in complex and interesting ways, reviewed in detail in Doherty (1985).

Fristoe and Lloyd (1977b) raised other questions concerning which signs to teach and how to teach them. They questioned whether the reinforcer for correct performance should be the sign's referent or some other reinforcer totally unrelated to the sign's meaning. Concerning the grouping of signs for instructional presentation, they indicated that categories that are conceptually or functionally coherent seemed to be preferable to alphabetic organization, which is used in most sign language manuals (alphabetic based on the equivalent English gloss). Two current studies have confirmed that this is so for hearing adults (Mills and Weldon, 1983; Fuller and Wilbur, in press). Stremel-Campbell and colleagues (1977) indicated that errors increased when two signs from the same category were included in a single learning set, and they suggested that the groupings of signs for presentation should be checked for similarities of handshape, motion, and place of formation. Fuller and Wilbur (in press) found that formation similarities continued to cause difficulties in learning and remembering signs even when the subjects were provided with "explanations" (metaphor cues) concerning the formation of the signs (see discussion of metaphor in signs in Chapter 7).

Another concern about the teaching of signs is the possibility that iconicity contained within the sign may contribute to the sign's learnability. Brown (1977) presented evidence indicating that hearing children with normal intelligence were better able to remember iconic signs paired with their proper meaning than signs paired with meanings that did not reflect the characteristics visible in the sign. Stremel-Campbell and colleagues (1977) and Kostantareas, Oxman, and Webster (1978) have indicated that iconicity may be a relevant variable in teaching intellectually handicapped individuals. However, Rogers (1976) did not find such an effect experimentally with four retarded adults. One major concern in attempting to answer this question is how iconicity is determined for experimental purposes. Lloyd and Fristoe (1978) analyzed the "guessability" or transparency of signs included in the vocabularies intended for retarded children. They indicated that the percentage of signs in these functional vocabularies that are guessable by adults who do not know any signs is higher than that reported by Bellugi and Klima (1976) or Hoemann (1975) for the language as a whole (see discussion in Chapter 7). Signs may be iconic, however, without being transparent or guessable. That is, a sign that is not guessable may still bear some relationship to its referent which might become more obvious when it is pointed out. In addition, guessability for adults does not necessarily mean guessability for children, especially retarded children. Bernstein (1980) demonstrated that although the signs IN, ON, and UNDER display in their formation the notations of "in," "on," and "under" (by the spatial arrangement of the two hands), deaf children learning ASL do not "see" these relationships in the sign until long after they have learned the concepts themselves; thus, the ability to see the iconicity requires the cognitive development of the concepts that are being iconically represented. In the case of retarded children, there is clearly a need to be concerned about what concepts each individual has already acquired. Furthermore, Bernstein's research indicates that the *presence* of iconicity in the signs does not contribute to the development of the concepts themselves, as the iconicity goes unnoticed until after the concept has been acquired and the relevant relationship has been brought to the child's attention (see the discussion of parents' strategies for signing to deaf children in Chapter 8).

OTHER POPULATIONS

Multiply Handicapped

The current work using signs with autistic, retarded, and other severely language-impaired populations is probably derived from the earlier work using signs with the "deaf retarded" (cf. Anthony, 1966, 1971; Butler, Griffing, and Huffman, 1969; James, 1963, 1967; Johnson, 1963; Sutherland and Becket, 1969). Manual communication intervention with this population was reported by Hall and Conn (1972), Hall and Talkington (1970), and Hoffmeister and Farmer (1972). Hoffmeister and Farmer reported an increase in receptive and expressive knowledge of signs through a special tutorial program for intellectually handicapped deaf adults, but no improvement through the same program for two others who were also considered autistic or brain damaged. In addition, subjects with vocabu-

laries greater than 200 signs were observed using two- and
three-sign productions in their spontaneous communication.

The *Perkins Sign Language Dictionary,* discussed in more detail
in Chapter 10, was constructed at the Perkins School for the Blind to
meet the communication needs of a population with the following
characteristics (Robbins et al., 1975):

1. multihandicapped (⅔ below 70 IQ.).
2. high incidence of expressive language problems: . . .
3. high incidence of motor difficulties;
4. acquisition of information (growth of concepts) is difficult. . . due
   to learning problems *and* the social and often physical isolating
   effects of dual sensory impairments.
5. the population includes a high percentage of deaf, partially seeing students whose learning needs and later social responsibilities are more similar to the non-professional, non highly-
   educated deaf than to any other group.
6. the population includes a high percentage of very visual children
   for whom visual imagery is most persuasive for thinking.

The program at Perkins, for which the dictionary was developed,
does not aim at teaching English as the primary goal. Instead, the
establishment of effective communication with whatever structural
means is of paramount importance.

The appropriateness of sign training with these and other multiply handicapped populations (deaf-blind) and hearing aphasics is
discussed in detail in Orlansky and Bonvillian (1983); Christopoulou
and Bonvillian (1985) pursue further the appropriateness of signing
for hearing aphasics.

Physically Handicapped

It might seem obvious that extreme motor control difficulties
would not make an individual a good candidate for learning signs.
Nonetheless, there have been some attempts, although the results
have not been systematically reported. In order to try to predict
which types of physical impairments might still allow an individual
to produce intelligible signs, Shane and Wilbur (1980) presented an
analysis of the motor components necessary for the signs in two vocabularies, the 840 signs in the functional vocabularies reviewed by
Fristoe and Lloyd (1979b) and the 1628 entries in the *Dictionary of
American Sign Language* (Stokoe et al., 1976). Location was separated into four main areas, chest, hand, face, and arm, with subareas
on the chest and face. An individual who is unable to bring the hand

to contact with the face, for example, would be unable to make 29 percent of the signs. However, if the person can make contact with the face but is unable to control the muscles well enough to distinguish between the cheek bone and the chin, only 11 percent of the signs are eliminated. Similar analyses are presented for handshape and movement. Inability to touch the fingers to the thumb eliminates only 5 percent of the signs, whereas inability to make a fist eliminates almost 15 percent of the signs, as the fist motor component is required for signs with S, A, Å, I, and Y handshapes. Flat handshape and the extended index finger are the two most prevalent (30 percent and 26 percent respectively), and an inability to produce them (and the handshapes that include them) would eliminate over 50 percent of the total vocabulary. Insufficient motor control to permit a movement to be repeated would prevent only 7 percent of the signs from being produced, whereas an inability to make a simple path movement in a straight line would eliminate over 50 percent of the signs. Using the data presented in Shane and Wilbur (1980), a clinical assessment of eligibility for signing could be conducted. Note, however, that an individual who cannot perform many of the required motor components could still benefit from a manual approach. This might occur in a situation where a motorically handicapped person uses only a limited number of motor approximations to sign targets. For example, Hoyt (1980) introduced a number of functional signs to severely physically handicapped individuals whose principle expressive communication was through the use of electronic aids. The individuals were able to communicate basic needs such as hunger and thirst through approximations to the sign targets, because there were so few signs involved and no possibility of confusion among them. The greater the number of signs needed, the more important accuracy of production becomes, making a clinical assessment of motor ability an important preliminary step.

DECIDING TO USE MANUAL COMMUNICATION

Because "other populations" includes a variety of possible problems, certain subdivisions must be made along with other than traditional labels:

1. There are individuals who, at some point during their lives, indicate that they are capable of both sophisticated comprehension and production but who do not choose to communicate.
2. There are individuals who have excellent comprehension and are

capable of good production but who suffer from performance dis-
fluencies (consistently improper word choice, disrupted switching
of stylistic level).

3. There are individuals who have excellent comprehension but who
   have difficulties in production attributable to speech problems.
4. There are individuals who demonstrate comprehension on tasks
   not requiring verbal output but who cannot speak.
5. There are individuals who demonstrate generalized learning difficulties, of which disturbed language is one manifestation; in
   such individuals there may be little or no evidence of comprehension or production.

These five general groups are not intended to be all-inclusive, or
necessarily mutually exclusive, and they do not take into account
etiology. They do, however, represent basic variables to be considered
in the remediation process. For example, the first group does not
have a language disorder in the *linguistic* sense of language. In most
cases of this type, some emotional disturbance is indicated, and unless the emotional problem is directly related to using speech (as in a
child who refuses to talk for fear of using up his breath), it is not
clear that switching to manual communication will provide any
benefit.

In the second group, the disorder can be considered paralinguistic, that is, it relates to factors concerned with socially defined usage
of language (conventional meanings of words, proper style for addressing friends as opposed to strangers). This type of problem has
been reported with autistic adolescents (Simmons and Baltaxe,
1975). It is not clear what benefit would be gained by using manual
communication with this population. The probability of similar
problems with ASL cannot be ruled out (that is, signs may be acquired, but paralinguistic difficulties may be manifest in the use of
those signs).

In those instances where there is an indication of aphasia (the
patient finds it difficult to find the right word or substitutes semantically similar or phonologically similar words for intended words),
some benefit may be gained by switching to ASL. Battison and
Markowicz (1974), Battison and Padden (1974), and Markowicz
(1973) reported that evidence from brain lesions indicate that signs,
fingerspelling, and speech are differentially located in the brain and
are differentially impaired by lesions. It is possible, then, for speech
to be lost while signs remain intact. Battison and Markowicz (1974)
suggested that "some hearing aphasics may have an intact system
capable of producing propositional gestures. That is, the language
disruption of some hearing aphasics may be limited to their speech,
and they may be capable of learning to sign, all problems of training
aside."

Individuals with speech problems may have either nerve problems (dysarthria) or motor coordination problems (oral apraxia). In the case of dysarthria, manual communication would seem to be indicated. In the case of oral apraxia, manual communication might be a beneficial alternative, unless of course the apraxia is actually more generalized to include manual apraxia also.

Individuals who exhibit no expressive language may demonstrate a wide range of comprehension, from nearly none (a few highly frequent utterances that require simple motor responses, such as "stand there" or "put on your jacket") to quite sophisticated (as, for example, reported in Lenneberg, 1967).

In the four groups discussed previously where some indication of comprehension was present and there was no indication of generalized learning difficulties, the focus of remediation is on providing a means for expresing language. With the intellectually handicapped, particularly the severely or profoundly retarded, the establishment of receptive language becomes as important as, if not more important than, teaching means of expression.

In order to acquire a minimal receptive knowledge of a language, an individual theoretically must be capable of symbolic representation, in that he must be able to use something (not necessarily a word) to stand for (refer to, represent) something else (an object or concept). The child who can take a rattle and pretend in overt play that it is a spoon (or some similar type of representation) has indicated the ability to substitute a symbol (the rattle) for the object (the spoon). Within Piaget's (1951, 1952, 1964) theory of cognitive development, the child begins to develop such symbolic representation at Stage 6 of the sensorimotor period (roughly 18 to 24 months of age in normal children). Inherent in Piaget's theory is the notion of "readiness" to acquire language (which does not mean that intervention should be postponed until the child is "ready"; see Chapman and Miller, 1980).

Woodward (1959) found that many profoundly retarded children and adolescents functioned at a level below Stage 6. In an explicit test of the relationship between Stage 6 functioning and the presence of meaningful language in the severely/profoundly retarded, Kahn (1975) compared a group of eight children who were able to use at least 10 words to ask for various objects with another group of eight children who used no words at all. On four Piagetian tasks of Stage 6 functioning, Kahn found that seven of the eight children who used words functioned at the Stage 6 level on all four tasks, whereas none of the eight children who did not use words functioned at Stage 6 on all four tasks. The two best children of the nonlanguage group were able to reach Stage 6 functioning on only two of the tasks. Kahn's findings were statistically significant: the language group functioned at Stage 6, the nonlanguage group did not. Kahn concluded that attainment of Stage 6 cognitive abilities are prerequisite to language development, therefore cognitive assessment should precede language training. Those children who are functioning at or above Stage 6 might reasonably be expected to profit from training, whereas those below Stage 6 might benefit from activities aimed at raising their cognitive functioning. Other researchers in the field have suggested that, cognitive level aside, language should be made available to children as early as possible to provide a communication system that will eventually result in further language and cognitive development. Yoder (1978) has argued that such communication should take place in an environment in which the child might be motivated to communicate, and that the communication method should be appropriate to the needs and abilities of the child.

WHY DOES IT WORK?

Many factors are involved in the acquisition of signs by these populations (as compared to their failure to acquire speech) and in the subsequent acquisition of speech (for those who do). The early emergence of signs in children who are learning ASL as a native language (see Chapter 8) suggests that signs are motorically simpler (although motor development alone is insufficient to account for the developmental stages observed in the acquisition of ASL). Another possible advantage in using signs is their visibility. The learner is able to see the shape and movement of the modeler's hands and, crucially, of his own hands. Signs are 100 percent visible, compared to speech, which may range from 10 percent to 40 percent visible via speechreading (Jeffers, 1967; Schlesinger, 1972). The two sets of hands can be held together to determine similarity, and the learner's hands can be corrected more easily than the learner's mouth. Signs can also be useful if an auditory perceptual disorder is suspected. That is, it might be possible to take advantage of the visual perceptual system if the auditory perceptual system seems to be impaired (not hearing impairment, but auditory attention focusing or short-term auditory memory) (Graham and Graham, 1971). This is particularly true because some signs can be held relatively stationary for a period of time, and can be produced more slowly without too much distortion.

Fristoe and Lloyd (1979a), in addressing the question Why does manual communication intervention lead to increased spontaneous vocalizations and even intelligible speech?, included some of the previous factors and several others. In all, they listed 16 factors that may be relevant to the effectiveness of the use of signs. The first two are relevant to all nonspeech communication (including the graphic and pictorial-type symbols): (1) removal of pressure for speech and (2) problems of auditory short-term memory and auditory processing circumvented. The next four highlight what nonspeech approaches force the trainer to do: (1) limit vocabulary, particularly to functional forms, (2) simplify the language structure used, (3) reduce excess verbiage (noise), and (4) adjust the presentation rate to ensure comprehension. The next four are training advantages of nonspeech approaches: (1) easier to determine student's attention, (2) enhance figure-ground differential, (3) facilitate physical manipulation (molding) if needed, and (4) facilitate observations of shaping to assess progress. The final six relate to stimulus and processing factors that are inherent in nonspeech approaches: (1) stimulus consistency is optimized, (2) both paired associate learning and match-to-sample learning are facilitated, (3) intramodal symbol meaning associations are simplified, (4) multimodal representation is possible, (5) duration of stimuli is adjustable, and (6) visual representation (iconicity, spatial modifications) is possible. Undoubtedly there are others at work, because these seem to be insufficient to explain why nonspeech approaches can lead to speech. (For discussion of the success of other nonspeech approaches, see Schiefelbusch, 1980).

One major problem faced by many programs is what sign system to use. The discussed populations represent groups that do not have their own communities as do deaf people. They do not have their own community organizations, social structure, and native language. In the absence of a communal language, there are no sociolinguistic grounds for choosing one signing system over another. One consideration would be that, given the structure of signs and the role of signs in memory, perception, and in reducing independent movement by the two hands, those forms of manual communication that use ASL signs would be preferable to those that do not. Many of the signs created by the manual systems violate the sign structure constraints, which are presumably perceptually based (Siple, 1973). Another problem that must be faced is that of choosing a limited system which conceivably could be mastered completely by the child, and then possibly having to switch to a different system in order to meet the increasing communication needs of the child, compared to choosing an infinitely expandable system, such as ASL or signed English. This last point is obviously only a problem if we are fortunate enough to have made significant progress with the child, but nonetheless should be considered beforehand, thus not limiting the child's eventual development by preconceived ideas as to his potential communication skills. Robbins (1976) argued that the goal of choosing such an intervention system should be "*not* to select *a* sign system, *not* to determine which system is the 'best', *nor* which system represents English the least imperfectly," but rather "for a preferred method for a particular child at a particular stage (Moores, McIntyre, and Weiss, 1973)." In addition, she indicated her personal preference for "language goals relating to functional use and development of meaning and of concepts which would enable the student to relate more completely to the world of objects, events and persons as he learns, than goals focusing on production of correctly formed English kernel sentences with perfect morphological components." Robbins also argued that the cognitive behavior of the child must be carefully considered before teaching particular signs. The child will demonstrate concepts such as possession, negation, and plurality, after which one can initiate teaching of such signs as MINE, NO, or MANY. As the child's cognitive level develops, different choices of signs and communicative structures will be appropriate. There is a need to monitor carefully both the input to the student and the output from the student, as well as to interpret the implications of the student's performance.

SUMMARY

Research studies on the effectiveness of sign intervention (alone or in simultaneous communication) indicate that when such visual systems are used, communication is enhanced and undesirable behaviors are reduced. The research has focused on issues such as the comparative benefits of sign only versus simultaneous signing and speech, the relative contribution of sign factors such as one versus two hands, contact versus no contact with the body or other hand, formational similarity in sign groups to be learned versus conceptual groupings, and learner characteristics that can increase the likelihood of success.

Further research on the use of signs with nondeaf populations needs to focus on the potential utility of such aspects of ASL as the use of space for grammatical information, facial expression for grammatical or adverbial information, and reduplication for its various purposes. Each of these devices allows a single sign to carry more information than a single word in English would: thus these devices may allow a child to convey or receive more information at the single sign stage than with uninflected, unmodified single signs.

For example, instead of signing NO MORE as a sequence of two signs, the sign MORE can be accompanied by a negative headshake and facial expression. Whether this will facilitate learning and retention remains to be determined (see further discussion of this topic in Wilbur, 1985d). Further research also needs to be addressed to those aspects of the sign training program that are making the contributions to the observed progress. Frequently, the implementation of signs is accompanied by other changes in routine, environment, personnel, or training procedures. It would be helpful to know how each of these affects the communication development of the individual. Also needed is more research on the use of signing with populations such as the reading disabled (Blackburn, Bonvillian, and Ashby, 1984) and hearing aphasics (Christopoulou and Bonvillian, 1985).

REFERENCES

Adams, C. (1979). *English speech rhythm and the foreign learner.* The Hague: Mouton.

Ahlstrom, K. (1972). On evaluation of the effects of schooling. In *Proceedings of the International Congress on Education of the Deaf.* Sveriges Läraförbund, Stockholm.

Allan, K. (1977). Classifiers. *Language, 53,* 285–311.

Allen, G., Wilbur, R., and Schick, B. (1986). *Determining the rhythm of American Sign Language.* Paper to be presented at the American Speech-Language-Hearing Association Convention, Detroit, MI.

Akamatsu, C. (1982). *The acquisition of fingerspelling in pre-school children.* Unpublished doctoral dissertation, University of Rochester.

Akamatsu, C. (1985). Fingerspelling formulae: A word is more or less than the sum of its letters. In W. Stokoe and V. Volterra (Eds.), *SLR '83: Sign language research.* Silver Spring, MD: Linstok Press, Inc. and Rome, Italy: Istituto di Psicologia, CNR.

Anderson, L. (1982). Universals of aspect and parts of speech: Parallels between signed and spoken languages. In P. Hopper (Ed.), *Tense-Aspect: Between semantics and pragmatics.* Amsterdam: John Benjamins Publishing Company.

Anthony, D. (1966). *Seeing Essential English.* Unpublished manuscript, University of Michigan, Ypsilanti.

Anthony, D. (1971). *Seeing Essential English* (Vols. 1 and 2). Educational Services Division, Anaheim Union School District, Anaheim, CA.

Ashbrook, E. (1977). *Development of semantic relations in the acquisition of American Sign Language.* Unpublished manuscript, Salk Institute for Biological Studies, La Jolla, CA.

Babbini, B. (1974). *Manual communication.* Urbana: University of Illinois Press.

Baker, C. (1976). What's not on the other hand in American Sign Language. In S. Mufwene, C. Walker, and S. Steever, (Eds.), *Papers from the Twelfth Regional Meeting, Chicago Linguistic Society.* Chicago: The University of Chicago Press.

Baker, C. (1977). Regulators and turn-taking in American Sign Language discourse. In L. Friedman (Ed.), *On the other hand: New perspectives on American Sign Language.* New York: Academic Press.

Baker, C., and Cokely, D. (1980). *American Sign Language: A teacher's resource text on grammar and culture.* Silver Spring, MD: T.J. Publishers, Inc.

Baker, C., and Padden, C. (1978). Focusing on the nonmanual components of American Sign Language. In P. Siple (Ed.), *Understanding language through sign language research.* New York: Academic Press.

Baker-Shenk, C. (1983). *A microanalysis of the nonmanual components of questions in American Sign Language.* Unpublished doctoral dissertation, University of California, Berkeley.

Bard, B., and Sachs, J. (1977). *Language acquisition patterns in two normal children of deaf parents.* Paper presented at the Second Annual Boston University Conference on Language Development.

Baron, N., and Isensee, L. (1977). *Effectiveness of manual versus spoken language with an autistic child.* Unpublished manuscript, Brown University, Providence, RI.

Barrera, R., Lobato-Barrera, D., and Sulzer-Azaroff, B. (1980). A simultaneous treatment comparison of three expressive language training programs with a mute autistic child. *Journal of Autism and Developmental Disorders, 10,* 21–37.

Battison, R. (1971). *Some observations of sign languages, semantics, and aphasia.* Unpublished manuscript, University of California, San Diego.

Battison, R. (1973). *Phonology in American Sign Language: 3-D and digit-vision.* Paper presented at the California Linguistic Association Conference, Stanford, CA.

Battison, R. (1974). Phonological deletion in American Sign Language. *Sign Language Studies, 5,* 1–19.

Battison, R. (1978). *Lexical borrowing in American Sign Language.* Silver Spring, MD: Linstok Press.

Battison, R., and Markowicz, H. (1974). *Sign aphasia and neurolinguistic theory.* Unpublished manuscript, Gallaudet College, Washington, DC.

Battison, R., Markowicz, H., and Woodward, J. (1975). A good rule of thumb: Variable phonology in American Sign Language. In R. Shuy and R. Fasold (Eds.), *New ways of analyzing variation in English II.* Washington, DC: Georgetown University Press.

Battison, R., and Padden, C. (1974). *Sign language aphasia: A case study.*

Paper presented at the 49th Annual Meeting, Linguistic Society of America, New York, NY

Bébian, R.-A. (1827). *Manuel d'enseignement pratique des sourds-muets* [Manual of practical teaching of deaf-mutes]. Paris: Mequignon.

Beckmeyer, T. (1976). Receptive abilities of hearing impaired students in a total communication setting. *American Annals of the Deaf, 121,* 569–572.

Bellugi, U. (1967). *The acquisition of negation.* Unpublished doctoral dissertation, Harvard University, Cambridge, MA.

Bellugi, U. (1972). Studies in sign language. In T. O'Rourke (Ed.), *Psycholinguistics and Total Communication: The state of the art.* Silver Spring, MD: National Association of the Deaf.

Bellugi, U. (1975). *The process of compounding in American Sign Language.* Unpublished manuscript, Salk Institute of Biological Studies, La Jolla, CA.

Bellugi, U., and Fischer, S. (1972). A comparison of sign language and spoken language: Rate and grammatical mechanisms. *Cognition, 1,* June: 173–200.

Bellugi, U., and Klima, E. (1972, June). The roots of language in the sign talk of the deaf. *Psychology Today,* 61–64, 76.

Bellugi, U., and Klima, E. (1976). Two faces of sign: Iconic and abstract. In S. Harnad, H. Steklis, and J. Lancester (Eds.), *Origins and evolution of language and speech.* New York: New York Academy of Sciences.

Bellugi, U. and Klima, E. (1980). *The structured use of space in a visual-manual language.* Unpublished manuscript.

Bellugi, U. and Klima, E. (1985). The acquisition of three morphological systems in American Sign Language. In F. Powell, T. Finitzo-Heber, S. Friel-Patti, and D. Henderson (Eds.), *Educating the Hearing-Impaired Child.* San Diego: College-Hill Press.

Bellugi, U., Klima, E., and Siple, P. (1975). Remembering in signs. *Cognition, 3,* 93–125.

Bellugi, U., and Newkirk, D. (1981). Formal devices for creating new signs in American Sign Language. *Sign Language Studies, 30,* 1–35.

Bellugi, U., Poizner, H., and Klima, E. (1983). Brain organization for language: clues from sign aphasia. *Human Neurobiology, 2,* 155–170.

Bellugi, U., and Siple, P. (1974). Remembering with and without words. In F. Bresson (Ed.), *Current problems in psycholinguistics.* Paris: Centre National de la Recherche Scientifique.

Belmont, J., Karchmer, M., and Pilkonis, P. (1976). Instructed rehearsal strategies' influence on deaf memory processing. *Journal of Speech and Hearing Research, 19,* 36–47.

Benaroya, S., Wesley, S., Ogilvie, H., Klein, L., and Meaney, M. (1977). Sign language and multisensory input training of children with communication and related developmental disorders. *Journal of Autism and Childhood Schizophrenia, 7,* 23–31.

Berko, J., and Brown, R. (1966). Psycholinguistic research methods. In P. Mussen (Ed.), *Handbook of research methods in child development.* New York: John Wiley & Sons.

Bernstein, M. (1980). *Acquisition of locative expressions by deaf children learning American Sign Language.* Unpublished doctoral dissertation, Boston University.

Bernstein, M., Maxwell, M., and Matthews, K. (1985). Bimodal or bilingual communication? *Sign Language Studies, 47,* 127–140.

Black, C. (1981). *It will never happen to me.* Denver, CO: M.A.C. Printing and Publications Division.

Blackburn, D., Bonvillian, J., and Ashby, R. (1984). Manual communication as an alternative mode of language instruction for children with severe reading disabilities. *Language, Speech, and Hearing Services in Schools, 15,* 22–31.

Bloom, L. (1970). *Language development: Form and function in emerging grammar.* Cambridge, MA: MIT Press.

Boatner, E., Stuckless, E., and Moores, D. (1964). Occupational status of the young adult deaf of New England and the need and demand for a regional technical-vocational training center. (Final report, Research Grant RD-1295-S-64.) Vocational Rehabilitation Administration, DHEW.

Bode, L. (1974). Communication of agent, object, and indirect object in spoken and signed languages. *Perceptual and Motor Skills, 39,* 1151–1158.

Bolton, B. (1976). *Psychology of deafness for rehabilitation counselors.* Baltimore: University Park Press.

Bonvillian, J. (1983). Effects of signability and imagery on word recall of deaf and hearing students. *Perceptual and Motor Skills, 56,* 775–791.

Bonvillian, J. and Blackburn, D. (1986). *Manual communication and autism: Factors relating to sign language acquisition.* Conference on Theoretical Issues in Sign Language Research, Rochester, NY.

Bonvillian, J., Charrow, V., and Nelson, K. (1973). Psycholinguistic and educational implications of deafness. *Human Development, 16,* 321–345.

Bonvillian, J., and Nelson, K. (1978). Development of sign language in autistic children and other language handicapped individuals. In P. Siple (Ed.), *Understanding language through sign language research.* New York: Academic Press.

Bonvillian, J., Nelson, K., and Charrow, V. (1976). Language and language-related skills in deaf and hearing children. *Sign Language Studies, 12,* 211–250.

Bonvillian, J. and Orlansky, M. (1984). Sign language acquisition: Early steps. *Communication Outlook, 6,* 10–12.

Bonvillian, J., Orlansky, M., and Novack, L. (1983). Developmental milestones: Sign language acquisition and motor development. *Child Development, 54,* 1435–1445.

Bonvillian, J., Orlansky, M., Novack, L., and Folven, R. (1983). Early sign language acquisition and cognitive development. In D. Rogers and J. Sloboda (Eds.), *The acquisition of symbolic skills.* London: Plenum.

Bonvillian, J., Orlansky, M., Novack, L., Folven, R., and Holley-Wilcox, P. (1985). Language, cognitive, and cherological development: The first steps in language acquisition. In W. Stokoe and V. Volterra (Eds.), *SLR '83: Sign language research.* Silver Spring, MD: Linstok Press, Inc. and Rome, Italy: Istituto di Psicologia, CNR.

Bonvillian, J., Nelson, K., and Rhyne, J. (1981). Sign language and autism. *Journal of Autism and Developmental Disorders, 11,* 125–137.

Bornstein, H. (1973). A description of some current sign systems designed to represent English. *American Annals of the Deaf, 118,* 454–463.

Bornstein, H. (1978). Systems of sign. In L. Bradford and W. Hardy (Eds.), *Hearing and hearing impairment.* New York: Grune & Stratton.

Bornstein, H., and Hamilton, L. (1972). Some recent national dictionaries of sign language. *Sign Language Studies, 1,* 42–63.

Bornstein, H., Hamilton, L., Kannapell, B., Roy, H., and Saulnier, K. (1973). *Basic pre-school signed English dictionary.* Washington, DC: Gallaudet College.

Bornstein, H., Hamilton, L., Kannapell, B., Roy, H., and Saulnier, K. (1975). *The signed English dictionary for pre-school and elementary levels.* Washington, DC: Gallaudet College.

Bornstein, H. and Saulnier, K. (1981). Signed English: A brief follow-up to the first evaluation. *American Annals of the Deaf, 127,* 69–72.

Bornstein, H., Saulnier, K., and Hamilton, L. (1980). Signed English: A first evaluation. *American Annals of the Deaf, 126,* 467–481.

Bornstein, H., Woodward, J., and Tully, N. (1976). Language and communication. In B. Bolton (Ed.), *Psychology of deafness for rehabilitation counselors.* Baltimore: University Park Press.

Boros, A. and Stuckless, R. (1982). *Deaf People and Social Change* (Social Aspects of Deafness Monograph, Vol. 6). Washington, DC: Gallaudet College.

Børrild, K. (1972). Cued speech and the mouth-hand system. In G. Fant (Ed.), *International Symposium on Speech Communication Ability and Profound Deafness.* Alexander Graham Bell Association for the Deaf, Washington, DC.

Boyes, P. (1973). *Developmental phonology for ASL.* Working paper, Salk Institute for Biological Studies, La Jolla, CA.

Boyes-Braem, P. (1973). *A study of the acquisition of the DEZ in American Sign Language.* Working paper, Salk Institute for Biological Studies, La Jolla, CA.

Boyes-Braem, P. (1981). *Distinctive features of the handshape in American Sign Language.* Unpublished doctoral dissertation, University of California, Berkeley.

Boynton, M. and Kossan, N. (1981). *Children's metaphors: Making meaning.* Paper presented at the Boston University Conference on Language Development, Boston, MA.

Brady, D. and Smouse, A. (1978). A simultaneous comparison of three methods for language training with an autistic child: An experimental single case analysis. *Journal of Autism and Childhood Schizophrenia, 8,* 271–279.

Bragg, B. (1973). Ameslish: Our national heritage. *American Annals of the Deaf, 118,* 672–674.

Bransford, J., Barclay, J., and Franks, J. (1972). Sentence memory: A constructive versus interpretive approach. *Cognitive Psychology, 3,* 193–209.

Bransford, J., and Franks, J. (1971). The abstraction of linguistic ideas. *Cognitive Psychology, 2,* 331–350.

Brasel, K., and Quigley, S. (1977). The influence of certain language and communication environments in early childhood on the development of language in deaf individuals. *Journal of Speech and Hearing Research, 20,* 95–107.

Brejle, H. (1971). *A study of the relationship between articulation and vocabulary of hearing impaired parents and their normally hearing children.* Unpublished doctoral dissertation, University of Portland.

Brennan, M., Colville, M., and Lawson, L. (1980). *Words in hand: A structural analysis of the signs of British Sign Language.* Edinburgh: British Sign Language Research Project.

Bricker, D. (1972). Imitative sign training as a facilitator of word-object association with low-functioning children. *American Journal of Mental Deficiency, 76,* 509–516.

Brown, R. (1973). *A first language: The early stages.* Cambridge, MA: Harvard University Press.

Brown, R. (1977). *Why are sign languages easier to learn than spoken languages?* Paper presented at the National Symposium on Sign Language Teaching and Research, Chicago.

Brown, R., and Hanlon, C. (1970). Derivational and complexity and order of acquisition. In J. Hayes (Ed.), *Cognition and the development of language.* New York: John Wiley & Sons.

Bunde, L. (1979). *Deaf parents — hearing children: Toward a greater understanding of the unique aspects, needs, and problems relative to the communication factors caused by deafness.* Washington, DC: Registry of Interpreters for the Deaf.

Butler, G., Griffing, B., and Huffman, J. (1969). Training program for the retarded blind and the retarded deaf children (Grant No. 2 R 20 MR02075-04). Sonoma State Hospital, Eldridge, CA.

Cairns, C. and Feinstein, M. (1982). Syllable structure and the theory of markedness. *Linguistic Inquiry, 13,* 193–225.

Carlson, F. (1982). *Alternate methods of communication.* Danville, IL: Interstate Printers.

Carmel, S. (1982). *International hand alphabet charts.* Rockville, MD: Simon J. Carmel.

Carr, E. (1979). Teaching autistic children to use sign language: Some research issues. *Journal of Autism and Developmental Disorders, 9,* 345–359.

Casey, L. (1978). Development of communicative behavior in autistic children: A parent program using manual signs. *Journal of Autism and Childhood Schizophrenia, 8,* 45–59.

Chall, J. (1967). *Learning how to read: The great debate.* New York: McGraw-Hill Book Co.

Chapman, R., and Miller, J. (1980). Language analysis and alternate communication systems. In R. Schiefelbusch (Ed.), *Nonspeech language and communication: Analysis and intervention*. Baltimore: University Park Press.

Charrow, V., and Wilbur, R. (1975). The deaf child as a linguistic minority. *Theory into Practice, 14*, 353–359.

Chinchor, N. (1977). *Problems in the study of aphasia*. Unpublished manuscript, Brown University, Providence, RI.

Chinchor, N. (1978a). *The structure of the NP in ASL: Argument from research on numerals*. Unpublished manuscript, Brown University, Providence, RI.

Chinchor, N. (1978b). *The syllable in ASL*. Paper presented at the MIT Sign Language Symposium, Cambridge, MA.

Chinchor, N. (1981). *Numeral incorporation in American Sign Language*. Unpublished doctoral dissertation, Brown University.

Chinchor, N., Forman, J., Grosjean, F., Hajjar, M., Kegl, J., Lentz, E., Philip, M., and Wilbur, R. (1976). Sign language research and linguistic universals. *University of Massachusetts at Amherst Working Papers, 2*, 70–94.

Chomsky, N. (1964). Current issues in linguistics. In J. Fodor and J. Katz (Eds.), *The structure of language: Readings in the philosophy of language*. Englewood Cliffs, NJ: Prentice-Hall.

Christopoulou, C. and Bonvillian, J. (1985). Sign language, pantomime, and gestural processing in aphasic persons: A review. *Journal of Communication Disorders, 18*, 1–20.

Clark, E. (1973). What's in a word: On the child's acquisition of semantics in his first language. In T. Moore (Ed.), *Cognitive development and the acquisition of language*. New York: Academic Press.

Clark, H. (1973). Space, time, semantics, and the child. In T. Moore (Ed.), *Cognitive development and the acquisition of language*. New York: Academic Press.

Cogen, C. (1977). On three aspects of time expression in American Sign Language. In L. Friedman (Ed.), *On the other hand: New perspectives in American Sign Language*. New York: Academic Press.

Cohen, C., and Shane, H. (1982). An overview of augmentative communication. In N. Lass, L. McReynolds, J. Northern, and D. Yoder (Eds.), *Speech, language, and hearing*. Philadelphia: Saunders.

Cohen, E., Namir, L., and Schlesinger, I. M. (1977). *A new dictionary of sign language*. The Hague: Mouton.

Collins-Ahlgren, M. (1986). *Word formation processes in New Zealand Sign Language*. Conference on Theoretical Issues in Sign Language Research, Rochester, NY.

Comrie, B. (1976). *Aspect*. Cambridge: Cambridge University Press.

Comrie, B. (1981). *Language universals and linguistic typology*. Chicago: University of Chicago Press.

Conley, J. (1976). The role of idiomatic expressions in the reading of deaf children. *American Annals of the Deaf, 121*, 145–162.

Conlin, D. (1972). *The effects of word imagery and signability in the paired-associate learning of the deaf.* Unpublished master's thesis, University of Western Ontario, London, Ontario.

Conrad, R. (1962). An association between memory errors and errors due to acoustic masking of speech. *Nature, 193,* 1314–1315.

Conrad, R. (1970). Short-term memory processes in the deaf. *British Journal of Psychology, 61,* 179–195.

Conrad, R. (1971). The effect of vocalizing on comprehension in the profoundly deaf. *British Journal of Psychology, 62,* 147–150.

Conrad, R. (1972). Speech and reading. In J. Kavanagh and I. Mattingly (Eds.), *Language by ear and by eye: The relationships between speech and reading.* Cambridge, MA: MIT Press.

Conrad, R. (1973). Some correlates of speech coding in the short-term memory of the deaf. *Journal of Speech and Hearing Research, 16,* 375–384.

Conrad, R. (1975). Matters arising. In Royal National Institute for the Deaf (Ed.), *Methods of communication currently used in the education of deaf children.* Letchworth, England: The Garden City Press.

Conrad, R., and Rush, M. (1965). On the nature of short-term memory encoding by the deaf. *Journal of Speech and Hearing Disorders, 30,* 336–343.

Cornett, R. (1967). Cued speech. *American Annals of the Deaf, 112,* 3–13.

Cornett, R. (1969). In answer to Dr. Moores. *American Annals of the Deaf, 114,* 27–33.

Coulter, G. (1979). *American Sign Language typology.* Unpublished doctoral dissertation, University of California, San Diego.

Coulter, G. (1982). *On the nature of ASL as a monosyllabic language.* Paper presented at the Annual Meeting of the Linguistic Society of America, San Diego.

Coulter, G. (1983). A conjoined analysis of American Sign Language relative clauses. *Discourse Processes, 6,* 305–318.

Covington, V. (1973a). Juncture in American Sign Language. *Sign Language Studies, 2,* 29–38.

Covington, V. (1973b). Features of stress in American Sign Language. *Sign Language Studies, 2,* 39–58.

Craig, E. (1976). A supplement to the spoken word — the Paget-Gorman Sign System. In Royal National Institute for the Deaf (Ed.), *Methods of communication currently used in the education of deaf children.* Letchworth, England: The Garden City Press.

Creedon, M. (1973). *Language development in nonverbal autistic children using a simultaneous communication system.* Paper presented at the Society for Research on Child Development Conference, Philadelphia.

Creedon, M. (Ed.). (1975). *Appropriate behavior through communication: A new program in simultaneous language.* Michael Reese Medical Center, Chicago.

Creedon, M. (1976). *The David School: A simultaneous communication model.* Paper presented to the National Society for Autistic Children Conference, Oak Brook, IL.

Crowder, R. (1972). Visual and auditory memory. In J. Kavanagh and I. Mattingly (Eds.), *Language by ear and by eye: The relationship between speech and reading.* Cambridge, MA: MIT Press.

Culhane, B. and Williams, C. (1982). *Social Aspects of Educating Deaf Per-*

sons (Social Aspects of Deafness Monograph, Vol. 2). Washington, DC: Gallaudet College.

DeMatteo, A. (1977). Visual imagery and visual analogues in American Sign Language. In L. Friedman (Ed.), *On the other hand: New perspectives in American Sign Language.* New York: Academic Press.

Dennis, R., Reichle, J., Williams, W., and Vogelsberg, R. (1982). Motoric factors influencing the selection of vocabulary for sign production programs. *Journal of the Association for the Severely Handicapped, 7,* 20–32.

Dixon, S., and Collins, C. (1981). *The development of metaphorical understanding.* American Speech-Language-Hearing Association Convention, Los Angeles.

Doherty, J. (1985). The effects of sign characteristics on sign acquisition and retention: An integrative review of the literature. *Augmentative and Alternative Communication,* 108–121.

Donahue, M. (1977a). *Conversational gimmicks: The acquisition of small talk.* Paper presented at the Second Annual Boston University Conference on Language Development.

Donahue, M. (1977b). *Conversational styles of mother-toddler dyads.* Paper presented at the American Speech and Hearing Association Conference, Chicago.

Donahue, M., and Watson, L. (1976). *How to get some action!* Paper presented at the First Annual Boston University Conference on Language Development, Boston, MA.

Ellenberger, R., Moores, D., and Hoffmeister, R. (1975). *Early stages in the acquisition of negation by a deaf child of deaf parents* (Research report #94). University of Minnesota, Research, Development, and Demonstration Center in Education of the Handicapped.

Engberg-Pedersen, E., Hansen, B., and Sorensen, R. (1981). *Døves tegnsprog* (Sign language of the deaf). Denmark: Arkona.

Erting, C. and Meisegeier, R. (1982). *Deaf children and the socialization process* (Social Aspects of Deafness Monograph Vol. 1). Washington, DC: Gallaudet College.

Ervin-Tripp, S. (1970). Discourse agreement: How children answer questions. In J. Hayes (Ed.), *Cognition and the development of language.* New York: John Wiley & Sons.

Fant, L. (1964). *Say it with hands.* Washington, DC: Gallaudet College.

Fant, L. (1972). *Ameslan.* Silver Spring, MD: National Association of the Deaf.

Ferreira Brito, L. (1985). A comparative study of signs for time and space in São Paulo and Urubu-Kaapor Sign Languages. In W. Stokoe and V. Volterra (Eds.) *SLR '83: Sign language research.* Silver Spring, MD: Linstok Press, Inc. and Rome, Italy: Istituto di Psicologia, CNR.

Ferreira Brito, L. (1986). *Epistemic, deontic, and alethic modalities in the Brazilian Sign Language.* Conference on Theoretical Issues in Sign Language Research, Rochester, NY.

Ferreiro, E. (1978, Fall). What is written in a written sentence? A developmental answer. *Journal of Education,* pp. 25–37.

Fischer, S. (1973a). Two processes of reduplication in American Sign Language. *Foundations of Language, 9,* 469–480.

Fischer, S. (1973b). *The deaf child's acquisition of verb inflections in ASL.* Paper presented to the Linguistic Society of America Annual Meeting, San Diego, CA.

Fischer, S. (1974). Sign language and linguistic universals. In *Proceedings of the Franco-German Conference on French Transformational Grammar.* Berlin: Athaenium.

Fischer, S. (1975). Influences on word order change in ASL. In C. Li (Ed.), *Word order and word order change.* Austin: University of Texas Press.

Fischer, S. (1978). Sign languages and creoles. In P. Siple (Ed.), *Understanding language through sign language research.* New York: Academic Press.

Fischer, S., and Gough, B. (1972). *Some unfinished thoughts on FINISH* (Working paper). La Jolla, CA: Salk Institute for Biological Studies.

Fischer, S., and Gough, B. (1978). Verbs in American Sign Language. *Sign Language Studies, 18,* 17–48.

Fitzgerald, E. (1929). *Straight language for the deaf.* Stauton, VA: The McClure Co.

Fouts, R. (1973). Acquisition and testing of gestural signs in four young chimpanzees. *Science, 180,* 978–980.

Franks, J., and Bransford, J. (1972). The acquisition of abstract ideas. *Journal of Verbal Learning and Verbal Behavior, 11,* 311–315.

Fraser, C., Bellugi, U., and Brown, R. (1963). Control of grammar in imitation, comprehension, and production. *Journal of Verbal Learning and Verbal Behavior, 2,* 121–135.

Friedman, L. (1974). *On the physical manifestation of stress in the American Sign Language.* Unpublished manuscript, University of California, Berkeley.

Friedman, L. (1975). Space, time, and person reference in American Sign Language. *Language, 51,* 940–961.

Friedman, L. (1976a). The manifestation of subject, object, and topic in American Sign Language. In C. Li (Ed.), *Subject and topic.* New York: Academic Press.

Friedman, L. (1976b). *Phonology of a soundless language: Phonological structure of American Sign Language.* Unpublished doctoral dissertation, University of California, Berkeley.

Friedman, L. (Ed.). (1977). *On the other hand: New perspectives on American Sign Language.* New York: Academic Press.

Frishberg, N. (1972). *Sharp and soft: Two aspects of movement in American Sign Language.* (Working paper). La Jolla, CA: Salk Institute for Biological Studies.

Frishberg, N. (1975). Arbitrariness and iconicity: Historical change in American Sign Language. *Language, 51,* 676–710.

Frishberg, N. (1976). *Some aspects of the historical development of signs in American Sign Language.* Unpublished doctoral dissertation, University of California, San Diego.

Frishberg, N. (1978). The case of the missing length. In R. Wilbur (Ed.), Sign language research [Special issue]. *Communication and Cognition.*

Frishberg, N., and Gough, B. (1973a). *Morphology in American Sign Language.* (Working paper). La Jolla, CA: Salk Institute for Biological Studies.

Frishberg, N., and Gough, B. (1973b). *Time on our hands.* Paper presented at the Third Annual California Linguistics Conference, Stanford.

Fristoe, M. (1975). *Language intervention systems for the retarded.* Decatur, AL: L. B. Wallace Development Center.

Fristoe, M., and Lloyd, L. (1977a). Manual communication for the retarded and others with severe communication impairment: A resource list. *Mental Retardation, 15,* 18–21.

Fristoe, M., and Lloyd, L. (1977b). *The use of manual communication with the retarded.* Paper presented at the Gatlinburg Conference on Research in Mental Retardation.

Fristoe, M., and Lloyd,L. (1978). *A first sign lexicon for nonspeaking severely profoundly impaired individuals, based on cognitive and psycholinguistic considerations.* Paper presented at the Gatlinburg Conference on Research in Mental Retardation.

Fristoe, M. and Lloyd, L. (1979b). Signs used in manual communication training with persons having severe communication impairment. *AAESPH Review, 4,* 364–373.

Fristoe, M. and Lloyd, L. (1980). Planning an initial expressive sign lexicon for persons with severe communication impairment. *Journal of Speech and Hearing Disorders, 45,* 170–180.

Fruchter, A. (1986). *Comprehension and use of idioms by deaf children.* Unpublished master's thesis, Tufts University.

Fruchter, A., Wilbur, R., and Fraser, B. (1984). Comprehension of idioms by hearing-impaired students. *The Volta Review, 86,* 7–18.

Fuller, D. and Wilbur, R. (in press). The effect of handshape metaphor cueing on the recall of phonologically similar signs. *Sign Language Studies.*

Fulwiler, R., and Fouts, R. (1976). Acquisition of sign language by a noncommunicating autistic child. *Journal of Autism and Childhood Schizophrenia, 6,* 43–51.

Furth, H. (1966A). A comparison of reading test norms of deaf and hearing children. *American Annals of the Deaf, 111,* 461–462.

Furth, H. (1966b). *Thinking without language.* London: Collier-Macmillian.

Gee, J. and Kegl, J. (1982). Semantic perspicuity and the locative hypothesis: Implications for acquisition. *Journal of Education,* 185–209.

Gentner, D. (1977). On relational meaning: The acquisition of verb meaning. (Technical Report No. 78). Cambridge, MA: Bolt, Beranek, and Newman.

Giorcelli, L. (1982). *The comprehension of some aspects of figurative language by deaf and hearing subjects.* Unpublished doctoral dissertation, University of Illinois, Urbana.

Godwin, E., Boyce, N., and Larson, V. (1980). *Acquisition of idiomatic expressions in normal children kindergarten through fourth grade.* Paper presented at the Boston University Conference on Language Development.

Goldin-Meadow, S. (1975). *The representation of semantic relations in a manual language created by deaf children of hearing parents: A language you can't dismiss out of hand.* Unpublished doctoral dissertation, University of Pennsylvania, Philadelphia.

Goldin-Meadow, S., and Feldman, H. (1975). *The creation of a communication system: A study of deaf children of hearing parents.* Paper presented at the Society for Research in Child Development Meeting, Denver, CO.

Goldin-Meadow, S. and Mylander, C. (1984). The development of morphology without a conventional language model. *Chicago Linguistic Society, 20,* 119–135.

Goodhart, W. (1978). *An analysis of the syntactic behavior of a deaf child of hearing parents.* Unpublished manuscript, Boston University.

Goodhart, W. (1984). *Morphological complexity, ASL, and the acquisition of sign language in deaf children.* Unpublished doctoral dissertation, Boston University.

Graham, J., and Graham, L. (1971). Language behavior of the mentally retarded: Syntactic characteristics. *American Journal of Mental Deficiency, 75,* 623–629.

Greenberg, J. (1966). Some universals of language with particular reference to the order of meaningful elements. In J. Greenberg (Ed.), *Universals of language.* Cambridge, MA: MIT Press.

Griffith, P. (1980). *The acquisition of the first few signs and words by a hearing child of deaf parents.* American Speech-Language-Hearing Association Convention, Detroit, MI.

Grosjean, F. (1977). The perception of rate in spoken and sign languages. *Perception and Psychophysics, 22,* 408–413.

Grosjean, F. (1978). *Crosslinguistic research in the perception and production of English and American Sign Language.* Paper presented at the National Symposium on Sign Language Research and Teaching, Coronado, CA.

Grosjean, F. (1979). A study of timing in a manual and a spoken language: American Sign Language and English. *Journal of Psycholinguistic Research.*

Grosjean, F., and Collins, M. (1978). Breathing, pausing, and reading. *Phonetica.*

Grosjean, F., and Deschamps, A. (1975). Analyse contrastive des variables temporelles de l'anglais et de français: Vitesse de parole et variables composantes, phénomènes d'hésitation [Contrastive analysis of temporal variables in English and French: Speech rate and related variables, hesitation phenomena]. *Phonetica, 31,* 144–184.

Grosjean, F., and Lane, H. (1977). Pauses and syntax in American Sign Language. *Cognition, 5,* 101–117.

Grosjean, F. and Lane, H. (Eds.). (1979). *La langue des signes [The language of signs]* [Special edition]. *Langages.*

Gudschinsky, S. (1964). The ABC's of lexicostatistics (glottochronology). In D. Hymes (Ed.), *Language in culture and society.* New York: Harper & Row Publishers.

Gustason, G., Pfetzing, D., and Zawolkow, E. (1972). *Signing Exact English.* Rossmoor, CA: Modern Signs Press.

Gustason, G., Pfetzing, D., and Zawolkow, E. (1973). *SEE supplement II.* Rossmoor, CA: Modern Signs Press.

Gustason, G., Pfetzing, D., and Zawolkow, E. (1974, September). The rationale of SEE. *Deaf American.*

Haiman, J. (1983). Iconic and economic motivation. *Language, 59,* 781–819.

Haiman, J. (Ed.). (1985). *Iconicity in Syntax.* Philadelphia: John Benjamins.

Hall, S., and Conn, T. (1972). Current trends in services for the deaf retarded in schools for the deaf and residential facilities for the mentally retarded. *Report of the Proceedings of the 45th Meeting of the Convention of American Instructors of the Deaf, Little Rock, AR, 1971.* U.S. Government Printing Office, Washington, DC.

Hall, S., and Talkington, L. (1970). Evaluation of a manual approach to programming for deaf retarded. *American Journal of Mental Deficiency, 75,* 378–380.

Hamacher, J. (1980). Deaf children's understanding of English metaphor. *Directions, 1,* 25–26.

Hanson, V. (1980). Implications of research on sign languages for theories of reading. In B. Frøkjaer-Jensen (Ed.), *The sciences of deaf signing.* Copenhagen: Audiologopedic Research Group.

Hanson, V. (1982). Short-term recall by deaf signers of American Sign Language: Implications of encoding strategy for order recall. *Journal of Experimental Psychology: Learning, Memory, and Cognition, 8,* 572–583.

Hanson, V. and Bellugi, U. (1982). On the role of sign order and morphological structure in memory for American Sign Language. *Journal of Verbal Learning and Verbal Behavior, 21,* 621–633.

Hedrick, D., Prather, E., and Tobin, A. (1975). *Sequenced Inventory of Communication Development.* Seattle: University of Washington Press.

Helmer, S., Layton, T., and Wolfe, A. (1982). Patterns of language behavior in autistic children. Paper presented at the American Speech-Language-Hearing Association Convention, Toronto.

Hewes, G. (1973). Primate communication and the gestural origin of language. *Current Anthropology, 14,* 5–24.

Hoemann, H. (1975). The transparency of meaning of sign language gestures. *Sign Language Studies, 7,* 151–161.

Hoemann, H., and Florian, V. (1976). Order constraints in American Sign Language. *Sign Language Studies, 11,* 121–132.

Hoemann, H., Oates, Fr. E., and Hoemann, S. (1981). *The Sign Language of Brazil.* Mill Neck, NY: Mill Neck Foundation.

Hoemann, H., Oates, Fr. E., and Hoemann, S. (1983). *Linguagem de Sinais do Brasil* [Sign language of Brazil]. Porto Alegre, Brasil: Centro Educacional para Deficientes Auditivos.

Hoemann, H. and Wilbur, R. (Eds.). (1982). *Interpersonal Communication and Deafness* (Social Aspects of Deafness Monograph Vol. 5). Washington, DC: Gallaudet College.

Hoequist, C. (1983). Syllable duration in stress-, syllable-, and mora-timed languages. *Phonetica, 40,* 203–237.

Hoffmeister, R. (1977). *The acquisition of American Sign Language by deaf children of deaf parents: The development of the demonstrative pronouns, locatives, and personal pronouns.* Unpublished doctoral dissertation, University of Minnesota, Minneapolis.

Hoffmeister, R. (1978). An analysis of possessive constructions in the ASL of a young deaf child of deaf parents. In R. Wilbur (Ed.), Sign Language Research [Special issue]. *Communication and Cognition.*

Hoffmeister, R., and Farmer, A. (1972). The development of manual sign language in mentally retarded individuals. *Journal of Rehabilitation of the Deaf, 6,* 19–26.

Hoffmeister, R., and Goodhart, W. (1978). *The semantic and syntactic analysis of the sign language behavior of a deaf child of hearing parents.* Paper presented at the MIT Sign Language Symposium, Cambridge, MA.

Hoffmeister, R., Goodhart, W., and Dworski, S. (1978). *Symbolic gestural behavior in deaf and hearing children.* American Speech-Language-Hearing Association Convention, San Francisco, CA.

Hoffmeister, R. and Wilbur, R. (1980). The acquisition of sign language. In H. Lane and F. Grosjean (Eds.), *Recent perspectives on American Sign Language.* Hillsdale, NJ: Lawrence Erlbaum Associates.

Hopper, P. (Ed.), (1982). *Tense-Aspect: Between semantics and pragmatics.* Amsterdam: John Benjamins Publishing Company.

Howlin, P. (1981). The effectiveness of operant language training with autistic children. *Journal of Autism and Developmental Disorders, 11,* 86–106.

Hoyt, J. (1980). Sign and the severely handicapped nonvocal devices user. *Exceptional Parent.*

Huffman, J., Hoffman, B., Granssee, D., Fox, A., James, J., and Schmitz, J. (1974). *Talk with me: Communication with the multi-handicapped deaf.* Northridge, CA: Joyce Motion Picture Co.

Hyman, L. (1984). *A theory of phonological weight.* Dordrecht: Foris Publications.

Hymes, D. (1971). *Pidginization and creolization of languages.* New York: Cambridge University Press.

Ingram, D. (1974). Phonological rules in young children. *Journal of Child Language, 1,* 49–64.

Ingram, D. (1976). *Phonological disability in children.* New York: Elsevier-North Holland Publishing Co.

Iran-Nejad, A., Ortony, A., and Rittenhouse, R. (1981). The comprehension of metaphorical uses of English by deaf children. *Journal of Speech and Hearing Research, 24,* 551–556.

Jackendoff, R. (1983). *Semantics and cognition.* Cambridge, MA: MIT Press.

Jackson, C. (1984). *Language acquisition in two modalities: Person deixis and negation in American Sign Language and English.* Unpublished master's thesis, University of California, Los Angeles.

Jakobson, R. (1968). *Child language, aphasia, and phonological universals.* The Hague: Mouton.

James, W. (1963). Mentally retarded deaf children in a California hospital.

Report of the Proceedings of the Forty-first meeting of the Convention of the American Instructors of the Deaf (pp. 573–577).

James, W. (1967). A hospital improvement program for mentally retarded children at Sonoma State Hospital. *Report of the Proceedings of the Convention of American Instructors of the Deaf* (pp. 272–276).

Jarvella, R. and Lubinsky, J. (1975). Deaf and hearing children's use of language describing temporal order among events. *Journal of Speech and Hearing Research, 18,* 58–73.

Jeffers, J. (1967). Process of speechreading viewed with respect to a theoretical construct. In *Proceedings of the International Conference on Oral Education of the Deaf.* Washington, DC: Alexander Graham Bell Association for the Deaf.

Johnson, H. (1980). *A longitudinal, ethnographic investigation of the development of interactional strategies by a normally hearing infant of deaf parents.* Unpublished doctoral dissertation, University of Cincinnati.

Johnson, R. (1978). A comparison of the phonological structures of two northwest sawmill sign languages. In R. Wilbur (Ed.), Sign Language Research [Special issue]. *Communication and Cognition.*

Johnson, R. (1986). *Metathesis in American Sign Language.* Conference on Theoretical Issues in Sign Language Research, Rochester, NY.

Johnson, R. K. (1963). The institutionalized mentally retarded deaf. *Report of the Proceedings of the Forty-first meeting of the Convention of American Instructors of the Deaf* (pp. 568–573).

Johnston, J. and Slobin, D. (1979). The development of locative expressions in English, Italian, Serbo-Croatian, and Turkish. *Journal of Child Language, 16,* 531–547.

Jones, M. (1976). *A longitudinal investigation into the acquisition of question formation in English and American Sign Language by three hearing children with deaf parents.* Unpublished doctoral dissertation, University of Illinois, Urbana-Champaign.

Jones, M. and Quigley, S. (1979). The acquisition of question formation in spoken English and American Sign Language by two hearing children of deaf parents. *Journal of Speech and Hearing Disorders, 44,* 196–208.

Jones, N., and Mohr, K. (1975). *A working paper on plurals in ASL.* Unpublished manuscript, University of California, Berkeley.

Jones, P. (1978). On the interface of sign phonology and morphology. In R. Wilbur (Ed.), Sign Language Research [Special issue]. *Communication and Cognition.*

Jordan, E. and Battison, R. (1976). A referential communication experiment with foreign sign languages. *Sign Language Studies, 10,* 69–80.

Jordan, E., Gustason, G., and Rosen, R. (1976). Current communication trends at programs for the deaf. *American Annals of the Deaf, 121,* 527–532.

Kahn, J. (1975). Relationship of Piaget's sensorimotor period to language acquisition of profoundly retarded children. *American Journal of Mental Deficiency, 79,* 640–643.

Kahn, J. (1981). A comparison of sign and verbal language training with nonverbal retarded children. *Journal of Speech and Hearing Research, 46,* 113–119.

Kanda, K. (1986). *Types of hand configuration: A contrastive analysis of HC in JSL and ASL.* Conference on Theoretical Issues in Sign Language Research, Rochester, NY.

Kannapell, B. (no date). *The presentation of the numbers in American Sign Language.* Unpublished manuscript, Gallaudet College, Washington, DC.

Kannapell, B., Hamilton, L., and Bornstein, H. (1969). *Signs for instructional purposes.* Washington, DC: Gallaudet College Press.

Kantor, R. (1977). *The acquisition of classifiers in American Sign Language.* Unpublished master's thesis, Boston University.

Kantor, R. (1978). Identifying native and second-language signers. In R. Wilbur (Ed.), Sign Language Research [Special issue]. *Communication and Cognition.*

Kantor, R. (1980). The acquisition of classifiers in American Sign Language. *Sign Language Studies, 28,* 193–208.

Kantor, R. (1982). Communicative interaction: Mother modification and child acquisition of American Sign Language. *Sign Language Studies, 36,* 233–282.

Karchmer, M., and Belmont, J. (1976). *On assessing and improving deaf performance in the cognitive laboratory.* Paper presented at the American Speech and Hearing Association Convention, Houston, TX.

Kegl, J. (1976a). *Pronominalization in American Sign Language.* Unpublished manuscript, MIT, Cambridge, MA.

Kegl, J. (1976b). *Relational grammar and American Sign Language.* Unpublished manuscript, MIT, Cambridge, MA.

Kegl, J. (1977). *ASL syntax: Research in progress and proposed research.* Unpublished manuscript, MIT, Cambridge, MA.

Kegl, J. (1978a). *Indexing and pronominalization in ASL.* Unpublished manuscript, MIT, Cambridge, MA.

Kegl, J. (1978b). *ASL classifiers.* Unpublished manuscript, MIT, Cambridge, MA.

Kegl, J. (1978c). *A possible argument for passive in ASL.* Unpublished manuscript, MIT Press, Cambridge, MA.

Kegl, J., and Chinchor, N. (1975). A frame analysis of American Sign Language. In T. Diller (Ed.), *Proceedings of the 13th Annual Meeting Association for Computational Linguistics. (American Journal of Computational Linguistics* Microfiche 35), Sperry-Univac, St. Paul, MN.

Kegl, J., and Farrington, W. (1985). *Formal properties of ASL word formation.* Linguistic Society of America, Seattle, WA.

Kegl, J., and Wilbur, R. (1976). When does structure stop and style begin? Syntax, morphology, and phonology vs. stylistic variation in American Sign Language. In S. Mufwene, C. Walker, and S. Steever (Eds.), *Papers from the Twelfth Regional Meeting, Chicago Linguistic Society.* Chicago: The University of Chicago Press.

Kiernan, C. (1977). Alternatives to speech: A review of research on manual and other forms of communication with the mentally handicapped and other non-communicating populations. *British Journal of Mental Subnormality, 23,* 6–28.

Kiernan, C., and Jones, M. (1985). The Heuristic Programme: A combined use of sign and symbols with severely mentally retarded, autistic children. *Australian Journal of Human Communication Disorders, 13,* 153–168.

Klima, E., and Bellugi, U. (1975). Wit and poetry in American Sign Language. *Sign Language Studies, 8,* 203–224.

Klima, E., and Bellugi, U. (1979). *The signs of language.* Cambridge, MA: Harvard University Press.

Klima, E., and Bellugi-Klima, U. (1966). Syntactic regularities in the speech of children. In J. Lyons and R. Wales (Eds.), *Psycholinguistics papers.* Edinburgh University Press.

Klima, E., Bellugi, U., and Poizner, H. (1985). Sign language and brain organization. In W. Stokoe and V. Volterra (Eds.), *SLR '83: Sign Language Research.* Silver Spring, MD: Linstok Press, Inc. and Rome, Italy: Istituto di Psicologia, CNR.

Kohl, F. (1981). Effects of motoric requirements on the acquisition of manual sign responses by severely handicapped students. *American Journal of Mental Deficiency, 85,* 396–403.

Konstantareas, M., and Liebovitz, S. (1981). Early communication acquisition by autistic children: Signing and mouthing versus signing and speaking. *Sign Language Studies, 31,* 135–154.

Konstantareas, M., Oxman, J., and Webster, C. (1978). Iconicity: Effects on the acquisition of sign language by autistic and other dysfunctional children. In P. Siple (Ed.), *Understanding language through sign language research.* New York: Academic Press.

Kotkin, R., Simpson, S., and Desanto, D. (1978). The effect of sign language and picture naming in two retarded girls possessing normal hearing. *Journal of Mental Deficiency Research, 22,* 19–25.

Kourbetis, V. (1986). *The deaf community in Greece.* Unpublished manuscript, Boston University.

Kourbetis, V., Hoffmeister, R., and Greenwald, J. (1985). *Greek Sign Language and education of the deaf in Greece.* Paper presented at the International Congress on Education of the Deaf, Manchester, England.

Kretschmer, R.E. (Ed.), (1982). Reading and the hearing-impaired individual [Special issue]. *The Volta Review, 84.*

Kyle, J., and Woll, B. (Eds.), (1983). *Language in sign: An international perspective on sign language.* London: Croon Helm Ltd.

LaBerge, D. (1972). Beyond auditory coding. In J. Kavanagh and I. Mattingly (Eds.), *Language by ear and by eye: The relationship between speech and reading.* Cambridge, MA: MIT Press.

Lacy, R. (1972a). *Development of Pola's questions.* Unpublished manuscript. Salk Institute for Biological Studies, La Jolla, CA.

Lacy, R. (1972b). *Development of Sonia's negations.* Unpublished manuscript, Salk Institute for Biological Studies, La Jolla, CA.

Lacy, R (1974). *Putting some of the syntax back into semantics.* Paper presented at the Linguistic Society of America Annual Meeting, New York.

Lakoff, G., and Johnson, M. (1980). *Metaphors we live by.* Chicago: University of Chicago Press.

Lane, H. (1980). A chronology of the oppression of sign language in France and the United States. In H. Lane and F. Grosjean (Eds.), *Recent perspectives on American Sign Language.* Hillsdale, NJ: Lawrence Erlbaum Associates.

Lane, H. (1984). *When the mind hears: A history of the deaf.* New York: Random House.

Lane, H., Boyes-Braem, P., and Bellugi, U. (1976). Preliminaries to a distinctive feature analysis of handshapes in American Sign Language. *Cognitive Psychology, 8,* 263–289.

Lane, H., and Grosjean, F. (1973). Perception of reading rate by speakers and listeners. *Journal of Experimental Psychology, 97,* 141–147.

Lane, H., and Philip, F. (1984). *The deaf experience: Classics in language and education.* Cambridge, MA: Harvard University Press.

Langacker, R. (1972). *Fundamentals of linguistic analysis.* New York: Harcourt Brace Jovanovich.

Langacker, R. (1982). Remarks on English aspect. In P. Hopper (Ed.), *Tense-Aspect: Between semantics and pragmatics.* Amsterdam: John Benjamins Publishing Company.

Launer, P. (1982). *"A plane" is not "to fly": Acquiring the distinction between related nouns and verbs in American Sign Language.* Unpublished doctoral dissertation, The City University of New York.

Lawson, L. (1983). Multi-channel signs, In J. Kyle and B. Woll (Eds.), *Language in sign; An international perspective on sign language.* London: Croon Helm Ltd.

Layton, T., Leslie, C., and Helmer, S. (1983). *A critical review pertaining to sign language acquisition in autistic children.* Unpublished manuscript, University of North Carolina, Chapel Hill.

Layton, T., and Stutts, N. (1985). Pragmatic usage by autistic children under different treatment modes. *Australian Journal of Human Communication Disorders, 13,* 127–142.

Lenneberg, E. (1967). *Biological foundations of language.* New York: John Wiley & Sons.

Levitt, L. (1972). A method of communication for non-speaking severely subnormal children — trial results. *British Journal of Disorders of Communication,* October.

Liddell, S. (1977). *An investigation into the syntactic structure of American Sign Language.* Unpublished doctoral dissertation, University of California, San Diego.

Liddell, S. (1978). An introduction to relative clauses in ASL. In P. Siple (Ed.), *Understanding language through sign language research.* New York: Academic Press.

Liddell, S. (1980). *American Sign Language syntax.* The Hague: Mouton.

Liddell, S. (1982). *Sequentiality in American Sign Language signs.* Summer Meeting, Linguistic Society of America, College Park, MD.

Liddell, S. (1984a). THINK and BELIEVE: Sequentiality in American Sign Language Signs. *Language, 60,* 372–399.

Liddell, S. (1984b). Unrealized-inceptive aspect in American Sign Language. *Chicago Linguistic Society, 20,* 257–270.

Liddell, S. (1985). Compound formation rules in American Sign Language. In W. Stokoe and V. Volterra (Eds.), *SLR '83: Sign Language Research.* Silver Spring, MD: Linstok Press Inc. and Rome, Italy: Istituto di Psicologia, CNR.

Liddell, S. (1986). *Thumb, finger, and local movement in ASL.* Conference on Theoretical Issues in Sign Language Research, Rochester, NY.

Liddell, S., and Johnson, R. (1985). *American Sign Language: The phonological base.* Unpublished manuscript, Gallaudet College.

Liddell, S., and Johnson, R. (in press a). Compound formation and compound structure: Evidence from American Sign Language. In D. Tannen and J. Alatis (Eds.), *Proceedings of the 1985 Georgetown Roundtable.*

Liddell, S., and Johnson, R. (in press b). ASL compound formation processes, lexicalization and phonological remnants. *Natural Language and Linguistic Theory.*

Liebovitz, S. (1976). *Sign versus speech in the imitative learning of a mute autistic boy.* Unpublished master's paper, McGill University School of Human Communication Disorders.

Livingston, S. (1981). *The acquisition and development of sign language in deaf children of hearing parents.* Unpublished doctoral dissertation, New York University.

Livingston, S. (1985). The acquisition of sign meaning in deaf children of hearing parents. In W. Stokoe and V. Volterra (Eds.), *SLR '83: Sign Language Research.* Silver Spring, MD: Linstok Press, Inc. and Rome, Italy: Istituto di Psicologia, CNR.

Lloyd, L. (Ed.). (1976). *Communication assessment and intervention strategies.* Baltimore: University Park Press.

Lloyd, L., and Fristoe, M. (1978). *Iconicity of signs: Evidence for its predominance in vocabularies used with severely impaired individuals in contrast with American Sign Language in general.* Paper presented at the Gatlinburg Conference on Research in Mental Retardation, Gatlinburg, TN.

Lloyd, L., and Karlan, G. (1984). Nonspeech communication symbols and systems: Where have we been and where are we going? *Journal of Mental Deficiency Research, 28,* 3–20.

Locke, J. (1970). Short-term memory encoding strategies in the deaf. *Psychonomic Science, 8,* 233–234.

Locke, J., and Locke, V. (1971). Deaf children's phonetic, visual, and dactylic coding in a grapheme recall task. *Journal of Experimental Psychology, 89,* 142–146.

Lodge, D., and Leach, E. (1975). Children's acquisition of idioms in the English language. *Journal of Speech and Hearing Research, 24,* 521–529.

Loew, R. (1983). *Roles and reference in American Sign Language: A developmental perspective.* Unpublished doctoral dissertation, University of Minnesota.

Logiadis, N., and Logiadi, M. (1985). *Lexiko noematikis glossas* [*The dictionary of sign language*]. Athens: Potamitis Press.

Long, J. (1918). *The sign language: A manual of signs.* Iowa City: Athens Press.

Lubert, B. (1975). *The relation of brain asymmetry to visual processing of sign language, alphabetic and visual-spatial material in deaf and hearing subjects.* Unpublished master's thesis, University of Western Ontario.

Lucas, C., and Valli, C. (1986). *Predicates of perceived motion in American Sign Language.* Conference on Theoretical Issues in Sign Language Research, Rochester, NY.

McCall, E. (1965). *A generative grammar of Sign.* Unpublished master's thesis, University of Iowa, Iowa City.

McCarthy, J. (1979). *Formal problems in Semitic phonology and morphology.* Unpublished doctoral dissertation, MIT.

McCarthy, J. (1981). A prosodic theory of nonconcatenative morphology. *Linguistic Inquiry, 12,* 373–418.

McDonald, B. (1982). *Aspects of the American Sign Language predicate system.* Unpublished doctoral dissertation, University of Buffalo, NY.

McIntire, M. (1974). *A modified model for the description of language acquisition in a deaf child.* Unpublished master's thesis, California State University, Northridge.

McIntire, M. (1977). The acquisition of American Sign Language hand configurations. *Sign Language Studies, 16,* 247–266.

McIntire, M. (1980). *Locatives in American Sign Language.* Unpublished doctoral dissertation, UCLA.

McIntire, M., and Groode, J. (1982). Hello, goodbye, and what happens in between. In C. Erting and R. Meisegeier (Eds.), *The deaf child and the socialization process* (Social Aspects of Deafness Monograph Vol. 1). Washington, DC: Gallaudet College.

McKeever, W., Hoemann, H., Florian, V., and Van Deventer, A. (1976). Evidence of minimal cerebral asymmetries for the processing of English words and American Sign Language stimuli in the congenitally deaf. *Neuropsychologia, 14* 413–423.

Madsen, W. (1972). *Conversational Sign Language II.* Washington, DC: Gallaudet College.

Maestas y Moores, J. (1980). Early linguistic environment: Interactions of deaf parents with their infants. *Sign Language Studies, 26,* 1–13.

Mandel, M. (1977). Iconic devices in American Sign Language. In L. Friedman (Ed.), *On the other hand: New perspectives in American Sign Language.* New York: Academic Press.

Mandel, M. (1979). Natural constraints in sign language phonology: Data from anatomy. *Sign Language Studies, 24,* 215–229.

Mandel, M. (1981). *Phonotactics and morphophonology in American Sign Language.* Unpublished doctoral dissertation, University of California, Berkeley.

Manning, A., Goble, W., Markman, R., and LaBreche, T. (1977). Lateral cerebral differences in the deaf in response to linguistic and non-linguistic stimuli. *Brain and Language, 4,* 309–321.

Markowicz, H. (1973). Aphasia and deafness. *Sign Language Studies, 3,* 61–71.

Markowicz, H. (1976). L'Epée's methodical signs revisited. In C. Williams

(Ed.), *Proceedings of the second Gallaudet symposium on research in deafness: Language and communication research problems.* Washington, DC: Gallaudet Press.

Markowicz, H., and Woodward, J. (1978). Language and the maintenance of the deaf community. In R. Wilbur (Ed.), Sign Language Research [Special issue]. *Communication and Cognition.*

Mayberry, R. (1976a). If a chimp can learn sign language, surely my nonverbal client can too. *ASHA, 18,* 223–228.

Mayberry, R. (1976b). An assessment of some oral and manual language skills of hearing children of deaf parents. *American Annals of the Deaf, 121,* 507–512.

Mayberry, R. (1978). French-Canadian Sign Language: A study of inter-sign language comprehension. In P. Siple (Ed.), *Understanding language through sign language research.* New York: Academic Press.

Mayberry, R., and Eichen, E. (1985). *Points and signs in memory for American Sign Language: The effect of age of acquisition.* Paper presented at the American Speech-Language-Hearing Association Convention, Washington, DC.

Mayberry, R., and Fischer, S. (1985). *Sign processing in sentences: The effect of experience.* Unpublished manuscript, University of Chicago.

Mayberry R., and Tuchman, S. (1985). Memory for sentences in American Sign Language: The influence of age of first sign learning. In W. Stokoe and V. Volterra (Eds.), *SLR '83: Sign Language Research.* Silver Spring, MD: Linstok Press, Inc. and Rome, Italy: Istituto di Psicologia, CNR.

Maxwell, M. (1983). Simultaneous communication in the classroom: What do deaf children learn? *Sign Language Studies, 39,* 95–112.

Maxwell, M., and Bernstein, M. (1985). The synergy of sign and speech in simultaneous communication. *Applied Psycholinguistics, 6,* 63–82.

Meadow, K. (1966). *The effects of early manual communication and family climate on the deaf child's early development.* Unpublished doctoral dissertation. University of California, Berkeley.

Meadow, K. (1976). Personality and social development of deaf persons. In B. Bolton (Ed.), *Psychology of deafness for rehabilitation counselors.* University Park Press, Baltimore, MD.

Meadow, K. (1977). Name signs as identity symbols in the deaf community. *Sign Language Studies, 16,* 237–246.

Meath-Lang, B., Caccamise, F., and Albertini, J. (1982). Deaf persons' views on English language learning: Educational and sociolinguistic implications. In H. Hoemann and R. Wilbur (Eds.), *Interpersonal communication and deafness.* (Social Aspects of Deafness Monograph Vol. 5). Washington, DC: Gallaudet College.

Meier, R. (1982). *Icons, analogues, and morphemes: The acquisition of verb agreement in American Sign Language.* Unpublished doctoral dissertation, University of California, San Diego.

Menn, L. (1976). *Pattern, control, and contrast in beginning speech: A case study in the development of word form and word function.* Unpublished doctoral dissertation, University of Illinois, Urbana-Champaign.

Menyuk, P. (1963). Syntactic structures in the language of children. *Child Development, 34,* 407–422.

Menyuk, P. (1964). Syntactic rules used by children from preschool through first grade. *Child Development, 35,* 533–546.

Menyuk, P. (1977). *Language and Maturation.* New York: Academic Press.

Miller, A., and Miller, E. (1973). Cognitive developmental training with elevated boards and sign language. *Journal of Autism and Childhood Schizophrenia, 3,* 65–85.

Miller, G., and Isard, S. (1963). Some perceptual consequences of linguistic rules. *Journal of Verbal Learning and Verbal Behavior, 2,* 227–228.

Mills, C., and Weldon, L. (1983). Effects of semantic and cheremic context on acquisition of manual signs. *Memory and Cognition, 11,* 93–100.

Monfort, M., Rojo, A., and Juarez, A. (1982). *Programa elemental de comunicacion bimodal para padres y educadores* [*Basic program of bimodal communication for parents and educators*]. Madrid: Ciencias de la Educacion Preescolar y Especial.

Montanini-Manfredi, M., Fruggeri, L., and Facchini, M. (1979). *Dal gesto al gesto* [*From gesture to gesture*]. Bologna, Italy: Cappelli.

Moores, D. (1969). Cued Speech: Some practical and theoretical considerations. *American Annals of the Deaf, 114,* 23–27.

Moores, D. (1971). *Recent research on manual communication.* University of Minnesota, Minneapolis: Research, Development, and Demonstration Center in Education of the Handicapped.

Moores, D. (1974). Nonvocal systems of verbal behavior. In R. Schiefelbusch and L. Lloyd (Eds.), *Language perspectives — Acquisition, retardation, and intervention.* Baltimore: University Park Press.

Moores, D. (1977). *Educating the deaf: Psychology, principles, and practices.* Boston: Houghton, Mifflin Co.

Moores, D. (1980). Alternate communication modes: Visual-motor systems. In R. Schiefelbusch (Ed.), *Nonspeech language and communication: Analysis and intervention.* Baltimore: University Park Press.

Moores, D., McIntyre, C., and Weiss, K. (1973). Evaluation of programs for hearing impaired children (Research report No. 39). University of Minnesota: Research, Development, and Demonstration Center in Education of the Handicapped.

Moores, D., Weiss, K., and Goodwin, M. (1977). *Early intervention programs for hearing impaired children: A longitudinal assessment.* (Asha Monographs).

Moskowitz, A. (1970). The two-year-old stage in the acquisition of English phonology. *Language, 46,* 426–441.

Moulton, R., and Beasley, D. (1975). Verbal coding strategies used by hearing-impaired individuals. *Journal of Speech and Hearing Research, 18,* 559–570.

Myklebust, H. (1964). *The Psychology of Deafness.* New York: Grune & Stratton.

Nagy, W. (1974). *Figurative patterns and redundancy in the lexicon.* Unpublished doctoral dissertation, University of California, San Diego.

Neisser, A. (1983). *The other side of silence: Sign language and the deaf community in America.* New York: Alfred A. Knopf.

Neisser, U. (1967). *Cognitive psychology.* Englewood Cliffs, NJ: Prentice-Hall.

Nelson, K. (1974). Concept, word, and sentence: Interrelations in acquisition and development. *Psychological Review, 81,* 267–285.

Neville, H., and Bellugi, U. (1978). Patterns of cerebral specialization in congenitally deaf adults: A preliminary report. In P. Siple (Ed.), *Understanding language through sign language research.* New York: Academic Press.

Newkirk, D. (1975). *Outline for a proposed orthography for American Sign Language.* Unpublished manuscript, Salk Institute for Biological Studies.

Newkirk, D. (1979). *The form of the continuative aspect on ASL verbs.* Unpublished manuscript, The Salk Institute for Biological Studies, La Jolla, CA.

Newkirk, D. (1980). *Rhythmic features of inflection in American Sign Language.* Unpublished manuscript, The Salk Institute for Biological Studies, La Jolla, CA.

Newkirk, D. (1981). *On the temporal segmentation of movement in American Sign Language.* Unpublished mansucript, The Salk Institute for Biological Studies, La Jolla, CA.

Newport, E. (1986). *The grammatical competence of native, early, and late learners of ASL: Critical period effects in the acquisition of a primary language.* Conference on Theoretical Issues in Sign Language Research, Rochester, NY.

Newport, E., and Ashbrook, E. (1977). The emergence of semantic relations in ASL. *Papers and Reports on Child Language Development, 13,* 16–21.

Nippold, M. (1982). *Perceptual and psychological concepts in children's understanding of predicative vs. proportional metaphors: A developmental investigation.* Unpublished doctoral dissertation, Purdue University.

Nolen, S. and Wilbur, R. (1985). The effects of context on deaf students' comprehension of difficult sentences. *American Annals of the Deaf, 130,* 231–235.

Norman, D. (1972). The role of memory in the understanding of language. In J. Kavanagh and I. Mattingly (Eds.), *Language by ear and by eye: The relationship between speech and reading.* Cambridge, MA: MIT Press.

Obler, L. (1980). Right hemispheric partipation in second language acquisition. In K. Diller (Ed.), *Individual differences and universals in language learning aptitude.* Rowley MA: Newbury Press.

Odom, P., Blanton, R., and McIntyre, C. (1970). Coding medium and word recall by deaf and hearing subjects. *Journal of speech and hearing research, 13,* 54–58.

Office of Demographic Studies. (1972). *Academic achievement test results of a national testing program for hearing impaired students: United States.* Washington, DC: Gallaudet College.

Oleron, P. (1974) *Elements de repertoire du language gestuel des sourds-muets [Elements of the gesture language of deaf-mutes].* Paris: Centre National de la Récherche Scientifique.

O'Malley, P. (1975). *The grammatical function of indexic reference in American Sign Language.* Unpublished manuscript. University of Minnesota, Minneapolis. Research, Development and Demonstration Center in Education of the Handicapped.

Orlansky, M. and Bonvillian, J. (1983). Recent research on sign language acquisition: Implications for multihandicapped hearing-impaired children. *Journal of the National Student Speech-Language-Hearing Association, 11,* 72–87.

Orlansky, M. and Bonvillian, J. (1984). The role of iconicity in early sign language acquisition. *Journal of Speech and Hearing Disorders, 49,* 287–292.

Orlansky, M. and Bonvillian, J. (1985). Sign language acquisition: Language development in children of deaf parents and implications for other populations. *Merrill-Palmer Quarterly, 31,* 127–143.

O'Rourke, T. (1973). *A Basic Course in Manual Communication.* Silver Spring, MD: National Association of the Deaf.

O'Rourke, T., Medina, T., Thames, A., and Sullivan, D. (1975, April). National Association of the Deaf Communicative Skills Program. *Programs for the Handicapped,* 27–30.

Owens, M., and Harper, B. (1971). *Sign language: A teaching manual for cottage parents of non-verbal retardates.* Pineville, LA: Pinecrest State School.

Padden, C. (1979). *Complement structures in American Sign Language.* Unpublished manuscript, University of California, San Diego.

Padden, C. (1981). Some arguments for syntactic patterning in American Sign Language. *Sign Language Studies, 32,* 239–259.

Padden, C. (1983). *Interaction of morphology and syntax in American Sign Language.* Unpublished doctoral dissertation, University of California, San Diego.

Padden, C. and Le Master, B. (1985). An alphabet on hand: The acquisition of fingerspelling in deaf children. *Sign Language Studies, 47,* 161–172.

Padden, C. and Perlmutter, D. (1984). *Evidence for sign language phonology.* Linguistic Society of America, San Diego, CA.

Paget, R. (1951). *The new sign language.* London: The Welcome Foundation.

Paget, R. (1971). *An introduction to the Paget-Gorman sign system with examples.* Reading, England: AEDE Publications Committee.

Paget, R., and Gorman, P. (1968). *A systematic sign language.* London: National Institute for the Deaf.

Panara, R. and Panara, J. (1983). *Great deaf Americans.* Silver Spring, MD: T.J. Publishers.

Paris, S., and Carter, A. (1973). Semantic and constructive aspects of sentence memory in children. *Developmental Psychology, 9,* 109–113.

Petitto, L. (1980). *On the acquisition of anaphoric reference in American Sign Language.* Unpublished manuscript, The Salk Institute for Biological Studies, La Jolla, CA.

Petitto, L. (1984). *From gesture to symbol: The acquisition of pronominal reference in American Sign Language.* Unpublished doctoral dissertation, Harvard University.

Petitto, L. (1985). From gesture to symbol: The relation of form to meaning in ASL personal pronoun acquisition. In W. Stokoe and V. Volterra (Eds.), *SLR '83: Sign Language Research.* Silver Spring, MD: Linstok Press, Inc. and Rome, Italy: Instituto di Psicologia, CNR.

Pettito, L. (1986). *Language vs gesture: why sign languages are NOT acquired earlier than spoken languages.* Conference of Theoretical Issues in Sign Language Research, Rochester, NY.

Phippard, D. (1977). Hemifield differences in visual perception in deaf and hearing subjects. *Neuropsychologia, 15,* 555–561.

Piaget, J. (1951). *Play, dreams, and imitation in childhood.* New York: International Universities Press.

Piaget, J. (1952). *The origins of intelligence in children.* New York: International Universities Press.

Piaget, J. (1964). Development and learning. *Journal of Research in Science and Technology, 2,* 176–186.

Poizner, H., Battison, R., and Lane, H. (1978). *Cerebral asymmetry for perception of ASL: The effects of moving stimuli.* Unpublished manuscript, Northeastern University, Boston.

Poizner, H., Kaplan, E., Bellugi, U., and Padden, C. (1984). Hemispheric specialization for nonlinguistic visual-spatial processing in brain damaged signers. *Brain and Cognition, 3,* 281–306.

Poizner, H., Klima, E., and Bellugi, U. (in press). *What the hands reveal about the brain.* Cambridge, MA: Bradford Books/MIT Press.

Poizner, H., and Lane, H. (1977). *Cerebral asymmetry in the perception of American Sign Language.* Unpublished manuscript, Northeastern University, Boston.

Poizner, H., Newkirk, D., Bellugi, U., and Klima, E. (1981). Representation of inflected signs from American Sign Language in short-term memory. *Memory and Cognition, 9,* 121–131.

Poulton, K. and Algozzine, B. (1980). Manual communication and mental retardation: A review of research and implications. *American Journal of Mental Deficiency, 85,* 145–152.

Power, D. (1974). Language development in deaf children: The use of manual supplements in oral education. *Australian Teacher of the Deaf, 15.*

Power, D. and Quigley, S. (1973). Deaf children's acquisition of the passive voice. *Journal of Speech and Hearing Research, 16,* 5–11.

Prinz, P. and Prinz, E. (1979). Acquisition of ASL and spoken English by a hearing child of a deaf mother and a hearing father: Phase I — early lexical development. *Papers and Reports on Child Language Development, 17,* 139–145.

Prinz, P. and Prinz, E. (1981). Acquisition of ASL and spoken English by a hearing child of a deaf mother and a hearing father: Phase II — early combinatorial patterns. *Sign Language Studies, 30,* 78–88.

Quigley, S. (1969). *The influence of fingerspelling on the development of language, communication, and educational achievement in deaf children.* University of Illinois, Institute for Research on Exceptional Children, Urbana-Champaign.

Quigley, S., and Frisina, R. (1961). *Institutionalization and psychoeduca-*

tional development in deaf children. Council on Exceptional Children, Washington, DC.

Quigley, S. and King, C. (1982). Language development of deaf children and youth. In S. Rosenberg (Ed.), *Handbook of applied psycholinguistics.* Hillsdale, NJ: Lawrence Erlbaum Associates.

Quigley, S. and Kretschmer, R. E. (1982). *The education of deaf children.* Baltimore, MD: University Park Press.

Quigley, S., Montanelli, D., and Wilbur, R. (1976). Auxiliary verbs in the language of deaf students. *Journal of Speech and Hearing Research, 19,* 536–550.

Quigley, S. and Paul, P. (1984). *Language and deafness.* San Diego: College-Hill Press.

Quigley, S., Smith, N., and Wilbur, R. (1974). Comprehension of relativized structures by deaf students. *Journal of Speech and Hearing Research, 17,* 325–341.

Quigley, S., Wilbur, R., and Montanelli, D. (1974). Question formation in the language of deaf students. *Journal of Speech and Hearing Research, 17,* 699–713.

Quigley, S., Wilbur, R., and Montanelli, D. (1976). Complement structures in the written language of deaf students. *Journal of Speech and Hearing Research, 19,* 448–457.

Quigley, S., Wilbur, R., Power, D., Montanelli, D., and Steinkamp, M. (1976). *Syntactic Structures in the Language of Deaf Children.* University of Illinois, Institute for Child Behavior and Development, Urbana-Champaign.

Rabush, D., Lloyd, L., and Gerdes, M. (1982a). Communication enhancement bibliography: Part I. *Communication Outlook, 3,* 4–10.

Rabush, D., Lloyd, L., and Gerdes, M. (1982b). Communication enhancement bibliography: Part II. *Communication Outlook, 4(1),* 4–12.

Rabush, D., Lloyd, L., and Gerdes, M. (1982c). Communication enhancement bibliography: Part III. *Communication Outlook, 4(2),* 4–12.

Rainer, J., Altshuler, K., and Kallmann, F. (Eds.). (1963). *Family and mental health problems in a deaf population.* Columbia, NY: State Psychiatric Institute.

Reddy, M. (1979). The conduit metaphor — a case of frame conflict in our language about language. In A. Ortony (Ed.), *Metaphor and thought.* Cambridge: Cambridge University Press.

Reichle, J. and Karlan, G. (1985). The selection of an augmentative communication system: A critique of decision rules. *Journal of the Association for Persons with Severe Handicaps, 10,* 146–156.

Remington, B. and Clarke, S. (1983). Acquisition of expressive signing by autistic children: An evaluation of the relative effects of simultaneous communication and sign-alone training. *Journal of Applied Behavior Analysis, 16,* 315–327.

Riekehof, L. (1963). *Talk to the deaf.* Springfield, MO: Gospel Publishing House.

Rittenhouse, R., Morreau, L., and Iran-Nejad, A. (1981). Metaphor and conservation in deaf and hard-of-hearing children. *American Annals of the Deaf, 126,* 450–453.

Rittenhouse, R. and Stearns, K. (1982). Teaching metaphor to deaf children. *American Annals of the Deaf, 127,* 12–17.

Robbins, N. (1976). *Selecting sign systems for multi-handicapped students.* Paper presented at the American Speech and Hearing Association Conference, Houston, TX.

Robbins, N., Cagan, J., Johnson, C., Kelleher, H., Record, J., and Vernacchia, J. (1975). *Perkins sign language dictionary.* Watertown, MA: Perkins School for the Blind.

Rodda, M. (1982). An analysis of the myth that mainstreaming and integration are synonymous. In A. Boros and R. Stuckless (Eds.), *Deaf people and social change* (Social Aspects of Deafness Monograph Vol. 6). Washington, DC: Gallaudet College.

Rogers, G. (1976). *The effects of iconicity on the acquisition of signs in Down's syndrome children.* Unpublished manuscript, Boston University.

Ross, J. (1967). *Constraints on variables in syntax.* Unpublished doctoral dissertation, MIT, Cambridge, MA.

Rupert, J. (1969). Kindergarten program using Cued Speech at the Idaho State School for the Deaf. *Report of the Proceedings of the 44th Meeting of the American Instructors of the Deaf,* Berkeley, CA.

Rutter, M. (1968). Concepts on autism: A review of research. *Journal of Child Psychology and Psychiatry, 9,* 1–25.

Sachs, J. (1967). Recognition memory for syntactic and semantic aspects of connected discourse. *Perception and Psychophysics, 2,* 437–442.

Sachs, J., Bard, B., and Johnson, M. (1981). Language learning with restricted input: Case studies of two hearing children of deaf parents. *Applied Psycholinguistics, 2,* 33–54.

Sachs, J., and Johnson, M. (1976). Language development in a hearing child of deaf parents. In W. Von Raffler Engel and Y. Lebrun (Eds.), *Baby talk and infant speech.* Lisse, The Netherlands: Swets & Zeitlinger.

Sanders, J. (Ed.). (1968). *The ABC's of sign language.* Tulsa, OK: Manca Press.

Sandler, W. (1986). The spreading hand autosegment of American Sign Language. *Sign Language Studies, 50,* 1–28.

Schaeffer, B. (1980). Spontaneous language through signed speech. In R. Schiefelbusch (Ed.), *Nonspeech language and communication: Analysis and intervention.* Baltimore: University Park Press.

Schaeffer, B., Kollinzas, G., Musil, A., and McDowell, P. (1977). Spontaneous verbal language for autistic children through signed speech. *Sign Language Studies, 17,* 287–328.

Schick, B. (1985a). *Morphosyntactic analysis of predicates in American Sign Language.* Unpublished manuscript, Purdue University.

Schick, B. (1985b). *The acquisition of complex classifier predicates in American Sign Language.* Unpublished manuscript, Purdue University.

Schick, B. and Wilbur, R. (1985). *Acquisition of complex morphology in American Sign Language.* Paper presented at American Speech-Language-Hearing Association Convention, Washington, DC.

Schiefelbusch, R. (Ed.). (1980). *Nonspeech language and communication: Analysis and intervention.* Baltimore: University Park Press.

Schiff, N. (1979). The influence of deviant maternal input on the development of language during the preschool years. *Journal of Speech and Hearing Research, 22,* 581–603.

Schiff, N. and Ventry, J. (1976). Communication problems in hearing children of deaf parents. *Journal of Speech and Hearing Disorders, 41,* 348–358.

Schiff-Meyers, N. (1982). Sign and oral language development of preschool hearing children of deaf parents in comparison to their mothers' communicative system. *American Annals of the Deaf, 127,* 322–329.

Schlesinger, H. (1972). Meaning and enjoyment: Language acquisition of deaf children. In T. O'Rourke (Ed.), *Psycholinguistics and Total Communication: The state of the art.* Silver Spring, MD: National Association of the Deaf.

Schlesinger, H. (1978). The acquisition of bimodal language. In I. Schlesinger (Ed.), *Sign language of the deaf: Psychological, linguistic, and sociological perspectives.* New York: Academic Press.

Schlesinger, H., and Meadow, K. (1972). *Sound and sign: Childhood deafness and mental health.* Berkeley: University of California Press.

Schlesinger, I. (1970). The grammar of sign language and the problems of language universals. In J. Morton (Ed.), *Biological and social factors in psycholinguistics.* Urbana-Champaign: University of Illinois Press.

Schlesinger, I., Presser, B., Cohen, E., and Peled, T. (1970). *Transfer of meaning in sign language.* (Working paper #12). Jerusalem: The Hebrew University.

Schmitt, P. (1968). *Deaf children's comprehension and production of sentence transformations and verb tenses.* Unpublished doctoral dissertation, University of Illinois, Urbana-Champaign.

Selkirk, E. (1982). *The Syntax of Words* (Linguistic Inquiry Monograph No. 7). Cambridge, MA: MIT Press.

Shaffer, T., and Goehl, H. (1974). The alinguistic child. *Mental Retardation, 12,* 3–6.

Shand, M. (1982). Sign-based short-term coding of American Sign Language signs and printed English words by congenitally deaf signers. *Cognitive Psychology, 14,* 1–12.

Shane, H. (1980). Early decision-making in augmentative communication system use. In R. Schiefelbusch and D. Bricker (Eds.), *Early language: Acquisition and intervention.* Baltimore, MD: University Park Press.

Shane, H. and Bashir, A. (1980). Election criteria for the adoption of an augmentative communication system: Preliminary considerations. *Journal of Speech and Hearing Disorders, 45,* 408–414.

Shane, H. and Wilbur, R. (1980). Prediction of expressive signing potential through assessment of motor capabilities in the severely handicapped. *Sign Language Studies, 19,* 331–348.

Shepard-Kegl, J. (1985). *Locative relations in American Sign Language word formation, syntax, and discourse.* Unpublished doctoral dissertation, MIT.

Shroyer, E. and Shroyer, S. (1984). *Signs across America: A look at regional differences in American Sign Language.* Washington, DC: Gallaudet College.

Shulman, J. and Decker, N. (Eds.). (1980). *Readable English for hearing-impaired students.* Boston: WGBH Educational Foundation.

Siegel, J. (1969). The enlightenment and a language of signs. *Journal of the History of Ideas, 3,* 96–115.

Simmons, J., and Baltaxe, C. (1975). Language patterns of adolescent autistics. *Journal of Autism and Childhood Schizophrenia, 3,* 333–351.

Siple, P. (1973). *Constraints for sign language from visual perception data.* Unpublished manuscript, Salk Institute for Biological Studies, La Jolla, CA.

Siple, P. (Ed.). (1978). *Understanding language through sign language research.* New York: Academic Press.

Siple, P. and Brewer, L. (1985). Individual differences in coding strategies for short-term retention of signs. In W. Stokoe and V. Volterra (Eds.), *SLR '83: Sign Language Research.* Silver Spring, MD: Linstok Press, Inc. and Rome, Italy: Instituto di Psicologia, CNR.

Slobin, D. (1973). Cognitive prerequisites for the development of grammar. In C. Ferguson and D. Slobin (Eds.), *Studies in child language development.* New York: Holt, Rinehart, and Winston.

Smith, N. (1973). *The acquisition of phonology: A case study.* London: Cambridge University Press.

Smith, W. (1986). *Evidence for auxiliaries in Taiwan Sign Language.* Conference on Theoretical Issues in Sign Language Research, Rochester, NY.

Smith, W. and Li-fen, T. (1979). *Shou neng sheng chyau [Your hands can become a bridge].* Taipei, Republic of China: The Sign Language Club and the Sign Language Training Classes.

Steitler, K., Cassell, J., and Webster, W. (1982). Self-concept and substance abuse intervention. In B. Culhane and C. Williams (Eds.), *Social aspects of educating deaf persons* (Social Aspects of Deafness Monograph Vol. 2). Washington, DC: Gallaudet College.

Stevenson, E. (1964). A study of the educational achievement of deaf children of deaf parents. *California News, 80,* 143.

Stohr, P., and Van Hook, K. (1973). *The development of manual communication in the severely and profoundly retarded.* Paper presented at the American Speech and Hearing Association Convention, San Francisco, CA.

Stokoe, W. (1960). Sign language structure: An outline of the visual communication system of the American deaf. *Studies in Linguistics Occasional Papers No. 8.*

Stokoe, W. (1970). Sign language diglossia. *Studies in Linguistics, 21,* 27–41.

Stokoe, W. (1972). Classification and description of sign languages. In T. Sebeok (Ed.), *Current trends in linguistics 12.* The Hague: Mouton.

Stokoe, W. (1985). Comment. *Sign Language Studies, 47,* 181–187.

Stokoe, W., Casterline, D., and Croneberg, D. (1976). *Dictionary of American Sign Language* (rev ed.). Silver Spring, MD: Linstok Press.

Stokoe, W. and Volterra, V. (Eds.). (1985). *SLR '83: Sign Language Research.* Silver Spring, MD: Linstok Press, Inc. and Rome, Italy: Istituto di Psicologia, CNR.

Stoloff, L. and Dennis, Z. (1978). Matthew. *American Annals of the Deaf, 123,* 452–459.

Strand, K. and Fraser, B. (1979). *The comprehension of verbal idioms by young deaf children.* Unpublished manuscript, Boston University.

Stremel-Campbell, K., Cantrell, D., and Halle, J. (1977). Manual signing as a language system and as a speech initiator for the non-verbal severely handicapped student. In E. Sontag, J. Smith, and N. Certo (Eds.), *Educational programming for the severely and profoundly handicapped.* Reston, VA: The Council for Exceptional Children.

Stuckless, R., and Birch, J. (1966). The influence of early manual communication on the linguistic development of deaf children. *American Annals of the Deaf, 106,* 436–480.

Supalla, T. (1982). *Structure and acquisition of verbs of motion and location in American Sign Language.* Unpublished doctoral dissertation, University of California, San Diego.

Supalla, T. (1985). The classifier system in American Sign Language. In C. Craig (Ed.), *Noun classification and categorization.* Philadelphia: John Benjamins.

Supalla, T. (1986). *Serial verbs in ASL.* Conference on Theoretical Issues in Sign Language Research, Rochester, NY.

Supalla, T., and Newport, E. (1978). How many seats in a chair? The derivation of nouns and verbs in American Sign Language. In P. Siple (Ed.), *Understanding language through sign language research.* New York: Academic Press.

Sutherland, G., and Becket, J. (1969). Teaching the mentally retarded sign language. *Journal of the Rehabilitation of the Deaf, 2,* 56–60.

Sutton, V. (1976). *Sutton movement shorthand: The sign language key.* Irvine, CA: The Movement Shorthand Society Press.

Swisher, M. V. (1985). Characteristics of hearing mothers' manually coded English. In W. Stokoe and V. Volterra (Eds.), *SLR '83: Sign Language Research.* Silver Spring, MD: Linstok Press, Inc. and Rome, Italy: Istituto di Psicologia, CNR.

Tervoort, B. (1961). Esoteric symbols in the communicative behavior of young deaf children. *American Annals of the Deaf, 106,* 436–480.

Thompson, H. (1977). The lack of subordination in American Sign Language. In L. Friedman (Ed.), *On the other hand: New perspectives in American Sign Language.* New York: Academic Press.

Thrasher, K. and Bray, N. (1984). *Effects of iconicity, taction, and training technique on the initial acquisition of manual signing by the mentally retarded.* Paper presented at the Seventeenth Annual Gatlinburg Conference on Research in Mental Retardation.

Todd, P. (1972). *From sign language to speech: Delayed acquisition of English by a hearing child of deaf parents.* Unpublished doctoral dissertation, University of California, Berkeley.

Todd, P. (1975). A case of structural interference across sensory learning modalities in second language learning. *Word, 27,* 102–118.

Tweney, R., and Heiman, G. (1977). The effect of sign language grammatical structure on recall. *Bulletin of the Psychonomic Society, 10,* 331–334.

Van Biervliet, A. (1977). Establishing words and objects as functionally equivalent through manual sign training. *American Journal of Mental Deficiency, 82,* 178–186.

Vanderheiden, G. and Grilley, K. (1976). *Nonvocal communication techniques and aids for the severely physically handicapped.* Baltimore, MD: University Park Press.

Vasishta, M., Wilson, K., Woodward, J. (1978). *Sign language in India: Regional variation within the deaf population.* Paper presented at the Fifth International Congress of Applied Linguistics, Montreal.

Vernon, M., and Koh, S. (1970). Effects of early manual communication on achievement of deaf children. *American Annals of the Deaf, 115,* 527–536.

Wagenen, L., Jenson, W., Worsham, N., and Petersen, B. (1985). The use of simultaneous communication to teach difficult verbal discriminations to an autistic and developmentally disabled child. *Australian Journal of Human Communication Disorders, 13,* 143–152.

Wampler, D. (1971). *Linguistics of Visual English.* Santa Rosa, CA: Early Childhood Education Department, Aurally Handicapped Program, Santa Rosa City Schools.

Wampler, D. (1972). *Linguistics of Visual English.* (Available from [2322 Maher Dr. 35, Santa Rosa, CA.])

Washabaugh, W., Woodward, J., and DeSantis, S. (1976). *Providence Island Sign: A context-dependent language.* Paper presented at the Linguistic Society of America Annual Meeting, Philadelphia, PA.

Washington State School for the Deaf. (1972). *An Introduction to Manual English.* Vancouver: The Washington State School for the Deaf.

Watson, D. (1964). Talk with your hands. (Available from [George Banta, Menasha, WI]). (Reprinted 1973.)

Watson, L. (1977). *Conversational participation by language-deficient and normal children.* Paper presented at the American Speech and Hearing Association Conference, Chicago, IL.

Webster, C., Konstantareas, M., and Oxman, J. (1976). *Simultaneous communication with severely dysfunctional nonverbal children: An alternative to speech training* (Working paper). University of Victoria.

Webster, C., McPherson, H., Sloman, L., Evans, M., and Kaucher, E. (1973).

Communicating with an autistic boy with gestures. *Journal of Autism and Childhood Schizophrenia, 3,* 337–346.

Wickelgren, W. (1965). Distinctive features and errors in short-term memory for English vowels. *Journal of the Acoustic Society of America, 38,* 583–588.

Wilbur, R. (1974). When is a phonological rule not a phonological rule? The morphology of Sierra Miwok. In A. Bruck, R. Fox, and M. LaGaly (Eds.), *Papers from the Parasession on Natural Phonology.* Chicago: Chicago Linguistic Society.

Wilbur, R. (1976). The linguistics of manual languages and manual systems. In L. Lloyd (Ed.), *Communication assessment and intervention strategies.* Baltimore: University Park Press.

Wilbur, R. (1977). An explanation of deaf children's difficulty with several syntactic structures of English. *The Volta Review, 79,* 85–92.

Wilbur, R. (1978a). On the notion of derived segments in American Sign Language. In R. Wilbur (Ed.), Sign language research [Special issue]. *Communication and Cognition.*

Wilbur, R. (Ed.). (1978b). Sign language research [Special issue]. *Communication and Cognition.*

Wilbur, R. (1978c). Review of "Cohen, Namir, and Schlesinger, *A New Dictionary of Sign Language.*" *Contemporary Psychology, 23,* 948–949.

Wilbur, R. (1979). *American Sign Language and Sign Systems.* Baltimore, MD: University Park Press.

Wilbur, R. (1981). Theoretical phonology and child phonology: Argumentation and implications. In D. Goyvaerts (Ed.), *Phonology in the 1980s.* Ghent: Story-Scientia.

Wilbur, R. (1982a). *A multi-tiered theory of syllable structure for American Sign Language.* Paper presented at the Annual Meeting, Linguistic Society of America, San Diego, CA.

Wilbur, R. (1982b). The development of morpheme structure constraints in deaf children. *The Volta Review, 84,* 7–16.

Wilbur, R. (1985a). Review of "Lane and Philip (Eds.) *The Deaf Experience: Classics in Language and Education.*" *Applied Psycholinguistics, 6,* 198–202.

Wilbur, R. (1985b). *The role of contact in the phonology of ASL.* Paper presented at the Annual Meeting, Linguistic Society of America, Seattle, WA.

Wilbur, R. (1985c). Towards a theory of "syllable" in signed languages: Evidence from the numbers of Italian Sign Language. In W. Stokoe and V. Volterra (Eds.), *SLR '83: Sign Language Research.* Silver Spring, MD: Linstok Press, Inc. and Rome, Italy: Istituto di Psicologia, CNR.

Wilbur, R. (1985d). Sign language and autism. In E. Schopler and G. Mesibov (Eds.), *Communication problems in autism.* New York: Plenum.

Wilbur, R. (1986a). *Why syllables?* Conference on Theoretical Issues in Sign Language Research, Rochester, NY.

Wilbur, R. (1986b). Interaction of linguistic theory and sign language research. In P. Bjarkman and V. Raskin (Eds.), *The real world linguist: Linguistic applications for the 1980s.* New York: Ablex.

Wilbur, R., Bernstein, M., and Kantor, R. (1985). The semantic domain of classifiers in American Sign Language. *Sign Language Studies, 46,* 1–38.

Wilbur, R. and Fristoe, M. (1986). "I had a wonderful, if somewhat unusual, childhood": Growing up hearing in a deaf world. In J. Christiansen and R. Meisegeier (Eds.), *Papers for the Second Research Conference on the Social Aspects of Deafness.* Washington, DC: Gallaudet College.

Wilbur R., and Goodhart, W. (1983). *Development of English modals by deaf students.* American Speech-Language-Hearing Association Convention, Cincinnati, OH.

Wilbur, R., and Goodhart, W. (1985). Comprehension of indefinite pronouns and quantifiers by hearing-impaired children. *Applied Psycholinguistics, 6,* 417–434.

Wilbur, R., Goodhart, W., and Montandon, E. (1983). Comprehension of nine syntactic structures by hearing-impaired children. *The Volta Review, 85,* 328–345.

Wilbur, R., and Jones, M. (1974). Some aspects of the bilingual/bimodal acquisition of sign language and English by three hearing children of deaf parents. In M. LaGaly, R. Fox, and A. Bruck (Eds.), *Papers from the Tenth Regional Meeting, Chicago Linguistic Society.* Chicago: Chicago Linguistic Society.

Wilbur, R., Klima, E., and Bellugi, U. (1983). Roots: The search for the origins of signs in ASL. *Chicago Linguistic Society, 19,* 314–336.

Wilbur, R., and Menn, L. (1975). Towards a redefinition of psychological reality: On the internal structure of the lexicon. *San Jose State Occasional Papers, 2,* 212–221.

Wilbur, R., Montanelli, D., and Quigley, S. (1976). Pronominalization in the language of deaf students. *Journal of Speech and Hearing Research, 19,* 120–141.

Wilbur, R., and Nolen, S. (1986). The duration of syllables in American Sign Language. Unpublished manuscript, Purdue University.

Wilbur, R., and Nolen, S. (in press). Reading and writing. *The Encyclopedia of Deafness and Deaf People.* New York: McGraw-Hill.

Wilbur, R., and Petitto, L. (1981). How to know a conversation when you see one. *Journal of the Student Speech-Language-Hearing Association, 9,* 66–81.

Wilbur, R., and Petitto, L. (1983). Discourse structure of American Sign Language conversations; or, how to know a conversation when you see one. *Discourse Processes, 6,* 225–241.

Wilbur, R., Quigley, S., and Montanelli, D. (1975). Conjoined structures in the language of deaf students. *Journal of Speech and Hearing Research, 18,* 319–335.

Wilbur, R., and Schick, B. (1985). *The effects of linguistic stress on sign movement in ASL.* The American-Speech-Language-Hearing Association Convention, Washington DC.

Wilson, K. (1978). *Syntactic features of sign languages in India.* Paper presented at the MIT Sign Language Symposium, Cambridge, MA.

Wilson, P. (1974). Sign language as a means of communication for the mentally retarded. Paper presented at the Eastern Psychological Association Conference, New York.

Wing, G. (1887). The theory and practice of grammatical methods. *American Annals of the Deaf, 32*, 84–89.

Winner, E., McCarthy, M., Kleinman, S., and Gardner, H. (1979). First metaphors. In D. Wolf (Ed.), *Early symbolization — New directions for child development.* Washington, DC: Jossey-Bass.

Woititz, J. (1983). *Adult children of alcoholics.* Hollywood, FL: Health Communications.

Woll, B., Kyle, J., and Deuchar, M. (1981). *Perspectives on British Sign Language and deafness.* London: Croon Helm Ltd.

Woodward, J, (1972). Implications for sociolinguistic research among the deaf. *Sign Language Studies, 1,* 1–17.

Woodward, J. (1973a). *Implicational lects on the deaf diglossic continuum.* Unpublished doctoral dissertation, Georgetown University, Washington, DC.

Woodward, J. (1973b). Some observations on sociolinguistic variation and American Sign Language. *Kansas Journal of Sociology, 9,* 191–200.

Woodward, J. (1973c). Interrule implication in American Sign Language. *Sign Language Studies, 3,* 47–56.

Woodward, J. (1973d). Some characteristics of Pidgin Sign English. *Sign Language Studies, 3,* 39–46.

Woodward, J. (1974a). Implicational variation in American Sign Language: Negative incorporation. *Sign Language Studies, 5,* 20–30.

Woodward, J. (1974b). A report on Montana-Washington implicational research. *Sign Language Studies, 4,* 77–101.

Woodward, J. (1974c). *Variety is the spice of life.* Paper presented at the First Annual Conference on Sign Language, Gallaudet College, Washington, DC.

Woodward, J. (1975). *Variation in American Sign Language syntax.* Unpublished manuscript, Linguistics Research Laboratory, Gallaudet College, Washington, DC.

Woodward, J. (1976a). Black Southern Signing. *Language and Society, 5,* 211–218.

Woodward, J. (1976b). Signs of change: Historical variation in American Sign Language. *Sign Language Studies, 10,* 81–94.

Woodward, J. (1977). *All in the family: Kinship lexicalization across sign languages.* Paper presented at the Georgetown Roundtable on Language and Linguistics, Washington, DC.

Woodward, J. (1978). Historical bases of American Sign Languages. In P. Siple (Ed.), *Understanding language through sign language research.* New York: Academic Press.

Woodward, J., and DeSantis, S. (1977a). Two-to-one it happens: Dynamic phonology in two sign languages. *Sign Language Studies, 17,* 329–346.

Woodward, J., and DeSantis, S. (1977b). Negative incorporation in French and American Sign Language. *Language and Society, 6.*

Woodward, J., and Erting, C. (1975). Variation and historical change in American Sign Language. *Language Sciences, 37,* 9–12.

Woodward, J., Erting, C., and Oliver, S. (1976). Facing and handling variation in American Sign Language phonology. *Sign Language Studies, 11,* 43–51.

Woodward, J., and Markowicz, H. (1975). *Some handy new ideas on pidgins and creoles: Pidgin sign languages.* Paper presented at the International Conference on Pidgins & Creoles, Honolulu.

Woodward, M. (1959). The behavior of idiots interpreted by Piaget's theory of sensori-motor development. *British Journal of Educational Psychology, 29,* 60–71.

Yoder, D. (1978). *Nonspeech communication.* Paper presented at the Boston University Miniseminar on Nonspeech Language Intervention.

Yoder, D., and Kraat, A. (1982). Intervention issues in nonspeech communication. In J. Miller, D. Yoder, and R. Schiefelbusch (Eds.), *Contemporary issues in language intervention.* Rockville, MD: The American Speech-Language-Hearing Association.

Yoder, P., and Porter, P. (1984). *Election and decision making: How to assess and train the relevant components.* Paper presented at the International Association for Augmentative and Alternative Communication Conference, Boston, MA.

AUTHOR INDEX

SUBJECT INDEX